*Whether you're a beginner, new to publishing, or an experienced hand, looking for greater success, this up-to-date and comprehensive book will show you everything you need to know to be successful at publishing. Step-by-step, following Avery Cardoza's advice, you'll learn all the essential tools necessary to produce, print, distribute and make money publishing books.*

*Avery Cardoza knows more about publishing, designing, writing and selling books, and the business of making it all happen in the real world, than anyone in the business today. His companies have the unique distinction of never having had a book go out of print. In this work, Cardoza brings together his vast experience in running a variety of successful typesetting, graphic, advertising, book, magazine and multimedia publishing companies to create the most complete and definitive book ever written on the subject.*

---

AVERY CARDOZA is the owner of two book publishing companies, Cardoza Publishing (www.cardozapub.com) and Open Road Publishing (www.openroadpub.com), a multi-media CD-ROM and interactive internet publishing company, Cardoza Entertainment (www.cardozaent.com), an internet game company, The Chronicles of Xandrea (www.xandrea.com), and an internet chess magazine (www.chesscity.com).

Cardoza Publishing is the world's foremost publisher of gaming and gambling books with almost 100 titles and five million books sold; Open Road Publishing, co-founded with partner Jonathan Stein, has a library of 75 travel guides in just the first four years, and is fast becoming a major player in worldwide travel guides; and Cardoza Entertainment a developer and publisher of high quality interactive CD-ROM game titles and a fully interactive online casino that accepts live wagering (www.cardozacasino.com). Cardoza is also a best-selling author of 21 books.

In addition to his multiple publishing companies, Cardoza has founded, owned and operated, two direct mail sales companies, a typesetting/graphics business, a dining club, and a full color lifestyle magazine.

This book, the *Complete Guide to Successful Publishing*, originally took Cardoza more than two years to research and write and had restricted him. to writing just five other books, publishing 27 titles, and starting just one company during that time. Since the first edition, he has started three other companies, and published more than 50 new titles using the techniques described in this book.

# BOOKS AND PRODUCTS PUBLISHED BY AVERY CARDOZA

(*Books written by Avery Cardoza - **co-written by Avery Cardoza)

## CARDOZA PUBLISHING
10 Most Common Chess Mistakes
303 Tricky Checkmates
Advanced Professional Winning Systems*
Avery Cardoza's Casino Strategy Guide
Avery Cardoza's Caribbean Stud Poker
   & Let It Ride*
Baccarat Master Card Counter*
Backgammon For Winners
Basic Endgame Strateg:
   Kings, Pawns and Minor Pieces
Basic Endgame Strategy:
   Rooks & Queens
Basics Of Winning Baccarat*
Basics Of Winning Bingo*
Basics Of Winning Blackjack
Basics Of Winning Bridge
Basics of Winning Caribbean Stud Poker
   & Let It Ride
Basics Of Winning Chess
Basics Of Winning Craps
Basics Of Winning Horseracing
Basics Of Winning Keno
Basics Of Winning Lotto/Lottery
Basics Of Winning Poker
Basics Of Winning Roulette
Basics Of Winning Slots
Basics Of Winning Sports Betting*
Basics Of Winning Video Poker
Beat The House Companion*
Beat The Odds
Beginning Chess Play
Cardoza 1-2-3 Multiple Deck Non-Counter*
Cardoza Base Count Strategy*
Cardoza Craps Master*
Cardoza School Of Blackjack -
   Home Instruction Course*
Caro's Fundamental Secrets Of
   Winning Poker
Casino Champion*
Casino Craps For The Winner*
Complete Defense to
   King Pawn Openings
Complete Defense to
   Queen Pawn Openings
Complete Guide To Successful Publishing*
Complete Guide To
   Winning Hold'em Poker
Complete Guide To Winning Keno
Encyclopedia of Chess Wisdom
Five Ball Lotto Wheels
Gambit Opening Repertoire for Black
Gambit Opening Repertoire for White
Gri Master Keno Strategy
Gri Roulette Master
Handbook Of Winning Bridge
Handbook Of Winning Poker
Horseracing Super Strategies
How To Play Winning Poker*
How To Win At Gambling*
How To Win At Horseracing
How To Win At Sports Betting
Master Checkmate Strategy
Master Greyhound Strategy
Master Lotto/Lottery Strategies
Oddsmaker*
Poker Champion*
Pro-Master II Lotto/Lottery Strategies
Professional Video Poker Strategy*
Secrets of the Sicilian Dragon

Secrets of Winning Roulette*
Secrets of Winning Slots*
Silberstang's Encyclopedia
   Of Games And Gambling
Standard Chess Openings
Ultimate Word Challenges
Unorthodox Chess Openings
Whiz Kids Teach Chess
Winner's Guide To Greyhound Racing
Winner's Playbook*
Winning Blackjack For The Serious Player
Winning Casino Blackjack For The
   Non-Counter*
Winning Casino Play*
Winning Chess Openings
Winning Chess Tactics
Winning Craps For The Serious Player
Winning Football Bettor*
Winning Lotto/Lottery For
   Everyday Players
Winning Poker For The Serious Player
World Champion Combinations
World Champion Openings

## OPEN ROAD PUBLISHING
America's Cheap Sleeps
America's Grand Hotels
America's Most Charming Towns
   & Villages
Arizona Guide
Austria Guide
Bahamas Guide
Belize Guide
Bermuda Guide
Boston Guide
California Wine Country Guide
Caribbean Guide
Caribbean With Kids
CDC's Complete Guide to Healthy Travel
Celebrity Weddings &
   Honeymoon Getaways
Central America & Caribbean
Central America Guide
Chile Guide
China Guide
Colorado Guide
Costa Rica Guide
Czech & Slovak Republics Guide
Disneyworld & Orlando Theme Parks
Egypt Guide
Florida Golf Guide
Florida Guide
France Guide
Golf Courses of the Southwest
Greek Islands Guide
Guatemala Guide
Hawaii Guide
Holland Guide
Honduras & Bay Islands Guide
Hong Kong & Macau Guide
Ireland Guide
Israel Guide
Italy Guide
Jerusalem Guide
Kenya Guide
Las Vegas Guide**
London Guide
Moscow Guide
National Parks With Kids
New Mexico Guide

New Year's Eve 1999!
Paris Guide
Philippines Guide
Portugal Guide
Prague Guide
Rome & Southern Italy Guide
San Francisco Guide
Smart Home Buyer's Handbook
Smart Runner's Handbook
Southern California Guide
Southern Mexico & Yucatan Guide
Spa Guide USA
Spain Guide
Tahiti & French Polynesia Guide
Texas Guide
Thailand Guide
Tokyo Guide
Turkey Guide
US Caribbean Guide
Utah Guide
Vietnam Guide
Washington DC Ethnic
   Restaurant Guide
World's Most Intimate Cruises

## CARDOZA ENTERTAINMENT
   (CD-ROM WINDOWS GAMES)
Avery Cardoza's Casino
Avery Cardoza's 100 Slots
Cardoza Entertainment's
   Internet Casino

## OTHER CARDOZA PUBLICATIONS
Bon Vivant Dining Guide
Bon Vivant Magazine
The Discount Guide (23 editions)
Direct Sales Technique (Unpublished)*

# THE COMPLETE GUIDE TO
# SUCCESSFUL
# PUBLISHING

*To Barbara Friedman*
She is the best.

## ACKNOWLEDGMENTS

This book is a compilation of knowledge and experience I've accumulated in more than 17 years in the publishing world, and a full list of acknowledgment would stretch more pages than I could realistically devote. Many people have been helpful along the way, and many names will go unmentioned - so I hope I'm forgiven.

My special thanks go to the front office staff at Cardoza Publishing, in particular, Tobasco, Brownstone, and Mary—they do a terrific job in running the business. For special editing work, and an overall outstanding performance, my partner and Open Road Publishing co-founder, Jonathan Stein.

Special acknowledgments certainly have to go to the Carol Publishing Group, my national distributor, in particular Gary Fitzgerald, who has been a star, and Steven Schragis, the chief, to the many companies we do business with, and to the book trade in general. Thanks to all.

# THE COMPLETE GUIDE TO
# SUCCESSFUL
# PUBLISHING

## Avery Cardoza

## CARDOZA PUBLISHING

**PRINTING HISTORY**

*First Printing*     *June 1995*
*Second Printing*    *September 1998*
*Third Printing*     *April 2000*

Library of Congress Catalog Card Number: 97-94721
ISBN: 0-940685-94-9

## CARDOZA PUBLISHING

P.O. Box 1500, Cooper Station, New York, NY 10276
Phone (718)743-5229 • Fax (718)743-8284
www.cardozapub.com

---

**COLLEGES, UNIVERSITIES, QUANTITY BUYERS**
Discounts on this book are available for bulk purchases.
Write or call for information on our discount programs.

# TABLE OF CONTENTS

## BOOK PUBLISHING

# 1. INTRODUCTION                                    19

# 2. OVERVIEW & THE BOOK MARKET                      20

INTRODUCTION                                          20
SETTING GOALS - BEING SUCCESSFUL                      21
SOME DEFINITIONS                                      21
FORMULA FOR SUCCESS - NICHE PUBLISHING                22
DIFFERENT TYPES OF BOOK PUBLISHING                    23
    How-to Publishing
    Fiction Publishing
    Non-Fiction Publishing
    Poetry
    Children's Books
    Religious Publishing
    New Age Publishing
    Fictional Genre Publishing
    Other Markets
OVERVIEW OF THE PUBLISHING PROCESS                    26
CHAPTER PREVIEW                                       28

# 3. GETTING STARTED                                 31

INTRODUCTION                                          31
SETTING UP THE COMPANY                                31
    The Company Name
OFFICIALLY ESTABLISHING THE COMPANY                   32
    Corporation vs. Single Proprietorship
    Setting Up a Corporation
    Setting Up a Single Proprietorship
    Opening a Bank Account
EQUIPMENT AND MATERIALS NEEDED                        34
    The Computer Set-Up
    Essential Hardware Set-Up
    Essential Software Set-Up
BASIC OFFICE SET-UP                                   39
    Office Supplies
    Stationery
    For Billing

For Packing Boxes
Fax Machine
START-UP COSTS                                                40
Profiting Where the Big Publishers Can't
First Book Budget
Break-Even Expectations


# 4. THE ELEMENTS OF A SUCCESSFUL BOOK          47

INTRODUCTION                                                 47
IDENTIFYING YOUR AUDIENCE                                    48
Running Book Example
Romance Book Example
Gaming Book Example
SELLING FEATURES OF A BOOK                                   51
THE COVER
The Title - How-to Books
The Title - Other Books
The Cover Copy
The Design
The Spine
TABLE OF CONTENTS
How-to & Non-Fiction
Fiction & Certain Genre
Other Categories
Positioning
THE INTRODUCTION
WRITING QUALITY
THE PRICE
PAGE COUNT
INTERIOR DESIGN
BLURBS
CONCLUSION                                                   63


# 5. THE AUTHOR & THE PROPOSAL          64

INTRODUCTION                                                 64
THE PROPOSAL                                                 65
FINDING A WRITER                                             65
They'll Find You
You'll Find Them
Finding Ideas for Books
SOLICITING OR ACCEPTING SUBMISSIONS                          67
JUDGING A BOOK PROPOSAL                                      70
EVALUATING WRITING                                           73
Evaluating  How-to and Non-Fiction Writing
Evaluating Fiction Writing

THE GOOD, THE BAD, AND THE UGLY                              75

    Good Signs in Writing
    Bad Signs in Writing
    Ugly Signs in Writing
NEGOTIATING THE CONTRACT      76
    Advances and Royalties
    Reporting & Paying Author Royalties
    Other Points
    Signing the Contract

# 6. INITIAL MARKETING & THE DECISION TO PUBLISH    80

INTRODUCTION      80
MARKETING DECISIONS      81
    Positioning a Book In the Marketplace
CHOOSING A BOOK'S DIMENSIONS AND BINDING      82
PAPERBACK (PERFECT BOUND) BOOKS      83
    Trade or Quality Paperbacks -
    5 1/2 x 8 1/2 or 6 x 9
    Mass Market Size - 4 1/4 x 6 3/4
HARDBOUND      87
OTHER BINDINGS      88
    Spiral Bound, Comb Bound
    Saddle-stitching
    Velo-Binding
SETTING THE LIST PRICE      89
    Initial Considerations
    Pricing a Book According to Cost
    Pricing a Book for Maximum Profit
    Price Points
    Pricing Higher or Lower than the Competition
PLANNING FOR SAVINGS - SIGNATURES      94
    More on Signatures

# 7. GETTING OFFICIAL/ COPYRIGHT/BAR CODE    96

INTRODUCTION      96
INTERNATIONAL STANDARD BOOK NUMBER (ISBN)      97
LIBRARY OF CONGRESS NUMBER      97
ABI FORMS      98
CATALOGING IN PUBLICATION (CIP)      98
COPYRIGHTING YOUR BOOKS      99
BAR CODES      100
    The Bookland EAN Bar Code
    Printing the Bookland EAN Bar Code

    UPC Bar Code

10

Getting Bar Codes Made
PLACES TO GET LISTED          102
    Places to List Your Books
    Places to List Your Company
    Places to List Your Authors
NATIONAL PUBLISHING ORGANIZATIONS    104
NORTH AMERICAN TRADE SHOWS    105

# 8. WORKING WITH THE MANUSCRIPT     106

INTRODUCTION    106
PROPER MANUSCRIPT SUBMISSION    107
    Instructing Authors on Disk Submission
WORKING WITH THE AUTHOR    109
    Coordinating with Authors for a Good Book
EDITING THE MANUSCRIPT    109
    Overview or Content Edit
    Copy Edit
    Design Edit
    Communicating on the Edits
ENTERING THE EDITS    114
    Double Check Edits
    Spell Check
THE NEXT STEP    115

# 9. BOOK DESIGN - TYPE, GRAPHICS, DESIGN BASICS     116

INTRODUCTION    116
TYPE DESIGN    117
    Working With Type
    Text Type
    Chapter, Headline and Sub-headline Type
    Principles of Using Typefaces
POINTS AND PICAS    121
    Picas
    Points
TYPE SELECTION    122
    Helvetica - Sans-Serif Type
    Serif Types
    Standard Text Point Sizes
    Samples of Styles
    Running Small and Large
BASICS THINGS YOU CAN DO WITH TYPE    127
    Leading
    Alignment
PAGE AND CHAPTER DESIGN    130

Paragraph Design
Running Headers
Page Numbers
Page Margins
Standard Minimum Text Margin Charts
Bleeding Print
Chapter Heads and Design
Chapter Size
STANDARD BOOK DESIGN................................137
GOOD DESIGN CONCEPTS..............................138
General Stylistic Guideline
Short Paragraphs and Headings
The Advantages of Using Graphics
Working with the Attributes of Type
COMPUTER DESIGN TECHNIQUES..................143
TRADITIONAL SCREENS.................................148

# 10. REPRODUCING GRAPHICS & PHOTOS 149

INTRODUCTION............................................149
USING A SCANNER......................................150
MANUAL PASTE-UP......................................150
Simple Tools for the Graphic Department
SIZING IMAGES..........................................152
Using the Proportional Wheel (Reduction Wheel)
Using a Calculator or Hand Measurement
The Correct Language for Percentages
Shooting Up and Shooting Down
CROPPING IMAGES......................................155
Cropping Example 1
Cropping Example 2
REPRODUCING IMAGES................................159
Reproducing Non-Photographic Images
Reproducing Black & White Photographic Images
Reproducing Color Slides as Black & White
Reproducing Color Prints as Black & White
Reproducing Color Photographic Images
DUOTONES, TRITONES, QUADTONES..............163
MANUALLY INSERTING GRAPHICS ON A PAGE..164

# 11. COVER DESIGN & PRODUCTION 166

INTRODUCTION............................................166
SELLING BOOKS BY THEIR COVER.................167
Designing Covers that Sell
Effective Design Principles
White Space
Designing Spines that Sell

    Some Key Points in Cover Copy
    Using Reviews & Endorsements
    The Importance of Color Covers

THE FOUR COLOR PRINTING PROCESS      175
    The Pantone Matching System
    Using the PMS books
    Understanding PMS colors

COLOR COVER COST COMPARISON      177
WORKING WITH COLORS      178
    Reverses

WORKING WITH BLACK COVERS      179
    Colors that Work With Black - Headline Type
    Colors that Work Against Black - Text Type
    Colors that Won't Work With Black
    Title Type

OTHER COLOR BACKGROUNDS      180
SETTING UP THE COLOR COVER      181
    Minimizing Color Costs - Trapping vs. Fifth Color
    Advantages of Trapping
    Advantages of Using a Fifth Color
    Color Conclusion

WORKING WITH A COVER DESIGNER      183
    Checking a Designer's Credentials

PROTECTING YOUR COVER      184
    UV Coating and Film Lamination

MAKING COLOR COMPS      185
    Strategy for Using Thermal Dye Transfer Printers
    Using High Quality Color Output
    Adding Photos to Your Comps
    Making Multiple Cover Comps

MAKING THE ACTUAL COVER      190
    Making Color Covers with Mechanicals
    Making Color Covers on Disk

PROOFING THE COVER      194
SUBMITTING THE COVER      195
COVER BLUES OR CROMALINS      195

# 12. PRODUCTION      197

INTRODUCTION      197
ORIENTATION - THE THINKING      198
THE THREE SECTIONS OF A BOOK      198
    FRONT PAGES
        Other Front Page Options
        Preface, Foreword
    BACK PAGES
    THE BODY TEXT

SETTING UP THE BOOK      202
    Crop Marks

WORKING WITH THE BOOK FILES      205
    Working with One File

Working with Multiple Files
Conclusion
TRANSFERING INTO THE PUBLISHING PROGRAM        206
WORKING WITH THE ROUGH PAGE COUNT              208
BOOK PLANNING - LOOSE OR TIGHT                 210
EXPANDING A BOOK'S PAGE COUNT                  212
REDUCING A BOOK'S PAGE COUNT                   215
FIRST TEST OF PAGE                             218
CHAPTERIZING A BOOK                            219
   How to Chapterize
   Adding Up the Chapter Count
LAYING OUT A BOOK                              222
ORGANIZATIONAL PAGE                            224
PROOFING                                       226
   Preparation for Proofing
GOING TO PRESS                                 231
   SUBMITTING CAMERA-READY ART
     Printing at an Output Shop
   ELECTRONIC SUBMISSIONS
     Submitting on Disk
     Getting the Job to the Printer
SEND THE WHOLE JOB AT ONCE                     235
GETTING THE BOOK PRINTED                       236

# 13. PRINTING     **237**

INTRODUCTION                                   237
THE THREE TYPES OF PRINTING PRESSES            238
   The Sheetfed Press
   The Web Press
   The Belt Press
GETTING QUOTES                                 240
LIST OF PRINTERS                               241
CHOOSING A PRINTER                             242
   Quality Issue
   Price Issue
   Turnaround Time
   Summing Up
UNDERSTANDING PRINTER'S QUOTES                 244
HOW TO ACCEPT A PRINTING QUOTE                 252
ORDERING THE PRINT RUN                         253
   Books With a Sales History
   New Books
   General Print Run Strategy
THE ACTUAL PRINTING BILL                       257
   Overs
   Shipping
   Extra Work
   Check the Bill
MAINTAINING A GOOD PRINTING PRICE              258

STORING NEGATIVES                                   259
PRINTING PROBLEMS                                   260
    Solutions to Pre-Press Problems
    Solutions to Printing Problems
ADDITIONAL PRINTING INSTRUCTIONS                    262
SHIPPING                                            262
    Shipping Instructions
    Order Extra Covers
THE BOOK HAS ARRIVED!                               263

# 14. DISTRIBUTION & SALES 264

INTRODUCTION                                        264
    Self-Distribution vs. Trade Distribution
NATIONAL EXCLUSIVE DISTRIBUTORS                     265
    Finding Distributors for Your Books
    Contacting Distributors
    What Do Distributors Want to Hear?
    Sales Technique
    Following Up
CHOOSING YOUR DISTRIBUTOR OR SALES REP              270
    Choosing a National Distributor
    Big or Little?
    List of National Exclusive Distributors
INDEPENDENT SALES REPS                              274
    Finding Rep Groups
    Computerizing Operations
LARGE PUBLISHERS AS DISTRIBUTORS                    277
WHOLESALERS                                         278
    National Wholesalers
    Regional Wholesalers
    Some Specialty Wholesalers & Distributors
JOBBERS                                             283
    Stripping Covers
WHAT HAPPENS IF YOU HAVE TROUBLE
   GETTING A DISTRIBUTOR?                285
DISTRIBUTING YOUR FIRST BOOK                        286
SALES AND SELF-DISTRIBUTION                         286
    Setting Your Terms & Discount Schedule
    How to Put Together Your Catalogue
    Mail Order Sales
    Toll-Free 800 Numbers & Credit Cards
AREAS TO GET EXTRA SALES                            291
    Specialty, Premium & Incentive Sales
    Selling to the Wholesale Clubs
    Catalog Sales
    Selling to Book Clubs
    Remainder Dealers
THE BOOK MARKET                                     295

TARGETING THE LIBRARY MARKET                        297

Library Distributors
LIBRARY-QUALITY BOOKS
   Library of Congress Number, ISBN, LC Number
   Index
   Acid Free Paper
SELLING TO THE ACADEMIC MARKET       300

# 15. MARKETING (ADVERTISING & PUBLICITY)   301

INTRODUCTION     301
PUBLICITY - GETTING REVIEWS     302
   PUBLICATION DATE/SHIP DATE     303
   PRE-PUBLICATION REVIEWS     303
      How to Submit Pre-Publication Books
      Along with the Page Proof or Galley
      Standard Book Announcement Information
      Where to Send Galleys - Trade Publications
      Where to Send Galleys - Newspapers
      Where to Send Galleys - Magazines
      Where to Send Galleys - Other Publications
      Where to Send Galleys - Book Clubs
   POST-PUBLICATION REVIEWS     309
      The Publicity Package
      The Cover or Pitch Letter
      The News or Press Release
      Following Up
      Other Review Sources
BOOK SIGNINGS/BOOK READINGS     315
ADVERTISING     315
      Advertising Directly to the Consumer
      Word of Mouth Advertising
      Co-op Advertising

# 16. RUNNING THE BUSINESS   319

INTRODUCTION     319
TAKING ORDERS     320
      The Order
      Setting Up Accounts
      Checking Credit References
      Invoicing Orders
      Collecting Money
      Increasing Orders
      Selling to Individuals
FULFILLMENT     326
STORAGE     326
PACKING BOXES     327
      How to Pack a Box

Taping the Box
Other Items on the Box
SHIPPING                                                     330
Shipping Packages with UPS
Shipping Boxes with the Postal Service (USPS)
Shipping Individual Books
Packing Individual Books
Stamps or Meters
Shipping Items You Resell
Shipping to Libraries
SENDING IMPORTANT DOCUMENTS                                  335
A NOTE ON BOOKKEEPING                                        336
Preparing the Accounting & Taxes
WAREHOUSING                                                  338
Outside Warehousing
RESALE NUMBER                                                338

# 17. MAKING MONEY      340

INTRODUCTION                                                 340
TYPICAL PUBLISHING COSTS                                     340
Production & Printing Costs
Employee Costs
Rent
Author Costs
Set-Up Costs
Marketing
Warehousing & Fulfillment
Postage and Shipping
Additional Costs
THE LIST/PRINT RATIO & PROFITS                               343
More on the 8-1 List/Print Ratio
WAYS TO INCREASE PROFITS                                     346
INCOME FROM DISTRIBUTION                                     348
Payment as Straight Percentage of List Price
Payment Based on Net Sales
ESTABLISHING A LINE                                          350
Keeping Within Your Strengths or Creating New Strengths
Developing a New Line
EXTRA MONEY ON THE BACK PAGES                                353
Doing the Order Form
TAKING CHANCES IN PUBLISHING                                 354
MAKING MONEY WITH NEW EDITIONS                               356
Improving Your New Edition or New Printing

# MULTIMEDIA PUBLISHING

# 18. MULTIMEDIA PUBLISHING 359

INTRODUCTION 359
STAYING TIMELY AND PREDICTING THE MARKETPLACE 359
THE SEVEN PERILS OF MULTIMEDIA PUBLISHING 361
    Financing
    Skilled Staff
    Post-Release Gotcha
    Retail and Distribution
    Packaging and Product
    The Product Must Sell
    Getting Paid
    Wrapping Up the Seven Perils
    The Good News
THE TYPES OF PLAYERS IN MULTIMEDIA 367
    Developers
    Publishers
    Hybrid Publisher-Developer Relationships
RETAIL AND DISTRIBUTIONS (AFFILIATED LABELS) 369
    Sales Force
    Distributors
    Distributor List
    Distributors and Exclusivity
    The Retailer
    Market Development Funds (MDF)
    Retail List
SALES AND DISTRIBUTION AS A PUBLISHER 373
THE DEVELOPMENT TEAM 376
    The Rules of the Staff
    Producer
    Programmers
    The Art Department
    Technical Writer
    Associate Producer/Audio Engineer
DEVELOPMENT AND PLANNING 379
    The Design Documents
    Pricing Your Product
    Manufacturing a Game
    UPC Code
    ESRB Rating
ESTABLISHING YOUR DOMAIN SITE 384
    Hosting Your Site

## LAST SECTION

# 19. FINAL THOUGHTS                                385

# 20. GLOSSARY                                      386

# 21. APPENDICES                                    404

APPENDIX A: SAMPLE AUTHOR CONTRACT              404
APPENDIX B: LIST OF US STATE ABBREVIATIONS      408
APPENDIX C: POINT SIZE CHART                    409
APPENDIX D: SOFTWARE REVIEW                     410
APPENDIX E: BOOK CHAIN LISTINGS                 418
APPENDIX F: RECOMMENDED RESOURCES               421

# 22. BOOK SECTION INDEX                            424

### LIST OF RESOURCES

Following is a list of resources to be found in this book.

| | |
|---|---|
| Bar Code Manufacturors | 102 |
| Book Chain Listings | 418 |
| Books on Publishing | 421 |
| Document Delivery Services | 336 |
| Jobbers | 284 |
| Library Distributors | 298 |
| List of Printers | 241 |
| Magazines to Send Galleys | 308 |
| National Exclusive Distributors | 273 |
| National Wholesalers | 279 |
| Newspapers to Send Galleys | 307 |
| Other Review Sources | 315 |
| Places to List Your Books | 102 |
| Places to List Your Company | 103 |
| Publishing Associations | 104 |
| Publishing Directories/Periodicals | 421 |
| Publishing Newsletters | 422 |
| Publishing Operations Software | 277 |
| Regional Wholesalers | 280 |
| Remainder Dealers | 294 |
| Software Programs | 415 |
| Specialty Wholesalers/Distributors | 282 |
| Trade Publications to Send Galleys | 306 |
| Trade Shows | 104 |
| Wholesale Clubs | 292 |

# 1. INTRODUCTION

You too can be successful in publishing books! Whether you're a beginner, new to publishing, or an experienced hand, looking for greater success, I'm going to show you everything you need to know to be successful at publishing.

Once you've read this book and absorbed the powerful information within, you'll not only have the skills to publish professional-looking publications, but you'll be successful in getting them sold and distributed. Step-by-step, from raw idea to the finished product, and from printer to the bookshelf, you'll learn how to produce, print, distribute and make money publishing books.

You'll learn what it takes to find and develop marketable ideas; how to set up the business from the ground up; how to choose type; how to design and layout a book; how to find authors, work contracts and negotiate deals; how to produce books that not only look good but *sell*; how to get your book distributed through the various channels; how to build upon success with even more success; how to expand your publishing company into a small empire; and much, much more.

For the first time, all the necessary ingredients of publishing books in the *real* world are under one cover, and that book is now in your hands. Many have achieved the dream of becoming a successful publisher, and many more will continue achieving it every year.

And the dream *can* be good; it's worked for me, and hopefully, after you finish reading this book, it will work for you. Read on! I'm going to show you how to be successful in publishing.

# 2. OVERVIEW & THE BOOK MARKET

## INTRODUCTION

The great advantage in being a publisher is that there are so many markets to sell your books, that if things are done right, you'll have a excellent chance at being successful. In addition to independent and chain bookstores, there are public libraries, military libraries, corporate libraries, supermarket and drug store outlets, specialty markets, gift markets, incentive and promotion sales, serialized and reprint sales, direct mail sales, catalogue sales, international sales, book club sales, foreign rights, and more.

But while the markets are there and hungry for new product - and they are *always* hungry for new product - the readers in that marketplace want products that appeal to and address their needs. No matter how you sell your book, through mail order, through bookstores, or through other outlets, that book has to *appeal*, or it's not going to be bought.

You're competing against many books on the shelves and in the open market, so however you do your books, and whatever subjects they cover, to be successful, you must give your target consumers a compelling enough reason to buy your titles. If you do your job well, and we'll spend a lot of time discussing how to do just that in these pages, than success will be yours.

There's a world of possibilities where the seed of success can be planted, but it all begins with careful planning, an understanding of the markets, and how to position yourself in them. Let's look at these concepts now.

# SETTING GOALS - BEING SUCCESSFUL

We all like to be successful in what we do. However, the concept of success means different things to different people, and of course, depends upon the situation. While one publisher might be ecstatic just to complete the publishing cycle - that is, create and publish a book, get that book into the bookstore, and have the consumer buy the book and take it home - even though few sales might be made - another publisher won't be satisfied until his line of books brings in untold millions in profits.

In between these two extremes are the majority of publishers, those who want their books to make enough money to not only be profitable, but to earn their living in publishing. Just getting a book into a few bookstores will be unsatisfactory, while on the other hand, making millions, though it might be nice, is not a requirement. They want to make a comfortable living and have the security of a line of books they can count on for their income year after year.

So, while financial goals are the objective of many publishers, others publish books as a labor of love or to support works they feel important or meaningful. For these publishers, success has an entirely different look and meaning to their program. The amount of money generated by their books is secondary to the fact that new people are getting exposed to their works. In truth though, all publishers probably share some of both traits; the financial goals and the labor of love.

Whatever your goal, we'll go over all the necessary steps to get your book to press and out into the market.

# SOME DEFINITIONS

Before we move on, let's go over some basic definitions, starting with what a publisher is and what he does. When I tell people I'm a publisher, they invariably ask, "well, what do you do?" I didn't know myself before I started. So perhaps it's best defined here.

A *publisher* is responsible for the entire process of making books, from finding the talent and overseeing the writing, editing and production, to the final printing and marketing. In a small publishing company, the publisher may do all of these functions himself or with a few employees or helpers. In larger publishing houses, individual people or entire departments will be devoted to each of these tasks. (In both cases, the printing will generally be hired out.) When the term publisher is used to denote the *publishing company*, which is usually the case, then it also includes the financing of the entire book process. Publishers take the risk, and if it all goes well, the lion's share of the profit.

A *book* is a bound publication of 49 or more pages that is not a periodical. (A *periodical* is a publication such as a magazine, issued at regular intervals). Less than 49 pages would technically be considered a booklet.

Now that we know what we are and what we're doing, let's take a look at the basic strategy for success in the book market.

# FORMULA FOR SUCCESS - NICHE PUBLISHING

Publishing books in a specialized field, **niche publishing**, is the most effective approach to selling books, provided of course, that the area chosen is marketable. By concentrating energies in a narrow market, being a specialist, you increase the chances of success. The book trade will take you more seriously if they see you have a coherent publishing program. Just as a book should target a specific audience, a concept we'll stress throughout this book, your publishing program should target a specific audience as well.

Coming right out of the chute as an unknown publisher doing three different titles on three completely different areas, leads to the perception that you have no focus, and the value of your line diminishes. And with three different types of titles, *you don't even have a line*, you have a mumble-jumble, and that's not a good perception to have when trying to get your company established. The question for the book trade becomes, *who are these people*? Without a coherent publishing program, it will be tough to give a satisfactory answer.

Thus, focus is vital. Zero in on the book publishing program you'll be starting with, and the books that will be following. To be successful, you must do a good job positioning your products into the market. Grab your share of shelf space, guard it jealously, and expand that share with solid follow-up books.

My initial strategy was to publish gambling books, the field of my expertise, and I built my program around that. Later on, when I was established, I was able to branch out into other areas because buyers respected the work I produced in my line. I produced quality books that sold, and that reputation carried over into my new venture.

But don't confuse this strategy of focusing, establishing yourself and developing one area before branching out to further areas, as being limiting. Within each specialty is an endless stream of books that an eager audience will eat up. Whether your subject is mountain climbing, gambling, writing skills, mystery, true crime or whatever, the possibilities of books within those niches are enormous.

Let's take a look at the various "niches" or areas of publishing out there, and some strategies you'll have to think about when entering these areas.

# DIFFERENT TYPES OF BOOK PUBLISHING

Books can be divided into three broad subject areas; **fiction, non-fiction** and **how-to**. And within these areas exist a wide range of categories, each one being a potential area of specialty for the budding publisher. For example, under the broad grouping of *non-fiction,* can be lumped biographies, exposés, political essays, certain reference works and more, and under the broad auspices of *how-to* are books from airplane flying techniques to designing costumes. Fiction of course, covers works of storytelling on anything and everything, and can technically include such genres as romance, mystery and thrillers.

Some categories present more difficulties to the publisher than others. The categories below are only a sampling, but will give you a sense of the type of effort needed and the available markets to make these books work.

You'll see that while I've addressed the main groupings of how-to's, fiction and non-fiction, I've also looked at subcategories by themselves to give you a broader look at different types of books.

## How-to Publishing

From a strictly business point of view, though perhaps I'm prejudiced because how-to books have given me a nice living, publishing how-to books is the easiest way to make money in the business. Books move themselves once they're on the shelf (presentation is essential!), and need no marketing to become established sellers.

But to be seen as important to the consumer, how-to books must stress an approach that makes it *different*, *unique* and *better* than others - and thus, a ***must-buy***. Get this message across, and you've got a book that will be consistently bought.

The range of possible how-to categories is enormous; from gambling titles (my specialty) to sporting books, to basket weaving, to camping and to meditation, these books present a bonanza of opportunity. Within the how-to umbrella are also giant selling categories such as cookbooks, dieting books, baby books, exercise books, and on and on.

## Fiction Publishing

While how-to books can sell themselves on a shelf; fiction titles on the other hand (excepting established authors) don't generally have that luxury. Readers need to be made aware that the work is out there and that it has merit. Unknown writers are *unknown*, and to make these writers and their works known, and ultimately under consideration as a possible purchase by a consumer, publicity, promotion, and reviews in key trade publications are often essential to their success.

Fiction is quite lucrative for the big publishing companies working with best-selling authors, but for smaller houses, and sometimes for larger houses working with lesser known authors, publishing fiction books can be a tough way to make a buck. If you'll be doing fiction, start with good authors, and plan on working hard to make it successful.

## Non-Fiction Publishing

Non-fiction is similar to fiction in that it's quite lucrative for big publishing companies who have the promotional budgets to make the most out of these titles. However, there's still lots of room for smaller publishers to get their share of the market with an interesting book.

*New Age*

Often, since sales are promotion driven, you'll need to organize your team and get all your ducks in line, so your non-fiction book can be released with the proper support it will need to become seen and purchased. You'll also want to make sure that the book you're publishing is interesting and has good sales possibilities to begin with.

## Poetry

Selling poetry books is the toughest way to make a buck in the publishing industry, so if this is your area of specialty, your main goal should be publishing for love, not money. Few poetry books make money for the publisher, and in general, poetry publishers have a tough go of it. There's only a small market for poetry books, thus marketing one's poetry list is essential to sales.

Poetry is best sold through book signings, author readings, and any promotion available to the poet. Being such a tough sell, you should be as flexible as possible when making sales. There aren't all that many places to sell poetry where you can afford to turn away possible sales.

## Children's Books

Books targeted for children are booming, and are considered one of the hot subject areas of the 90's. Attesting to their popularity, *Publishers Weekly* (PW), the established voice of the book world, publishes a weekly list of best-selling children's books.

There's a lot of competition in this lucrative category, but that could be said of just about any category. While the competition does exist, the demand is high. It's certainly worth a go if children's books are your thing.

## Religious Publishing

Religious books have a surprisingly large market - it is said that the bible is the best-selling book in the world - and if your expertise and inclinations get you involved as a religious publisher, the market is there.

## New Age Publishing

New age books are hot, and getting hotter by the month. The interest in these titles is huge and enjoys the advantage not only of a large base of the regular bookstore venues, but the additional bonus of a wide net of metaphysical bookstores, health food stores and the like. Like other avenues of books, there's an insatiable demand for more new age titles.

## Fictional Genre Publishing

Areas such as mystery, science fiction, romance, horror and the like have tremendous followings and are fields wide open to niche publishers. The demand is steady, but you'll have to fight your way on and off the shelves. Once you get a strong title, develop an exciting lineup of books around it.

## Other Markets

We've only touched on some of the many types of book categories, and there are many others out there, but hopefully, this sampling gives you some preliminary feel for the types of books you may be publishing.

# OVERVIEW OF THE PUBLISHING PROCESS

Following is an overview of the steps and processes involved in the making of a book from start to finish; from the thin air of a thought, into the actual printed book many steps down the food chain.

This brief look below will be explained in greater detail throughout this book, along with the business aspects of making and selling books, so that by the time you finish all the chapters, you'll have the tools to be a successful publisher. How you use these tools, and how much effort you put into your publishing venture will determine the success you'll have out in the marketplace.

### 1. Establish a Business
Get your company officially set-up and ready to conduct business.

### 2. Book Idea
Once your business is established, the first step is to have a solid book proposal, an actual manuscript, or simply an idea. The proposal must be one that fills a need for a large enough potential audience to succeed.

### 3. Decision is Made to Publish the Book
Deciding to publish is the most important decision you'll make in the publishing process. At this point, you're also making specific decisions as to the book's focus, list price, page count and its size.

## 4. Contract a Writer

If everything looks good, get a contract signed, and set the author in motion. However, make sure that you and your author are in agreement about what the book will cover and the tone it will take.

## 5. The Book Gets Written

The idea needs to be brought to fruition by the writer, who at the very least, writes competently, and at the very best, gives you an *exciting* manuscript.

## 6. Edit the Book

Upon submission of the completed manuscript, the book gets edited. If the book is not already entered into a word processing program, it gets done now.

## 7. Book Plan and Design

After the book is edited and ready to go, you decide upon the typestyles and sizes, the margins, the page, chapter and book designs, and the preliminary front and back page sections.

## 8. Book Production

Carry out the book plan and design so that a finished book is laid out and all pages are in order and ready to be mass produced.

## 9. Proof Book

Go through all the stages of proofing to ensure that the book is ready for press.

## 10. Send Book to Printer

The book gets sent to the printer with the proper instructions including the number of books to print.

## 11. Your Book Arrives!

Four to five weeks later, your books are shipped from the printer - you're ready to roll!

# CHAPTER PREVIEW

Following is a brief preview of the *remaining* chapters in this book and some of the items covered in them.

## 3. GETTING STARTED

We go over the basics of establishing a publishing company, choosing a business entity, the basic equipment needed to start the company, and the start-up costs involved.

## 4. THE ELEMENTS OF A SUCCESSFUL BOOK

We'll show how to identify and target your audience, and go over the various selling features that will make your book both competitive and marketable.

## 5. THE AUTHOR AND THE PROPOSAL

In this chapter, we show how to come in contact with potential authors, how to evaluate their proposals for marketability and writing quality, and finally, how to negotiate a contract and come to agreement with authors.

## 6. INITIAL MARKETING AND THE DECISION TO PUBLISH

We'll look at each of the decisions we must make in targeting our book; the best type of binding and format for our market, how we price the book according to our needs and the market, and how to set the best list price for the book we're doing.

## 7. GETTING OFFICIAL/COPYRIGHT/BAR CODE

We learn how to officially announce our books to the book trade, how to get Library of Congress Numbers, ISBN's, and bar codes, and how to copyright the book. We also show how and where to get our books, authors and company listed.

## 8. WORKING WITH THE MANUSCRIPT

Working with the author toward producing the best possible book are the important issues we'll look at in this chapter. A book should go through three edits - overview, copy, and design - and we'll show the basics of each step.

## 9. BOOK DESIGN - TYPE, GRAPHICS AND DESIGN BASICS

We go over all the aspects of working with type and type design in a book, page and chapter design, and the important basics of working with graphics, including reproduction, sizing and cropping.

## 10. REPRODUCING GRAPHICS AND PHOTOS

This chapter shows how to reproduce photographic images for both black and white and color printing in your book. You'll learn how to size and crop images, and how to use the simple tools needed for manual paste-up.

## 11. COVER DESIGN & PRODUCTION

Books sell by their covers, and we go over the essentials of design, cover production, and working with color. You'll learn how to save on color printing, work with cover designers, and how to design your own covers.

## 12. PRODUCTION

Here we discuss the strategies for putting together and laying out a book, from overall book design and pagination to the final proofing before the book goes to the printer. We go over the three parts of a book, front, body and back, and how to coordinate them into an actual book ready for the printer to produce.

## 13. PRINTING

You'll learn about the process of printing and the terminology used, how to bid a job and understand estimates, how to save money while getting high quality printing, how to properly submit books, how to deal with problems should they occur, and all the ins and outs associated with printing books.

## 14. DISTRIBUTION & SALES

Distribution is the key to selling books, and in this chapter, we talk about self-distribution versus using a distributor, the different types of players involved in distribution, how to find and choose the best distributors, the terms of doing business, about discount schedules, and overall, how to sell your books through traditional and non-traditional channels.

## 15. MARKETING (ADVERTISING & PUBLICITY)

You'll learn how to promote books both before publication and after, and how to work with the general media and the book trade media to bring attention to your books and get them reviewed.

## 16. RUNNING THE BUSINESS

Once your books are out in the market, you've got a business to run. We'll go over basic bookkeeping, invoicing, packing, shipping, sending important business papers, organizing, and the like.

## 17. MAKING MONEY

We'll discuss the profit structure, some basic principles of pricing books, how to develop a line and expand your growing publishing empire, the list/print ratio, strategies for earning extra income from your books, and overall, some strategies to maximize profits.

## 18. MULTIMEDIA PUBLISHING

An overview to show you the basics of succeeding and the perils in multimedia CD ROM publishing.

## 19. FINAL THOUGHTS

Some final thoughts before you're on your way.

## 20. GLOSSARY

The jargon and terms used in the graphics, printing and publishing industry are explained.

## 21. APPENDICES

The appendices provide additional supporting information such as sample author contracts, book chain contacts, and more.

## 22. INDEX

A thorough index to help you find items faster.

*world of publishing*

# 3. GETTING STARTED

## INTRODUCTION

The world of publishing awaits, and the good news is that you can get your foot in the door for under five or ten thousand dollars, which isn't a whole lot of money to start a business with unlimited potential. Of course, you can spend more money, but if you're on a tight budget and know what you're doing, professional-looking books with excellent potential can be produced inexpensively.

If you haven't started a business before, you'll be in for a nice surprise: Getting a business established is a straightforward and easy process. Once you establish the name of your company, the type of organization you'll be setting up (single proprietorship, partnership or corporation) and get that name registered, you'll be able to set up a bank account so you can accept and issue checks. Once these basics are taken care of, you've got an official business and you're ready to start making books.

We're going to cover all these basics in this chapter, how to start a business, the equipment and setup you'll need to get started, and the money you'll need to get your first book produced and printed.

Well, the books are waiting for us, so let's get going. We'll first look at how to officially establish your company.

## SETTING UP THE COMPANY
### The Company Name

The first step in establishing your company is to choose a business name. It makes no difference whether your last name is included as part of the company name or is the name of the company itself or you name it after an historical event, or even name it after a character you like out of a book. Any company name will do as long as you're not using any trademarked name (such as Mickey Mouse) and infringing on someone else's rights.

I called my company Cardoza Publishing, but I could have used Press or House instead, or something entirely different. You can use an image you like as in Big Mountain Publishing, Rusty Railing Press, Double Dribble, or Waddling Duck.

If you don't use your name as part of the company (no advantage or disadvantage in doing so), then the best name to use is one that is descriptive of the work you'll be publishing. If you'll be publishing light-hearted material, say comics, humor, children's stuff, whatever, you can use a fun title that's evocative of the books you'll be publishing - Crazy Five, Loony Lou - or you can go on the authoritative side with Children's Majesty Publishing or some such name. If you're doing tennis books, you can use company titles like Hard Volley, Love 40, Matchpoint, whatever.

Have fun with your company name, or make it authoritative, but above all, make it a name that *feels good*, one you want to associate with.

# OFFICIALLY ESTABLISHING THE COMPANY

There are three basic business entities available to you as a new business; single proprietorship, partnership, and corporation, and you'll have to choose one of these forms to get your business going. There are disadvantages to each form, and we'll discuss these briefly.

A single proprietorship and partnership are basically the same type of set-up except that in a partnership, of course, two or more people are involved in the ownership. For purposes of this discussion, we'll group partnerships under the banner of the single proprietorship, since the discussions for one more or less applies equally to the other.

Keep in mind that this discussion is legal in nature, and since I'm not a lawyer, use the following discussion only as a general guideline for understanding the differing nature of single proprietorships and corporations. You should confer with a lawyer and an accountant about the advantages and disadvantages for your particular situation in choosing one form of business entity over the other.

## Corporation vs. Single Proprietorship

The main reason people set up their business as a corporation is to limit their personal liability. If the business goes bankrupt, or if there's a giant lawsuit levied against the business, then unless there is serious wrongdoing, the individual himself is not financially liable. The disadvantage of the corporation, on the other hand, is double taxation, more paperwork involved (quarterly taxes should be filed), and stricter rules on bookkeeping.

Also, technically speaking, you don't own the corporate funds (though you may control the corporation). The corporation owns those funds. Thus, different rules apply as to how the money might be handled.

## Setting Up a Corporation

Corporations are filed with the state to become valid, a process that can take several days to several weeks, depending on how fast the people involved in filing move. You can hire a lawyer to do this for you (approximately $200-$500 including the filing or registration fee), or you can file yourself (a filing fee is involved) if you know what to do.

If you're new to establishing a business, using professional legal help may be the preferable way to set up the corporation so that you fully understand the legalities involved.

Once the corporate name is filed, a search will take place to make sure that the corporate name is not already being used within that state. Lawyers generally recommend that you give them two alternate corporate names, so that if your first choice is already taken, there will be no delays and you can file under one of the alternates.

When the search is concluded and all is in order, you'll receive corporate resolutions, stock certificates, and some other paperwork, and you'll also receive a corporate seal. You'll now be a corporate type - congratulations.

## Setting Up a Single Proprietorship

As in a corporation, you must first name your company before you can officially file any papers at the local **County Clerk's** office, where this will be done.

At this office, you must file what is called a **Fictitious Business Name Statement** if you'll be using a name other than your own to conduct business. This name is called a **DBA - Doing Business As**. Forms will be readily available at this office. They're simple to fill out and you can do it on the spot. The form establishes the name of the business, the type of ownership - single proprietor or partnership (corporations don't get filed here - they're done at the state level) and the owners involved. Usually, there's either no fee or a minor one required for the filing.

The office will do a quick search for you, or may even require you to do it, to make sure no one else in the jurisdiction has the same company name.

Once the forms are filed, you are required by law and the banks to publish that Fictitious Statement for four weeks in a local general circulation paper. The office will likely have a list of publications that meet this requirement. Once this process is concluded, you'll be official.

## Opening a Bank Account

With Fictitious Business Name Statement in hand and proof of publication for single proprietors and partnerships (which will automatically be sent by the paper after the ad has been published for four weeks), or the corporate seal and Minutes for corporations, you'll be able to open a bank account under the company name.

That's all there is to it. The bank account allows you to receive and write checks - you're in business!

# EQUIPMENT AND MATERIALS NEEDED

Publishing is one of the great start-up businesses available, because it can be done from any location, and even on the move. On the most basic level, only a phone, mailing address and a computer set-up is needed to run the business. Everything else can be winged.

If expenses are tight in the beginning, employee costs, typically the largest expense of many companies, can be minimized. You can run the business by yourself, out of your home or apartment, or even a post office box, if you're on the move a lot.

The business can be set up on a shoestring, and as things get established, an office can be set up and extra employees and overhead that will make your job easier can be added. In the beginning though, you won't even need an office at all. A corner space in your home or apartment will be sufficient.

It can be done. I know, for that's how I started in 1980. I moved around a lot, using my post office box as a base, while my distributor handled all the day to day operations of sales - all for a percentage I was glad to give them. Back then, and even until 1990, I didn't have a computer to do my books. They were typeset onto long galleys and hand cut into pages ready for the printer. But that's the dinosaur age now.

In the early 1990's, a new direction has completely changed the way books are put to press, and that's the onset of **desktop** or **computer publishing**. Now the complete production process is done on the computer itself.

The computer revolution in publishing, dating from about the mid-1980's and going full steam ahead in the 1990's, has advanced the world of publishing so that now an entire book can be processed - text and graphics can be entered, designed and paged right on the computer - and delivered to your printer either as camera-ready copy, on computer disk or even through the phone lines by modem.

No longer do galleys need to be entered into a typesetting machine, developed through a chemical processor, and manually cut and paged as before. The computer eliminates all these steps. You go right from data entry to camera-ready copy. In terms of the final process in book-making, the printing of the book itself, that will always be hired out to print shops, so it's equipment you don't need to worry about. The cost of these high speed machines are in the millions of dollars, and are way out of the range for all but the very largest of publishers.

Galleys: indicate a pre-publication version of a book.

Let's now look at the computer set-up needed to get going and then show a sample low budget book to give you a preview of what's involved.

---

# TYPESETTING

The traditional way of putting books to press was through a process called **typesetting** or **phototypesetting**, a process that is outdated, and so much more expensive - maybe 5-10 times as much as desktop publishing - I really don't understand why anyone would use it anymore. Typesetting is a complete dinosaur and should not be used to produce books .

I'll quickly explain the typesetting process though so you're aware of how books were commonly produced as recently as a five years ago (and still today by companies short on brains) and why you should not typeset your books.

To be ready for the typesetter, your book must be completely edited and designed with instructions on how the book is to be set. A data entry person will enter your book according to your preset instructions, run the generated film through a photographic process, and ultimately, produce long unpaged sheets of type. These long strips of type are called **galleys**. Galleys could be as long as 10 feet or more, depending upon how much is read out, but the length is unimportant. The graphic artist now has the arduous process of measuring and individually cutting out each page for final copy. (Today galleys indicate a pre-publication version of a book.)

Your proofing not only consists of manually spell-checking the finished type for errors, something your word processing program, for the most part, would do automatically, but of checking the alignment of the layed-out copy, a process automatically done on your program. If you change your mind, or have spec'd your type wrong, you're in for added expenses. Every change that's made must be reset on the typesetter (at a charge) and then layed-out again by the graphic artist (more charges).

Why would any publisher still use typesetting? Beats me.

---

# The Computer Set-Up

All the type in a book, whether created by the author or the publisher, will be designed and produced on the computer. Other than setting your book up on a typewriter, which would be limiting and amateurish, or through traditional typesetting, which is expensive and outdated, there is no other way to efficiently and inexpensively get your type ready for the printing press.

So, if you haven't joined the computer age yet, it's time to get your wheels in motion. There will be a couple of bumps in the road if you're new to computers and the programs, but that's part of the learning process. Though books can be published without using computers, those methods are antiquated, expensive, and simply make no sense. Therefore, settle in, and get used to the computer age.

A proper computer set-up has several elements; the **hardware** consisting of the CPU (the computer itself) and hard drives (for storing documents), computer monitor (the screen by which you view what's going on), keyboard, and a printer, to print pages that will be needed. While each piece can be purchased separately, typically, they'll be bought together since they're all necessary components of the whole system.

There is one other element vital to any computer system, and that is the **software**, the programs that give the CPU the capabilities of doing all the wonderful things a computer can do.

Let's go over the basic hardware setup, and then talk about the software you'll need to get going in publishing.

## Essential Hardware Set-Up

The basic computer system is the shell which gives you the power to run the various software (programs) you'll be using. This unit is called the **hardware**, and is the guts and power that will run your system.

It's best to work with either the Macintosh line of computers (or new compatibles) made by Apple, or the IBM compatible computers, the latter, more commonly referred to as PC's. Either system will work great for producing books. While many in publishing started with and stay faithful to the Macintosh environment - that's the system we use - the great advances made in the PC platforms with the Windows operating system have made the IBM and compatibles a serious choice as well.

*Technically, PC stands for any personal computer, but it has come into vogue to refer to IBM-compatible systems as PC's, and Apples as Apples, Macintoshes, or Macs.

Even though Windows architecture has made the IBM world a lot more user-friendly, the Macintosh system is still easier to use than the PC's, and the preferred pre-press system in use among publishers. PC's will get the job done as well, and for those devoted to the IBM compatible, they will make their case for the PC being a better computer just as Mac devotees will stubbornly back their systems. The fact is though, either system will get the job done.

The IBM compatibles - and these include computers with brand names such as Compaq, Toshiba, Mitsubishi, Dell, Gateway, and many others - have the advantage of being lower priced. Other operating systems, such as the long-gone Commodore platform, are not readily used in the industry and can create problems, possibly insurmountable ones, if you need to interface with authors, output houses, and printers. If you're not already set up with a computer, just make sure that whichever one you purchase is either in the Mac or IBM-compatible family. Most likely, you probably can't even find any other type of system so this is really not a big concern.

Most configurations of the IBM compatibles and Macintosh computers will be adequate for handling your work. A basic Macintosh or PC set-up should have a minimum of 16 megs of RAM (Random Access Memory) with 32 megs or more preferred, and 500 megs hard drive, with one, two, or more gigs preferred. While older configurations work well in the Macs, I would recommend at least a Pentium model or better for the PC. And by the time you read this, at the speed in which computers are developing, the minimum requirements needed to efficiently run the latest software will most likely be raised higher.

If you're not computer literate, don't worry. Ask your dealer to recommend a set-up that will handle your needs.

It's best to own your own computer, but if your budget cannot accommodate that, you'll need to either borrow one from a friend, or rent one from either a shop where you can rent by the hour (see computer rentals in the yellow pages or check the weekly papers in your area for advertisements), or by the month. Many of the quick-print type shops often carry a computer department where machines are available for on the spot rental.

## Essential Software Set-Up

The essentials of book publishing require a word processing program and preferably, also a publishing program, so that you can process your book in the computer, and get it ready for press.

Theoretically, you could get by with just a strong word processing program (as you could theoretically get by with a souped-up typewriter turned word processor), but due to the limits of these programs which are set up for word processing and not publishing, you'll really need a publishing program to do a proper job in getting the book ready for press.

Your first order of business is to have a good word processing program. I have worked with Microsoft Word for the Macintosh (also available for IBM compatibles) and found it to be an excellent word processing program. It does everything you'll need it to do and comes with an excellent spell check. WordPerfect is another popular program (available on both platforms). There are other word processing programs that may be just as good.

I recommend Pagemaker, available on the Macintosh and PC platforms, or Quark (both platforms), as your basic publishing software. These are the most widely used publishing programs and would be your best choice. There are other readily available programs, such as Ventura Publishing for the IBM compatibles, that ought to work for you as well. Basically, if a program gets the job done, that's all that counts.

There are also graphic programs, ones that can create illustrations and logos, and which can alter photographs, and there are computer attachments which allow you to scan images into the computer and alter them, but none of these are necessary to publish top quality books. As with any tool, they can very useful, but until you're versed in their workings, I would concentrate instead on the other aspects of book publishing, and keep the basic book-making process simple in the beginning. (See Appendix D for further discussion of software programs.)

# BASIC OFFICE SET-UP

Following is a list of items that are basic to any business and can be bought and supplied when deemed necessary. We're making certain assumptions below, such as that you already have a chair, desk, lamp, phone, etc.

## Office Supplies

The following items will be helpful in organizing your papers and doing the regular things that are done in any office:
• **Colored folders** - To keep everything organized. Organization is the key to efficiency.
• **Papers** - You'll need extra paper for your printer, fax machine, stationery, etc.
• **Office Stuff** - Pens (regular black or blue ink pens plus red for editing), pads, paper clips, rubber bands, scotch tape, white-out, stapler, scissors, etc. You can figure out the rest.

## Stationery

• **Business cards, Envelopes, Letterhead** - You can get these run off at a local printer or through a mail order company.

## For Billing

• **Invoices** - Three part NCR (Non-Carbonless Reproduction) blank invoices will work in the beginning. However, once you start writing a lot of invoices, you'll find it easier to have your company name, address and phone number already printed on the form. This is easily done at your local print shop or through a mail order company.

## For Packing Boxes

• **Packing Paraphernalia** - You'll need good packing tape, thick magic marker (for marking), packing slip pouches and packing slips, and mailing labels.

## Fax Machine

The fax is now almost a mandatory business tool. If you're on a tight budget, don't worry about the fancy machines; a basic fax will get the job done for you.

# START-UP COSTS

Compared to most businesses, a publishing company needs very little start-up capital to get things up and running. The major expenses of the typical business, employees and rent, can be minimized, since the publishing business can be done from any location (no storefront required), and employees, especially in low-budget operations, are minimal if any. Compared to a retail store, where a huge inventory of many products must be kept, our inventory is restricted only to the books we publish, an expense that won't occur until we're ready to print.

Later on, as the business grows, the normal trappings of any business are added to those printing costs. Overhead and expenses such as rent, payroll and the like become part of the cost formula. But at the point where a business has these added expenses, there is also income from books to pay for them, and hopefully, profits with everything working well.

But the important thing, especially for start-up companies, is that a publishing business can be started with a relatively small investment. A start-up investment of under $5,000 will be enough to order a print run of 3,000-5,000 books - prices will vary depending upon page count and quantity ordered - and few other expenses need apply to the process. Add another $2,000-$5,000 for the basic computer set-up we discussed earlier, if you do not already have a computer, and we have a total of under $10,000, perhaps even as little as $5,000, to get things rolling.

That's not bad at all for a business with the tremendous potential and freedom that publishing offers.

## Profiting Where the Big Publishers Can't

While large publishers have the advantage of major resources to back their big books, the smaller independent publishers have a big advantage as well; our break-even point is so much smaller than major publishers that we can make good money on books that the larger publishers wouldn't even consider. And in the marketplace, that leaves a large number of titles we can market successfully, books which a big publisher would lose money on.

In some sense, while it's hard to compete with the big publishers on their turf, rolling out major books with big promotion campaigns, at the same time, it's hard for big publishers to compete with us on ours - producing steady creative titles which they're too top-heavy to be profitable on. We have a smaller overhead and a streamlined, less-expensive publishing process that allows us lots of room for profits. The big publishers, on the other hand, need a lot of grease to keep their machinery rolling.

While one, two or even three people may be involved in our book-making process, they'll need entire departments of workers. Each step of the way, an individual, or team of individuals is involved in a big publishing house. This slow train through the company builds up expenses at every stop. By the time the train has arrived and the book is camera-ready, its pre-press costs have grown into a frighteningly high level and it will need to produce big sales to make the large publisher a profit.

Thus, we see a large measure of success from small publishers who are able to compete with larger publishers, for the simple reason that the small publisher's expenses are comparatively minimal in putting out a book, and profit levels are not hard to reach.

The definition of break-even and profit for large and smaller publishers is different as a result. As a matter of fact, while a small publisher may consider sales of 5,000 copies on a particular book to be profitable and a healthy success, a larger publisher with the big overhead might consider that same book a giant bust.

Let's look at some examples of the costs of doing a book with real dollars and cents figures. (Keep in mind that paper prices skyrocketed in 1995, and that actual printing prices may be somewhat higher)

## First Book Budget

In the examples we'll be showing below, you will be doing the data entry, design, text and production - all of which we'll show you how to do in this book. If you happen to be the author as well, even more savings will be had.

We're coming in lean and mean with our only major cost being the printing of the book itself. Compared to a major publisher, which has tremendous pre-press costs, our break-even will be significantly lower and less risky. It also means we can make nice profits on books that big houses wouldn't consider. Those are sizeable advantages we have over the big boys.

We'll look at three models with each succeeding model encompassing more work and thus costing more. There are ways to economize on some of these costs, as well as ways to incur greater ones. It's all a function of your skills, how much work you want to farm out, what price that costs you, and the nature of the book you're doing.

If you follow the advice in this book, you'll be able to work pretty close to Model 1, the least expensive one. In each of these three theoretical examples, we're assuming a 176 page book with a 3,000 copy print run. The print costs shown can be higher or lower for a number of reasons - including the printer used, extra work performed by the printer, the paper used, page count, number of books printed, etc. - but for purposes of this discussion, you'll get a general sense of the costs involved.

## Model 1 - Basic Printing Plus Cover Costs
Model 1 is a basic book with the only extra expenses incurred being the $500 budgeted in for the cover costs, either in the form of a cover designer, reproduction of color images or both combined, (money that can be saved if you do the cover yourself, and also if you're not reproducing color photos), and $500 for Miscellany and Promotion.

**Model 1**
**TOTAL PRODUCTION AND PRINTING COSTS**

**PRE-PRESS**
| | |
|---|---|
| Data Entry | $0 |
| Production | $0 |
| Photos | $0 |
| Illustrations | $0 |
| Cover Costs | $500 |

**PRINTING**
| | |
|---|---|
| Print + Ship | $3500 |

**MISCELLANY AND PROMOTION**
| | |
|---|---|
| Miscellany and Promotion | $500 |

**TOTAL**
| | |
|---|---|
| Pre-press + Printing | $4500 |

If we charged $9.95 retail for our book, for example, at the approximate $4.00 wholesale price we would receive, we need sell only between 1,000-2,000 copies to break even (depending upon our individual situation). That's it! And in the book business, that is not hard to do at all, especially with how-to titles. Even figuring in extra overhead and expenses, 2,000 sales of our most expensive book easily puts us into profits.

Keep in mind that these low break even points are possible only because we are not figuring in any overhead or employee costs. When you add them to the mix, and there would be no reason you need to if you are a low budget start-up company, than the break-even point becomes higher, but still very manageable.

Let's move on and look at the elements of a successful book.

# 4. THE ELEMENTS OF A SUCCESSFUL BOOK

## INTRODUCTION

There's a lot of competition to be found on a bookshelf. Some books on these shelves will be purchased at a brisk pace, other books will go at a slower pace, and still others won't get bought at all. And there's one more category - the books that don't even make it to the shelf in the first place - books that couldn't find distribution, and those that did find distribution but weren't purchased by the retail store.

What's the difference between these different books? Why do some books sell well, others sell poorly, and still others not at all?

The difference is really quite simple: The publishers who understand the needs and concerns of their audience, and the factors that move books in the marketplace, are the ones who will have their imprint on the books that are good sellers. And the ones who have no clue as to why someone buys a book - these are the publishers whose books will make it directly into remainder bins, if that far.

Many factors influence a consumer in the purchase of a book, and in this chapter, we're going to go over them so you best understand what goes into a consumer's buying decision. We'll go over how to identify and target your audience, the various selling features that will make your book both competitive and marketable, and how to design your book into an appealing format and price it at a level that the market will bear.

Let's now look at the secrets of successful books.

# IDENTIFYING YOUR AUDIENCE

Your very first step toward publishing books that will sell on the open market, *the very first step*, is to identify your audience *and* its needs. The level of your success with a particular book rests on your success in appealing to (and of course, reaching) your audience. The better you achieve that goal, the more books you'll sell. It's a simple formula, but one you must execute well.

And you must go deeper than the obvious. Once you've chosen a type of book and a direction, you must really hone in and segment your market so it hits the nail right on the head. The basic sales goal with a book is to reach out and touch as many interested people as possible, and thus give yourself maximum sales potential. To do this you must understand what the majority of readers in this field desire so your book can appeal to them.

Let's look at some examples to see this principle in action.

## Running Book Example

Let's say an interesting proposal comes in from a marathoner and he wants to write a book on running. So we look at the issue further.

The first thing we have to ask ourselves is; who exactly among runners or would-be runners are we targeting and what is it that this potential audience wants to get out of the book? Is this book for beginning runners or advanced? Is the running market audience interested in learning about the psychology involved, the equipment needed, about medium distance or marathon skills, the importance of a runners diet, how to prevent injuries, or all of these and perhaps other things?

If we focus on the importance of a runner's diet, and all the average runner is interested in is the basic running skills to keep himself or herself fit, we've missed the boat - we haven't addressed our audience. Or if runners want to know about improving their performance skills and conditioning, and the book focuses on ultra-marathon running, we've really missed the boat. We could of course really specialize and target the ultra-marathoner, but then the concern arises whether this market is broad enough to give us the sales we need.

Thus, our ability to identify the needs and desires of the particular type of runner we're targeting and the size of that book-buying market not only makes a huge difference in our chances for successfully marketing this book, but also, in how well the author can focus in on his subject and give us the best material to work with.

A little market research will go a long way. In the case of this projected running book, we'll find it helpful to talk with regular runners - perhaps family, friends or colleagues who like to run - in addition to the author so we get a better understanding of where they're coming from and what we'll have to do to give them a book they'll enjoy reading.

Alternately, we could go for the various sub-markets and target say, ultra-marathoners, but again, we'll be limiting our market to just a small segment of possible runners. But that could be a strategy as well. Or perhaps, it would be better to go for the more general approach and target a wider running audience while still fielding a unique angle. These are decisions that have to be made.

> In real estate they say the three most important things are *location, location, location*. In publishing, a similar thing can be said about selling books; *address your audience, address your audience, address your audience.*

## Romance Book Example

The tremendous success of writers in the Danielle Steele-romance-Harlequin-authors ilk is an excellent example of targeting one's audience for success.

You can say whatever you want about the literary quality of these books, but you can't argue with their success. The best-selling romance writers *address their readers desires* and understand their audience perfectly. Consequently, they write best-seller after best-seller.

Some critics may downgrade their work by saying it's just a formula; ravishing woman meets handsome man, falls in love, there are difficulties, then a resolution, whatever the plot might be. Maybe every book in the series may be a variation on the same story, with different characters. But if the formula works, as far as I'm concerned, it works. These books make both the publishers and their authors tons of money, while at the same time, filling the needs of millions of readers.

We're in business to entertain or educate our audience, and if we can come up with a formula that readers enjoy and benefit from, and there's profits to be made and books to be sold, then by all means, you should consider a marketable formula that serves a readership.

## Gaming Book Example

When I wrote and published my first book, *Winning Casino Blackjack for the Non-Counter*, I targeted that book to the segment of the blackjack audience that comprised 95% of the blackjack player market - those players who want to win money at blackjack without counting cards. I let the readers know right off the bat, in the title, that the book is about winning and that they can win without counting cards (addressing a misconception).

Blackjack players, like all gamblers, want to win, and they want to win the easy way, so I addressed those issues through every aspect of the book, from the writing to the packaging, format and price of the book, originally $3.95 in 1981.

My formula for success was simple; appeal to the average player - 95% of the market. I could just as easily have written a book to appeal to the 5% of advanced blackjack players looking for super-advanced concepts, but how many copies would this book have sold? This is now 10 printings and hundred of thousands of copies later, and *Winning Casino Blackjack for the Non-Counter* is selling as well as ever. This book is exceptionally successful for I gave the average blackjack player - 95% of the market - exactly what they wanted - a quick but easy reading book that shows them how to win.

And if you can do that too, identify your market and then serve them in the way you put together your book, than you'll have a winner as well.

The question then becomes; once you've identified your audience, how do you target your book so that it appeals to them?

*First Impressions* ✳

COMPLETE GUIDE TO SUCCESSFUL PUBLISHING     51

---

## THE FIRST IMPRESSION

The buy or no buy decision on a book is often rendered in a matter of seconds. Sometimes it may be as little as five seconds, other times it may take as long as a minute or more. But however it measures out in any individual case, we have just a brief amount of time before that decision is made.

Thus, a buyer's initial impression is crucial to our chances for success in selling a book so we've got to make that first impression good. Unless the consumer comes in the bookstore looking for a particular book, he only has the book he holds in his hands, and the competing books in the shelf next to this book, to judge from in making a buying decision. So we've got to make consumers feel that this book was written for their needs - that it's just the book they were looking for.

And we get our game plan together. Once we identify our market and its needs, we're ready to formulate and execute our plan.

---

# SELLING FEATURES OF A BOOK

There are several factors which influence a buyer's decision to buy a book, and each plays a part toward the whole, but the factor most influential of all is clearly the cover. You've heard the expression, "Don't judge a book by its cover." Well, in a bookstore, where the buyer doesn't have time to read the book, and may give the book just seconds of his or her time, that cover is the flower that attracts the bee. The cover helps define a book, gives it a "feel" and a personality, and lets a reader know just what that book is about.

And when it all boils down, a book *is* greatly judged by the cover. But other things are considered as well.

Besides the *cover* (which *must* grab the browser) and its *spine* (gets the book plucked off the shelf) both critical tools to sell your book, these sales tools must be supported by the book itself. After examining the cover, the typical browser will quickly flip through the book to get a feel of what's happening (*interior design*), perhaps read a few random lines or paragraphs (*writing quality*), and will examine the *introduction* and *table of contents* to see if the book addresses their particular interests. The *page count* and *price* will be checked for comparative value.

These supporting items are then weighed, measured, and added up in the human calculator. They can either make the sale, or they can postpone the consumer's decision to buy, and lose the sale. And there will be a decision. If the consumer feels that a combination of the above factors work to address his needs in buying this book, there's a deal. If the consumer is not convinced, then no deal.

And that is why we must put a lot of emphasis on making the book look as strong as possible in all areas: Cover, spine, interior design, writing quality, introduction, table of contents, page count and price - they all must be given careful thought and must, as best as possible, serve the audience we're selling.

Let's go over each selling item in detail and talk about it's role in the sale of the book and what you've got to do about it.

## THE COVER

A book cover is composed of various items of sales importance; the *title* of the book, the *sales copy*, the *design*, and the *spine type*. The cover is such an important element in the creation of a successful book that besides stressing its importance throughout this work, we've devoted an entire chapter to the cover itself.

## The Title - How-to Books

As a very basic principle, the title should clearly let the reader know what the book is about and how it benefits them. Great titles can make a two, three, or even five-fold or more difference in sales over mediocre titles. Consider your title carefully, keeping in mind the key principle of success - *address your market*.

For example, in my gambling books, I stress *winning*. *The Basics of **Winning** Slots, How to Play **Winning** Poker, **Winning** Craps for the Serious Player*. *Winning* is what gamblers want to hear - they're going to win. The other words, *Basics, Serious Player*, sends a message as well. Listing the name of the game in the title leaves no doubt what the subject matter is.

If you're writing a book on meeting singles, go for the title that sells over a hokey title. *How to Meet Singles* is infinitely better than *Singles Mingle*. The first title lets you know what the book is about and addresses an interest, a need. The second title doesn't tell you anything.

It's a turn-off. Is the book about singles meeting (?), some self-indulgent fiction rag, a chemical study - what is it?

Similarly, the *Art and Science of Hunting* interests and addresses the hunter far more than, *Is the Bear in the Woods?*, while *Dance the Mambo Tonight* easily is better than *1-2-3 Footsteps*.

Titles of books cannot be copyrighted, so you can use any title you want for your book as long as it doesn't infringe on anyone's trademark.

## The Title - Other Books

Where the emphasis on how-to books is in addressing practical needs, with fiction, poetry, certain genre (such as mystery, romance, true crime, and others), art, photography, historical fiction, and non-fiction, the emphasis in the title is more on catching an *emotional* nerve, getting the reader *intrigued* with the book, perhaps telling a story.

Titles such as *The Grapes of Wrath, You Can't Go Home Again, Gone With the Wind, Great Expectations,* are great titles that conjure up images and thoughts on their own. Of course, these books are classics in their own right, but the titles certainly lend to their aura.

Many classics and best-sellers have made it with titles that on their own are flat or uninspiring, but why not give your book that extra push an exciting title can provide?

A photography book titled *The Mystery of the Killer White Shark* gives us a little more emotional appeal than simply *The White Shark*. A detective or horror story entitled *Dr. Sullivan's Dark Secret* commands more oomph than simply *Dr. Sullivan's Secret*. Often, an extra word or two in a title, as we see above, can do wonders. Don't be afraid to put a little extra spice in the formula; jazz up your book title.

## The Cover Copy

There's only one point to your cover copy - and that's to sell your book. Make no mistake about it. Put your cannons on the cover and set all guns blazing. Strut your stuff. *Make an impact. Address your audience!*

Regardless of the type of book you're doing, fiction, romance, how-to, photography, or whatever, the cover copy is an essential part of sales.

In our travel guides, we use the logo line on every cover, *Your Passport to Great Travel*. Our message: "You want to have a great trip, buy this book". We're targeting an audience of pleasure seekers, people that just want to have a good time on their vacation.

If you're publishing a book on women's fashion, your copy should be stressing how young and beautiful the reader will look by using your design suggestions. If you're doing a book on gardening, the reader wants to hear about the beautiful flowers or wonderful produce they'll grow. If you're doing a cookbook, make the reader *salivate* with your descriptions (and use a damn good picture).

Get those powerful adjectives in motion. Women's fashion - beautiful, attractive, young, inspiring, sexy. Gardening - fresh, healthy, fragrant. Cookbook - appetizing, delicious, salivating, tantalizing.

Look at best-selling horror books. Sinister black and red covers predominate the field. The cover copy has people imagining the horror of the storyline, gets their flesh creeping. *And when the lights went out...* And then???

Fiction covers should pull the readers into the story, make the book a *compelling* buy; poetry books should grab the readers ethereal senses; photography books must capture the mood of the artist's work.

Work the readers' imagination. Work the copy. Make sure the cover *rock and rolls*.

## The Design

The cover design hits the reader first and sets a mood and tone to the book. You must make this design *inspiring*. We'll talk a lot more about the cover in the *Cover Design and Production* chapter.

## The Spine

The book with the most attractive spine, is most likely the first book pulled off the shelf. It's noticed first. In psychology we learn that first impressions are the strongest if many items are sampled. Let the other books compare to the tone you've set. Get in the readers' hands first.

Quite often, the most attractive spine simply means, the easiest seen. Make your letters as big and bold as you can and use colors that stand out. Check the shelves for spines that grab your attention. Make your spine a screamer.

## TABLE OF CONTENTS
### How-to & Non-Fiction

The table of contents should be attractive and show the reader, especially in how-to and non-fiction books, that your book is interesting and chock-full of information. The contents are extremely important in these categories because it gives the browser a definitive look at what the book contains. You want to give the appearance that your book is comprehensive and all-encompassing. The more that's listed in the contents, the more information you appear to be giving the reader. A book with a three page table of contents appears to have a lot more information than a table of contents with simply one page.

### Fiction & Certain Genre

In fiction and some genre books, the table of contents is usually not listed or even used as a sales tool, so it's not a factor. However, this doesn't mean that you can't use one yourself for the proper book and add a little extra interest. Conventions are good, but don't always have to be followed.

### Other Categories

For books where the table of contents can be used as a sales feature, you want the reader to get a nice feeling for the book you're presenting and have them make that purchase. Intriguing or informative chapter heads add interest and can help sell books.

Following is a comparative look at the table of contents for the first edition of *The Basics of Chess*, compared to the second edition. The difference in *perceived* information is significant - the second edition's contents appear to be more informative and comprehensive. Both books however, contain the same information. (Note also how we changed the title to include the word *Winning*.)

# THE BASICS OF CHESS
## First Edition

# Table of Contents

I. Introduction ......................................... 5

II. The Fundamentals Of Chess ............ 6

III. Additional Rules of Play ................ 18

IV. Chess Notations ............................ 21

V. Principles of Play ........................... 29

VI. Tactical Maneuvers ........................ 38

VII. Standard Openings ........................ 44

VIII. Representative Games ................. 49

IX. The Chess Clock ............................ 55

X. Five Minute Chess ........................... 57

# THE BASICS OF WINNING CHESS
## Second Edition

# Table of Contents

**I. Introduction** .......................................... 5

**II. The Fundamentals Of Chess** ............ 6
The Players • The Chessboard • The Pieces and Pawns •
Pawns • The Rook • The Bishop • The Queen • The King •
The Knight • Symbols of the Pieces • Castling

**III. Additional Rules of Play** .................. 18

**IV. Chess Notations** ............................... 21
Algebraic System • English System • Symbols Common to
Both Systems • Notating a Game • The Ruy Lopez Open-
ing

**V. Principles of Play** ............................. 29
Opening Principles • Middle Game Principles • End Game
Principles

**VI. Tactical Maneuvers** ......................... 38
The Pin • Discovered Check • Double Check • Knight Fork
• Combinations

**VII. Standard Openings** ......................... 44
King's Pawn Openings (Ruy Lopez, Sicilian Defense,
French Defense) • Queen's Pawn Openings (Queen's Gam-
bit Declined • Queen's Indian Defense)

**VIII. Representative Games** .................. 49
Karpov vs. Spassky • Fischer vs. Petrosian

**IX. The Chess Clock** ............................. 55
The Element of Time • Types of Chess Clocks

**X. Five Minute Chess** .......................... 57
Introduction • Special Five Minute Rules • Five Minute
Chess Strategy

## Positioning

The table of contents should *always* start on a right-hand side page. It's one of two premium pages in the book where we make maximum sales impact, the other one being the introduction.

It's a known fact in advertising that right-hand pages get more attention than left hand pages, and thus advertisers often get charged premiums for requesting this right-side position. Make sure the table of contents receives this premium position.

## THE INTRODUCTION

The main purpose of an introduction is to sell books. The introduction, like the table of contents, is the other most important sales section within a book. Due to its sales importance (and like the table of contents), the introduction must always be on a premium right hand page. Make no exception to this rule.

Whether you're publishing how-to's, non-fiction, or any other category of appropriate books (fiction, for example, may not be appropriate), the introduction, like the cover copy, should pack big-time wallop and be given careful attention. You want your potential readers to be wowed, and to feel the quality and scope of the book right off the bat. An effective introduction should immediately address its intended audience, get them excited by what the book has to offer, and move them to make the purchase. A good introduction should convince a browser that this is a book that needs to get bought.

Forget the drab, senseless introductions of most books. *Get your readers into the book, make the purchase compelling.*

A properly written introduction is the hardest page in the book to write, for it's here where you address your readers and appeal to their needs. If necessary, make your writer redo the intro five times or more until it's right. But get it right.

We'll look at two introductions of books I've published for examples of introductions that attempt to sell the reader. (Also, look at the introduction to this book.) You'll see that I immediately get the reader excited by the possibilities of publishing and the benefits of this book.

Compare these introductions to books where the author rambles on about all the things he's not going to do that others do. *An introduction should talk about what the author will write about and what the reader will learn, not the things that won't be done.* A good introduction must be relevant and interesting, and must draw the reader into the book. Basically, if the introduction does not make the reader want to read the book, it is poorly written and worthless.

The first introduction we'll look at is from my book, *Winning Casino Blackjack for the Non-Counter,* and the second, from the *Las Vegas Guide,* which I co-wrote with Ed Kranmar.

The following two pages shows these examples.

## WRITING QUALITY

In your book, you want the reader to find the writing to be of excellent quality, just as you want your reputation of producing fine books to be of similar stature. Good writing is immediately apparent to sophisticated readers while bad writing sticks out like a sore thumb and can turn readers off to current and future books you may publish.

Book buyers respect quality, and will respond to that quality by buying your books.

## THE PRICE

The browser must view the book as a good or at least fair value to allow the reader to act upon his or her impulses to buy the book. If the book is priced too high, some readers will think twice and shy away, while if it's priced inexpensively, some readers will go for the value.

In all cases, the price is a function of the book itself - its subject matter, dimensions, page count, and competition, if any, all adding up to a perceived value.

Basically, you want to price your book so that you get maximum value for the sales you make. Pricing your book correctly is an important issue. We'll discuss increasing your profits through pricing and other related concepts in greater detail in the *Making Money* chapter.

## Winning Casino Blackjack for the Non-Counter

# I. Introduction

Blackjack can be beaten! Once you've finished reading this book and learned the skills presented, you'll find that there will be one major difference between you and 95% of the other players - you'll be a winner at blackjack!

We'll teach you how to win without the blind memorization and boring tedium usually associated with learning blackjack. Our computer-tested basic strategies are carefully explained so that every play you make is easily learned. In addition, all the winning strategies are presented in easy-to-read charts.

You'll learn how to beat the single deck game without counting cards and how best to adjust your play for multiple deck games whether you're a player in Las Vegas, Northern Nevada, Atlantic City, the Mississippi riverboats and Indian reservations, or you're heading for play in Europe, Asia, the Bahamas, the Caribbean or anywhere else blackjack is found.

You'll receive a wealth of information from this book. We cover the fundamentals of casino blackjack - the rules of the game, the player's options, the variations offered in casinos around the world, how to bet, casino jargon, how to play and everything else you'll need to know about playing winning casino blackjack.

Not only will we teach you the skills of winning, but just as important, we'll teach you how to walk away a winner. Money management is carefully explained to insure your success as a blackjack player. We also discuss emotional control, how to minimize losses when losing, and how to let your winnings ride, so that when you lose, you lose small, and when you win, you win big - the overall result being that you walk away a winner!

For the first time, the winning concepts that have been successfully taught at the Cardoza School of Blackjack are now presented here so that you can win without counting cards.

So read this book carefully, and you'll be among those players that the casinos fear, and for good reason - you will be a consistent winner at blackjack!

## Las Vegas Guide

# 1. INTRODUCTION

Las Vegas is America's most exciting city, and in this book we'll show you all that this great town has to offer. If you follow our advice, and we have plenty of it, you'll have the time of your life!

Of course, Vegas is built around gambling, but the city that never sleeps is much more. It's good, clean fun for families with its theme parks and video arcades, and it's also *Sin City* and topless numbers in the big casino production shows. It's a fun raft trip on Lake Mead, it's a breathtaking hike in Valley of Fire State Park, and it's also a visit to the "Eighth Wonder of the World" - monumental Hoover Dam.

We'll show you unexplored Las Vegas; where to go Country and Western dancing; how to rediscover Elvis and Liberace; and where to find delicious 99¢ shrimp cocktails. You'll find out where to go to enjoy some of the country's finest golfing, tennis, boating, and swimming, and if solitude and nature is desired, where to go to explore one's soul in the vast magnitude of the desert.

For people who never sleep or love to gamble, Vegas is paradise. While other travel guides may tell you how to play, we'll show you how to *win*. Armed with Avery Cardoza's inside tips, you'll learn everything you need to know to win money gambling.

It all adds up to excitement and thrills. We'll show you all the possibilities to help make your trip to Vegas one of the best you've ever taken!

## PAGE COUNT

Sometimes your marketing strategy with a book is to keep the book thin, and super-easy to read. This is what I did with my *Basics of Winning Series*, where each book is kept to just 64 pages. You may also take the other end of the spectrum, and push the complete type of book, or look to charge a certain amount and need bulk. Thus, you may do a 320 page book, or even a 128 page or 224 page book printed on high-bulk stock for a thicker book.

In either case, the page count affects the decision-making process of the consumer only as a function of the price (see above) where perceived value is the key.

## INTERIOR DESIGN

A clean, easy-to-read and professional look will make a reader feel comfortable with your product and will induce sales. Readers typically flip through a book upon picking it up, and if you do a good job with the layout and overall design, you can greatly increase the chances that the book will be bought.

Interior design is important to sales, and a big part of production, so you want to do a good job. In the *Book Design* chapter, we'll go over the general concepts of a quality, attractive design, and then in the *Production* chapter, show how to put these concepts together into a book.

## BLURBS

Praiseworthy reviews of your book or author, given in appropriate abbreviated form, called **blurbs**, give a book more credence and help sell a book, especially if given by experts or known personages. If you get good blurbs, by all means, use them on the cover, front or back, and also, on the very first page of the book as it opens. If you got it, strut it.

---

### STUDY BUYING HABITS

You'll find it valuable to observe browsers in a bookstore mulling over possible books to buy. After watching these potential book buyers examine the front and back covers, flip through the book, look at the price, think, look again, and then make their purchase - or not make the purchase, you ought to get some more good insights into what a consumer considers before buying a book.

# CONCLUSION

To be successful, all the elements of the publishing process, from the format and price, to the writing and book design (text and cover), must be aligned toward the market you're addressing.

Your job as a publisher is to make your books as sellable as possible. By following the guidelines we laid out in this chapter, you'll be well on your way toward properly executing that plan. We'll talk a lot more about using strong design concepts to improve the salability of our books in our design and cover chapters, and from there, in production, put the whole thing together.

Blurbs: If you get good blurbs, by all means, use them on the cover, front or back, + also, on the very first page of the book as it opens.

# 5. THE AUTHOR & THE PROPOSAL

## INTRODUCTION

There are thousands of ideas, manuscripts and book proposals from published and unpublished writers, that are marketable and lack only the connection with the right publisher at the right time to become a published book.

For this connection between writer and publisher to occur, each side must be accessible in some form so that one side can find the other. For the author, this typically takes the form of sending out queries and manuscripts to potential publishers; and for the publisher, it typically means having a certain visibility so that authors can find them. These roles can be reversed as well. Rather than the author with the good idea going after the visible publisher, the publisher with the good idea may go after the visible writer.

There's one more aspect of the magic formula, and that is that a quality proposal must encompass the promise of both a quality manuscript and a marketable idea. If the idea is not marketable in the financial sense, then at the least, for certain publishers, it should be marketable in a creative way (a good idea that should be brought to fruition).

In this chapter, we'll talk about all these things; how to come in contact with good manuscripts and opportunities, how to evaluate among these possibilities for marketability and for quality of writing, and additionally, how to shape a contract and come to agreement with the author.

But the whole process starts off with the proposal, so let's begin our discussion here.

*From a tiny acorn, grew the mighty oak!*

# THE PROPOSAL

In a famous poker scene from one of his classic movies, *My Little Chicka-dee*, the great comedian W.C. Fields, shocked upon receiving just one chip for his $100 entrance into the game exclaimed, *From the tiny acorn, grew the mighty oak!* Our acorn here, the seed of our book-making process, starts with a serious proposal for a book. If the proposal looks intriguing, and merits consideration, we've got some serious thinking to do.

The proposal can be in the form of an idea, an outline and/or sample chapters, a completed manuscript, or even as a previously published book. The book idea can come as an unsolicited submission, it can be a self-written book or one written by a friend or acquaintance, or the proposal can be received from an outside source, either with or without a writer.

But however a proposal comes to our attention, a manuscript must be written before a book can be produced, so our first step in publishing a book, is to find ourselves a writer who can give life to an idea.

There's an abundance of aspiring writers with marketable ideas and the talent to put them together into a solid book, and by the same token, there are lots of ideas waiting for the writer. Many writers have even written their book, and only await the match with a publisher to get their break and become published.

The trick is to get the two sides together and form the marriage. Either the author finds you, or you have to find the author. Let's look at how to help this process along.

# FINDING A WRITER
## They'll Find You

Once a publisher is established and has listings in the *Literary Market-place, Writers Market,* or some of the other valuable publications we've listed in this book, or has books already on the shelves, manuscripts and proposals will come in unsolicited. Most of these submissions won't be very good, but now and then some gems will sneak through and give you something interesting to think about.

See the *Places to Get Listed* section on pages 102-104 for a listing of directories that will get your company exposed to potential writers looking for a publisher.

Writers will also find you through books that are already published and in the bookstore. They'll see a book on a similar category as the one you're publishing and send a query. And there's always friends, friends of friends, friends of friends of friends, and friends of authors you've already published. Word will get out there and ideas and books will start coming your way. I've received quality submissions all the above ways.

## You'll Find Them

If the writer you need doesn't come to you, you've got to go to them. As a new publisher or one who has a particular book in mind and lacks only the writer, there are a wealth of places where, with a little sleuthing, the right writer can be tracked down.

The best place of all to find qualified writers is in the magazines, newspapers, and other publications which publish articles on a similar subject. For example, if you're looking for writers to do new age books, a really hot field now, begin your search with the magazines and newspapers targeted to the new age audience. If you want to do a gardening book, buy the gardening publications and get in touch with writers doing articles there, or check out the gardening sections of either your local paper or ones in other cities. These publications are chock-full of budding talent waiting for their break.

The great thing about finding talent this way is that you already have a sampling of what the writer can do, and know that he or she has enough skills or recognition to at least be published in the place you located him or her. It doesn't necessarily mean the writer is good (some editors can do wonders fixing up inferior writing), but then again, the writing is right in front of you and most likely was good to begin with.

You can place ads yourself in these specialized publications, and let the writers come to you with their proposals - there should be plenty of them - or contact the editors. They may be interested in writing a book for you, and if not, will certainly know writers who might be. You may even want to try ads in magazines targeted to the writers themselves.

The local library is a great source for finding potential writers. Have the librarian point you in the right direction for articles and books on the relevant topics.

The search for talent should not be limited to the written word resources. There are other good places to look. Go right to the experts in their workplaces, track down potential candidates through trade associations, get recommendations from friends or acquaintances who might have a connection with the subject matter. Teachers at universities, extension programs, private schools, and private clubs, are other ideal places to find ready and willing experts on a variety of subjects that just may make a great book. Places such as the Learning Annex, Discovery Center, the local high school and community extension programs are goldmines of potential authors as well.

## Finding Ideas for Books

Get leads for books just like a news editor or fiction writer get leads for their stories — search through the media for leads. Special interest, regional and local magazines, newspapers and weeklies, in your city and others are packed with articles written by experts or about experts, which could be expanded into books. This search is promising for all types of publishers short on ideas, from fiction and poetry, to how-to's and biographies.

Magazines, newspapers, talk shows, specialty associations, and previously published authors are all great places to get ideas. Keep your ears and eyes open, and you'll be amazed at the possibilities.

# SOLICITING OR ACCEPTING SUBMISSIONS

Below, we've listed five parts of the book proposal that should be required of an author before you can properly consider his or her submission.

However, while the first two parts of the submission, sample writing and the outline/table of contents, in themselves may be adequate for a decision to publish, the other three parts should be required as well to help provide the full flavor of the book and its place in the market.

## 1. Two Sample Chapters or Sufficient Previous Work

To be able to make an intelligent decision on a writer's manuscript, you must see enough of their writing to make a good judgment, and that writing must *interest* you. Whether it's two sample chapters of the book under consideration (generally you'll require those chapters anyway), or the submittance of previously written work for examination, you need to feel 100% sure that the writer can produce the quality book you need.

The proof is only in the pudding: Without seeing samples of an author's writing, there's little to discuss unless you like spinning wheels. Talk usually sounds good, but writing is what we're interested in. Make sure you get enough of a sample to be able to make ane educated judgment.

## 2. Outline and/or Table of Contents

An outline and/or a table of contents, like nothing else in the proposal, tells us what the book will be about, the depth and scope it will encompass, and how the author will go about developing the subject. From the outline and table of contents, we start getting a good feel of the insight the author brings to the idea.

Later, when we actually make the book, we'll be using the table of contents as a sales feature (for certain types of books). Seeing the author's viewpoint in this area helps us to envision its sales potential.

## 3. The Intended Market

There's nothing more important in selling a book than knowing the intended audience. Thus, the proposal should tell us who the book is targeted to, the size of that audience, and why this book will serve their needs. This element of the book proposal gives us a good feel and perhaps some convincing arguments why the book should be done.

## 4. Closest Competition & Sales Angle

Ask the author to list the closest existing competitors to the proposed book, the author's names, the dimensions of the book (mass market, trade, oversize), the page count and price, and the success of the books if known.

This lets you know what you're up against, and how best the book can be positioned in the marketplace. As part of this discussion, let the author briefly outline, in a sentence or two, what makes this book different than the other books in this list.

## 5. The Author's Qualifications

If the author has qualifications and credentials relevant to the writing of the book, we want to know what they are. We're always looking for a way to position our book in the marketplace and show it's unique voice compared to the competition. If the author has credentials that will help sell the book, so much the better.

Credentials are especially important to books where the author's knowledge, insight and experience are vital to the subject. How-to's and non-fiction books demand that the author has control of his subject matter, while books in the general area of fiction simply require flat out talent - it's the book itself which must do the talking, unless the author is popular enough to sell by name alone.

You want to make sure the writer is qualified in the field he or she is writing and that the information provided is reliable, but really, the main concern with a book is whether the writer can do a terrific job on the subject. Whether the author is a so-called expert, a "verified" expert, or an unknown and unlettered person who has greatly studied the situation, if the book is written clearly and with intelligence, for all intents and purposes, you have an expert.

Keep in mind that "credentials" are often born when a person's book goes into print. Suddenly, a previously unknown entity has become an expert, and verifiably so. The author has proven a capacity to present the subject in documented form, and there it is, a book to prove it and give voice to his or her expertness.

Thus, the first question we must ask of the author in non-fiction and how-to books, is, "What are your qualifications to write this book." We don't need the world's most impressive answer, for bottom line, we want good, clear writing, but we do want to feel secure that there's a real book here.

A good writer can write clearly and authoritatively on any subject if the proper research is done. You're better off with an excellent writer's work on a thoroughly prepared subject over an expert (who doesn't write well) any day, just as you're better off learning from a superior teacher who happens only to be an average skill level on a subject, than the world's number one expert who can't explain his technique. Of course, if you can combine the two, an expert who writes extremely well, you've got yourself the ideal combination.

## FOR AUTHORS - NOTE

If you're an author reading this book, and want to get published, send proposals to publishers according to the outlines discussed above to give yourself the best shot of gaining a contract. If a publisher shows some interest in your work, don't be afraid to follow up with a call to move that publisher along.

# JUDGING A BOOK PROPOSAL

Following are the three criteria that must be met for you to move ahead with a book project.

## 1. Quality Writing

An absolute must for any proposal is that, unless you're publishing books where you can get away with inferior writing and don't mind doing so, the writing must be good. Quality writing is the basis of good books; good books are the basis, not coincidentally, of good sales.

To be a publisher who's taken seriously, you must only work with *real* writers. Don't even consider publishing hacks. We'll talk more about how to recognize and judge quality writing, and the importance of working with good writers below in the section, *Evaluating Writing*.

## 2. Good Potential Market

For a proposal to be taken seriously, we have to feel that a book can command enough of an audience to make the project, from a financial frame of reference, a *worthwhile* project. In terms of a goal needing to be met, "worthwhile" is a relative term whose definition is going to vary from publisher to publisher.

For some publishers, the goal might be to support a great new author, or a book that *needs* to get published regardless of the sales, though of course good sales is a goal as well. For others, break-even or near break-even might be an acceptable minimum goal, while for many publishers, ones running their companies like a business, the expectation of certain profit levels must be met for any publishing effort. Publishing is a business, and generally speaking, the business must at the very least, make enough to further its existence and hopefully, accrue profits for the owners.

Often, the goals of a company are tied in with the types of books published. Houses publishing religious, philosophical or poetry books may have different goals than say, business publishers; disseminating their important works, with profit desirable, but not absolutely necessary.

On the other hand, non-fiction, how-to, and most medium and large publishers might be more profit-driven. Payroll, overhead and the authors must be paid. Growth is generally desirable and attention is paid toward improving profit margins and increasing market share. While there may be the labor of love involved in the publishing process, the bottom line is that money must be made to drive the machine. The break-even point may not be sufficient; a certain profit level is the goal.

Books need an audience, a market to sell to, and our job as a publisher is to make sure our books have enough potential to fit into our minimum sales and break-even or profit goals.

### 3. There Must Be a Place to Sell the Book
Just as important as having a potential market for our books, is having a place where that audience can find our books and buy them. If we can't reach our potential audience, we're going to have a hard time selling books.

The basic market for a book is not just in the bookstore, *but a particular section within the bookstore.** Books are shelved in categories according to the types of books they are. There are sections for fiction, poetry,

---

*There are many other markets as well, as we'll discuss in the distribution section, but if your book is intended for the bookstore trade, there's got to be a section in that store for your book to be found and displayed.

historical romance, religion, philosophy, history, biography, sports, computer books, art, photography, film, and many others. If a true-crime book or dance title is stocked, they'll go into their appropriate section.

But if we're publishing a book that doesn't happen to fit into any of these sections cleanly, we've got a potential problem in selling this book. Let's look at an example.

Several years ago we received a proposal for a book, *The Family Guide to Shooting Video Tape*. A quick examination of the material showed me that the book was a serious possibility for publication. It was well-written and organized, and there certainly was a good potential market for this title. There are millions and millions of families with video camcorders.

I liked the proposal and took the next step for book proposals I take seriously. The bookstore. We always want to see what competition is out on the book shelves and how our book can be positioned in the marketplace. Understanding the marketplace is crucial for the success of any product and nothing reveals more about the marketplace and our competition than a trip to the bookstore and a first-hand look at what's going on.

I went to several bookstores and ran into a big obstacle. *There was no section for home videotaping.* Some stores had videotape books in the film section, others had them in photography. One store didn't even know where to suggest I look. I felt the film section was a more natural place, film and video being close, but there was certainly disagreement among individuals I asked, and more importantly, in the bookstore itself. Others argued that videotape books belonged in the photography section. Thus, without having a clear-cut direction, I decided against the book.

Had my main interest in this book been to other markets outside the book trade, for example, trying to sell this book to camcorder manufacturers as an incentive, or positioning the book as a mail order item, then I may have given the book a further look. But since the main energies of my company are in the direction of publishing for the general book trade, we had to turn down the book.

I've long liked the idea of publishing reprints of great explorers (more for personal interest than for profit), but have been held back somewhat because there really is no place in the store to sell them. Sections such as history, travel (under country headings), travel writing, biography, all sort of fit the bill, but not really. These books need a travel and exploration section, and though some stores now have such a section or a related one, not many do.

On the other side of the coin, a book such as, *Raising Toddlers* faces no such difficulty. This one's easy, it goes in the parenting section, while books such as *Crochet Patterns*, *Investing on the Cheap*, and *The Mystery Readers Handbook* have clear-cut places on the shelves. People can wander over to that section, and find the book.

Usually, there is a clear-cut section for your book, and it won't be an obstacle to find a fit on the shelves. If in doubt about a possible book, do your research at several bookstores, and ask the clerks there for assistance.

# EVALUATING WRITING
## Evaluating How-to and Non-Fiction Writing
I look for the following clues, good and bad in someone's writing.

First and foremost, as we discussed under submissions, *the writer must be able to write*. If it's obvious from the writing you've received, that the book is poorly written and unclear, and that the writer's thoughts are badly organized, don't waste your time reading any more than you have to. When you find that you're spending a lot of time just trying to make sense of someone's writing, you've got inferior writing.

On the other hand, sometimes you'll get writing that's somewhat inconsistent but shows many good signs, or writing that is strong but the author tends to get lost in his direction. That's a different story than an out and out bad manuscript.

If the work shows a lot of promise and you feel the writer can be worked with, then give the manuscript some consideration. Some writers have the talent, but sometimes, perhaps, need a helping hand.

There are particular signs that can clue you in on the writer's skill level. I look to get impressed right away, immediately, in the very first paragraph. A good writer gets right to the point in his work, and in subsequent paragraphs and chapters, stays on the point. At any place in the book, the writing should be tight and concise, a pleasure to read. He or she makes the subject *interesting*; we feel we're learning things, or being entertained.

Bad writing stands out because it is loose and confused. With a poorly written piece, we find ourselves thinking about things other than what the writer is trying to say. These are not good signs.

If the book is about hiking, for example, I'm going to be turned off real fast about asides that have nothing to do with hiking or the mentality involved, unless, and we're talking rare occasion here, the writer is really good, and can make those discussions both interesting and relevant. But I don't want to hear about the writer's brother-in-law's golf game, who while hitting a birdie thought about hiking, etc.

Sometimes good writers do get off the track, and some editing will polish the rough into a gem. And sometimes writers are good, but just haven't learned certain basic skills that would improve their work, so there's glitches in the writing. Such imperfections don't matter - if the talent is there, you can work with the writer. But if there's no sparkle under the dust, don't bother. There's more fish in the sea. Get someone who *can* write the book.

## Evaluating Fiction Writing

Fiction is an entirely different type of horse than how-to and non-fiction writing. It's more creative and free-flowing, and fewer rules and forms apply. While the writing still has to be good, it doesn't have to be logical, at least not in the same formula as in how-to's and non-fiction. Creativity abounds, there are different rules. A writer who can excel in non-fiction or how-to may not necessarily be able to write fiction. These are very different types of writing.

As fiction is tougher to sell than other types of writing it is also more difficult to judge a talented manuscript from the chaff. If you're going to publish fiction books, you must have an understanding of what is good, and equally important, what others will find good.

Fiction is somewhat subjective as well. One man's pearl is another's crustacean. My advice here, if you know what you're doing, then go to town. If not, choose a line of books you better understand.

# THE GOOD, THE BAD, AND THE UGLY
## Good Signs in Writing
- The writing gets to the point.
- The writing makes you interested in the subject. You may have something here.
- The writer makes points and illustrates them with clear examples. Many writers are good, but don't necessarily provide good examples. (This is easily taken care of with advice to the author.)
- When a point or interesting observation is made, the writer completes the thought and makes it relevant.
- You feel the *power* of the author's work. Wow! - you've got a good one here. Time to talk.

## Bad Signs in Writing
- A writer constantly writes about what they're going to do, rather than how to do the thing.
- The writing is boring. If you're bored, forget the manuscript. Others will be bored also.
- The approach is too stiff or textbook-like. Words like empirical, didactic, and other overstuffed gems clue me in that a long, tedious hike will be needed to get through the book.
- Long irrelevant analogies. Get to the point.
- The writer makes obvious inaccuracies in the subject matter. When you see this, and believe me, I've seen this often in people passing themselves off as experts, you're dealing with a sub-brain.
- Sentences and thoughts aren't connected. Call the electrician.
- The writer or writing appears confused.

## Ugly Signs in Writing
- The average "humorous" manuscript by hacks who think they're funny. No writing is more depressing or nauseating than this excreta.

# NEGOTIATING THE CONTRACT

Once a qualified author is found, we'll need to come to terms with him or her, and begin a happy arrangement. A book contract has many clauses each side will need inserted to protect their interests, and we'll cover the main items of importance here. In Appendix A, we've reproduced a sample contract that you can use as a base to form your own.

Advances and royalties are the two most important issues that will need to be agreed upon, so let's look at them first.

## Advances and Royalties

The main issues of concern are the size of the **advance**, the amount of money paid to the author before publication of his or her book and before the first royalty check is due, and the **royalty percentage**, the percentage paid to the author for each book sold.

The usual arrangements publishers make with authors is to pay them an **advance against royalty**. This is usually split into two parts, half on contract and half upon receipt of the final acceptable manuscript. You can even split the advance into three parts, 1/3 on contract, 1/3 on a certain performance level (say 1/2 or 2/3 of the book being submitted - judged by page count) or on submission of first draft, and 1/3 upon receipt of the final acceptable manuscript or on publication.

While authors will sometimes begin work without an advance (though most won't), I believe an advance should always be given to the author. The exchange of money for contract makes the book real, and shows commitment on both sides - an important issue for me - the publisher in tendering money for the work to be performed, and the author in accepting that money and the responsibility that goes with it.

There are various formulas you could work with, but whatever you use, I would target an advance equal to the projected first six months sales, with the upper limit set at projected first year sales for any advance agreed upon. If you fail to sell enough copies to cover this advance, practically speaking, it's the authors money to keep, so you want to be careful in how you structure your advances.

The amount of royalty and advance is totally negotiable, but the key

List Price = full retail price
Flat Pay: Paid a set fee to write the book.

**COMPLETE GUIDE TO SUCCESSFUL PUBLISHING** 77

consideration in my mind is that it's a fair arrangement for both sides. Give the author a fair share, but at the same time, ensure that your company gets a fair share concomitant with the money you risk and the skills you bring to the table.

Fair has different meanings to different people and situations, but in my mind, I use the figure of 5%-7% of the *list price* as a fair share for the author. **List price** is the full retail price of the book which is printed on the cover. With the discount I must give my distributor, that comes close to 15% of net which I feel is a good arrangement on both sides. Authors can also be paid as a percentage of **net price**, the amount of money the publisher receives for sales of the book.

You'll hear of some publishers paying authors as high as 10% or even 12% of list, but these percentages are given by large publishing houses with their own sales force to better-selling and star authors, or by established publishers with excellent markets for their books who can afford these high rates (and need to pay them to get their high-priced authors). However, if you're going through a distributor, and receiving only 40% percent or so of the list price, I believe these rates are too high to stay profitable unless you really have a gem of a seller.

On the other hand, you'll also hear of many, many publishers who pay less than the rates I mentioned, and I believe these publishers are not giving their authors a fair shake.

Authors can also be hired on a **flat pay** basis, where they're paid a set fee to write the book. The advantage of paying on a flat pay basis is that once the author is paid their fee, all income from the book stays with the publishing company. This can be a very profitable arrangement for the publisher if the book is a steady seller. The disadvantage is that you'll have to pay more up-front to the author to write the book since he or she won't be sharing in profits down the road.

Most authors will not work on a flat pay basis, but will insist on royalties, as well they should. If the book sells well, they would like to share in its monetary success and continue to feel part of the book.

## Reporting & Paying Author Royalties

Royalties are typically paid twice yearly, based on the sales (less returns) for the January-June and July-December accounting periods.

In the contract, you should allow two months after the accounting period has ended before issuing a **royalty report**, an accounting of sales, so that all your sales information can be received and compiled, and three months after the accounting period before money is due the author, to allow time for the revenues for books sold to be received.

Royalties should be based on books sold less returns. For example, if 1,570 books were sold during the sales period, and 170 books were returned, the royalties are based on 1,400 sales.

Royalty reports should be done timely, and payments made promptly to the author, according to the terms of the contract.

## Other Points

There should be provisions in the contract as follows: the due date of the manuscript, the approximate number of words or final page count for the book to be considered of acceptable length; the number of free books provided to the author upon publication and the discounted price if the author wishes to buy further books; a non-competition clause to prevent the author from engaging in a similar book that will compromise this one's sales; and certainly an author's warranty that indeed, he or she is the author of this book.

The other points not discussed here, can be gleamed from a perusal of the sample contract in Appendix A.

## Signing the Contract

When the decision to publish has been made, a topic we'll cover in greater detail in the following chapter, you'll need to make it official. Prepare two signed contracts according to the terms you've discussed and agreed upon with your author, and send them off to the author.

When a signed original contract is received back and in your possession, send off the first part of the author's advance - and you've got a deal.

Let's move on to the next chapter, *Initial Marketing & The Decision to Publish*, and look more at what's involved in making the publishing decision and doing the initial planning.

Advance = paid to the author before publication. + before the 1st royalty ck is due.

Royalty % = % paid to the author for each book sold.

Advance against Royalty = split into 2 parts. ½ on contract + ½ upon Receipt of the final acceptable manuscript.

List Price = full retail price of the book which is printed on the cover.

Net Price = amt of $ the publisher receives for sales of the book.

flat pay = paid a set fee to write the bk.

Royalty Report = acctg of sales.

*1st make intelligent decisions in regard to the price, format + page count of the proposed bk.*

# 6. INITIAL MARKETING & THE DECISION TO PUBLISH

## INTRODUCTION

When the time comes to seriously consider a book proposal, we must examine the marketing decisions that will best address our audience and bring in the maximum sales and profits. Our goal is to create a book that sells, and to do so, we must make the book both appealing to our audience and competitive in the market.

Before we make the ultimate decision - to publish a book - we must first make intelligent decisions in regard to the price, format and page count of the proposed book. We need to get a sense of how this book will shape up and fit into the marketplace, and how we're going to go about putting this book together. For example, is the book best done at 400 pages with a retail price of $14.95, or are we better off positioning the book at a smaller page count and at a $9.95 retail price? These are marketing decisions that must be considered now, before the book is accepted.

We'll look at each of the decisions we must make in targeting our book, so that by the time we emerge from this chapter, we've got a firm idea of the audience we're targeting and the nature of the book we're going to publish.

And if all looks right, we'll go ahead with the decision that sets all the wheels in motion - the decision to publish.

We've discussed understanding our market and serving them. Now it's time to make the decisions that turn this idea into a growing reality - a book!

# MARKETING DECISIONS

We start our thinking by looking ahead, and understanding how we will market the final product. Given the nature of the book, what price can we charge, *or do we need to charge,* and what does the book have to look like to support that price.

For a book to be successful, we must understand our audience, what they want, and how much they'll pay for it. By always keeping our audience in mind, and *addressing that audience,* we're likely to produce a book that will appeal to this target audience and gather in its share of sales.

We'll also want to think about the types of books we plan on publishing and what it will take to make those books successful. For example, will promotion or advertising be needed to get the book off the ground, and if so how much? Is the book worth it given these parameters for success, or will just getting the books on bookshelves be satisfactory?

Thus, we need to get a good sense of the type of book we're getting involved in, and the effort and money it will take to make it successful. For example, lots of attention may be needed to make a poetry book work, knowing in advance that there may be dim prospects of widespread distribution and profitability. On the other hand, a strong true-crime title may seem to hold good potential but will need "x" amount of dollars to make it work. Or perhaps our writer has an excellent idea and has executed it well, but the market is too narrow for the proposed book's needs.

No book can be considered seriously for publication until we can visualize its final price, page count and dimensions, and how that combination may be received in the markets we'll be targeting. If the book is targeted to the bookstores, it must be competitive in its section and be able to grab the attention of the reader. If the book is targeted for mostly mail order sales, the price we'll need to charge must be worth the costs needed to be successful - and the product must be able to stand up to that price.

All this thinking goes into the weighing of factors as to whether a book should be accepted for publication.

## Positioning a Book in the Marketplace

To be successful, especially in a crowded field, you need to come out with a different angle - an approach that's attractive to consumers and either hasn't quite been done or hasn't been done well. There are lots of excellent approaches to any subject that has yet to be tackled properly. Put a fresh wrinkle on an old theme; show readers a new way.

Talk to friends, look around carefully. There's no limit of good ideas, or better ways to do something. You can package the book differently. If everything is trade size, maybe you can go mass market or 6 x 9. Maybe the books are all thick tomes. Surely then, there's room for a shorter version, one that can be read and digested quickly. If many of the books are smaller, go with a comprehensive version. Go thinner in page count, go thicker in page count. Find a better angle, do a better cover, address a different need.

The market is always there. It's hungry, it needs to be fed. Tap into it with more product.

A first glance at the competition may be intimidating and a bit sobering. Perhaps there are lots of books on the shelf that are seemingly well done, and books that seem firmly ensconced. Maybe there are even eight books along the general lines of what you have in mind and most of those eight titles are books you perceive or know to be good sellers. You get scared a little. You think, *"Can I compete?"*

But look again. Not every angle is covered, no matter how big the section is, no matter how many books are printed on the subject. There's always room for fresh ideas, for more books. Maybe all the books have been around for a long time. How about a *new* approach?

Let's now go over the various aspects of a book's dimensions and binding to get a better understanding of what we'll need to do to best appeal to our market.

# CHOOSING A BOOK'S DIMENSIONS & BINDING

Most books you'll see in the bookstore are paperback (paperbound) books printed in the following three sizes - 4 1/4 x 6 3/4, 5 1/2 x 8 1/2 or 6 x 9. Their actual size will usually be an 1/8 or 1/16 of an inch less or so, depending upon the amount of trimming done by the printer during binding.

Most publishers print in these dimensions for they are standard printing sizes, and will assure us of the best prices. Printing outside standard press dimensions requires extra work, and thus extra expenses, possibly considerable ones, in producing a book.

While we'll often refer to books in terms of their size, such as **mass-market** *size* (books that are 4 1/4 by 6 3/4) or **trade** *size* (books that are 5 1/2 x 8 1/2 or 6 x 9), **trade paperbacks** are actually any book targeted to the book trade regardless of size (even though they may be mass-market size). This is opposed to **mass market paperbacks**, bestseller type books that are targeted to racks such as are found in newsstands and drugstores. There is some confusion over these labels in the industry, but referring to books by their size, as in *mass market size*, makes your description clearer.

In addition to the paperback format of the books we discussed above, we'll go over four other types of bindings that may be appropriate for your publications. In all, we'll discuss five types of bindings - paperbound (actually *perfect bound* - books bound so that the spine is flat and can be printed on), hardbound, spiral/comb bound, saddle-stitching and velo-binding.

We'll go over each trim size in turn, and discuss the advantages and disadvantages for each. We'll start this discussion with paperbound (perfect bound) books, the most common type of binding.

# PAPERBACK (PERFECT BOUND) BOOKS

Paperback (paperbound), or perfect bound books, have the advantage over hardcovers in that they're cheaper to produce and have a much higher sales potential. The lower list price charged for paperbacks translates to more book sales and thus greater overall profits.

For example, peeling off $7.95, $9.95 or $12.95 for a book is no big deal for the average consumer. He or she won't think twice about this purchase. However, departing with 2 1/2 - 3 1/2 times that much, the price for the average hardcover, is another story altogether. Paying $20-$40 for a book needs a lot more thought than paying just $9.95.

# Trade and Mass Market Sizes

The larger box shows the size of a 5 1/2 x 8 1/2 inch book (*before* trimming), and the smaller one, a 4 1/4 x 6 3/4 inch book (also *before* trimming). This page itself was setup as a 6 x 9 but now is slightly less because the book has been trimmed. It is almost the same size as the 5 1/2 x 8 1/2 untrimmed page.

**5 1/2 x 8 1/2**

**4 1/4 x 6 3/4**

The lower list prices of paperbacks might also translate into more library sales as well (though this will likely be only a secondary market). Big budget cuts have steered libraries into buying more paperbacks than before and have opened the market up somewhat to these sales.

Unless you have a major book that can be promoted, creating an urgency for the public to buy, or specifically targeting the library or some specialized market like the gift market, your best way to proceed into the book market is with paperbound books. Sure, you'll make more per issue with hardcovers, but you'll sell fewer copies, and will greatly increase your chances of having a loser in the general book trade. While readers may be willing to part with $8.95 or $14.95 for a paperback without a second thought, that same book as a hardcover at $24.95 or $34.95 will cause second thoughts and perhaps cost too many sales.

Let's now look at the two types of paperbacks, trade and mass market.

## Trade or Quality Paperbacks - 5 1/2 x 8 1/2 or 6 x 9

Unless you're publishing a mass-market best-seller or have a special smaller-sized project in mind, you're most likely going to be publishing trade paper size books, the successful approach that many small to medium-sized publishers use, and the one that gives you the best chances of success in the general book trade.

This is the optimal book size for publishing fiction, non-fiction and how-to books and is the first size you should consider when contemplating a book. The larger format allows us to charge a higher price and make more money per book sold than if we published smaller mass-market sized books, and at the same time, keeps the price low enough to allow mass sales.

Perceived value is important when selling books (as with anything else), and the trade size allows us to get a higher price than a mass market sized book even though the book may contain 200 fewer pages!

You could charge $6.95, $7.95, $8.95 or even $9.95 for a 112 page how-to book and have it perceived as a fair price, while that same price for a 320 page mass market size book on the same subject would be viewed as expensive. A 320 page trade paper book, on the other hand, could command a list of $14.95 without any price resistance at all.

Trade paperback publishing is a great way to enter the market. We get an excellent print cost to list price ratio with this size book, a larger "look," and bottom line, more profits for our efforts.

## Mass Market Size - 4 1/4 x 6 3/4*

The main reason to choose a mass market size for your title would be if a significant part of your projected market will be in locations where books are sold in racks. Racks are made for books of this size, mostly to take advantage of the big money best-sellers put out by the major publishers. But other books go into these racks as well, and if you've got a good title for a particular market, you can get some of this premium space as well.

For example, we publish a series of 14 games and gambling books (the *Basics of Winning* series) that are extremely successful sellers in newsstands, airports and other rack locations. Had this series been done in a larger format, a large portion of these sales wouldn't have happened.

Racks can be found at airports, drug and convenience stores, groceries, newsstands and in countless other locations including big chains such as Target and K-Mart. If you can tap into these markets, there are a lot of sales that can be made.

Readers are attracted to these smaller-sized books, because they're less bulky than bigger books and easily fit into a woman's pocketbook or even a man's hip or jacket pocket if the book is thin enough.

Mass market titles have been creeping up in price over the last few years, from $3.95 to $4.95 to $5.95, to $6.95 and higher. You are limited to what the market is doing in terms of your pricing for these mass market titles. Of course, as the publisher, you can charge anything you want for the books, but it doesn't mean people have to buy your books. If you exceed the perceived value of a mass market title, which at this time is $5.95-$6.95 (and creeping up to $7.95), then people may perceive your book as overpriced and you'll lose sales.

*(Note that the trim size of mass market size paperbacks will vary. While the typical trim size of a web press might be an eight or sixteenth of an inch less than the 4 1/4 x 6 3/4 size, the final trim on a belt press will be slightly larger, closer to 4 1/4 x 7 *after* the book has been trimmed.)

# HARDBOUND

**Hardbound** or **hardcover** titles, books bound in stiff boards, command a higher price on the market and allow you to charge significantly more than the same book with a paper cover. Hardbound books have an aura of value and quality that paperbacks just don't have, and consumers are often willing to pay for that value.

Hardbound books cost more to produce, but if the book you're doing is appropriate to the market you're reaching, and is successful, the extra costs will more than be offset by a greater amount of revenue. Typically, hardcover books work well for library editions, reference works, gift and collectors' items, and books, whether fiction or non-fiction, that can be backed by big bucks and big influence.

For example, the major publishing companies make fortunes on hardcover publishing, but they're big players with major authors, major presence, and a major publicity machine that can propel "big books" to the bestseller lists. Works produced under their auspices generate a large demand-driven audience willing to pay upwards of $30 for the latest works of their favorite writers. The big publishers can generate this type of major interest in a hardcover, but you may not be able to.

Don't produce a hardbound book unless you're reasonably certain that this is the best way to go with your title. The problem with hardbound books for most consumers is that they're too expensive, and you certainly don't want to price yourself out of a potentially successful book. Of course you would like to get maximum dollars for your book, and a hardbound book will get you those bigger bucks, but the book has to be appropriate for the particular market you're selling.

The old rule of thumb was that books strictly targeted to the library market, especially important reference works, should be hardbound. While this statement still has some validity, severe budget cuts in many library systems have created somewhat of a shift toward less expensive paperbound titles. Budget cuts notwithstanding, heavily thumbed "serious" reference books may be more attractive to libraries if produced as a hardcover.

As with everything in the book trade, it's a question of knowing your intended audience, and meeting their needs. If you're producing reference works for doctors, expensive editions are probably the way to go. MDs are accustomed to spending big bucks on their research materials and most likely prefer the more weighty authoritative volumes.

Keep in mind that many books for the general bookstore trade are most appropriately produced as softcover titles and not as hardcovers (though there are always exceptions) and give you the most chances for success. If you do opt for hardcover, make sure your marketing plan has convincing reasons for this decision.

There are two basic hardcover bindings, smythe-sown and adhesive bound. **Smythe-sown** is where the signatures - groups of 16 or 32 pages printed as one long sheet of paper and folded - are first sewn together and then glued into the cover. This is a more durable form of binding and allows the book to lie open flat. Not surprising, this is the more expensive of the two ways. **Adhesive** hardcover binding is where the signatures are collated and glued to a fabric, which in turn is glued to the end sheets of the book (the first page of the first signature and the last page of the last signature), and then glued to the hardcover binding itself.

If you'll be publishing a hardcover edition, you'll want to work closely with your printer to produce the type of book that will work best for your project.

# OTHER BINDINGS
## Spiral Bound, Comb Bound

Comb binding8

**Spiral binding** is the binding of preference in school notebooks, and is a thin metal wire wound along one side of a book. **Comb binding** uses a similar process, except with plastic, and can have a spine which can be imprinted on.

The advantage of spiral and comb binding is that they allow a book to lie flat when open. Workbooks, cookbooks and the like, often use comb binding to allow their readers hands-free use while reading. Cookbook publishers especially find that a "lay-flat" binding format can be advantageous to their sales: Cooks appreciate the fact that they can keep both hands free to do the cooking.

## Saddle-Stitching

Signatures held together with staples through the spines, **saddle-stitch-ing**, is a less expensive way to bind books than perfect binding, how-ever, the disadvantage of this binding method is that it doesn't create a flat spine to print on.

While saddle-stitching is often used to hold together magazines, re-ports, or mail order publications, it should never be used for books to be sold in bookstores. Browsers must be able to see the spine of a book as it sits on a shelf. Many bookstores won't even consider carrying a saddle-stitched book.

## Velo-Binding

Another good way to hold together reports and books sold through the mail is by **velo-binding**, a patented binding process that punches holes in the material to be bound, and affixes two long strips of plastic outside the holes to hold them together. Typically, the outside covers are of a medium-stiff colored plastic (about 10 colors available), though other covers are possible.

The velo-bind process is most appropriate for publications that will be produced in small numbers either from the office, or from a copy shop or small printer providing this service. Like saddle-stitching, how-ever, velo-binding is not used for serious bookmaking.

# SETTING THE LIST PRICE   List Price — WHAT CUST. PAY FOR BOOKS,

Pricing a book, that is, setting the retail **list price** which consumers will pay for the book, is one of the most critical and difficult decisions you'll make in the marketing of your book. It involves coordination of various elements in your publishing decisions; the factors that affect perceived value - the size of the book, the type of binding, the page count - and of course the type of book you're publishing. Obviously, you can charge more for a law textbook than for a mass-market thriller.

On one hand, we want to maximize the amount of profit we can make in our print run by charging as much as the market will bear for our books, but at the same time, we don't want to price ourselves out of sales.

If the price is too high, we'll sell fewer books than we should, and will cost ourselves profit. By the same token, if the price is too low, we won't be getting enough income from the books we do sell. Trying to find the balance between being too high and too low is where serious thinking must be done.

There are two ways to approach the pricing issue; the amount of money we *need* to charge to make the book profitable, and the amount we *can* charge to bring us the biggest net income. What can be charged for a book is a function of many things; the book's size, the number of pages, the competition, the publicity involved, if any, and the price point beyond which consumers have resistance to purchasing the book.

## Initial Considerations

Before we even think of setting the retail price, we must make decisions on the dimensions of the book, and at the first stages, at least have a general idea of what the page count might be so that we're selling a book that's perceived to be of good market value. The size of the book is the first decision to be made and is not all that difficult once it's determined which segment of the market we're targeting the book towards. Once this is set, we should be able to narrow down the possible prices to two or three choices.

If the book is targeted for sales in airports, gift stores and the general rack trade, we want to price the book in the general parameters of mass market size books. For this determination, we need to be on top of current trends and prices. For example, when we chose to publish the first edition of our *Open Road Publishing* title, *Las Vegas Guide*, as a standard mass-market sized book (4 1/4 x 6 3/4) we had a choice of two prices in the current market; $4.95 on the lower end, and $5.95 on the higher end. We could even have tried $6.95, and it may have worked, but it may not have. We chose to go with the price we were sure would be acceptable, and not risk killing the title by exceeding current prices levels for that size book. So we priced the first edition at $5.95.

Best-sellers priced at $7.95 have quickly replaced $6.95 titles. In the early to mid-90's, best-seller type books started moving from $4.95 to $5.95 to $6.95, somewhat pushed along by a rising price of print paper. Soon enough, the $7.95 price level will be $8.95, then $9.95.

*Maximize the Profit for every title we produce!*

## Pricing a Book According to Cost

At the bare minimum, if profit or at least continuity and growth of your publishing program is important, you'll need to post a high enough list price so that reasonable sales ensure reasonable income.

One formula is to set your list price at a minimum of five times your production costs (pre-press plus printing), and ideally, at eight times or higher. In addition to covering production costs, you need to pay your author, your overhead, your time, plus have a profit window. See the *Making Money* section, for a further discussion of pricing as it relates to costs and profit.

Let's now look at pricing a book according to what the market can bear, that is, what we can get.

## Pricing a Book for Maximum Profit

We want to maximize the profit we can get for every title we produce, but determining just what price brings us the best results is not so easy. While we make more money per book at a higher price, it doesn't follow that overall profit will be more.

For example, if we can sell 3,500 copies of a book at $9.95 for a gross income of $34,825, but only 3,000 at $10.95 for a gross income of $32,850, we'll certainly come out better with the $9.95 price. If the choice were that clear, the decision in the above example would be easy - price the book at $9.95. Unfortunately though, we'll never have numbers like that to work with. We just won't know how many more books will sell at a particular price, let alone how many will sell at any given price at all.

So it comes down to making good judgments. We need to get a feel for what price consumers think is fair for a particular book, and at what prices they'll start resisting.

Some market research is in order here. Start out by talking to friends who are interested in the field; bookstore workers and managers who know the appropriate section; buyers who you deal with and anyone else you can think of who has a good educated opinion on the particular field. People who buy books, either as a buyer for a bookstore or as an individual making their own purchase, are market conscious and have a great feel of what the market will and will not bear. Book-buying consumers have excellent opinions on prices they would pay for a book, and prices they might not pay. Consulting with these consumers, whether they're friends or family, will provide excellent information that will help you in making a final price determination for your book.

## Price Points

Thus, we need to be conscious of the **price point** of a book, a point at which a book is perceived to be in a different, higher class of price, and thus result in fewer sales. A retail price of $4.95 appears to be much cheaper than $5.95; $9.95 much cheaper than $10.95; $14.95 much cheaper than $15.95; $19.95 much cheaper than $20.95; and $24.95 much cheaper than $25.95. These commonly accepted price points are important factors that need to be considered when pricing a book.

But how about the decision to go $8.95 against $9.95 (or $13.95 against $14.95)? Here's a tough one. The extra $1.00 would be nice and a big boost to our net, but do we need that extra sales push from the "discounted" $8.95 price? This decision should be looked at carefully.

What exactly does that $1.00 more or less mean to our bottom line?

## Pricing Higher or Lower than the Competition

If I'm going head to head against real heavyweights selling at $9.95 and I need to get my book established, I may go for the $8.95 price if I feel the consumer is choosing either my book or theirs. If I feel they'll buy both anyway, I'll go $9.95, or if I feel my book is the leader, I'll take the higher price. Let the others chase me.

If you're giving the reader more perceived value, you go for the $9.95 list. You may have a more recognizable author or company, or your book may be thicker or have a bigger page count, or your book is simply worth the money, competition be damned! They'll buy the book.

If your book is unique, or you feel it is *perceived* to be a better quality book then the competition, than you're not competing against other books - just against the price a buyer is willing to pay. So you weigh that factor in your decision and lean toward a higher list price.

*Always try to set the higher list price* unless you have a compelling reason to do otherwise. If you've done a good job with your book, then you've got something the consumer will pay for. Go the extra buck, keeping the price points we've discussed in mind.

In super-competitive fields, where your book must fight side by side with many other titles serving a similar purpose, and with all else equal, you might want to choose a list price $1.00 less than the main competitors, especially if those competitors are well-entrenched.

Why $1.00 less and not more? Simple. The $1.00 discount presents the consumer with a value, a *discount* if you will, that can push the consumer to make your book the book purchased. It gives you a pricing edge over the competitors. You may get the sale if you've done a good job with your book. While a $2.00 discount makes that same statement, it does so at the cost of that much more off your profit line, an extra discount you don't need to give to make that sale.

## Case Study - Backgammon for Winners

In 1993, I decided to publish a backgammon book and thought about the marketing choices. I had the option of producing the book as a mass-market size book, 4 1/4 x 6 3/4, and making it a 64 page book, $3.95 list price, as part of my 14-book *Basics of Winning Series*, or expanding the concept into a trade paper book and getting either $6.95 or $7.95 with a modest page count, or $9.95 or more with an even larger volume page count.

In this particular case the choice was clearly to go for the trade size. The strength of my smaller books was in sales directly to casino gift shops and rack jobbers who serviced casino areas. Since backgammon is not a casino game and wouldn't be carried by my important vendors there, I had nothing to gain by the smaller size. The trade size gave me a higher list price and profit margin, and better visibility on the shelves in the bookstore itself.

I priced the book at $6.95, and made the decision to go for an 80 page title, making the book an easy-to-read primer for backgammon players. I could also have chosen a larger book, perhaps 192 pages and $9.95, or 208 pages and $12.95, but felt there was no rush. These could be follow-up books. Meanwhile, the 80 pages would be easy to publish, would find good acceptance among an audience I was accustomed to selling to, and would test the particular audience for a backgammon book at a lower print cost and risk.

In 1997, we moved the price to $9.95 with no apparent drop off of sales.

# PLANNING FOR SAVINGS

To get the best savings in printing, books should *always* be planned so that the page count ends up in multiples of 16 or 32 pages. Just as we plan a book's dimensions to fit standard sizes for the best printing prices, we must also plan the page count according to the number of pages that will be bound and printed together.

In the printing process, pages are printed together in even multiples of 4, 8, 16 or 32 pages - depending upon the press - and then stacked and bound to make books. These groups of pages, called **signatures**, are formed from one large sheet of paper that is printed on both sides and then folded. The final book is produced by binding signatures one upon the other.

You should always strive to get your final page counts evenly divided into these 16 or 32 page signatures. For example, if there's a choice of sending your book to the printer at either a 150 or 160 page count, choosing the 160 page one is definitely the wiser choice. Divided evenly, the 160 page book breaks down into five 32 page signatures. The 150 page book, on the other hand, is way more expensive because you're requiring the printer to customize the book outside of the standard signatures of his printing press. This requires extra work, and thus an unnecessary charge that can be avoided with proper planning.

The chart below shows 32 page signature counts up to a 704 page book.

## 32 PAGE SIGNATURE CHART

| | | | | | | | |
|---|---|---|---|---|---|---|---|
| 32 | 64 | 96 | 128 | 160 | 192 | 224 | 256 |
| 288 | 320 | 352 | 384 | 416 | 448 | 480 | 512 |
| 544 | 576 | 608 | 640 | 672 | 704 | | |

A 176 page book will be built by the printer as five 32s and one 16, and a 336 page book will be printed as ten 32s and one 16. Smaller number counts than this, such as 2s and 4s will not be economical and will cost more money to print than expanding the page count to a 16 or 32. It's actually cheaper to print a 176 page book - which is a standard job - than either a 172 or 166 page one.

Depending upon the printer - and you must coordinate with your printer to see the signatures that work best with the type of press they'll be using for your book - eight page signatures will often be economical as well when they're added on *after* a 32 page signature count. Thus, if you were doing a 320 page book and realized you needed to add some pages, you may find it less expensive to go to 328 pages as opposed to 336. What you won't find cost-effective is a 24 page addition to 344 pages in this example. In this instance, you're probably better off adding eight more pages for a full 32 page signature and a 352 page book. Again, you'll need to check with your printer on the cost viability of the eight page signature versus 16s or 32s.

Following is a chart showing 16 page signatures up to 704 pages. The bold listings indicate the 32 page signatures.

## 16 PAGE SIGNATURE CHART

| **32** | 16 | **32** | 16 | **32** | 16 | **32** | 16 |
|---|---|---|---|---|---|---|---|
| **32** | 48 | **64** | 80 | **96** | 112 | **128** | 144 |
| **160** | 176 | **192** | 208 | **224** | 240 | **256** | 272 |
| **288** | 304 | **320** | 336 | **352** | 368 | **384** | 400 |
| **416** | 432 | **448** | 464 | **480** | 496 | **512** | 528 |
| **544** | 560 | **576** | 592 | **608** | 624 | **640** | 656 |
| **672** | 688 | **704** | | | | | |

## More on Signatures

On a 32 page signature, 32 pages are printed *1-up* on one large sheet of paper, and then folded to make 32 pages. A 16 page signature is printed *2-up*, and folded to make two sets of 16 pages. An eight page signature is printed *4-up*, and folded to make 4 sets of eight pages. Some presses have now started printing in 48 page signatures, with 16's and 24's being economical page counts. Check with you printer to see what kind of signatures they will be using so you can plan your book in the most efficient fashion possible.

### *Let's Move On and Make the Book Official*

Now that we've got a decision to publish and have a rough idea of how we're positioning the book into the marketplace, it's time to move on to the next chapter and get our book announced into the book trade.

# 7. GETTING OFFICIAL/ COPYRIGHT/BAR CODE

## INTRODUCTION

Once we've decided on publishing a book, there are a few things we'll need to take care of to make our book official and get it announced properly to the book trade. These steps are best taken care of well ahead of publication, so that our books can be listed in the appropriate places. Additionally, when it's crunch time, we want to concentrate on getting our book to the printer and not worrying about taking care of things that could have been taken care of earlier.

For one thing, we'll want to get your books listed in official publications such as Books in Print and the other databases published by R.R. Bowker. These references are important sources to the book trade, and can be found in just about all bookstores and libraries. In addition to the Bowker publications, we may want to get our company or books listed in other trade publications for even more exposure. We've included a listing of these sources at the end of this chapter.

We'll also want to obtain an ISBN number and a Library of Congress Number. These numbers get printed on the copyright page.

We'll also go over the process of copyrighting your book and protecting your rights, and how to go about bar-coding your book so that it conforms to the practices used by the book trade.

We'll go over each of these items in turn, beginning with the ISBN number.

# INTERNATIONAL STANDARD BOOK NUMBER

Issued by the ISBN agency, a division of Bowker, these numbers are used in the book trade to identify each individual title. The ISBN consists of 10 numbers which overall identify the country of origin, the publisher and the book itself. The last number in the ISBN is an automatic check digit that makes sure the other numbers are correct.

The ISBN for this book is 0-940685-94-9. The first number, 0, shows that the book is from the United States or Canada (French speaking Canada would use 2), while the next six numbers, 940685, identify Cardoza Publishing. The next two digits, 94, in combination with the first seven, identify this particular book, *The Complete Guide to Successful Publishing*. The final digit, the 9, is the check digit. No other book will share these numbers. The old style of numbers has run out, and new ISBN's have the hyphen moved one digit to the left, for example, 1-58042-009-5.

It costs $195 to register a set of numbers (they come in blocks of 10, 100, and 1,000 numbers). These numbers are processed within 15 business days and then mailed out. For priority service, ISBN numbers will be shipped out by overnight mail in three business days for $165. While the application can be faxed and paid for by credit cards, the numbers will not be faxed back. Bowker insists that they be mailed. To receive an application for ISBN numbers, contact: The ISBN Agency, 121 Chanlon Road, New Providence, New Jersey 07974, (908)665-6770.

# LIBRARY OF CONGRESS NUMBER

Library of Congress numbers allow users of the Library of Congress catalog card service to track down your book in their system. These numbers are essential for selling book into the library trade. The LC number gets printed on the copyright page of your book, and thus gets obtained *before* your book goes to press. Once your book is printed, it's obviously too late to print the number.

This Library of Congress program prepares pre-publication cataloging records for those books most likely to be acquired by libraries nationwide. This includes almost all types of books (though not vanity publishing), and excludes non-book items such as calendars, brochures, certain religious materials and pre-college textbooks, publications of less than 50 pages, journals, and other items not commonly thought of as "books". Library of Congress numbers are obtained by calling (202)707-6372, or writing to the **CIP Office**, Library of Congress, Washington, DC 20540. Forms will then be forwarded.

Changes in a book's basic information subsequent to receiving the LC number should be reported back to the CIP Office in writing to keep your book information accurate and up-to-date. Changing title, price or page count does not affect the number assigned though - that number remains the same. On new editions however (as opposed to new printings), a new LC number will be required.

While there is no charge to get an LC Number, a complimentary copy should be sent immediately after printing to the CIP office (they supply postage-free mailing labels) for final cataloging.

# ABI FORMS

You should fill out the **Advanced Book Information** (**ABI**) forms from Bowker to get your books listed in their publications, **Books in Print**, **Forthcoming Books in Print,** and **Subject Guide to Books in Print**. It's a good idea to get your book listed here, as these guides, used heavily in the book trade, are the authoritative reference tools to English language books in print. Virtually every important library and bookstore in the country carries a current set of these annuals. Being listed here lets the book trade know that your books exist.

Get the ABI forms by calling (800)521-8110 or (908)665-2882 ext. 2881, or by writing to: ABI Department, R.R. Bowker Co., 121 Chanlon Road, New Providence, NJ 07974.

# CATALOGING IN PUBLICATION (CIP)

The CIP information, also provided by the CIP Office at the Library of Congress, has a history dating back to the early 1900s. The basic premise of the program is to catalogue books centrally, just once, so that local libraries around the country (the main constituents of the this program) don't have to independently obtain this information themselves - at duplicate effort and cost.

The CIP data helps librarians properly catalog the book in their files and is thus important information to include when the libraries are an important market for your book. While most small publishers are excluded from directly participating in the program (self-published and books that *seem* self-published from small publishers will generally not be listed), an equivalent and respected listing can easily be obtained from the library distributors, Quality Books and Unique Books.

The scope of the CIP program is restricted to publishers who are US-based, or foreign-based with US editorial offices.

Publishers who fit within the confines of the program submit their pre-press galleys along with a complete application to the CIP office. Within 10 days, sometimes even as little as five days, the CIP bibliographical data will be returned to the publisher for setup in their text. This bibliographical information gets printed on the copyright page. This helps libraries categorize books in the proper section.

Publishers who seek to be listed within the program should contact the CIP department to see if their books qualify for the program. To apply for a CIP, contact: The Library of Congress, Cataloging in Publication Division, Washington, DC. 20540, (202)707-9812.

## COPYRIGHTING YOUR BOOKS

Beginning in 1989, when the US ratified the Bern Convention (an international copyright agreement), publishers were no longer required to publish copyright notices in the book to be protected by copyright law. Books and other printed matter are now automatically protected by copyright when they are first written or published, regardless of whether a copyright notice is published or not.

Though it is no longer mandated that this notice be published, it is still recommended that you do so since it gives you added legal protection against would-be violators. It also gives notice to the public and formally announces that you are the copyright owner of the book.

The copyright protects the owners' rights to the text, illustrations, and photos for the author's life plus 50 years. By U.S. and international law, it is illegal for someone to infringe on any of these rights and to reproduce another's materials without permission.

To formally register a copyright, request **Form TX** from the **Register of Copyrights**, Library of Congress, Washington, DC 10559. Call (202)707-9100 for forms or (202)707-3000 to reach a copyright specialist. After the book comes off the press, send the completed TX form, two copies of the book and the $20 registration fee. The Copyright Office will send a photocopy of the registration with their official seal.

# BAR CODES
## The Bookland EAN Bar Code

In the last five years or so, bar codes have become an essential part of the book business. The computerization of the industry relies on bar coding for fast information processing, from receiving books, to ringing them up on the register and reordering. In one scanning, the bar code identifies the ISBN, publisher, title, author, edition, and price, and allows stores to keep track of inventory sold and place a book on automatic reorder. The ISBN itself is printed above the bar code, and in a way, becomes part of the bar code you'll be printing. See the bar code on the back cover of this book for an example.

The major book chains and most independent bookstores require that books be bar-coded, so if you haven't been using bar codes, make absolutely certain that all future printings contain them.

There are several types of bar codes, but you need to be concerned with just the Bookland EAN type, in particular, the **Bookland EAN/5**. The "5" signifies the price add-on. The bar code contains 13 numbers, plus the five number price add-on and is configured as follows:

**a.** The first three digits are always: **978**

**b.** The following 9 digits are the first nine numbers of your bar code. We'll use the bar code for this book as an example: **0-940685—94**

**c.** The final digit is computed from the first 12 as a countercheck and will be automatically generated by bar code suppliers, or by your bar code program. The bar code thus becomes: **9 780940 685949**

**d.** The five digit add-on begins with a 5 for US publishers followed by the price. A book under $10.00 will be listed as a 0 and then the price,

and one over $10.00 will be the straight four digits. Thus, the final four digits on a $6.95 book will be 0695, and on a $14.95 book will be 1495.

Add the 5 before each one, and we get the following price add-ons:

**$6.95 book - 50695**
**$14.95 book - 51495**

The bar code on the back cover of this book shows the complete configuration of what we've just put together.

The **Book Industry Study Group** at 160 Fifth Avenue, #604, New York, NY 10010 (212)929-1393 puts out a useful pamphlet for $7.50 called *Machine-Readable Coding Guidelines for the U.S. Book Industry* which explains more about established Bar Code printing guidelines. A free copy is also available from **Fotel/GGX Associates** 41 Westhome Ave., Villa Park, IL 60181, Phone (630)834-4920, fax (630)834-5250.

## Printing the Bookland EAN Bar Code

The Bookland EAN bar code gets printed on the bottom of your back cover with the ISBN printed above it. This should automatically be generated by your bar code maker or bar code software program in the correct location with the letters ISBN preceding the numbers. (If it isn't, make sure you get it done.)

Color combinations such as black or dark blue on white or light colors can be read easily by scanners. However, if you're looking to get fancier with your color combinations on the bar code, you'll want to contact the Book Industry Study Group or their publication (see above) to see which color combinations will work.

## UPC Bar Code

The UPC code is predominantly used only for mass-market books sold at non-book store accounts like drug, grocery, variety stores and the like. If your book will sell big-time in these accounts you may need a UPC bar code as well, though I've not found it necessary with my titles in these locations. If you're doing business with a retailer or wholesaler who will get your books into these markets, coordinate this part of the bar-coding with them to see if they'll require you to print the EAN Bookland/5 on the inside front cover as well.

Just because you may not have a bar code on the inside front cover doesn't mean you can't get into these accounts either. I've been selling books through wholesalers into many UPC type accounts for years without a UPC or any other bar code printed on the inside cover.

## Getting Bar Codes Made

Obtaining bar codes for your books is a fairly easy process. You can order bar codes from suppliers at a cost of $10-$20 each. We've listed a few bar code manufacturers below.

**Fotel Inc.,** 41 Westhome Ave., Villa Park, IL 60181, Phone (630) 834-4920, fax (630)834-5250.

If you'll be doing a lot of books, you'll save money by ordering a software program that makes the bar codes right on your computer. A company called ComputaLabel makes an excellent bar code program for Macintosh computers called *MacBarcoda Professional*.

The new version of MacBarcoda allows you to produce both color and black and white bar codes in every conceivable configuration. For $295, the program comes equipped with the capabilities to make a full range of bar codes. See the full revew in Appendix D for more information on this program.

This excellent program is easy-to-use and well worth the money if you publish books on a regular basis. You can order this program direct from the company at:
        **MacBarcoda**: (800)289-0993 • (978)462-0993

# PLACES TO GET LISTED

You may want to get your books, company and authors listed in the following publications.

## Places to List Your Books

**Books in Print** and **Forthcoming Books in Print**. ABI Department, R.R. Bowker Co., 121 Chanlon Road, New Providence, NJ 07974, (800)521-8110, (908)665-2882. The authoritative guide to English language books in print. Used by libraries and bookstores worldwide.

**Cumulative Book Index**, H.W. Wilson Company, 950 University Avenue, Bronx, NY 10452. Phone (800)367-6770, fax (800)590-1617 for further information. Used as a buying guide and acquisition tool worldwide, the Cumulative Book Index is published in print format and online. A listing here is free. Send cover letter along with finished book.
**Small Press Record of Books in Print,** Dustbooks, P.O. Box 100, Paradise, CA 95969. Phone (916)877-6110. A *Books in Print*-like publication for small press books. Now published only on CD ROM.

## Places to List Your Company

**Directory of Poetry Publishers,** Dustbooks, P.O. Box 100, Paradise, CA 95967; (800)477-6110, (530)877-6110. For poetry publishers, this is an excellent place to be listed.
**F and W Publications**, 1507 Dana Avenue, Cincinnati, OH 45207; (513)531-2222. F and W publishes a line of well-known directories - a listing in the appropriate one will get you a steady stream of manuscript submissions. Call to have the listing questionaire sent.

| | |
|---|---|
| Writer's Market | Artist & Graphic Designer's Market |
| Children's Writer's Market | Guide to Literary Agents |
| Romance Writer's Sourcebook | Mystery Writer's Sourcebook |
| Photographer's Market | Novel and Short Story Market |
| Poet's Market | Science Fiction Writer's Sourcebook |

**International Directory of Little Magazines & Small Presses**, Dustbooks, P.O. Box 100, Paradise, CA 95967; (800)477-6110, (530)877-6110. Lists over 6,000 book and magazine publishers with full subject and regional indexing. Directed towards writers, this directory allows potential authors to be aware of your publishing program.
**Literary Market Place (LMP)**, R.R. Bowker, 121 Chanlon Road, New Providence Road, NJ 07974. Phone (908)464-6800. Invaluable research tool in the book trade. Excellent place to be listed. Requirement is that three books are published a year.
**Publishers Directory**, Gale Research Company, 835 Penobscot Building, Detroit, MI 48226 (800)877-4253, fax (800)414-5043. This directory is distributed worldwide and includes a thorough listing of North American book publishers along with their contact information.
**Publishers, Distributors, Wholesalers of the United States**, R.R. Bowker, 121 Chanlon Road, New Providence, NJ 07974. Phone (800)521-8110. Legitimate publishers automatically get listed in this publication when they fill out ABI forms (also through Bowker).

## Places to List Your Authors

**Contemporary Authors**, Gale Research Company, 835 Penobscot Building, Detroit, MI 48226 (800)877-4253, (800)414-5043.Listing is free in this reference directory of authors. Don't be shy with the form - generally, the more you write, the longer the reference you get.

# NATIONAL PUBLISHING ORGANIZATIONS

Below, we've listed two national publishing organizations, Publishers Marketing Association and SPAN, both of which you should consider joining. The fees are reasonable, and basically, all it takes is one good idea and membership will pay off in spades. With either of these organizations (and why not join both?), you'll receive plenty more than just one valuable idea. Call PMA and SPAN for a sample newsletter and membership information.

**Publishers Marketing Association**, 627 Aviation Way, Manhattan Beach, CA 90266, (310)372-2732, Fax (310)374-3342. The PMA, starting with a core group of 15 members in 1983, has grown to over 2000 book, audio, and video publishing members. For an annual membership of $80, you receive an excellent 48 page monthly newsletter loaded with valuable cost-saving and money-making tips, get access to effective cooperative marketing programs, and perhaps best of all, have a forum to meet and exchange ideas with other members. As their tag line says, *Helping each other to achieve and succeed.*

**SPAN**, P.O. Box 1306, 425 Cedar Street, Buena Vista, CO 81211. Phone (719)395-4790, (719)395-8374. Another valuable publishing organization worth joining, SPAN is a new organization that began operations in early 1996 to pick up the pieces left when the COSMEP, an organiztion that had close to 1500 members, closed its doors at the end of 1995. For an annual membership fee, SPAN members receive a monthly newsletter loaded with good ideas, networking with other members, cooperative advertising programs, and other benefits.

In addition to PMA and SPAN, there are regional and local publishing organizations across the US and Canada, and you should check into these groups as well. Meeting and networking with other publishers will not only provide a wealth of information that you can use to further your business, but may present some opportunities as well.

# NORTH AMERICAN TRADE SHOWS

**ABA Convention,** American Booksellers Association, 828 South Broadway, Tarrytown, NY 10591; (914) 591-2665, (800) 637-0037; Fax: (914) 591-2720. This is the convention of the book trade, and anybody who is anybody in the book business attends.

Publishers come from around the world to display their books at this fascinating show, do a lot of talking, and generally have an exhausting, but fun time. While it's not a show where many books get sold, you meet the people you've been doing business with, and make contacts that lead to foreign rights deals, new distribution outlets and new authors. Takes place Memorial Day Weekend every year in Chicago.

**ALA Convention,** American Library Association, 50 East Huron Street, Chicago, IL 60611, (800)545-2433 (312) 944-6780. The ALA's annual conference takes place the end of June every year in a different city. The show features more than 1,000 exhibitors, and is attended by thousands and thousands of library buyers from across the country.

**Canadian Booksellers Convention,** Canadian Booksellers Association, 301 Donlands Avenue, Toronto, Ontario M4J 3R8, Canada, (416)467-7883. Takes place late June.

## THINGS TO DO BEFORE YOUR BOOK IS PRINTED

**1. Order ISBN Number**
These are obtained from R.R. Bowker.
**2. Order Library of Congress Number**
These are issued from the Library of Congress
**3. Fill Out ABI Form**
Forms are available from R.R. Bowker
**4. Obtain CIP Data**
Contact Library of Congress, or alternative issuers
**5. Make a Bar Code**
You can order from a supplier, or create with a software program.
**6. List Your Copyright Notice**
This gets printed on the other side of your title page.

# 8. WORKING WITH THE MANUSCRIPT

## INTRODUCTION

The difference between a mediocre and a good book, or one that is excellent as opposed to just good, is often a direct result of the editorial process. An editor's guidance is crucial to keeping authors on track with their work and in producing superior books. Manuscripts lacking an editor's experienced hand generally suffer for it, much to the detriment of the book. On the other hand, books helped by the touch of a good editor can really shine.

To get the best and the most marketable book possible, we need to work closely with our authors from the very start. It's important that we're working toward a *common, stated and understood goal*. This requires open communication between the author and the publisher. If we start assuming things, we'll most surely be in for a surprise. After all, how is our author supposed to know what to expect if it hasn't been discussed?

It doesn't matter how experienced or how many books the author has written. The publisher and the author must be speaking the same language to produce this superior book. While the author, after all, is the author, and the expert on the subject he or she is writing, we must make sure that the author stays focused. This guarantees the highest quality book, and not coincidentally, the most marketable one as well.

We'll look at the editorial processes in this chapter including the three editing stages a book must go through before being ready for production. But since nothing can be done until the manuscript is entered into the computer, let's begin our discussion there.

# PROPER MANUSCRIPT SUBMISSION

In the last few years alone, typewriters have been relegated to antique level, and the computer has risen to the forefront as the instrument of choice for writers. The power of the computer to save text in a format that can be shifted around, saved, transferred and spell-checked has made it such a powerful tool, that it's difficult to imagine a writer using the typewriter anymore, though of course, there are still human dinosaurs roaming the country, creating their books on the typewriter.

You should make it a requirement for your authors to submit their manuscripts on computer disk along with a hard copy printout of that disk. If the book is not submitted on disk, you'll need to hire a data entry person to enter the hard copy manuscript onto the computer (at significant cost), or you could make the writer responsible for getting it done. In any case, before any publishing work occurs, the manuscript must already be entered onto a word processing program. Having the entire manuscript pre-entered saves time and money in the publishing process and allows you to concentrate on your job - getting the book edited, designed and paged for press.

If the disk is done on an IBM compatible computer and you have a Macintosh, you can use the pre-installed conversion program (Apple File Exchange) to convert the files into Macintosh files. If no conversion program has been installed, you can buy one at your local software store. If you use a DOS system and the disk is on Macintosh, a service can be hired to transfer the disk onto a compatible system if your computer doesn't have a conversion program. Computer rental departments at copy shops or other locations often have such a service and you shouldn't have too much trouble locating one. Disk conversion fees are usually nominal, in the range of $10-$25 for many jobs.

Often though, a word-processing program created in one computer system, can be opened by a word-processing or publishing program in another, and thus compatibility problems might be kept to a minimum.

## Instructing Authors on Disk Submission

There are ways to create more work and cost for your computer pre-press people, and that is to let your authors submit their material on floppies without any instructions at all.

Every step the author takes toward designing his or her own book, is one step more you have to undo to make the book work in the format you like best. And that can turn into a lot of work.*

Provide the author with direction on the following four items.

**1. No boxes or graphic elements.**
Trying to remove graphics could become more than time consuming - especially when converting from one program format to another - it could become a nightmare. Have the author indicate appropriate suggestions either on the hard copy accompanying the disk, or with a brief indication near the text itself.

**2. Instructions on Paragraph Indenting.**
The author may indent paragraphs with an automatic formatting tool, but should not do so with spaces or tabs.

**3. Usage of Bolds, Italics, and Underlines.**
Bolds, italics, and underlines may be programmed, but make sure you're in agreement with the author on their usage.

**4. Guidelines for Paragraph Spacing.**
Paragraph spacing must be done according to agreed-upon guidelines. If you like an extra return at the end of each paragraph, and the author submits the book without any, or visa-versa, then more steps have been created in getting the book ready for press.

## DEVELOPING A STYLE GUIDE

As your publishing concepts develop and you establish an identity, you will want to develop a style guide for your authors that clearly spells out what you expect from their writing and the form in which the manuscript should be presented to make it acceptable for submission. Style guides are a great way to ensure clear communication between yourself and your authors.

*Note: The major word processing and publishing programs have sophisticated search and replace features that can change and undo tabs, extra spaces, bolds, italics, caps and a host of other text attributes and formats virtually at a snap. Thus, many formatting changes can be done automatically and with a minimum of extra work.

# WORKING WITH THE AUTHOR
## Coordinating with Authors for a Good Book

Once a proposal is accepted, you must exercise your skill at helping direct the author in producing the best book he or she can write for the intended market. Whether it's fiction, where we want to make sure the author stays on track with the creative flow, or a how-to, where the author must provide clear and full explanations of his or her topic, the editorial and guiding processes are an essential part of the formula for creating quality books.

It's a good idea to have authors submit a sample chapter early on, so that we can keep the manuscript on track and make sure that the approach the author is taking is the approach we expect them to take.

## HOW TO DO A BOOK THE EASY WAY...

Get a good writer and coordinate with him or her so that you're both working on the same page. Don't leave the process vulnerable to big surprises. The editing process will flow.

## ...HOW TO DO A BOOK THE HARD WAY

Hire a bad writer. There will be no end to the work you'll have to make that work competent. Or, alternately, hire a good writer, have no communication at all, and get something back you didn't expect.

# EDITING THE MANUSCRIPT

Once the final manuscript is submitted, the book is in our creative hands now - the author's work is done. There are three editing processes the manuscript should go through before we transfer it from our word processing program into the publishing program.

The first and most important edit is the **overview** or **content edit,** where the book is checked for organization, continuity and flow of thought; the second is the **copy edit**, where basics such as spelling, grammar and punctuation are corrected; and the third is the **design edit**, where we make some preliminary decisions on how breakouts of the text, such as subheads and charts, will be handled.

By nature, there will be a lot of overlap between the different stages, and you may find that reversing the process, or even doing all the edits together will be more comfortable for your style.

These are all important edits in preparing the book for the production stage. We may make further edits later on during production if it's determined some shifting around will be necessary to get the book settled into the right page count - perhaps moving a few lines so we can gain or lose a page in a chapter - but before we move on, we should feel comfortable that our edits were carefully completed.

Let's look at each edit in turn.

## Overview or Content Edit

A good organizational edit makes the difference between an excellent book and a mediocre one. This is the stage in a book's early development where the editor lends a skilled hand to make sure that the author's writing is organized, focused and relevant to the work, and that sentences, paragraphs and thoughts follow in a cohesive manner.

We also do the *preliminary* **chaptering**, dividing the book into chapters we feel are the most logical, which is not necessarily the way the author has laid it out.

Though some grammatical errors may be fixed at this stage, the real purpose of the overview edit is to make sure that the train of thought running throughout the book remains consistent.

For example, in how-to writing, if an author introduces a thought, that thought must be developed and complete, and the author's explanations must make sense. If the gist of a particular discussion is murky to you, it doesn't matter that you don't understand the subject. What matters is that you can't understand the point, and thus there's a problem in that passage. If the idea is not an easy editorial fix, have the author rewrite the idea more clearly. For the best explanations of all, nothing works better than showing an example.

In fiction, non-fiction and certain genre writing, continuity of the story, character development and the proper development of the dramatic flow are key concepts you must make sure the author achieves in their work. The overview edit makes sure that the various aspects of the novel contribute to the whole.

A good editor should work within the framework of an author's style and what he or she is trying to do, and not impose his own way of doing things on the manuscript. How an editor would write a thought is not necessarily how the author should write that thought. Authors have different styles and skills, and perhaps different viewpoints than one's own, and allowances must be made for that. The editor's purpose is to enhance an author's style and let it come out and flourish.

It's probably a good idea to read the manuscript a minimum of two times in an overview edit.

The first read should be thorough and focus on the overall continuity of thought and how the author is handling his or her subject; the second (and third or more) edit should concentrate on the organization of the book, the breakdown of the chapters, and how the parts contribute to the whole. Quality overview editing really makes the difference between a good book and a great book.

## Copy Edit

The basic elements of editing such as sentence structure, grammar, word usage, spelling and the like are given careful attention during the copy edit, which should be the third read of a manuscript. Some of these items will be caught during the overview edits - there will always be some overlap between the three edits - but now the fine-toothed comb is taken page by page.

In addition to the above-mentioned copy edit basics, I use this edit to break up long paragraphs into smaller paragraphs easier for the reader to digest, to apply subheads to the text to break up the book further in how-to's, and to retitle chapter heads if needed. I'm looking for ways to improve the readability and organization of a book. Additionally, I make sure all my subheads coordinate well with the text.

If you're working with a professional level writer, or at least a very good one, the edits should be mostly on the straightforward side. Good writing is easy to edit. If the book is a real mess and needs serious editing, then you probably made a mistake in the first place by working with a writer who isn't very good.

During this edit, the hard copy of the manuscript should be marked with the symbols for the data-entry person to go by when making the changes on the computer. The following chart shows the symbols I use to spec out my type instructions. This is just a simple list of the basic things I may do to a manuscript.

# PROOFREADING MARKS

| Proofing Mark | | Example | After Change |
|---|---|---|---|
| / | lowercase | Great force | great force |
| ⫢ | capitalize | the simplest | The simplest |
| __ | italics | sweet offerings | *sweet offerings* |
| ∿ | bold | tremendous show | **tremendous show** |
| ≈ | bold italics | I'm published! | ***I'm published!*** |
| ⊙ | add period | then sleeping ⊙ | then sleeping. |
| ∧ | insert (comma) | green red and blue | green, red and blue |
| ∧ | (space) | gravytrain | gravy train |
| ⌒ | close space | riding the tid e | riding the tide |
| ℮ | delete | he went went | he went |
| ¶ | start paragraph | ¶ On the second day... | |
| ∾ | transpose | rivne | river |

## Design Edit

We have one final edit to make before we transfer the book into our publishing program and that is the **design edit**. Now we must go through our manuscript, and spec the details out so that we can transform the manuscript into a book.

For certain fiction, genre and non-fiction books, books where the flow of type is just a long uninterrupted stream of type, this is easy. How the type falls on a page makes no difference at all. Once the typestyle is chosen, there are few design decisions needed to lay down with the text. We have the basic decisions of our page margins and chapter heads, but other than that, the book flows smoothly from chapter to chapter.

On the other hand, how-to's, guides, instructional manuals, children's books, and other types of books which feature headings, tables, charts, illustrations, photographs and other graphics, are the most labor-intensive books in production. Every page requires decision-making. It matters where type falls on a particular page for these types of books. Headings and graphics must be positioned with accompanying text *on the same page.*

You don't want to have a subhead by itself with no text underneath. That's a no-no. Similarly, graphics such as illustrations and photos need to be placed near the appropriate text. Charts and tables should be integral to one page as opposed to being broken up across two pages. Each page requires individual treatment to ensure that it makes sense and can stand as a whole. (We'll deal with these issues later on in the production chapter.)

In the design edit, we want to go through the text and indicate the charts, sidebars, chapter heads, subheads, bolds, italics, and any other design work we'll be doing so that your data entry person can input these changes. The actual decisions on the typestyle to be used and its attributes can be made at this point, or they can be saved until later when the book is transferred into the publishing program.

## Communicating on the Edits

My feeling, which is not necessarily shared by all publishers, is that edits in the manuscript that concern anything other than minor changes should be communicated with the author to get his or her feedback. I always want to make sure that everybody is in agreement on what is being done to improve the writing in the book, and that when the book is published, there are no surprises sprung on the author.

If the edits are correct, the author will recognize their validity. Perhaps the author will disagree with an edit, and with proper reasoning convince you of such and improve the book yet again.

I like this communication for the first two types of edits, the overview and copy edits. It gives myself and the author the best quality control.

However, as concerns the design edit, there is no reason to consult with an author since it's not their expertise, and in a sense, not their concern. Designing a book falls under the domain of the publisher.

# ENTERING THE EDITS
## Double Check Edits

Once the edits have been completed and marked onto the hard copy of the final manuscript, they should be entered in the word processing program by your data entry person. These changes should then be double-checked by the editor in charge of the book to make sure they were entered properly.

It is better to catch errors now where changes are easy, than later, when actual pages have been layed out and it becomes a problem. That's why double-checking is important at all stages of the publishing process. Like anything else, it's easier to fix problems when first caught, than later on, when small problems can exacerbate into larger problems.

## Spell Check

The computer software programs are filled with marvels, and one of them is the wonderful spell-checks that come along with good word-processing programs such as Microsoft Word. The publishing programs are equipped with spell checks as well. While a spell check is no substitute for an actual page by page and word by word proof which must be done carefully, it will catch almost all your spelling errors.

What spell checks won't catch are misspelled place and proper names, words out of context, missing text or text entered twice (though it will get *words* entered twice), text designed wrong, and correctly spelled words in the wrong part of a sentence.

And you'll have to put up with unusual words tagged as misspelled words. For example, *a fish and ice dinner*, where the author meant *a fish and rice dinner*, won't be picked up by the word processing or publishing program's spell check. Also a word such as *flibbertigibbet*, meaning a silly and restless person, will show up as being misspelled because it's not in the dictionary base of the program. (Words used frequently, which are not in the dictionary's base, such as your company name, can be added though.)

## THE NEXT STEP

A fine proofing beyond the computer's spell-check won't be necessary at this stage, only later on, when it's time to get the book ready for press. We have performed the last step we take in our word processing program. Now it's time to get down and dirty. After discussing the basics of type and graphics in our next chapter, and making some decisions, we'll be ready to put our book together.

# 9. BOOK DESIGN - TYPE, GRAPHICS, DESIGN BASICS

## INTRODUCTION

The inside pages of a book are physically composed of two elements; the *type* which consist of all *written* text in a book, and the **graphics** or **artwork**, which is all else that gets printed on the page, including photographs, drawings and materials such as maps, charts and the like.

While we generally think of a book as being comprised of the written word, this is totally a function of the book itself. Books in categories such as poetry, and fiction and its various genres, usually have little if any graphics, while art-oriented titles such as photography and children's books, are predominately graphics-based with comparatively little type. How-to's and instructional books fall in the middle; they generally use a wide mix of graphics to go along with the type.

The number of graphic elements - photos, illustrations, charts and the like - included in a book, is a marketing decision whose main considerations boil down to the demands of the book itself and the market being targeted. Basically, what elements will be needed to make the book more attractive and useful to a reader, and ultimately, a better seller? These are creative decisions made by the publisher or editor in charge of production.

In this chapter, we'll look at each element of the book separately, both type and graphics, and show how to work with them to not only create the finished book, but to create an *attractive* one.

# TYPE DESIGN

**Typefaces (typestyles)**, the families of similar types that are designed as a group, and **fonts**, the individual styles within that group, are the styles of characters including the letters themselves, numbers and punctuation marks, that make up printed text. In the industry, there is a certain amount of confusion over the exact usage of these terms, *typestyles*, *typefaces (faces)* and *fonts*, but really they all amount to the same thing, and you'll confuse no one by using these terms interchangeably, as I'll be doing throughout.

**Typography**, or type design, is an art in itself, and is the term used in graphics to describe the usage of type. While typography is wielded wonderfully by talented designers (especially on cover design), for the purposes of designing and making books, the choosing of appropriate typefaces and their implementation into a strong design is a straightforward and relatively easy task - you'll have no problems getting the basics down.

There are thousands of typestyles available for you to use in making books, from straightforward faces designed for reading to highly stylized ones made for specific moods. New ones are being created all the time. If you look hard enough, you'll find fonts with about any design imaginable. There are faces created for wedding invitations, and others designed for an art deco look. Big, thin, expanded, scripted, bolded, slanted, whatever - if someone has thought of it, it's been created. You can even buy programs that help you design your own.

But don't get intimidated with this huge selection. There's a logic to using type, and we'll break that down for you, and show you an easy way to choose appropriate faces for your book. Let's look at that now.

## Working With Type

We choose typefaces for three basic reasons; the ability of the face to be read easily at the point size we choose; the amount of space we need to fill; and the typeface's *look* - the feel it gives the type we'll print.

While the type used for a book must be readable since the book must be able to be read, a typeface might also be chosen for the amount of space it consumes in a book - we may need to expand or condense the pages - or for the *look* or *feel* it lends a book.

There are also different types of typestyles such as **decorative type**, stylized fonts which are used for creating a look such as a logo; **headline type**, type best used as headings (and can sometimes be considered a decorative face); and **text type**, which are all-around faces good for both text and headlines.

Decorative and headline faces are effective when used sparingly for items such as logos, type headers and covers, but are difficult to read as passages of text. For example, Aachen Bold, the typeface used in this book for the headers and chapter heads, is a headline type, and looks fine the way we've used it. But watch what happens when we use Aachen Bold for text. Try to read the following passage. Yugh!

**For example, Aachen Bold, the typeface used in this book for the headers and chapter heads, is a headline type, and looks great the way we've used it. Look what happens when we use this for text. This headline type becomes very hard to read when used as text type.**

And that is the basic distinction between text type, and non-text type. Text type, such as we're using in this paragraph, is easily read as sentences or paragraphs of type, while decorative and headline type, usually distinctive because it's designed as bold or script, is not easily read except as a one liner such as a headline.

## Text Type

The main function of **text type**, the sentences, paragraphs, and charts that make up a book, is that it must be *readable*. It sounds like common sense, but you would be surprised at the number of publications and ads that ignore this basic principle. Unless you're doing an "artsy" type of book (where weird might be wonderful), you should use easy-to-read type for passages where there is more than one or two sentences of type - that is, if you want people to be able to read what's written.

*Easy-to-read* is not just a function of the typeface itself, but also, of the size of type used. Text type that is either too large or too small can be difficult to read, and thus, can really hurt a book's presentation and its sales. So, when dealing with passages of text, you must make sure that the typestyle chosen is of sufficient style *and* size. We'll cover exactly what that means in a little bit. Meanwhile, have a look at the chart for examples of type that is either too large or too small.

---

## TYPE TOO SMALL, TYPE TOO LARGE

### TYPE TOO SMALL

Here's an example of a point size that is too small to be used as text type. We're using ITC New Baskerville for this illustration, a great text font when used as 11 point (as we've done in the book) or even 10 point. Using 9 point New Baskerville borders on being too small, eight point or lower, has really passed the limits. This example shows New Baskerville at 7 point.

## TYPE TOO LARGE

Here's an example of a point size that is too large to be used as text type. We're using ITC New Baskerville 16 point for this illustration, a great text font when used as 11 point or even 10 point. Using 12 point borders on being too large (for regular books, that is, books not geared for children or those with weaker eyesight), thirteen point or higher, begins to pass the limits.

---

## Chapter, Headline and Sub-Headline Type

Besides the type used to create the basic text in a book, we'll be working with **chapter headings**, the text used to indicate and announce a chapter; **heading**s, text used to announce or lead off a passage of text, and **subheadings** or **subheads**, lesser headings.

Chapter headings are typically the only headline type used in fiction books, while books such as how-to's and references may use frequent headline type to guide the reader and make the book easier to follow and more practical to use.

Typically, the type used for these various types of headings are darker and larger, so that they easily stand out against the text type.

# Principles of Using Typefaces

The hallmark of good design is consistency. Despite the large variety of typefaces available, you must avoid the temptation to use too many of them in one project. The difference between working with the same typestyle for variety, as opposed to mixing in a cauldron of typestyles, is that in the first case, we get a *coordinated*, professional look. In the second case, the hodgepodge of faces can hurt a book's look and make it appear confusing, and even unprofessional.

For text copy, as a rule, one typestyle should be used throughout a book. Now, there are various things one can do with the text itself to highlight passages - using bolds, italics, caps - which we'll get into later, but there's no reason to change styles within text passages themselves. It is with the chapter and headline types that another style can be used effectively, to bring out a strong design and sharp look.

You can either mix two typestyles together, one for the text and one for the headlines, as we did with this book, to create a particular look for your book, or you can use the same typeface for both text and headers in a book. Either style will give your book a strong and professional design, and the choosing of one design or the other is a matter of personal preference .

When choosing typestyles, remember that the guiding principle is consistency. Whatever typestyle is used for headers, should be used for all headers, and whatever is used for body type, should be used for all body type.

Consistency must be maintained among the sizes of typestyles used as well. Straight text passages should be of uniform size throughout a book. For passages treated differently, such as footnotes, sidebars, charts and the like, it is okay and even preferable to change the size (though the typestyle should be the same), but all footnotes, for example, should maintain that same size. Chapter heads can (and should) be of different size than headings, which should be different than subheadings; but the same design principle remains - all like elements should be treated the same.

You can sometimes effectively mix in a third typestyle for the front and back pages (such as the table of contents, copyright page, ads), or for your chapter heads, as long as the mix works. Usually though, you'll find that one or two typefaces will be sufficient (and often preferable) for a powerful design.

Before we move on to the fundamentals of working with type, let's get familiar with the measurements systems used in publishing and graphics.

# POINTS AND PICAS

The standard units of measurements used in graphics and typesetting are *picas* and *points*. *Picas* are used to measure widths and lengths of objects such as text blocks on a page or graphic elements that need to fit on a page or resized. *Points* are used for smaller measurements such as the size of a character (letters, numbers and symbols), the distance between sentences (called *leading*) and the thickness of lines (known as *rules*).

These graphic units are actually easier to use than inches for they give us more precise measurements to work with. Once you're accustomed to thinking in terms of these measurements, picas and points, you'll actually find them easier to use than inches.

Since points and picas are the language of graphics, you should get familiar with these terms right away.

## Picas

There are six picas to every inch. Thus, three picas equals half an inch, and 18 picas, three inches. The advantage of using picas over inches is that since the unit of measurement is smaller, we end up working with whole numbers, or at the very least, easy fractions in our calculations.

While inches might give us unwieldy fractions such as 1/3 of an inch or 5/6 of an inch, picas gives us whole number units to work with. In this example, 2/6 or 1/3 of an inch equals two picas, and 5/6 of an inch equals five picas; these are more manageable for our purposes. If you want to indicate that your text or line should measure 4 1/2 inches, you could indicate *27 picas*. If it was 2 picas less, you could indicate 25 picas; or 2 1/2 picas less, 24 1/2 picas. Try working those out in inches, and you end up with sixths and twelfths.

Rather than translating everything from inches to picas, you should get yourself a **pica rule** and get accustomed to using picas from the outset. A pica rule is just like a regular inch ruler except that it measures distances in picas (and points). Often, the pica rule will have an inch measurement on it as well.

## Points

Points are an even finer measurement than picas and will often be found on the pica ruler as well. We most commonly use points to refer to the size of type, the thickness of a line, or the space between lines.

There are 12 *points* to every pica, thus, 72 points to an inch. The higher the type size, the larger the character. For example, 54 point type is larger than 18 point type. (Both of these are larger, headline sizes.)

# TYPE SELECTION

While you're limited to using the fonts you have loaded on your computer system, it's easy to expand your choices by buying font packages readily found in any software store or mail-order catalogue. Though there's a wide choice of typestyles available, there's really only a few basic ones you'll be using anyway, so don't worry about the endless possibilities. You may already have the fonts needed on your system anyway.

If there's a particular typestyle you're fond of and feel will really help the look of your book, go out and purchase it - get the look you want. But otherwise, don't worry about every type possibility that exists. Choose a couple of basic fonts you're comfortable with, and concentrate your efforts on the energies needed to get your book done right, not on amassing typestyles you won't even be using.

## Helvetica/Sans-Serif Type

The most commonly found type - and you'll see it everywhere, on ads, in books, and in catalogs - is **Helvetica**, the real iron horse of typefaces. If you have nothing else in your type arsenal and you're doing how-to, reference or instructional books, you'll get by fine with this face. It's straightforward, easy to read, and while perhaps a little on the plain side for cover titling, will serve every other type function, text, headings and cover copy with aplomb.

Helvetica is best used in books where the type is frequently broken up by headings and subheadings. For books with long continuous streams of type or larger page counts though, publishers have found that serif typestyles (see below) make for smoother reading.

Helvetica has other names, depending upon the company which manufacturers a compatible face. Helvetica-type fonts are also found as Ariel, Helios, Megaron and Triumverate.

Helvetica is a **sans-serif** type, which means the characters themselves, if you look carefully, lack the flourishes and hooks you'll find in **serif types**, which do have the flourishes and hooks.

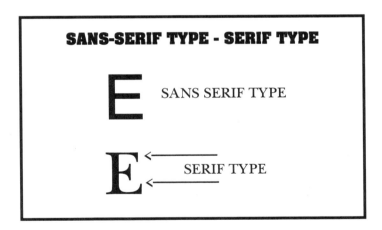

## Serif Types

Books with long unbroken strings of text, such as you'll find in most books outside the how-to categories, are most easily read in serif types. Thus, you'll see almost all books in the fiction and non-fiction categories using serif typestyles for their text.

In this book, we chose to use 11 point New Baskerville, a serif type, for the text, and Aachen bold for the chapter and subheads.

There are many serif typestyles that work great for text. One of the most popular faces is **Times Roman**, which may also be called **Times,** depending upon the manufacturer. Other excellent serif fonts include such popular ones as **Century Schoolbook, Garamond**, **Cheltenham**, and **New Baskerville (Baskerville)**. These are all standard and easy-reading book faces, commonly used by publishers and designers.

There are many, many other serif type styles that are excellent for text copy, so don't limit yourself to the above choices. Just make sure you see a full page of printed text before deciding upon any typestyle you might use. If the typestyle proves readable, consider using it.

If choosing a serif or non-serif style for your book becomes a difficult decision - make life easy - simply go with one of the excellent faces we've suggested above and move on to the next aspect of getting your book done.

## Standard Text Point Sizes

Standard text sizes for most books run between 10 and 12 points. Below 9 point gets to be a little on the smallish side for most readers, though you will see books using 9 point type. Above 12 point type, the type starts getting to be noticeably large and often hard to read as well. How the type appears at different sizes is a function of the typestyle itself, and the way it's used.

For example, we recommend against using 12 point or higher Helvetica as text. It's a heavy typestyle that's clean 11 point or under, but at 12 point or higher, it begins to take on aspects of headline type and becomes difficult to read as text. On the other hand, 12 point Times is excellent as text.

Special projects have special needs, so you may find a need to run point sizes for text outside this general range depending upon your market, and sometimes, the way a particular font sizes out.

For example, you'll want to use larger type for children's books and books targeted to the elderly. On the other hand, you might opt for smaller type for instructional and technical manuals, publications where more information needs to be printed on fewer pages.

Let's talk a little more about these variances in typestyles.

## USING HELVETICA

Here's a couple of quick pointers for using Helvetica.

**For Straight Text**
Helvetica can be a good choice for how-to and other books where the text is frequently broken up by headings, though you may prefer to use a serif type, as most publishers do, for text type.

Helvetica is super easy to read at 11 point or smaller sizes. Over 11 point, however, long stretches of text done in 12 point Helvetica or larger is tough on the eyes and not recommended. Helvetica is a heavy type that starts taking on characteristics of headline type at the 12 point size.

**For Headlines**
Helvetica can be used an effective and strong headline type when made bold. It's easy-to-read and has a strong, straightforward look. Run the bolds at the same size as the text or a few points larger.

**For Small Type**
For type 8 point or smaller, Helvetica is the easiest to read of all type-faces. Even at smaller sizes, such as 5 or 6 point, Helvetica comes across clean and readable. See samples on pages 145-147.

## Samples of Styles

Following are samples of a few typefaces in 11/13 (11 point letters/13 point leading).

This is **Helvetica** shown in 11/13 type. The first number, the 11, shows the point size; the second number, the 13, shows the leading, the space between lines. Compare this typestyle to the other examples shown here to see how type can vary from one font to another.

This is **Times** shown in 11/13 type. The first number, the 11, shows the point size; the second number, the 13, shows the leading, the space between lines. Compare this typestyle to the other examples shown here to see how type can vary from one font to another.

This is **New Century Schoolbook** shown in 11/13 type. The first number, the 11, shows the point size; the second number, the 13, shows the leading, the space between lines. Compare this typestyle to the other examples shown here to see how type can vary from one font to another.

This is **Courier** shown in 11/13 type. The first number, the 11, shows the point size; the second number, the 13, shows the leading, the space between lines. Compare this typestyle to the other examples shown here to see how type can vary from one font to another.

## Running Small and Large

While a rose is a rose is a rose, 10 point is not 10 point is not 10 point. Typestyles, even though they may be the same point size, do not take up the same amount of space either vertically, or horizontally. Some typestyles *run small*, which means the actual characters print smaller than the standard point size, while other ones *run large*, that is, print larger than the standard size.

*Running small or large* affects how much space the text takes up over the course of a book, and even over the course of a page. This is a function of the width of the typeface. While a page may hold 350 words of a standard face, a style *running large* may need 1 1/4 pages to fit the same amount information, while one *running small* may use only 4/5 of a page.

So, just as increasing or decreasing the point size increases or decreases the number of pages a type will fill, so too will changing the typeface. For example, the chart following this section compares 11 point Times Roman, a typestyle that runs small, with 11 point Helvetica, a typestyle that runs standard.

If you have a ruler that measures points, usually found on your pica rule, you can see the vertical difference as well. Helvetica at 11 point is an exact 11 point, while Times at 11 point is somewhere between 10-11 point. And they're both 11 point. Thus, when you measure certain fonts for the purpose of matching them with previously printed text or for figuring out the type size, you cannot rely solely on the pica rule (except for Helvetica). The only accurate way to measure type and see how it falls on the page is to actually print out a sample page.

Why the size difference? It's just a matter of how the typefaces were designed. Sometimes we choose one typestyle over another for just this reason - we may need to fill a certain number of pages in a book and one typestyle consumes more or less pages than another under consideration. We'll go over this later in the *Production* chapter.

# BASIC THINGS YOU CAN DO WITH TYPE

You can design type in other ways than simply choosing typestyles and altering their size. Following is a chart that shows the basic things you can do with type:

| **TYPE ATTRIBUTES** | |
|---|---|
| Medium | Not bold. The standard version of a *text* type (not to be confused with headline type which is made bold). Medium may also be called, depending upon typestyle, book, regular and normal. |
| **Bold** | **A heavier thickness of type than the normal.** |
| *Italic* | *A type with the letters slanted.* |
| Underline | A line going under the text. |
| ***Bold Italic*** | ***Bold and italic at the same time.*** |
| ALL CAPS | WHERE ALL THE LETTERS ARE CAPITALIZED. |
| SMALL CAPS | WHERE ALL THE LETTERS ARE CAPITALIZED, BUT THE FIRST LETTER OF EACH WORD IS IN LARGER CAPS. |
| Upper/Lower | With capitalized letters capitalized according to standard punctuation, and other letters in the small face. Abbreviated as U/L. |

## Leading

**Leading**, pronounced *ledd-ing* the space between lines of type, is measured from the bottom of the text line to the bottom of the line above (or below), or in the jargon of the graphics industry, from *baseline* to *baseline*. The standard leading used for text passages is either one or two picas more than the point size. Thus, if you're using 10 point type, you can spec out the leading at 11 or 12 point.

Leading is indicated in written instructions as, for example, 10/11. The first number represents the point size, 10 point; the second is the leading, which is 11 point. 10/12 would indicate 10 point type with 12 point leading. 36/40 indicates 36 point type and 40 point leading (an indication you might see for cover type).

## HOW TO MEASURE LEADING

**Leading**, pronounced *ledd-ing* the space between lines of type, is measured from the bottom of the text line to the bottom of the line above (or below), or in the jargon of the graphics industry, from *baseline* to *baseline*. This is 12 point leading.

This passage is also 10 point type as above, but the leading has been increased to 14 point in this example.

Publishing programs assign automatic leading to your characters by default so this makes life easy. On text, the automatic leading features work perfectly fine for giving you the proper look to the spacing. It is only when you really need to control the leading in the book for specific spacing purposes, or are working with larger point sizes of text, especially on cover type, that you might want to override this default feature by assigning your own leading.

Word processing programs account for leading in a slightly different manner with their default functions, though you can override this too with specified instructions. For example, Microsoft Word gives you the basic option of single space (12 points), one-and-one-half space (18 points), and double space (24 points).

## SAMPLES OF LEADING
## 10/11, 10/12, 10/14, 10/9

This is an example of **10/11** leading. We're using 10 point type for all these examples so you can see the effect of using different leading. Book type is typically in the range of 9/11, 10/12 and 11/13, though many other possibilities including 10/11.5, 10/11, 10/13, 11/12.5, 9/11, 14/15, etc., are valid as well.

This is an example of **10/12** leading. We're using 10 point type for all these examples so you can see the effect of using different leading. Book type is typically in the range of 9/11, 10/11 and 11/13, though many other possibilities including 10/11.5, 10/11, 10/13, 11/12.5, 9/11, 14/15, etc., are valid as well.

This is an example of **10/14** leading. We're using 10 point type for all these examples so you can see the effect of using different leading. Book type is typically in the range of 9/11, 10/12 and 11/13, though many other possibilities including 10/11.5, 10/11, 10/13, 11/12.5, 9/11, 14/15, etc., are valid as well.

This is an example of **10/9** leading. We're using 10 point type for all these examples so you can see the effect of using different leading. Book type is typically in the range of 9/11, 10/12 and 11/13, though many other possibilities including 10/11.5, 10/11, 10/13, 11/12.5, 9/11, 14/15, etc., are valid as well.

## Alignment

Type can be aligned in four different ways; flush left, flush right, justified and centered. The text in most books, newspapers and magazines is justified, while headlines are often centered or flushed left.

**Flush left** (also called **ragged right**) is when the type along the left side is aligned along an imaginary margin, while the right is uneven. **Flush right** (also called **ragged left**) is the opposite, the type along the right imaginary margin is flush, while the type on the left is ragged. **Justified** copy is text that's both flush left and flush right; neither side has a ragged edge. **Centered** copy is where the copy is centered in the middle of an imaginary horizontal margin line.

Following is a chart showing examples of each alignment.

## ALIGNMENT CHART

### Flush left
Type can be aligned in four different ways; flush left, flush right, justified and centered. The text in most books, newspapers and magazines is justified, while headlines are often centered or flushed left.

### Flush right
Type can be aligned in four different ways; flush left, flush right, justified and centered. The text in most books, newspapers and magazines is justified, while headlines are often centered or flushed left.

### Justified
Type can be aligned in four different ways; flush left, flush right, justified and centered. The text in most books, newspapers and magazines is justified, while headlines are often centered or flushed left.

### Centered
Type can be aligned in four different ways; flush left, flush right, justified and centered. The text in most books, newspapers and magazines is justified, while headlines are often centered or flushed left.

As a rule, book text should be justified.

# PAGE AND CHAPTER DESIGN

We've discussed the various ways to work with type, from choosing typestyles and *speccing* (specifying) their point size, to leading and alignment. The next step is to see our options for putting the type together into paragraphs and pages, and after, how to use good design principles to make these pages look good.

## Paragraph Design

There are two basic ways to present your paragraphs. Each paragraph can be separated by the previous one with a return, as we've done in this book, or instead of using the return, the paragraph can lead in with an indent.

The convention with many books is to indent each paragraph and have no returns between, while how-to's can be found either way. (Your publishing and word processing programs will give you the option of indenting the first line of every paragraph.)

A good indent size is 1 1/2 picas (1/4 of an inch). Other size indents will work as well. We see what paragraphs look like with the extra return between them. Following is an example of the above three paragraphs presented with a first line indent and no extra return.

---

### FIRST LINE INDENT EXAMPLE

There are two basic ways to present your paragraphs. Each paragraph can be separated by the previous one with a return, as we've done in this book, or instead of using the return, the paragraph can lead in with an indent.

The convention with many books is to indent each paragraph and have no returns between, while how-to's can be found either way. (Your publishing and word processing programs will give you the option of indenting the first line of every paragraph.)

A good indent size is 1 1/2 picas (1/4 of an inch). Other size indents will work as well. We see what paragraphs look like with the extra return between them. This is an example of the previous three paragraphs presented with a first line indent and no extra return.

---

## Running Headers

**Running headers** are type that run consistently from one page to another above the main text across the top of a page. They're called *running*, for they appear consistently throughout either the chapter or even throughout the entire book - they *run* through the pages.

Running headers typically represent the title of the book, the chapter's name or perhaps the author's name. In this book, you see the running header on the left or **verso** page indicating the author's name, *Avery Cardoza*, and on the right or **recto** page, the name of the book, *Complete Guide to Successful Publishing*.

Running heads add a smart design element to books. They bring a consistency to the look of each page, help break up the otherwise flat look of pages that are text only. They also provide an easy reference feature in books where they are used to title each chapter. Running heads are used on both the left and right pages in the body of a book, except for the first page of each chapter on which they're generally omitted.

It is not necessary to use running heads within a book, but as you'll see with some perusal through the bookstore and your personal collection, they're favored by most publishers.

Overall recommendation: take the extra design feature of the running heads and use them in your design.

Running heads can be sized and specified in all sorts of ways, from all caps, or bold, to a variety of other attributes. See what grabs your fancy by comparing to other books you like. Sizing your type in the 10-12 point range, medium, all caps, is a safe way to go.

## Page Numbers

Publishing programs have a feature which allows you to automatically insert page numbers that will run through the book. You can independently control the right and left pages, and once the command is set, each page in the file, starting at whatever page number is set, will consecutively number itself in the position desired.

There's several basic places to put your page numbers. Perhaps the most commonly used way is to place the page number on the upper outer edges of the page. Thus, the right hand page will have the number on the upper right, in the margin above the text area, and the left hand page will have the number in the corresponding place in the upper left. You may also see the number centered in the margin. You can also center the page number along the bottom of the page, in the white margin area, or gracing the outside edges. These are the standard locations used.

If you choose to put your page numbers on the outer corners, remember that odd numbers go on the right hand page and even numbers on the left side.

Compare other books to see what size page numbering you want. From smallish 9 point, to largish 14 point or higher, medium, italic or bold, you'll find a whole range of possibilities that will work. You should keep your page number type consistent with your running heads, though this is not a necessity.

## Page Margins

**Page margins** are the space between the outside of the main printed text area and/or graphics area, both length and width, and the physical end of the page. These margins may contain running heads and page numbers, but otherwise are filled with white space.

The main purpose of these margins is to allow your printer a sufficient amount of room to print the book without chancing error. Using smaller margins than the amounts I recommend is asking for potential big trouble. If there's a small shifting during the printing process or a tight cut at the trimming or binding stage, there's a good chance that your book will have type print right to the edge of the paper, or even worse, lose type right off the edges - and that's not a good scenario.

## ILLUSTRATION OF MARGIN AREAS ON A PAGE

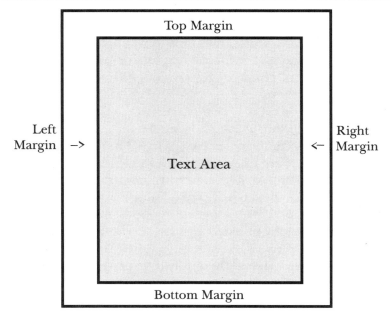

There are four margins; top, bottom, left and right. You should plan the white space you'll want ahead of time for each of these areas. You must leave *at least* three picas or preferably four picas of white space for each of these margins.

Theoretically, you could use two pica margins and get away with it, and definitely no smaller margins than that, but three picas would be a better minimum if space were tight.

When page numbers or running heads are designed at the top margin, give yourself a minimum of four and a half or five picas of space outside the main text area instead of the suggested four picas. You still need that minimum of two, and preferably three picas of margin space outside *any* printed area. Similarly, if page numbers or running footers are placed at the bottom of the page, that same four and a half or five picas of margin should be left. If there's a combination of page numbers on the bottom margin and running heads on the top, or other combination, the four and a half and five pica margins apply to each.

Where there is no running head or foot, three or four picas will suffice as a minimum margin. I would use this range of margin numbers as the minimum requirements for 4 1/4 x 6 3/4 and 5 1/2 x 8 1/2 books.

On bigger books, 6 x 9 or larger, you may want to leave a little more "air." Maybe go with a minimum of four picas all around, or five picas, and six picas or more where there's headers or page numbers on the bottom or top margin. These suggestions fall within the standard range used by many publishers.

On the following page are charts showing the minimum recommended margins for various trade size books. Wider margins than those suggested in these charts are often used, and will work quite well with any type of book. For example, left and right margins can be 4 or 5 picas, and top and bottom can be 6 or 7 picas. Using even larger margins will add class to a book, and look especially good in creative titles such as fiction and photography books.

When setting up your page in the publishing program, don't forget to account for these margins.

## Standard Minimum Text Margin Charts

We've used the following standard minimum margins for this chart: Three picas each for the left, right and bottom margins, and five picas for the top on the 4 1/4 x 6 3/4 and 5 1/2 x 8 1/2 books, and four picas on three sides, and six picas for the top on the 6 x 9 books. Two extra picas are added to the margins in each case.

As we discussed, other sized margin configurations are possible, and extra room should be allowed on the bottom margin if page numbers or a running footer is used.

In the charts below, the **Final Text Area** shows the main print area for the text or graphics after the margins are subtracted from the size of the book. Thus, on a 5 1/2 inch wide book, taking 3 picas off both the left and right margins gives us a print area of 4 1/2 inches, or 27 picas.

The first chart shows the recommended minimum margin area in picas; the second chart shows these same measurements in inches.

## MINIMUM MARGINS CHART
### Standard Minimum Text Margin Chart in Picas

| Size Book (in inches) | MARGINS | | | | FINAL TEXT AREA | |
| --- | --- | --- | --- | --- | --- | --- |
| | Left | Right | Top | Bottom | Width | Height |
| 4 1/4 x 6 3/4 | 3 | 3 | 5 | 3 | 19 1/2 | 32 1/2 |
| 5 1/2 x 8 1/2 | 3 | 3 | 5 | 3 | 27 | 43 |
| 6 x 9 | 4 | 4 | 6 | 4 | 28 | 44 |

### Standard Minimum Text Margin Chart in Inches

| Size Book (in inches) | MARGINS | | | | FINAL TEXT AREA | |
| --- | --- | --- | --- | --- | --- | --- |
| | Left | Right | Top | Bottom | Width | Height |
| 4 1/4 x 6 3/4 | 1/2 | 1/2 | 5/6 | 1/2 | 3 1/4 | 5 5/12 |
| 5 1/2 x 8 1/2 | 1/2 | 1/2 | 5/6 | 1/2 | 4 1/2 | 7 1/6 |
| 6 x 9 | 2/3 | 2/3 | 1 | 2/3 | 4 2/3 | 7 1/3 |

## Bleeding Print

Alternately, you can print right to the edge of the page, called *bleeding*, but this will require a different printing process for your inside pages. It will also make the printing much more expensive. For this reason, you rarely see bleeds in a standard book design, and where you do see them, it's on books that are artistically-oriented. Typically, it's only on the cover where bleeds are used.

If you will be printing bleeds on your inside pages, you *must* coordinate with the printer on the best way to prepare your artwork. You'll also need to ask that your estimate include charges for bleeding, or you'll be heading for a basketful of surprises and problems on both the printing and pricing ends.

## Chapter Heads and Design

A **chapter** is a distinct division in a book, usually, but not always, begun on a new page. Chapters are separated from one another by a demarcation known as the **chapter head**, type set in a distinct style from the text type, and usually preceded by extra space. When begun on a new page, chapter heads are usually positioned one fourth to one third the way down the page.

Chapter heads can be designed in a wide variety of styles, from using small bold or decorative type, to screaming bold type, from type run vertically, up and down (as opposed to horizontally), to mixing a variety of typestyles and sizes within the chapter head itself. They can be spiced up by the addition of quotes or drawings underneath the title, enclosed in a box, or underscored with a thick rule (line). Basically, the design possibilities are endless, and most ideas will work as long as the design is appropriate to the book and its audience.

For a straight and simple approach, use a bold, decorative or headline type 18-36 points or larger, flushed left or centered, and begun about 1/3 the way down the page. This will give your book a strong look and make life easy if you're prone to endless agitation over every decision. The type itself that you use can be the same type as used in the text, but made larger and in bold, or it can be any type under the sun that is readable and meets your fancy.

Chapters are often designed to start on the first right hand page, thus leaving the facing left page blank if the previous chapter had ended on a right page as well, but you can start your chapters on the left page as well, or even begin your chapter right after the last chapter ends, without starting on a new page. Sometimes this decision is a function of space.

The final decision on chapter design should be held off until the production stages, where we see what chapter style best fills our needs for meeting the 16 or 32 page signatures.

## Chapter Size

Chapters can be any size you feel comfortable with, from 1 to 50 pages or more, and you can mix and match within a book. There's no problem having several large chapters, say 45 pages each, then a two page chapter.

It's preferable even to have some small chapters - they psychologically give the reader a break and make the book easier to read.

I would caution though against overly long chapters for the same reason. A chapter that never seems to end can be tiresome to get through and burn out a reader. What's a long chapter? I'm not sure where you draw the line, but I would certainly say 100 pages is excessively long, perhaps even 70 pages. If your book does run long chapters, think about mixing in some shorties as well to cut the reader some slack.

# STANDARD BOOK DESIGN

It's easy to get overwhelmed by the huge variety of typefaces available, the sizes of type you can use, and the leading, format and dimensions of a book. But there's no reason to get intimidated by all the variety - the process need not be complicated.

To make life simple, I've narrowed your choices to a few strong designs. The recommendations listed in the *standard book design* chart on the following page will work well and provide a strong presentation with most any type of book you might do.

# STANDARD BOOK DESIGN

**Type Style:**

Use Helvetica, Times Roman, Garamond.

**Type Size:**

10, 11 or 12 point.

**Leading:**

Automatic; or if manual, add two points to the type size.

**Alignment:**

Justified.

**Page Numbers:**

11 point medium, placed on top outside corners.

**Page Margins:**

• 4 1/4 x 6 3/4 and 5 1/2 x 8 1/2 size books, leave three picas (1/2 inch) on the left, right, bottom margins, 4 picas on top.

• 6 x 9, 4 picas on the left, right, bottom margins, 6 picas on top.

**Paragraph Style**

First line indent of 1.5 picas, 1/4 inch.

**Subheads:**

12 or 14 point bold, same face as text, flush left.

**Chapter Size:**

Any size you feel comfortable making them.

**Chapter Heads:**

18 or 24 point bold, all caps, beginning 1/4 the way down from top margin.

**Other:**

If you use running heads, cover them over on the first pages of new chapters.

# GOOD DESIGN CONCEPTS

The key to strong interior design in books is making the text easy-to-read. On books other than those that are composed of straight type, such as fiction, this is done by breaking up the text out of straight type as much as possible.

We do this by making judicious use of short paragraphs, subheadings, graphics (such as charts, illustrations and photos), screens, and by altering type (bolds, italics, etc.). All these factors improve the readability, feel, and organization of a book. And thus, they increase sales.

In how-to and artistic books, where creative use of white space brings out the best in a book, readers have more difficulty navigating through straight running type such as would be found in fiction, and thus interior design takes on more sales importance. (In fiction and non-fiction books, we still want a nice design, but other than doing a good job with type, there are few design decisions. These books are pretty much straight text.)

## General Stylistic Guideline

A cardinal rule in publishing is to design your books the way *you* feel best presents their material for the potential audience as opposed to the style in which the author has handed in his manuscript. Sometimes the two may coincide, though generally they won't. Just because an author has suggested a certain format or happens to hand in a manuscript in a particular style doesn't mean you have to follow it. Authors should not design their books; they're writers, not designers or marketers. If the latter two designations applied, they would be the publishers. But since this is not the case, and you are the one responsible for making the sales and putting the book together, keep those distinctions clear in your head and do the book in the manner you feel is best.

It's your job to design the book, to have the final say on chapter titles, chapterization, charts, subheads and all other features that make the book a book. The author has already done his part; he's *written* the book. His job is officially over. You are the person *marketing* that book, making sure that it's presented in its best form with the maximum potential of sales.

## Short Paragraphs and Headings

The two main techniques for breaking up text are the use of short paragraphs and frequent headings.* There's nothing wearier to read than one long, paragraph with no breaks. The eyes need a break, a resting point that headings and paragraphs provide.

Breaking up text is especially important in how-to and reference books, where information needs to be as accessible as possible. Imagine this

*This discussion excludes books such as the fiction category where books are typically published as straight text - headlines being rarely used.

Book with no subheads to break up the text. For example, if the type in this book was comprised of chapter heads and long streams of text without headings, this book would be extremely hard to get through.

You want to present the manuscript in the most readable form possible, and you do this by carefully combing the manuscript and looking for ways to break up long streams of text. Besides inserting charts, illustrations, photos and other graphics, you do this by breaking up the text. Long paragraphs should be cut to smaller paragraphs, and wherever possible, headings should be inserted over the text.

Don't rely on the writer for this aspect of the design. The writer's job is to write a good manuscript. Your job is to go through the manuscript and break it up into headings and paragraphs where appropriate - to do the overall design. This stage in the design and editing process is where books with a superior design get created.

Below, we'll compare the same material presented in three ways; first as a solid long paragraph; second as a text block broken into several paragraphs, and third, using short paragraphs and headings. You'll see that each successive version gets easier to read.

## LONG PARAGRAPH EXAMPLE

**One Long Paragraph** - Breaking up text is especially important in how-to and reference books, where information needs to be as accessible as possible. Imagine this book with few subheads to break up the text. For example, if the type in this book was comprised of chapter heads and long streams of text without headings, this book would be a very hard read and tough to get through. It's the editor's job to go through the manuscript and break it up into headings and paragraphs where this is appropriate. This phase of a book is extremely important, and separates books with superior designs from books with mediocre designs. Long paragraphs should be cut to smaller paragraphs, and wherever possible, headings should be inserted over the text. You want to present the manuscript in the most saleable form you can, and you do that by carefully combing the manuscript and looking for ways to make it more presentable. Don't rely on the writer to do this. The writer's job is to write a good manuscript. Your job is to make a book out of it.

*Compare now to the examples on the following page*

## SHORTER PARAGRAPH EXAMPLE

**Broken Up Into Smaller Paragraphs** - Breaking up text is especially important in how-to and reference books, where information needs to be as accessible as possible. Imagine this book with few subheads to break up the text.

For example, if the type in this book was comprised of chapter heads and long streams of text without headings, this book would be a very hard read and tough to get through. It's the editor's job to go through the manuscript and break it up into headings and paragraphs where this is appropriate. This phase of a book is extremely important, and separates books with superior designs from books with mediocre designs.

Long paragraphs should be cut to smaller paragraphs, and wherever possible, headings should be inserted over the text.

You want to present the manuscript in the most saleable form you can, and you do that by carefully combing the manuscript and looking for ways to make it more presentable. Don't rely on the writer to do this. The writer's job is to write a good manuscript. Your job is to make a book out of it.

## SHORTER PARAGRAPH EXAMPLE WITH HEADINGS

### BROKEN UP INTO SMALLER PARAGRAPHS
Breaking up text is especially important in how-to and reference books, where information needs to be as accessible as possible. Imagine this book with few subheads to break up the text.

### CHAPTER HEADS
For example, if the type in this book was comprised of chapter heads and long streams of text without headings, this book would be a very hard read and tough to get through. It's the editor's job to go through the manuscript and break it up into headings and paragraphs where this is appropriate. This phase of a book is extremely important, and separates books with superior designs from books with mediocre designs.

Long paragraphs should be cut to smaller paragraphs, and wherever possible, headings should be inserted over the text.

### THE PUBLISHER'S JOB
You want to present the manuscript in the most saleable form you can, and you do that by carefully combing the manuscript and looking for ways to make it more presentable. Don't rely on the writer to do this. The writer's job is to write a good manuscript. Your job is to make a book out of it.

## The Advantages of Using Graphics

The more charts, illustrations and photos you have, the better.* Absolutely. Graphics break up text blocks nicely, add a richer dimension and texture to a book, and without doubt, make a book more pleasant and easier to read. There's no two ways about it. Adding graphics to a book greatly increases its value in the consumer's eyes. And that means more sales.

However, if you're going to use graphics, make sure that they're quality graphics. Including *cheesy* illustrations in a book is worse than having no illustrations at all. Graphics reflect on the overall quality of the book you're publishing, so you want to maintain a high standard. You want to avoid **clip art**, generic artwork, that is sold for general use. It can come in the form of software programs or clip art books that may be found in art supply stores. But wherever and however you may see it, avoid it just the same. Clip art looks unprofessional, cheap, and generic - which is exactly what it is - generic art that looks generic - and will make your book look like a high school production.

## Working with the Attributes of Type

There are various styles we can apply to type - Medium, **Bold**, *Italic*, <u>Underline</u>, ***Bold Italic***, ALL CAPS, SMALL CAPS - but like anything else, there's good and bad usage. We'll provide a few hints here to keep you on the right track.

Type attributes are best used for highlighting text and not overwhelming it. If you constantly apply underline, bold, parenthesis, italics, all caps, and other attributes to your type, sentence in and sentence out, you'll create a monstrosity to read. Too much highlighting throughout a passage or book makes a book look amateurish and the passage, instead of being emphasized, becomes a distraction.

Some bolding or underlining certainly adds value and emphasis to selected text, but don't overdo it. Let the writing speak for itself. If a point is strong, it will stand out on its own.

*This discussion excludes books (such as fiction) that are straight text - where graphics are typically not used. By the same token, though it is not standard convention, using graphics in fiction books, such as illustrations or woodcuts, would add to a book's value and could be used as a marketing tool.

The following paragraph shows what happens when too many styles are added to a paragraph. Try to get through this baby.

For example, we get proposals WHERE THE WRITER CONSTANTLY UNDERLINES OR CAPITALIZES TEXT TO STRESS HIS OR HER POINT. What really happens is that - THEY'RE HARD TO READ. **If a point is strong, it will stand out on its own!!!** Perhaps you'll use an exclamation point, or bold or italicize a word a two. **PERHAPS NOW AND THEN MAYBE AN ENTIRE LINE.** *BUT, LET THE WRITING DO ITS OWN SPEAKING!*

Continuous bold or continuous caps makes text quite difficult to read. In this next example, we'll look at this paragraph in all caps and bold (below). It's no coincidence that my phone bills, when I lived in California, were always bold and in all caps - the most difficult kind of type to read. The phone company didn't want their customers looking at the bills too carefully. If you thought the previous example was hard to read, how about this one!

**CONTINUOUS BOLD OR CONTINUOUS CAPS MAKES TEXT QUITE DIFFICULT TO READ. IN THIS EXAMPLE, WE SHOW A PARAGRAPH PRINTED IN UPPER CASE (ALL CAPS) AND WITH THE TEXT BOLD AS WELL. MY PHONE BILLS, WHEN I LIVED IN CALIFORNIA IN THE EARLY 1980'S, WERE ALWAYS BOLD AND IN ALL CAPS - THE MOST DIFFICULT KIND OF TYPE TO READ. THE PHONE COMPANY DIDN'T WANT THEIR CUSTOMERS LOOKING AT THE BILLS TOO CAREFULLY.**

Attributes used frequently in short bursts, and in the right situation, do wonders for breaking up a text and making it easy to read. The key, as we've shown negatively in these examples, is to keep the design *clean*.

# COMPUTER DESIGN TECHNIQUES

The tremendous flexibility of computer publishing programs allows us to add depth and dimension to a book without increasing costs. We can add boxes, lines, circles, and most interesting of all, *screens* over and around type to make great-looking pages. Sidebars and charts are easily created, and type can be set to run around a pre-set area such as the outline of a bicycle. Books can take on a look that simply wasn't possible ten or even five years ago without adding lots of expenses.

**Screens** or **tints** are dot patterns of various percentages that tone down a solid color and appear as shades on the printed page. When printing black on white, a screen gives you a gray look, the intensity of which is controlled by the coverage of the screen used. Printing black at 100% is solid black. Printing that same black at 5% would produce a light gray scale.

The new computer technology is greatly advantageous for it allows us to use screens over text at no additional printing or setup cost. This is opposed to pre-computer technology where the printer and/or the graphic artist had to manually cut screens each time they were used - and the publisher was charged for each screen made and shot. The computer-generated screens on our publishing program needs no adjustment or work to be reproduced by the printer and thus the page can be shot as a straight line shot by the printer.

A light screen placed over type makes a marvelous effect and breaks up a page nicely. Screens of 10%-20% work best over type, with screens greater than 20% tending to run a little dark for the text within. Screens are patterns of black dots placed over type, so you must also be aware of the type style and size you're using. The eye sees dots as a solid gray coverage, but if the type runs too small, it will get lost among the dots and be difficult to make out. Thick, bold letters will show against many screens, but a thinner type style such as Times Roman printed at below eight point could get lost in the shuffle and be difficult to make out.

Screens can be made using any color at all, but since we're dealing with black only on the inside of the book - for standard books - your screens will be in various shades of gray depending upon the percentage screen used. If you do use a second color on the inside, you can do wonderful things with screens and make a book really look beautiful.

On the following page are sample computer generated screens of 10%, 20% and 30% with type shown in 7, 9 and 10 point Times and Helvetica, with Headings in 12 point bold caps for each. You'll see for yourself the differences in typestyles, sizes and screens, and how it affects the readability of the type. Some text, as you see, can be difficult to read.

## 7, 9 AND 11 POINT HELVETICA - 10% SCREEN

Screens of 10%-20% work best over type, with screens greater than 20% tending to run a little dark for the text within. The eye sees dots as a solid gray coverage, but if the type runs too small, it will get lost among the dots and be difficult to make out. Thick, bold letters will show against many screens, but a thinner type style such as Times printed below eight point could get lost in the shuffle and be difficult to make out.

Screens of 10%-20% work best over type, with screens greater than 20% tending to run a little dark for the text within. The eye sees dots as a solid gray coverage, but if the type runs too small, it will get lost among the dots and be difficult to make out. Thick, bold letters will show against many screens, but a thinner type style such as Times printed below eight point could get lost in the shuffle and be difficult to make out.

Screens of 10%-20% work best over type, with screens greater than 20% tending to run a little dark for the text within. The eye sees dots as a solid gray coverage, but if the type runs too small, it will get lost among the dots and be difficult to make out. Thick, bold letters will show against many screens, but a thinner type style such as Times printed below eight point could get lost in the shuffle and be difficult to make out.

## 7, 9 AND 11 POINT TIMES - 10% SCREEN

Screens of 10%-20% work best over type, with screens greater than 20% tending to run a little dark for the text within. The eye sees dots as a solid gray coverage, but if the type runs too small, it will get lost among the dots and be difficult to make out. Thick, bold letters will show against many screens, but a thinner type style such as Times printed below eight point could get lost in the shuffle and be difficult to make out.

Screens of 10%-20% work best over type, with screens greater than 20% tending to run a little dark for the text within. The eye sees dots as a solid gray coverage, but if the type runs too small, it will get lost among the dots and be difficult to make out. Thick, bold letters will show against many screens, but a thinner type style such as Times printed below eight point could get lost in the shuffle and be difficult to make out.

Screens of 10%-20% work best over type, with screens greater than 20% tending to run a little dark for the text within. The eye sees dots as a solid gray coverage, but if the type runs too small, it will get lost among the dots and be difficult to make out. Thick, bold letters will show against many screens, but a thinner type style such as Times printed below eight point could get lost in the shuffle and be difficult to make out.

## 7, 9 AND 11 POINT HELVETICA - 20% SCREEN

Screens of 10%-20% work best over type, with screens greater than 20% tending to run a little dark for the text within. The eye sees dots as a solid gray coverage, but if the type runs too small, it will get lost among the dots and be difficult to make out. Thick, bold letters will show against many screens, but a thinner type style such as Times printed below eight point could get lost in the shuffle and be difficult to make out.

Screens of 10%-20% work best over type, with screens greater than 20% tending to run a little dark for the text within. The eye sees dots as a solid gray coverage, but if the type runs too small, it will get lost among the dots and be difficult to make out. Thick, bold letters will show against many screens, but a thinner type style such as Times printed below eight point could get lost in the shuffle and be difficult to make out.

Screens of 10%-20% work best over type, with screens greater than 20% tending to run a little dark for the text within. The eye sees dots as a solid gray coverage, but if the type runs too small, it will get lost among the dots and be difficult to make out. Thick, bold letters will show against many screens, but a thinner type style such as Times printed below eight point could get lost in the shuffle and be difficult to make out.

## 7, 9 AND 11 POINT TIMES - 20% SCREEN

Screens of 10%-20% work best over type, with screens greater than 20% tending to run a little dark for the text within. The eye sees dots as a solid gray coverage, but if the type runs too small, it will get lost among the dots and be difficult to make out. Thick, bold letters will show against many screens, but a thinner type style such as Times printed below eight point could get lost in the shuffle and be difficult to make out.

Screens of 10%-20% work best over type, with screens greater than 20% tending to run a little dark for the text within. The eye sees dots as a solid gray coverage, but if the type runs too small, it will get lost among the dots and be difficult to make out. Thick, bold letters will show against many screens, but a thinner type style such as Times printed below eight point could get lost in the shuffle and be difficult to make out.

Screens of 10%-20% work best over type, with screens greater than 20% tending to run a little dark for the text within. The eye sees dots as a solid gray coverage, but if the type runs too small, it will get lost among the dots and be difficult to make out. Thick, bold letters will show against many screens, but a thinner type style such as Times printed below eight point could get lost in the shuffle and be difficult to make out.

## 7, 9 AND 11 POINT HELVETICA - 30% SCREEN

Screens of 10%-20% work best over type, with screens greater than 20% tending to run a little dark for the text within. The eye sees dots as a solid gray coverage, but if the type runs too small, it will get lost among the dots and be difficult to make out. Thick, bold letters will show against many screens, but a thinner type style such as Times printed below eight point could get lost in the shuffle and be difficult to make out.

Screens of 10%-20% work best over type, with screens greater than 20% tending to run a little dark for the text within. The eye sees dots as a solid gray coverage, but if the type runs too small, it will get lost among the dots and be difficult to make out. Thick, bold letters will show against many screens, but a thinner type style such as Times printed below eight point could get lost in the shuffle and be difficult to make out.

Screens of 10%-20% work best over type, with screens greater than 20% tending to run a little dark for the text within. The eye sees dots as a solid gray coverage, but if the type runs too small, it will get lost among the dots and be difficult to make out. Thick, bold letters will show against many screens, but a thinner type style such as Times printed below eight point could get lost in the shuffle and be difficult to make out.

## 7, 9 AND 11 POINT TIMES - 30% SCREEN

Screens of 10%-20% work best over type, with screens greater than 20% tending to run a little dark for the text within. The eye sees dots as a solid gray coverage, but if the type runs too small, it will get lost among the dots and be difficult to make out. Thick, bold letters will show against many screens, but a thinner type style such as Times printed below eight point could get lost in the shuffle and be difficult to make out.

Screens of 10%-20% work best over type, with screens greater than 20% tending to run a little dark for the text within. The eye sees dots as a solid gray coverage, but if the type runs too small, it will get lost among the dots and be difficult to make out. Thick, bold letters will show against many screens, but a thinner type style such as Times printed below eight point could get lost in the shuffle and be difficult to make out.

Screens of 10%-20% work best over type, with screens greater than 20% tending to run a little dark for the text within. The eye sees dots as a solid gray coverage, but if the type runs too small, it will get lost among the dots and be difficult to make out. Thick, bold letters will show against many screens, but a thinner type style such as Times printed below eight point could get lost in the shuffle and be difficult to make out.

# TRADITIONAL SCREENS

Material to make screens can be purchased at graphic arts stores and cut and placed by hand over areas as an actual screen, or as a **rubilith**, a red acetate exactly cut out over the area to be screened. The printer, with proper instructions, can make the screens for you as well.

Screens come in a variety of percentages at the store, but you'll need a steady and precise hand to lay them down right. If you're not adept at this and want high quality screens that your publishing program may not allow you to do, you should have the printer make the screens, since their screens are of higher quality anyway. Having the printer screen text for you adds expenses to a bill, so get quotes first to see if they're costs you want to take on.

As we said earlier, the cheapest and easiest way to make screens is on the publishing program itself. These screens are shot like regular text and thus add nothing to the bill.

## SUMMARY TO THE DESIGN DECISIONS ON A PAGE

### Text Decisions

Choose Typestyle and Point Size
Size for Text
Leading for Text
Alignment for Paragraphs
Paragraph Style - Extra Return or Indent

### Heads and Subheads

Choose Typestyle and Point Size
Align Center or Left
Return After or Directly Above Text

### Page Decisions

Margins on Page
Running Heads? and Point Size
Point Size, Typestyle, Placement of Page Numbers

### Chapter Decisions

Size of Chapter Head
How Far Down the Page?
Start Text How Far Below Chapter Head?
Chapter Head on Its Own Page?
On Right Side of Page?

# 10. REPRODUCING GRAPHICS & PHOTOS

## INTRODUCTION

We'll often want to reproduce **artwork**, or simply **graphics** - drawings, maps, photos and the like - to be placed into our book. We can reproduce the **original**, the image from which we'll be copying, at either **100%** (the original size), or at sizes larger or smaller than the original, called respectively, **enlargements** (increasing the size of the original) or **reductions** (decreasing the size of the original).

The final image size that will be inserted onto a page can be any size we desire, as long as it fits on the printed full page or **facing pages**, two pages that face each other when the book is opened to them. We may want to have a graphic fill one half or one third of a page, with the type filling the rest, or we may decide to print a full or facing page graphic. These are design decisions.

Sizing decisions are often a function of practicality. For example, large originals such as maps may lose too much detail if shrunk below a certain size and will need a full page to be seen properly. For extra large images, we may need to run the image across facing pages. Printers call this type of image a **cross gutter**, since it goes across the *gutter*, the inside spine of the book.

There are two ways to insert graphics into a book. The first, which we'll cover in great detail in this section, is to reproduce the images and place them *manually*, by hand, onto the camera-ready page itself. Until recently, before the advent of the scanner, this is the way all graphics were done. The second way, *scanning*, which is now gaining in popularity but may not be for everyone, is to scan the image onto the computer and insert it directly into the book file.

# USING A SCANNER

If you're set up and conversant with a scanner, you can scan most graphics directly into the computer and work with them almost like you would with text - placing them where you wanted, or increasing or decreasing their size. While in the computer, the images can be manipulated and changed to meet the particular requirements of the book or page. Elements and type can be edited in or out, resized, and moved around at will within a file or many files.

There are definite advantages with this new technology, and you should familiarize yourself with it when you get a chance.

For a scanner to work for you, the following three conditions must be met: You must know how to use a scanner and have access to one; the scanner must produce high quality reproductions of your artwork; and the files created don't overload your capacity to either work with the file or access it to your printer. Additionally, manipulating scanned images and editing these files takes time and familiarity with the appropriate programs.

If you're like many publishers, and are not familiar or comfortable with the quality and proper use of a scanner and their output results, and don't yet have the time or inclination to learn the software that will give you the full advantage of scanning, then traditional reproductions and manual paste-up will be the easiest way to go.

# MANUAL PASTE-UP

There's still a place in publishing for manual paste-up techniques, and I'll discuss them in this section so you have options, often easier options, to insert graphics into your book and get it ready for press. Keep in mind that just because images can be scanned onto your computer, doesn't mean it's the only way, the easiest way, or even the best way.

**Paste-up**, the manual placement of artwork or text on a page, is necessary when you'll be inserting graphic elements such as illustrations, halftones (photos) and line drawings that you either cannot or are not set up to do on the computer.

The steps involved in paste-up are simple. Once we figure out the re-production size we'll need, we reproduce the image on either a copy machine or stat camera, wax the back surface, and then, paste the copy down on our camera-ready page.

We'll cover this in greater detail, but first let's take a look at the basic equipment used in graphics.

## Simple Tools for the Graphic Department

Only simple, inexpensive tools are needed to get the graphic depart-ment in working order and ready to handle basic projects. We'll look at these now.

Whether scanning or doing manual paste-up, you'll need a **pica rule**, a ruler that measures in the finer increments of points and picas, and a **proportional** or **reduction wheel**, a round, hand-held thin plastic de-vice with one wheel set atop another, that is used to figure the enlarge-ment or reduction of images. Alternately, you could use a calculator instead of the proportional wheel to size items properly.

For manual paste-up, I recommend all publishers have these simple tools. You should also have a **ruler with a hard edge** (preferably metal or hard plastic - wood splinters and becomes uneven), an **exacto cut-ting knife** or **straight edge blade**, and a **hand waxer**, a simple unit that melts wax and dispenses it onto the back of items to be manually placed.

There's one additional item needed, and that's a cutting surface to work on. A good **stiff piece of cardboard** will work perfectly well. The cardboard surface will not give you a "professional setup," you'll need a drafting or art table and T-square for that, but the cardboard will get the job done and that's all that counts. I still use cardboard for my cutting surfaces.

I have put together hundreds of publications using the simple tools described above: hard-edged ruler, blade, waxer, pica rule, proportional wheel, cardboard - that's all you'll need. All of these can be bought in your local art supply store for well under $100.

# SIZING IMAGES

Once a graphic has been chosen to be inserted into a book, and the area on the page where you'll be placing that image has been determined, then you'll need to get the graphic sized for proper reproduction.

To correctly size an image, you first measure both the size of the original, the **original size**, and that of the **reproduction size**, the end size after the image has been reduced or enlarged. Line these two measurements on the wheel, or figure it out by hand or on a calculator as we'll show in the next section, and you'll have the percentage needed to shoot the image.

If a final image is to be inserted as a **full page graphic**, meaning there will be no text, or at most a caption or heading on the page, you only need center the graphic element within the text area to be printed.

If the final image after reproduction is part of a page containing other text or graphics, proper room must always be left so that the image fits within the margins for the text and so that it doesn't cover over any other elements on the printed page. Also, the image should have white space around it so that it can "breathe" and achieve the full visual impact intended.

## Using the Proportional Wheel (Reduction Wheel)

The proportional wheel does two things; it can either show how to enlarge an image to a larger size, or reduce that image to a smaller size. If the image used is to be the same as the original size, then there's no need to size it - you'll be shooting it at 100%.

The proportional wheel has two round wheels set atop one another. The smaller wheel represents the size of the **original**, the slide, photo or artwork you're working with, and the larger outer wheel, shows you the **reproduction size**, the final image area after you've enlarged or reduced the original. There will also be a cut-out in the smaller circle showing numbers. The numbers on the top show the enlargement, the numbers on the bottom will show the reduction.

# PROPORTIONAL WHEEL

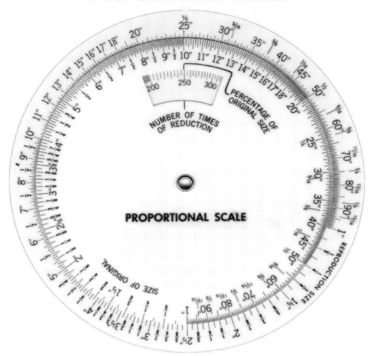

The wheel shows an example where a 10 pica object
gets enlarged to 25 picas - a 250% enlargement.

To size an image, you line up the height (or width) of the original area - this is found on the smaller, top circle - with the intended height (or width) of the image; this final reproduction size is lined up on the larger, bottom circle. Height always gets sized with height, and width with width. For example, if you have a 5 pica high object and want to make it a 17 pica high object, align the 5 on the small wheel, with the 17 on the larger wheel. The cut-out of the proportional wheel shows the percentage enlargement or reduction. In this example, the image should be shot at a fraction under 340%.

The reduction wheel doesn't care whether you're working with points, picas, millimeters, inches, yards, miles or whatever; just as long as you're not mixing apples and oranges. If you use the wheel to work with inches, the reproduction area will be in inches.

Thus, if you start with 2 inches and blow that up 200%, you'll get the identical answer, except in a different language, as using 12 picas, the same measurement area. Two inches blows up to 4 inches; 12 picas become 24 picas - the same four inches. Similarly, 2 miles at 150% become 3 miles, and 18 millimeters at 50% become 9 millimeters.

## Using a Calculator or Hand Measurement

You can also make enlargement and reduction sizes by hand, or with a calculator. Basically, you do so by dividing the original size into the size to be reproduced, and multiplying it by 100. Let's say you want to take an original that is three picas long and enlarge it to six picas. Three divided into six equals 2, and multiplied by 100, equals 200%.

Here's a more difficult example. Your original is 14, the final size is to be 37. Fourteen into 37 gives us 2.64, multiplied by 100, equals 264%. You'll shoot the image at 264% to get the desired result.

If you're *reducing* the image, as opposed to enlarging, it's the same formula, the original size divided into the final size. For example, your original is eight inches, and you want it reduced to three inches. Eight divided into three equals .38, and multiplied by 100% (you move the decimal point over two places), and you get 38%. You'll shoot the image at 38% of the original size.

The advantage of the proportional wheel is that it does these calculations automatically for you, but if one is not available, you can use the above method for getting the identical answer.

## The Correct Language for Percentages

The language for reproducing images is in percentages. Shooting at 100% indicates that the shot should be reproduced at the original size; 50% would be one half the original size; 10% would be one tenth the original size; and 250% would be two and a half times the original size.

Always specify that you want an image *shot at X%*, X being the size desired. Never indicate that you want the image *enlarged* or *reduced* to a specific percentage, only that you want it shot *at that percentage*. For example, if you ask an image to be blown up to 100%, there is legitimate confusion over whether you want the image at double the original size (a 100% blow up) or at the original size (at 100%). There are two interpretations and both are correct.

To leave no room for confusion, indicate your percentages not as an enlargement or reduction, but as a straight % of the original. *Shoot it at "X"%.*

## Shooting Up and Shooting Down

You should keep in mind that the larger you blow up an image, the more quality you will lose, since the pixels and dots that make up an image get further and further apart, and thus, more noticeable. On the other hand, the more you reduce an image up to a point, the tighter the pixel and dot patterns, and the sharper it will look. In the first instance, weak lines will break up when enlarged, and in the second instance, they'll appear to solidify when reduced.

Thus, for best reproduction quality, it's better to start with a larger-sized image and reduce it, than a smaller-sized image and enlarge it. Be careful with reducing images too much. Though lines may tighten, type in the image may gets smaller and more difficult to read.

# CROPPING IMAGES

There's two basic tools we have at our disposal to size an image properly. The first is **sizing**, which we discussed earlier; the second is **cropping**, trimming an image on any or all of its four sides (top, bottom, left side, right side).

Cropping is somewhat of an art because you have to take an imperfect situation and make it perfect. You need to be able to judge what is the *essential* part of the image, and what can be dispensed with by cropping.

The first step in cropping is to establish the **key area**, the essential area in the original photograph which must appear in the final image. For example, let's say we have a close-up photograph of a model's face, and the way the picture is framed, we cannot crop either the lower or upper portion of the photo without cutting out part of the face. That vertical dimension, in this example, would be the *key area.*

## CROP OF PHOTO BEFORE AND AFTER

The current size of the photo below, the orginal, is 24 by 16 picas (4 x 2 21/32 inches). However, it needs to fit in an area 18 picas wide by 15 picas high. This is no problem though. By cropping 6 picas off the width, and one pica off the height, we can achieve a perfect fit.

**Original Image - 24 picas x 16 picas**

**Cropping image to fit into the above 18 x 15 pica box**

By cropping from the left and off the top, we size the photo to the exact size required - and still retain, if not improve the essential image.

Working with the key area, the area that cannot be cropped, you should test both the horizontal and vertical planes for sizing. If the essential image area on a slide is six picas high and four picas wide, *use these essential area measurements as the starting area for the sizing*, not the eight by five and one half pica area of the slide itself. We're only interested in the essential part of the picture, the area we'll use.

Let's say you want to enlarge an image to fit a 40 pica vertical space. (We'll forget about the width for now to make this example easy.) If you're going to crop out one pica from the top and two picas from the bottom of an eight pica original, than your vertical starting plane measures five picas. Thus, you'll shoot the essential five pica image size at 800% (five picas enlarged to 40 picas). You won't enlarge the image at 500% (eight picas enlarged to 40 picas) because we don't care about the entire eight pica original image, only the five pica essential image.

Before you submit an image for reproduction, you should know exactly what size enlargement or reduction you're going to need, and the crop you'll be making for that image to fit.

## Cropping Example 1

Let's say we have an 8 x 10 inch graphic that needs to be reduced exactly into a 4 x 4.5 inch area. (The first number given is always the width, the second is the height.) If we shoot the photo at 50% (half-size), the 8 x 10 reduces to 4 x 5 . The four inch width, the horizontal plane, fits perfectly, but the five inch height, the vertical plane, is one half inch too high.

If we shoot the 10 inch side to reduce to four and one half inches, at 45%, then the eight inch side reduces under four inches and we have a problem - it isn't high enough for the area.

With cropping, you can still use the 50% reduction. Starting with the perfectly-sized four inch width and cropping one half inch off the five inch high side gives us an exact vertical fit of 4.5 inch. Looking at our image, a photograph of mountains and lots of sky, we see that cropping out one half inch of sky not only doesn't hurt the image but improves it. Thus, we do the crop, and now have a perfect 4 x 4.5 fit onto our page.

## Cropping Example 2

Let's say we decide that final image area is to be 20 picas wide (about 3 1/3 inches) by 24 picas high (four inches). Since the top is longer than the side, we're dealing with a vertical image.

Our original is a beautiful horizontal slide of an old stone house surrounded on both sides by thick forest, with a bright blue sky above. The image we're trying to project is that of great country living. However, one thing mars the slide. Along the left side of the image, about 1 pica into the photo, is a deep shadow that throws off the picture. But that's easily taken care of with a judicious crop.

There are two ways to approach the enlargement; from the width, or from the height. We'll show what happens both ways so you understand the slight dilemma we're going to have, and then show how to size the image properly so the image will fit perfectly into the space.

Let's try the width first. Using the wheel, we line up the original size, the slide, of 8 picas, with the desired blow-up on the outer wheel, 20 picas, and get a result of 250%. Now, whatever we do to the width, happens equally to the length. Keeping the wheels aligned at the 250% mark, we locate 5 1/2 (5.5) on the smaller wheel, the original size. It matches up just before 14 at 250%.

We can see right away this won't work. Though we sized our width to be perfect, the length is way too short. While cropping is always a possibility to trim an image and make it fit, we can't stretch that image without resizing it.

Let's try the enlargement using the length now. 5.5 picas to 24 picas is an enlargement of 435%. That same 435% makes a starting width of 8 picas into 35 picas, 11 picas too wide. However, if we can crop 11 picas off the width, we'll have a perfect fit.

Let's examine the slide again. The house itself is four picas wide, while the forest on either side is 2 picas. When the image is blown up 435%, of the 35 picas total width, the house becomes 17 1/2 picas, and the forest 8 3/4 picas on the left and right sides. We know we need the 17 1/2 picas of the house in the picture, and by cutting equally left and right, we're left with 3 1/4 picas (just over 1/2 inch) of forest on either side of the house, and an image of 24 picas width - a perfect fit. In the process, we cropped out the dark shadow off to the left.

## SOME CROPPING TIPS

Rather than imagining what a crop may look like, you should cover various side areas with a straight edged paper to see how the picture as a whole will look. You can use a business card, an envelope, a piece of paper - whatever is handy - as long as the edge covering the image is straight.

Test each of the sides, top, bottom, left and right, and see how it affects the rest of the picture. Cover two, three or four sides at once, if need be, to get the best look. When in doubt on the best crop, trust your instincts.

# REPRODUCING IMAGES
## Reproducing Non-Photographic Images

With the improved quality of the copy machine, most non-photographic images can be resized at percentages from 50% to 200% with excellent results for prices as little as 5¢ a copy! Copy machines have become so sophisticated that quality that formerly could only be achieved on stat cameras can now be approached at the local copy shop.

Or if you're conversant with scanning and have access to a machine (they're easily rented at places that rent computer time), then scanning is a great way to go as well. Once an image is scanned into the computer, it is easily manipulated to any size that is needed. And the great advantage to scanning is that you can alter the image once it's in the computer. Lines can be darkened if necessary; extra elements can be added to the image; the image can be used as a template to redraw it in better form or quality - pretty much anything that's artistically possible can be done to enhance or change that image to your needs.

Previously, the **stat camera**, a machine that photographically reproduces images, was the only available high quality option as recently as the mid 1980s. However, while the stat camera can produce superior reproductions in many instances, this extra quality is often not needed for your reproductions. The standard high quality copiers will do the job equally well and at a quality level that will generally be perfectly acceptable. And the main reason to use a copier first, is for the savings (5¢ a copy beats $5+ per image anyday), and for the ease of use. Good quality copiers are easily found.

You may still need to use the stat camera at times when the copy machine (or scanner) just won't give you the quality you need. For example, poor quality originals such as those needing to be reproduced from newsprint (like a newspaper) or from a colored original with shadings may need to be shot on the stat camera.

Copies needing to be shot at under 50% must be shot and reshot on the copy machine to achieve the proper size (copy machines don't generally reduce less than 50%). That's usually too many generations to maintain the quality you'll need, and in these instances, the stat camera (or scanner) is the better option for reproduction. The stat camera will handle any percentage size in one pass, no matter how small.

Stat cameras can be found at graphics, typesetting, and printing shops, while high-end copying machines are easily accessible in many locations nowadays. Stats generally cost $5 and up per camera shot.

## Reproducing Black & White Photographic Images

Black and white photographs cannot be reproduced for the printing process on a regular copy machine, but instead must be shot as a **halftone**, a dot pattern specially used for photographs to make them suitable for printing. Using a copy machine to reproduce black and white photographs will result in poor quality since the machine isn't equipped with the dot patterns needed for proper reproduction of your photographs.

Halftones have to be made on either a stat camera, or processed on a high quality scanner, and converted with software such as Photoshop into halftones. When processed on a stat camera, a halftoned image can be manually pasted onto a camera-ready board for printing; and when processed on a scanner, the halftone can be submitted on disk to the printer or run out as negatives. (When submitting a halftone electronically, on disk or modem, it's best to position the scanned halftone onto the file and let the printer run it out as part of the page, but if that's a problem, the printer can set up the page.)

In drum scanning, halftones are shot from the print itself and not from the negatives, so if only negatives are available, you'll need to develop them into prints before a halftone can be taken.

Halftones have various screens associated with their reproduction, and the type of screen you'll need for your printing must be coordinated with your printer *in advance*. Books printed on high quality web printers often use 133 line screens for black and white photographs, while newspapers often get printed with an 85 line screen.

Again, coordinate with your printer before shooting your halftones. You may even find that the printer will give you a competitive price on shooting halftones along with a higher quality than available locally.

---

## NOTE ON MARKING PHOTOGRAPHS

Do not place any mark on the back of original glossy photographs to be reproduced. The pressure from the writing instrument may go through and mar the front side. Indicate placements, cropping instructions or percentage reproductions on a separate sheet or overlay. Similarly, do not put scotch tape, crop marks or any other writing on the original.

---

## Reproducing Color Slides as Black & White

The best way to reproduce color slides as black and white printed images, that is, halftones, is to scan the images using either a traditional drum scanner, or the new desktop scanners with a slide attachment. You can either have a service bureau or separation house do the scanning for you, or you can rent a scanner, or buy one, and do it yourself.

Color slides won't always convert well into black and white, but through programs like Photoshop, you can color correct, actually, *tone correct*, for improved results. There's a big difference between good quality scans and poor quality scans and you'll have to trust your eyes and gather some experience to know the difference. But basically, if it looks poor to the eye, it probably will look poor after being printed.

Color slides can also be converted into black and white through a photographic process known as an internegative, but since this results in inferior quality, and creates extra unnecessary generations for this result, I can't recommend it.

For the best quality halftones, you'll want to start with black and white images, but of course, you usually won't have that choice.

## Reproducing Color Prints as Black & White

It is better to start with color prints if available, for this gives you the option of making the halftone right on the stat camera, something that can't be done with a slide. Prints can also be scanned for good results. As with the slides, color prints don't always reproduce well as black and white halftoned images, and it is only experience that will show which images may convert well and which won't.

## Reproducing Color Photographic Images

Color photographs and slides, to be reproduced, must be separated into four negatives, called **separations**, one representing each of the process colors - black, magenta, process cyan, and process yellow. High quality color separations, which is what the four negatives that make up a color image are called, cost $20-$100 and up, depending upon size, quality of the shop and equipment, and where they're done.

High quality color printing generally requires a 150 line screen for color separations, but, as with the black and white halftones, you'll need to coordinate with your printer to find the best line screens for their equipment.

There are shops that do excellent quality color separations across the United States and Canada, and these can be found locally in your yellow pages, through recommendations of printers, graphics shops, other publishers, and through advertisements in trade magazines. If you have a lot of separations, you may even consider farming them out to one of the Asian countries like Singapore or Hong Kong, places with exceptionally low prices for a lot of work, and exceptionally high quality.

The most economical way to separate color slides or prints is to contract for the work yourself at the production house of your choice. If you let the printer send the separations out, which they'll probably do - most printers don't have the equipment - they'll add their own markup to the work, and you'll end up paying considerably more.

Separations can be done one of two ways; either traditionally, on a drum scanner and output as film, or using the latest technology, actually scanned onto disk, and output either as film, or submitted electronically to your printer along with the rest of your files. For all high quality color work, you'll need to ask for a Cromalin or Match Print with the separations, so that the actual quality of the work can be seen. Also, the printer will not print without having these high quality proofs.

Cromalins and Match Prints are made from the negatives themselves. (Iris prints, made as a continuous tone, are high quality as well, but are not a substitution for a Cromalin or Match Print since they are not made from the negatives.)

Traditional drum scan separations can be made directly from a color print or color slide, but not from a color negative. The traditional drum scanners, unlike the new scanning equipment, scan what they see, and thus, negatives, which are a reversed image, will come out reversed and be unusable. If you do have a color negative to start with, you'll first need to get a print made, that is, a positive image, so that image can get separated.

Scanned separations, on the other hand, can be made from a color negative as well as a color print or color slide. These machines have no problem inverting the negative image into a positive one, such as is seen on a print. However, if you'll be getting a scan directly from a negative, which is preferable over the print in the scanning process, then a color print should be supplied as well so that the separator can best match the proper colors.

# DUOTONES, TRITONES, QUADTONES

Duotones, tritones and quadtones, are respectively, two, three and four color halftone reproductions made from a one color original. These beautiful effects cannot be done on a black and white printing, of course, because they use additional colors, but when used effectively - wow!

If you'll want to print duotones, tritones, or even quadtones on your color pages or cover, you'll need to coordinate carefully with your printer as to how to submit and process the image for best results.

# MANUALLY INSERTING GRAPHICS ON A PAGE

Once an image is reduced to the proper size, you'll often have to cut away extraneous material around the image itself so that the reproduction can fit in the space allotted on the page. For example, if you've shot a drawing at 50% at your local copy shop, you'll need to cut away the extra paper around the drawing so that you can affix the image to the page.

There's no need to trim the image exactly if the surrounding area is white because white won't print. You just want to make sure that the extra area doesn't obscure the other material on the page. Areas within the live image that you don't cut but which you don't want reproduced either (black dots, imperfections, or information you don't want printed, for example) can also be cleaned up by using the white-out liquid available in stationery stores everywhere. Simply apply the liquid over the offending area - *white it out*. Be careful however that you don't white-out print you'll need. Once the liquid is affixed, you can't undo it.

For easy cuts, an exacto knife, razor or scissors will work fine. On fine cuts though, where there's danger of cutting the image itself, use a hard ruler (preferably hard plastic or metal - wood splinters) as a guide and a straight edge blade. A straight edge is preferable over scissors because it's more exacting and helps prevent you from accidentally clipping off material you may need.

To affix the graphic onto your page, you'll first need to plug in your waxer and get it hot (it takes about 15 minutes) so that the wax will melt and apply to the image. Then you wax the back of the graphic being careful that you don't get wax on the graphic itself. Never put your graphic face down on a surface that has wax on it for the wax will transfer to its surface and possibly mar the image.

The image can now be placed where it belongs and shifted around easily as needed. And that's the beauty of wax. It holds the graphic in place while at the same time, allowing you to shift it around the page, or remove it and place it on another page altogether.

If you don't have a waxer, clear tape will work as well. Though your eye can see the tape's placement, the camera won't, so it's press-safe. However, try to avoid placing the tape over the image itself, for if you try to lift the tape later for some reason, it might pull off some of the image. There's also a glue-stick which serves a similar purpose as wax but is not as versatile (it hardens after a while), and plain glue, which will get your image to stay, but gives you no maneuverability at all once it's been placed.

# 11. COVER DESIGN & PRODUCTION

## INTRODUCTION

A good cover sells books, and an outstanding cover sells lots of books. In strictly sales terms, a great cover on a lousy book is much better than a lousy cover on a great book. A great cover can make a terrible book sell, while a bad cover can kill a great book. Never, ever, underestimate the importance of having a good cover.

A consumer or trade buyer who receives a favorable first impression in the first few seconds of looking at a book is more likely to buy that book than the person who either gets turned off by the cover or doesn't get moved by it. First impressions are extremely important. In the book business, you need to capture a person's interest immediately, and get him or her interested enough about your book to consider buying it. That's the job of the cover, your main sales tool.

Chains and independent bookstore buyers, who generally see only the cover when making their buying decisions, ask themselves: Will people buy this book? Consumers, on the other hand, who see the whole book, but make value judgments largely on the strength of the cover, ask themselves: Is this book for me (or whoever they're buying the book for)? The cover must answer those questions favorably. If a person *is* moved by your cover, you'll most likely make the sale. And if they're not, you've probably lost the sale.

So your cover has got to be good.

# SELLING BOOKS BY THEIR COVER

It will help for you to understand the importance of a good cover when you learn how books are actually sold in the industry.

Salespeople, representing your distributor or sales rep group, will set up appointments with the buyers from independent and chain book-stores with the purpose of presenting many books and lines for sale, not just your own, and they won't have much time to spend with any one book. With a lot of books to review, and a minimal amount of time for the entire process, each title will only get a brief presentation. The buyer will quickly make his decision on whether the store will carry that particular book; and then it will be time to present the next book.

In this brief time, buyers will see a rendition of the book's cover, and perhaps some catalogue copy. These are generally the only two sales items the salesperson will have with them for that book. The buyer will not actually see the book itself, for with all the titles a rep is presenting in that appointment, there's no way the salesperson can lug around the hundreds of pounds that would require. In all likelihood, the sales rep hasn't seen the book either, and most probably, if you're dealing with advanced sales, you haven't even seen the book and may still be waiting to receive the final manuscript from the author!

So the buyer sees a cover, maybe some catalogue copy, and listens to the salesperson extol its features. And while the salesperson is talking, the cover promenades in front of the buyer's eyes, the only visual rendition the buyer will see of your book before he makes his purchase.

If purchasing decisions in a bookstore by a consumer are based largely on a book's cover, imagine the importance of the cover on *this* sales presentation, when the buyer doesn't even have the luxury of a book to thumb. Thus, you see the importance of a good cover.

## Designing Covers that Sell

The purpose of a cover is to sell books, and all items you work with in your design and copy should be aimed toward that goal. Yes, you want to make the cover look great, but more importantly, you want to *sell* it to the reader. There's a difference.

For example, a reproduction of a Renoir or Picasso might look great on the cover of your dieting or beer-making book, but those paintings won't influence readers to buy. As a matter of fact, they'll kill your book. These two painters have nothing to do with either of these subjects, and their work, great as it might be, adds nothing to your sales effort - those paintings do not address your audience.

Success in selling books, as we've stressed over and over again, is all about addressing your audience and appealing to their needs and desires.

One of the best ways to hammer home your message, in all books regardless of subject or field, is through the use of powerful images. Well-chosen graphics make a huge difference in a cover's success, especially good photos or stylized drawings and you want to employ them in your design as much as possible. A picture is worth a thousand words as the saying goes, and it's true. If that image can touch a positive emotion, it will help make the sale. If the audience can identify with the image shown and get moved by it, *then you've got yourself a cover graphic.*

In my gambling books, my readers want to be winners. I address those needs with the photos I use on the cover. They show game situations with chips and money; these images suggest playing and winning. Readers identify with these winning images, and picture themselves with those winning piles.

My golfing guides show people enjoying themselves at the golf course, and my travel guides show the images people expect to see in their destination. Similarly, a running guide should show a well-toned runner, a dieting book should show a slim, healthy person - a success story, and a cookbook should show a meal you just have to eat - *now*. These images appeal to their audience and suggest to them the advantages they'll get buying the book. They are to the point. They are selling the reader.

On the other hand, a picture of a heavy and unhappy person on the dieting cover or of an uncooked chicken on the cookbook, do the opposite. They turn off the reader as opposed to turning them on. They're negative images. That uncooked chicken doesn't exactly make you want to chow it down. Looking at an obese woman doesn't exactly suggest a successful diet to potential buyers of a diet book either.

However, a beautifully roasted, savory chicken, dripping with flavor and dressed and decorated with nice fixings, might just want to get you to the table like you can't believe. Ummm, baby - feed me! And an attractive, slim woman on the cover of the diet book suggests a diet that works. Potential female buyers may think, "*I wish I looked like that,*" and associate the graphic with the benefits of buying that book.

Similarly, the use of your typestyles has a selling message to do as well. Get that message across loud and clear - no pussyfooting around here. The cover title is not the place to be subtle, not if you want to sell books. Use a font and color combination that dominate the cover, or at the very least, are easily visible at a quick glance. The more powerful-looking the title, the more effective the message. By the same token, avoid subtle, hard-to-read, and small type. A fancy typeface on your cover done in small letters may be real artsy and get oohs and ahs from your friends, but if that small, hard-to-read type doesn't sell books, you're making a big mistake using it.

Again, don't lose sight of what the purpose of cover design is all about; it's to sell books, not be pretty.

## Effective Design Principles

You want your cover to reach out and grab the reader. But to do that, you must allow its message to come through loud and clear without being hampered by type running amok, lines, boxes and doodads going every which way, and design elements or colors that just don't work.

The cover must be **clean**, uncluttered by elements that obscure its message. At a glance, the reader should clearly see the title, perhaps a strong sell line, the graphic, and the author's name. *And nothing more.* That's *clean*, and that sells. It sells in advertising and it sells in books.

Trying to bring more elements into visual play loses the whole image entirely, and you get muddy water. And you see it so often with things in print, where amateurs and professionals with no talent or insufficient training (and there are plenty of them) try to make everything stand out, and bring colors or design elements for each item to glow.

It's like a band where each musician is trying to stand out or is playing a different song - it doesn't work and it's lousy.

Anything that pulls away from the main message of the cover - title, sell line, graphic, author - is clutter, gets in the way of that message and weakens the effectiveness of the cover. Great ads of any nature, whether mail order advertising, print ads or the cover of a book (which is in effect an ad for the book) share one thing in common - the message is not only compelling, but comes through loud and clear. It comes through *cleanly*.

If you do have many items you want to stress on the cover, definitely do so, but in smaller print. If the reader is brought in by your main message, they'll read on. If you lose them in your main message by highlighting too many things, your highlighting effort will be self-defeating. The human eye can only handle so much emphasis before nothing is emphasized. Make too many bolds, as we did in an earlier example bolding an entire paragraph, and you won't see anything. The same principle holds true in a cover.

The eye must be kept centered toward the message - if you bounce the reader's eye all over a cover, you may lose them. As much as possible, strive for consistency in typefaces, sizes, leading, and attributes. Too many different things going on can overload and distract the eye. Also avoid "artsy-fartsy," "cutesy," "pretty" and busy covers, covers with images and type all over the place. Just get right down to the main message - here's what I have, here's what you need.

Simple works and always has. Don't "design" your message away. No matter what other design elements are brought into play to make the book attractive, keep that message up front, strong (sometimes "screaming") and straightforward. This is the cover, your sales tool, so don't be shy.

Study covers of successful books, and go up and down the bookstore shelves getting the essence of what turns you on in a cover, and try to get those elements you like on your cover. The examples on the following pages will show the difference between a clean cover and one where the message is hard to find.

## BUSY COVER DESIGN

# WINNING
# CASINO PLAY

### HOW TO PLAY • HOW TO WIN
### BEAT THE CASINO AFTER ONE EASY READING!

**You can be a winner. This book shows you how! Learn blackjack, craps, slots, video poker, roulette, more!**

*Be a loser no more! You can win by following the advice of this book and the world's number one gambling expert!*

### PHOTO

# AVERY CARDOZA

Too many design elements - boxes, treatments of type - and too much type obscure the message on this cover. There's so much going on, it's difficult to read. Also, notice how the photo has no "air" above and below it. Reducing the height of this image will greatly improve this cover. Yes, you always want to give your image a powerful presence on the cover (provided it's a good image, otherwise don't overemphasize it), but not to the point where it clutters the type.

## CLEAN COVER DESIGN

# WINNING CASINO PLAY

### HOW TO PLAY • HOW TO WIN
### BEAT THE CASINO AFTER ONE EASY READING!

PHOTO

# Avery Cardoza

This is a classic example of a *clean* cover. This cover can sell books - and actually does! It is vastly superior to the mess on the previous page. That cover is unprofessional looking and wouldn't be taken seriously by buyers for a simple reason - it won't sell books. On this cover, notice the strong use of title type, and how all the important element of the cover - title, sell lines, image (photo in this cover), and author - combine for a powerful message. (See pg. 193 for the back cover.)

## White Space

A primary tool in designing clean covers is the effective use of **white space**, unprinted "open" spaces devoid of design and type. Let your cover *breathe*. White space doesn't have to be white, it can be a color or montage of colors where there is no print. For example, if your cover is solid green, the blank green is your "white space."

Many designers do not understand the concept of white space. Just because there's space, doesn't mean it should be filled. If your designer is good, yet tends to produce cluttered work, make it clear to him or her that the cover must breathe, or better yet, find one who is talented and understands this important concept.

## Designing Spines that Sell

The spine of a book is the first thing a potential book buyer sees (most books are shelved spine out and not face out), and thus, has a large influence over whether that book is plucked off the shelf to be examined.

To help influence a browser's decision to examine your book, you'll want to make your book more noticeable than others. A great spine is one seen easily among others, a poor spine is one whose title gets lost in the crowd. The hallmark of a great spine is one in which the type is prominent and noticeable.

First impressions are the strongest - if your book is the first off the shelf, it has a head start in getting purchased.

## Some Key Points in Cover Copy

You've got a ton of competition on the shelves so you've got to differentiate your book from the rest, and show why it's different, why it's better, and why the reader must buy the book. You do this with powerful cover copy that addresses the readers needs and brings out the benefits of the title.

If the book is a how-to, readers should know what they'll learn, and how the book will benefit them. Fiction, poetry, certain genre and non-fiction buyers must be appealed to through their emotions. The cover copy should draw them into the book, stir up feelings, touch them in a way they can relate to. It should not only make them interested, it should draw them into the book and make them anxious to buy it.

## Using Reviews & Endorsements

People always want to feel that they're buying a good product and nothing works better than another reader's recommendation.

Testimonials from experts, well known writers or other public figures, or from reviews in appropriate media, are effective forms of recommendation that lend legitimacy and familiarity to a book. The book becomes "bigger," more important, more of a must-have, when an important name says that this book is good.

For example, if Stephen King endorses your mystery book, or John Grisham says your thriller is a great read, everybody in the business, from bookstore buyers to the casual reader, takes that book a lot more seriously. If a heart expert endorses a book on preventive health care for seniors, more credence and legitimacy is given to that book. A lot more.

Use endorsements, testimonials and positive reviews as much as possible. This big-time strategy is used by many publishers with great success, and one you should employ as well.

## SOME KEY POINTS IN COVER DESIGN

- Address your audience
- Stress main points: title, sell line, graphic, author
- Make title large and easily seen
- Make spine large and easily seen
- Keep message simple
- Don't feel that because there is space, you have to fill it.
- Don't be afraid of white space.
- Don't overdo use of point sizes, leading, styles - be consistent as much as possible.

## The Importance of Color Covers

Whatever the venue, whether it's mail order pieces, catalogues, or book covers, it's been proven thousands of times over and over, across the board, that color sells far better than plain black on white. Color covers are simply more attractive than black and white covers, and make a book seem more weighty and professional.

In most cases, your book will not even be taken seriously unless it has a color cover. You hand a buyer a book with a black and white cover, that buyer is going to think your book is small-looking, that you're *small press*, some mom and pop operation making homemade books. You want a bigger look, a cover that says professional, one that appeals and attracts, and that means a color cover.

There's a trade-off in doing color covers as opposed to black and white, and that is that color covers cost more to produce. But it is a trade-off that should not only be made, it is one that should be considered automatic. A given. Forget the savings a black and white cover can give. Whatever the savings might be, it's not worth it.

Color covers are the only way to go.

# THE FOUR COLOR PRINTING PROCESS

All colors can be made from the basic four colors - yellow, blue, red and black. In printing, these colors are referred to as process colors, respectively, as **Process Yellow** (bright yellow), **Process Cyan** (bright, light blue), **Process Magenta** (bright pink) and **Black** (black).

By mixing the process colors skillfully, any color under the sun can be formed. Thus, a green can be made from combining equal parts Process Yellow and Process Cyan, and a darker green can be made by combining these two colors in differing percentages, say 6 parts Cyan to 4 parts yellow. Or a heavier green can be made by adding a touch of black to the mix. Add more yellow to the mix instead, and the green becomes lighter.

To achieve this process in printing is called **trapping**. Your printer can achieve virtually any color possible through this method.

Color photos for example, are separated into four different negatives, one each for the process colors. When these four negatives are placed one above the other, they create the full color image of the original. Whenever you print a color photograph, no matter the simplicity or complexity of it, you'll be using the four color process.

The printer will send the four color image one time each through the press, four times total, to achieve the final full color look, as opposed to just one time for a simple black on white image. In printing terms, the cover will make four *passes*. (There are actually covers that will need more than four passes through the press - we'll discuss that later.)

You don't have to be a color genius to figure the percentages needed when choosing any of the myriad of colors that you'll be using in your design. You only need to refer to a Pantone Matching System (PMS) color book to choose your colors. The printer will take it from there.

## The Pantone Matching System

A standard and acceptable system for indicating colors in the printing industry is the **Pantone Matching System**, or **PMS** colors. PMS books show almost a thousand colors in various shades, and give you an exact language to communicate with your printer.

PMS books combine process colors in various amounts to produce colors in a rainbow of choice. This give you an excellent range of colors to choose from. The printer prints these colors in the exact combinations specified, to give you a very close approximation to the color specified.

PMS books are readily available from your printer or art supply store at a cost of about $50-$75 and are necessary pieces of equipment that must be purchased if your plan is to publish books on a regular basis.

## Using the PMS books

PMS books typically have two sections: The front section shows colors printed on **coated** stock, and the back section shows colors printed on **uncoated** stock. These will be indicated by the letter **C** for coated following the color number, or **U** for uncoated. For example, the sample for 350C, dark green, will show dark green printed on coated stock, and 350U will show that same color printed on uncoated stock.

## Understanding PMS Colors

There are many more colors possible than the ones shown in the typical PMS books - in fact the range of colors is almost endless. But unless you're a color wiz, in which case you'll know how to get fancy with mixing colors and instructing your printer, the range generally shown will be all the color you'll need.

You must know the surface you're printing on and match the colors shown for the same type of surface. If you're printing on uncoated stock, make sure that you're looking at the colors as they appear on uncoated stock. Comparing colors on different surfaces is like comparing two unlike things. They can't be compared on the same terms. Your PMS color book will show differences for the same color printed on uncoated and coated stocks. These colors will look different, just as they would look different if printed on wood, glass, metal, or any other surface that will impart different tones and feels to colors on them.

Don't choose PMS colors taken off your computer screen or a color printer and expect that they'll come out anywhere the same when printed on paper - they won't! For one thing, and we discuss this elsewhere as well, *colors on the computer screen are generally not accurate,* nor is the standard color printer you may use in your computer rental or output shop. These copies which will cost $1-$10, depending upon where they're done, do a nice job, an okay job, but not an accurate job.

Only Cromalins, Match Prints, Iris prints and the like, color prints of higher quality, will give you reasonably accurate color renditions.

If you want accuracy in your final printed colors, that is, no surprises, you must refer to your PMS book. And if you want accuracy in your prints, you must get either a Cromalin or Match Print.

# COLOR COVER COST COMPARISON

I'll list here in order, the least expensive to most expensive way to do color covers.

**1. Black and White** - The least expensive and least effective way to do a cover. Except under exceptional circumstances, this is not the way to go with a book needing to command market appeal. A black and white cover done by a talented artist can be effective, but I would be real hesitant to produce a book of this nature for the bookstore market.

**2. Two-Color** - With judicious use of color, you can make a very nice-looking book. You can use black plus one color, or two colors with no black. By reversing, you make use of white for free and seemingly have three colors. And by combining colors, but you better understand your colors to do this, you can effectively achieve a wider range of colors. My first book, *Winning Casino Blackjack for the Non-Counter,* reversed out of blue, used some yellow type, and combined the two to get green. In effect, I achieved four colors; blue, green, yellow and white.

**3. Three-Color** - One more pass, more color possibilities.

**4. Four Color** - When printing color photographic images on your cover, you will automatically use the four color process. By trapping within this range, you can achieve any other colors you want. Extra colors can also be created by printing five colors and up (below).

**5. Five Color and Up** - A fifth color entails an additional plate, a press wash-up on a fifth unit, and a fifth pass through the press. Similarly, you can call out for six colors, seven colors or more. Each pass and wash of a color adds to the complexity and expense of the printing job. We'll discuss trapping vs. five color or more printing on page 181.

# WORKING WITH COLORS

Choosing the right colors for your book is difficult, especially if you have little experience in combining colors to get the right look. The best crash course you can take is right in your local bookstore or even your personal library if you've got a number of books on the shelves.

See what works for other books, and what doesn't work. It's important to get a feel for things you don't want to do as well. Look not only at the color combinations but how those colors are affected. As you move along from book to book, begin forming ideas that fit your ideas of successful cover design.

We'll discuss two basic but strong designs that are effective with covers, reverses and the black cover.

## Reverses

One of the strongest and most effective looks you can give a cover is by *reversing* the type out of a dark background color. A **reverse** is type that prints in white against any colored background. Technically, what is black on the mechanical gets printed white, and what is white, gets printed in black or whatever other color is specified.

White type against dark backgrounds such as dark greens, blues, reds, purples and browns, is super-readable, clean, and really stands out well. Reverses are simple to design, and effective on covers, much more so, I think, than black or other colored lettering on white or other colors.

You'll see many reverses in the bookstore, and how effectively they stand out against other books.

# WORKING WITH BLACK COVERS

When all ideas fail, go with a black background on the cover. Whether fiction, non-fiction or how-to, black presents a strong and classy look. And the advantage of working with a black background is that you don't need to know much about color theory - just about every color used with black not only works, but looks great.

Black may not be appropriate for certain types of books such as baby, children's, and wedding books, where a lighter, more wholesome background may be preferable (though I personally don't completely rule out the use of black), but like clothing, black looks sharp in most situations.

## Colors that Work With Black - Headline Type

For *headline* type, bright colors such as process blue, process yellow, and process magenta really scream off a black cover and will get the customer noticing what you've got. Oranges and light greens are colorful and fun, light and bright reds and blues are strong as well. All bright and toned down colors will show strong against black and give you a nice look. White against black, comes out strong, though uncolorful.

## Colors that Work Against Black - Text Type

For *text* type, white type, the straight reverse, is far and away the best type to use against black, as it is against any dark background. It is the most readable type color with all other colors being second.

Yellows and oranges work as well for smaller blocks of text to counter-balance white type, and throw more color and life on the cover, though I would be hesitant to use these colors for all the text type. On the other hand, multiple lines of smaller text in red, green or blue type, say 12 point or smaller (forget about less than 8 point) can be tough on the eyes and hard to read.

One line of red or blue can be effective for brightening up a cover and perhaps "pick up" red or blue elsewhere on the cover, but more than one line of these colors can be tough reading. Even multiple lines of process cyan, the brightest of the blues, doesn't read well against the black background and is best used in one-line highlights.

Where there is a doubt how any color will work, go the safer route and choose another color. Why risk your cover with such an uncertainty?

## Colors that Won't Work With Black

Colors that are dark themselves will not work against black unless used as design elements as opposed to type. Dark greens, dark blues and purples will be lost and virtually unreadable, especially if the lettering is small. Reds will have impact as big type, but in multiple lines of text can be harsh on the eyes.

For text type, you'll want to stay with lighter colors against the black background.

## Title Type

For the title of the book itself, white and yellow are the best for straight ahead and strong looks, and are my favorites. Toned down colors will show nicely and perhaps fit the exact image you're portraying. Bright reds, blues, greens and oranges used as headline type work great but I would be careful using any of these as the type for the title itself, unless you've got a very particular look in mind and really know what you're doing with color.

# OTHER COLOR BACKGROUNDS

Dark reds, greens and blues work nicely as backgrounds, with white or yellow being effective for the title colors. Black titling on a yellow background presents a strong image; black on white may be too plain, but with other colors mixed in on the cover, the overall image can be effective. When using white, yellow or other light backgrounds, black and other dark types such as strong reds, greens and blues should be used so that the print reads clearly.

# SETTING UP THE COLOR COVER

There are various ways to set up a color cover for printing, and we'll discuss these below with an eye towards savings.

## Minimizing Color Costs - Trapping vs. Fifth Color

The best way to minimize costs associated with printing four color covers is to request that your printer *trap* extra colors and use the four color process to create additional colors as opposed to picking up the costs associated with a fifth color or more.

Color photos and slides, as we discussed earlier, are separated into four color separations (four negatives) to be reproduced in the printing process. Each negative requires a separate pass through the press. Let's say that in addition to these separations, you request PMS 202 (wine red) and PMS 299 (sky blue) to be printed on the cover. To enjoy savings on the printing, you can instruct your printer to "trap for extra colors, print as process colors".

*Trapping* allows the printer to mix the process colors so that you're still using the four passes to create these two colors. There will be some expense setting up the traps, but not as much as paying for two extra passes, two plates, and two wash-ups, expenses you would incur to create these two colors without trapping.

Again, as with all other technical questions, go over this issue with your printer when setting up your cover. Each printer works differently, and coordination with your printer will avoid problems and give you the best and most efficient results.

There are reasons not to trap as well, and sometimes to request a fifth color instead. Let's compare the two processes.

## Advantages of Trapping

Trapping works best when the actual color match you require does not need to be absolutely perfect and when the area trapped is a smallish area as in type, lines, or small graphic areas.

In terms of color match, unless you are Joe Artist or are working with Joe Artist, selling lipstick or creating color-exacting print, where the color *really* must be perfect, it will not make a bit of difference in the world if the color printed is a fraction off from what you ordered. First of all, good printers produce output that is very close to any PMS color specified, and if they were off a bit, you probably wouldn't notice. Second, it won't make any difference in sales, one minor shade to the other, no matter what any artist with an attitude problem tells you. If you've designed an effective cover, it will stand powerfully even if one color is slightly off.

Trapping for an extra color in large areas, as in the background color, has some disadvantages, and we discuss them below.

One other thing to keep in mind. Some colors, particularly certain yellows, browns and purples, may be difficult to trap, so check with your printer before setting up your cover.

## Advantages of Using a Fifth Color

You get better color integrity and registration on large surfaces, for example on solid stretches of background color, when using a fifth color. Using a specific color allows the printer to maintain the integrity of the color throughout the print run. Though I haven't had problems on my covers - and I trap background covers all the time - trapping process colors to achieve an extra color can lead to some inconsistencies (in initial and future print runs) due to more colors being involved in the making of the specific color.

How critical is color integrity and some inconsistencies on the background color? Usually, not critical at all. Some minor variations, which would be the extent of the issue, wouldn't be a problem and won't hurt your book. It may even be nice to have some different shades. But like all quality issues, you should coordinate with your printer before printing, for best results and to understand the variations you might expect if any, and the best way to set up your cover.

There can also be a cost savings if changes are made to the cover. For example, minor changes in the cover such as bar codes, a line of type and price might only affect one negative, that of the fifth color (if it's the background color). If the fifth color, the background color, was trapped, up to four pieces of film could be involved in what would otherwise be a change to one piece of film.

## Color Conclusion

Try to trap where possible for maximum savings, but as I've stressed throughout this book, you must keep a dialogue open with your printer to assure best quality of the finished product. The printer will be happy to discuss any quality issues involved in making your book perfect. It not only makes their job easier, but keeps you as a happy customer.

# WORKING WITH A COVER DESIGNER

Unless you've worked with the cover artist before and he or she knows what you want, don't expect the designer to divine your will and do the entire cover with the simple instruction, "go to it," and then expect perfect results. It won't happen. You must communicate clearly with your designer and demand the same open communication. If this is not done, you're almost ensuring a problem.

The designer must be given a distinct direction to work with, and must understand the basic elements and *feel* you want brought out in the cover. He or she should be clear on who the book is appealing to, what the cover is trying to do, and what elements in that cover are important to you.

If your designer hands you a cover that's not what you want - don't accept it, especially if it's not what you asked for. Or, if there's something you don't like about the design they've submitted, have it altered, and then altered again if need be, until you get what you want.

Don't change your decision on a cover design because your cover artist makes a good case for it, unless of course you agree with what he or she is saying. The designer's job is to bring out *your* message on the cover as clearly as possible, not to express his or her own. Designers know how to design, they don't necessarily know how to sell books. There's a difference.

Always remember that you're the boss. Some cover designers can be difficult to work with - and that's the price of working with creative people - but the bottom line is that your money is on the table with your book and you're the one who does the snapping and they the jumping, not the other way around. If you lose sight of this, you'll lose control of the most important sales feature of your book, the cover.

Again, remember that you are the marketing person, the one responsible for selling books, so make sure that what you get is what you want.

## Checking a Designer's Credentials

Choosing a designer among many candidates is not as difficult as it may first sound. It's really quite simple. If you like a designer's work, better yet, *if you're impressed by their work*, then you have a legitimate candidate to design your cover.

If you don't like a designer's work, don't use them. I don't care what covers they've done or what their credentials are. It doesn't matter; *you don't like their work*. End of story. Always go with what *feels* right and stick with your instincts - with your cover design, or any other aspect of your business for that matter. Don't make the mistake of going against your feelings.

# PROTECTING YOUR COVER
## UV Coating and Film Lamination

Color covers must *always* be coated with the extra protection afforded by **UV**, ultra violet coating, by **film lamination**, a thin plastic coating, or by similar protections, as a standard part of your printing job. Your covers need to be protected against normal wear and tear, and UV coating or lamination is the way to do it.

Film lamination costs more than UV, but for the extra money you spend, you get some nice advantages. Besides giving your book extra protection against scuffing and fingerprinting compared to UV, the colors will shine through more brilliantly. If you feel that the little extra shine or protection offered by film lam is not worth the extra cost, you might opt for the savings of UV coating.

UV will normally provide adequate cover protection, but if you're printing books with very dark solid color coverage, such as dark greens, dark blues and of course, black, colors which scuff easier than light colors, or at least show scuffing easier, you may want the extra protection of film lamination.

If you do use film lamination, you must insist that the lamination be *curl resistant*. It's more expensive than standard film lamination, but the standard stuff, in my opinion, shouldn't be offered by any printer. It is not print quality. Sure, the extra brightness of film lam coating looks great, but watch out if humidity gets hold of it. Those covers will curl like crazy, sometimes embarrassingly so. Ask your questions carefully when ordering film lamination - make sure it's curl resistant.

# MAKING COLOR COMPS

Once you're plugged into the distribution system and are getting advance book sales based on upcoming books, you'll be expected to provide **cover comps**, color reproductions of your covers. These are used for advance sales purposes.

We've already discussed how books sell by their covers, literally - the reps bring copies or representations of your covers to buyers so that purchasing decisions can be made. Now, we'll show how to make color comps of your covers.

Color comps of your cover can be created fairly easily on publishing programs, a great advantage over publishers ten and even five years earlier, who went through a great deal more expense and trouble to make a color comp.

The process is easy; once your color rendition is in place on your computer, make a copy of the file on your disk and drop it off at a color output place, or alternatively, you can rent computer time at a business that has color printers (if any are in your area), and send them through yourself.

## A WORD ON FONTS

If you're using fonts that are not generally available, you'll need to bring them with you to the color output place. Make sure that both the Screen Font and Printer Font are supplied.* Adobe and Bitstream family fonts should print out without a hitch. However, some fonts that come supplied with your computer (and some fonts made by other companies) are not "real" fonts and may not print on another system. Fonts named after places such as Switzerland, New York, and Avalon, for example, while based on actual font families, may be problematic for electronic output, whether at your service bureau or your printer.

*In the Macintosh Font folder in the System folder, copy both the Suitcase and Postscript font files.

Previously, the lower end of quality color printers, machines with brand names such as Seiko, QMS, Océ, and Tektronics, cost in the range of $7,000 or more, and gave you color output on glossy paper at 300 DPI. They use a process called **thermal dye transfer**, which provides output that is not great, but it is acceptable for purposes of a color comp.

However, there's good news. Prices on color printers are dropping precipitously, and quality is going way up. As we go to press, pretty good quality ink jets are available for around $500 - and with surprisingly good color quality! Quality is so good in fact, that you'll get comparable results to the thermal dye transfer machines listed above - and more than twice the DPI! The ink jets do have the disadvantage in that they're slow, and the quality for black and white printing isn't very good. (Your 300 DPI laser will produce much better results.) But for color, you'll really be amazed at what these machines can do.

Output will cost you in the general range of $5 to $10 per printout (plus computer time if you're renting a workstation) at a service bureau, a price that can be brought even lower by combining more than one cover on the page if there is room. Typically, an output service will give you output ranging from 8 1/2 by 14 up to 11 x 17.

The main advantage of these machines is acceptable color output at relatively inexpensive prices.

## Strategy for Using Thermal Dye Transfer Printers

While the advantage of using thermal dye transfer printers are inexpensive output, the disadvantage of these machines is the lack of color trueness, and the visible dot patterns of many colors. You'll see those 300 dots per inch, and will often get weak color coverage on colored lettering 18 point (or so) and under against dark backgrounds. You can however, make reasonable comps on these machines as long as you know how to work with their deficiencies, and can live with them.

First and foremost, you must be aware that the colors that you spec (specify), will most likely not be the colors you get. Black, process yellow, and to a lesser extent, magenta, should hold true to form. After that, either you get lucky and your colors are close, or the people at the computer rental service had enough foresight to print a sample color guide so that customers can see how the colors actually print.

It's just like your computer; the colors that you see on your monitor don't necessarily resemble the actual PMS colors that you'll get on thermal dye transfer printers.

I get around the color guessing by making 20-30 colored boxes around the edge of my cover and giving them each a different PMS color. This way, when my cover prints out, if the colors I chose did not work out well, I see how similar colors actually print, and can make the immediate adjustment. My next printout won't be guesswork, and I won't have to keep on experimenting at $X per page until it comes out right.

## Using High Quality Color Output

Match Prints and Color Keys, available from high-end service bureaus, provide color trueness and high quality professional output to please everyone but the most finicky of artists. Output from these machines are significantly more costly (check for prices) and may take 24 hours to process unless you're willing to pay premium for rush service.

Your printer also can also make match prints and color keys of your cover when it is in the printing process. Usually this is not a realistic option because these cover comps are generally needed months before the actual cover is being printed anyway.

This process is relatively easy if you're not reproducing photos on the cover comp. Let's see how to get actual photos on your comps.

# Adding Photos to Your Comps

There's several ways to add photos or slides to your cover presentation. The easiest way is to have the photographic images scanned and then positioned onto the cover file itself. This can be done by an output bureau, or you can scan them yourself. When done this way, the entire cover emerges as a complete unit. An alternative and less expensive method is to actually output the cover *sans* photo, and add the photo afterwards. The final way is to use the actual color proof from the cover image. We'll discuss each method in turn.

### 1. Scanning Photos Onto Your Comps

The easiest option, scanning, runs into more money than using a color copier, and will generally give you better quality than the second method we'll show. You can scan your photos yourself if you're skilled enough - scanning is a skill that needs to be learned - or you can have the scans of your photographic image done at a service bureau.

At service bureaus, there are also two quality levels of scans; **FPO**, **For Proof Only**, scans of lower quality; and high resolution scanning, the real McCoy, which costs more, and provides superior quality output. FPO's by themselves may not give you good enough quality for your presentation - you'll probably need to tweak the image to get pleasing enough results. Again, this is a skill you must have to use this method.

High resolution scanning that can be imported onto a computer disk, at $20-$100, depending upon the place used, will give you good enough quality. But several conditions must be met for this to work for you. First, you must be willing to pay this much for the image. If this image will be your final cover shot, then it's money well spent. If not, it's up to your budgetary considerations. Second, you must have a storage device such as a Syquest to hold the scanned images since the files will generally be larger than the 1.4 megs your floppy disk holds. You can alternatively have the service bureau place the image in place on your cover and print out the cover on one of their high output machines, but again, this add more costs, and you can't take the scan with you if you don't have the storage unit to hold the scan.

You'll need to size your picture properly, as we discuss in the sizing section, before having it scanned. If you alter the reproduction size after the scan, which programs such as Photoshop can do, you lose quality, especially if you enlarge the image. (If altering the size is simply a matter of cropping, then the quality of the scan is not affected.).

If you're working with color slides, you'll need to find a place that has a slide attachment if you'll be scanning the images yourself. Actual color prints will scan easily on any standard flatbed scanner.

### 2. Using Color Copies to Reproduce Photographic Images
The cheapest option for adding photos to a cover comp, at just $1-2 per print, is having your images reproduced on a color copier and then manually inserting them on the physical cover printout. Color copiers won't do a great job, but there should be enough quality to give pleasing results. You even get a nice bonus sometimes - the copier may throw in some cool (cool as in hip) color tones that weren't in the original.

If you're working with a color print, simply instruct the color copy operator at what percentage you want the photo enlarged or reduced. If you're starting with slides, you'll have to look a little harder to find a place with a slide attachment on their copier. (When enlarging slides, copy shops often measure percentages based on their machines full page output, not the true percentages. To get the correct final image, you'll need to base your percentages on *their* 100% image size.) For even better quality working with a slide, and at a greater cost, you can have a film service customize your image to the exact size needed.

With the properly sized image, you'll now need to hand crop the reproduction so that it fits into your color printout perfectly. Grab a sharp straight edge blade, a ruler for precise measuring, and a cutting surface - stiff cardboard will do for this operation. Work under decent light if possible. Take your time in this process and make sure your measurements are exact before you begin cutting.

I suggest you wax the back surface first before cutting to keep your photo repro from moving, but this step is not mandatory or necessary - just helpful. Once your image is cut to fit, with extraneous background and white space removed, affix it to the space provided for on your cover. Lo and behold - you've got a finished comp!

Making comps in this manner, as opposed to scanning, takes a little more work but could well be worth it for the savings, as long as the cover comp is of adequate quality. It usually will be.

### 3. Using the Actual Color Key From the Final Separations
The best choice of all, if you know you're going to use an actual image, is to separate the slide or photograph ahead of time - you'll be doing it anyway - and to use the color proof that comes along with it. Rather than cropping this proof, cut out the space from the back of your color printout and attach the proof to the back. You don't want to mangle the image; your printer will need the color proof later on in the printing process. Alternatively, you can make copies from this original. Since it's of high quality, the color copies will be pretty good as well. Even better, have the image scanned onto a disk, and print the complete cover at once for highest quality and easiest effort.

## Making Multiple Cover Comps
If making more originals is either difficult, or too expensive for what you need, the color copier found at your print or copy shop will most likely give you an acceptable rendition.

The downhill quality on color goes much faster than black and white, so you want to make your color copies from the best copy (the original if possible). Each generation is a big step downwards in quality. If you need three copies, make them at once before your original is sent away.

If you need to make a copy from a copy later on, you'll have to settle for less quality than you might desire. I'm sure you've seen black and white copies of pages that had been reproduced so many generations, that the current page really looked bad. Keep in mind that with color, this deterioration process is accelerated and pronounced.

# MAKING THE ACTUAL COVER
Your publishing programs give you the tools to create covers right on the computer. The typestyles, spacings, boxes, lines, and colors you'll use are all available within the program and easily accessed into a viable cover. This cover can be submitted either as *black and white camera-ready artwork*, or *electronically*, as a file already set up with the colors. We'll look at each way briefly.

## Making Color Covers with Mechanicals

Until several years ago, we submitted all our covers as **mechanicals**, camera-ready black and white artwork with instructions for the color placements. This traditional way of doing covers is rapidly being replaced by electronic submissions, but is still a viable way to get your cover produced.

To do mechanicals, you'll need a crisp black on white printout of the cover itself of at least 1,000 DPI quality - the *camera-ready original*, and a second copy to serve as your printers instructions. The camera-ready original must be crisp and of high quality (not a copy) for the printer will shoot negatives from it. The printer instruction sheet can be of any quality since it won't be shot, but it should be an accurate duplicate of the original. A transparent plastic or thin tissue **overlay**, material placed over the original, with clearly marked instructions, will serve the same purpose.

On the printer instruction sheet, which really doubles as a proof of the cover, or the overlay, you clearly mark down each element's PMS color so the printer knows how to shoot the film and put together the cover. If the cover title is going to print in process yellow, mark the black type on the proof, *print in process yellow*. If the sales line goes in PMS 350, and the box it is enclosed in is black, indicate that as well. Covers which will be shot as reverses present no problem. Simply indicate on the top, Reverse out of PMS——, and all area's that are white on the original will be whatever PMS color is chosen, and whatever area is black - all the type - becomes white, or whatever color you spec for that type. You could also set the reverse up on the computer itself.

Screens, boxes and traps that your program or printer may not set up well due to limitations, can be indicated by hand on the instruction sheet for the printer to set up, or the element's outline can be created on the computer with instructions given for the printer to trap or screen whatever color is specified.

Make sure that each element on the cover is assigned a color on the printer instruction sheet, and that instructions are provided for any blank spaces that are left for outside graphics. If graphics are supplied separately, for example, a bar code or a four color separation (color photo), then the printer instruction sheet should indicate its placement and cropping instructions.

Mechanicals can be prepared without a computer or typesetter as well. You can buy **press-type** - type that can be pressed onto a surface - from graphic arts stores and lay down the type by hand on a white background. On an overlay or separate instruction sheet, you would call out the colors in the same method as we've described above.

And that's all there is to it. The printer will shoot film and set up your cover according to the instructions - color will be born.

## Making Color Covers on Disk

The cover will be set up on the publishing program much as you did to create your mechanicals, only here you'll specify the color information on the file itself, and submit that file electronically to the printer either by sending a disk through the mails, or by modem over a phone line.

There will be a library of PMS colors you can assign to the background or type to see a close rendition of the cover on the screen itself, keeping in mind, as we discussed earlier, that colors on the screen are not true, and you'll need to rely on the PMS book for accuracy.

As with the camera-ready copy, a printer instruction sheet must accompany the disk to the printer. You can alternatively send an actual color proof that will serve the same purpose, but you should call out those colors anyway to be safe. Files often read differently from one computer system to another - this is not an unknown occurrence - and this printing instruction sheet or color proof ensures that if elements do change or get corrupted, the printer knows what was intended and can call if there are discrepancies.

> The following example shows a sample printer instruction sheet. This instruction sheet could accompany an electronic submission on disk, or could be a copy of the actual artwork the printer uses to print from. (You don't want to write on the artwork itself.) The author photo indicated could come as part of the file if submitting electronically, or as four color separations to be inserted by the printer as part of the electronic submission, or as camera-ready art.

## SAMPLE COVER INSTRUCTION SHEET

# BE A WINNER NOW!

PMS
354
(Green)

| Author photo gets placed here. | *The book that shows you how to play and beat the casino in one easy reading!* |

Print in
Process
Yellow

Two point PMS 1665 border

# PLAY TO WIN MONEY!

PMS
354

America's foremost authority on beating the casino shows you how to have fun and win at the same time!

White

## FEATURING

Process
Cyan

Easy Steps for Winning Players
The Rules and Winning Strategies for Blackjack,
Craps, Roulette, Slots, and Video Poker
Charts, Illustrations and Examples for Easy Reading
Casino Basics & Money Management

White

The World's Foremost Publisher of Gaming and Gambling Books

PMS
1665
(Orange)

ISBN 0-940685-47-7

5 0 5 9 5

9 780940 685475

CARDOZA
PUBLISHING

$5.95

White

Bar code
prints
black on
white

REVERSE COVER OUT OF BLACK

The instruction to reverse the cover out of black, tells the printer that all type that is black should become white (actually the colors indicated above), and that everything that is white, becomes black.

# PROOFING THE COVER

You need to be particularly careful on the cover proof, since this is obviously the most important part of the book. Carefully check the following items:

**1. Bar Code -** Check that the bar code accompanies the cover, that it belongs with this particular book, and that it has the correct ISBN and price add-on. If doing a new edition, check that the *new* Bar Code, and not the previous one, is in place.

**2. Price -** Don't screw up here. Make 100% sure that the correct price is printed on the cover (and that it matches your Bar code price add-on).

**3. Color Check -** Verify extra carefully that you have indicated the correct colors in the correct places. Say the colors out loud - you never know, maybe this will catch an error you may miss with the silent mutter.

**4. Spine and Title -** Check that spine type is correct for the book you're printing and runs the correct direction, that the title matches the one printed on the front cover, that the author's name is correctly spelled on front and spine, and that your publishing company has its logo in place on the spine and/or back cover. Finally, check to see that these are in the proper color.

**5. Photos -** If you use photos, verify that they're properly marked so that the printer knows where they get placed. If cropping, indicate exact instructions so that the printer is perfectly clear on what needs to be executed. Indicate borders, and color of borders if applicable.

**6. Cover Copy -** A careful reread of the cover copy is always in order and really should be done many times before a book goes to press. You want your absolute best copy here, thus, the more proofs, checks, and reads, the better.

If you have a series and are in the habit of copying the design from one book to another before editing for the current edition, make 100% sure that you have changed the type so that it matches the current book. Again, read the copy out loud for best safety.

**7. Once-Over -** If you're submitting electronically, open up the disk that will be sent to the printer, and give it the once-over. Make sure the cover is on the file (it would set you back some days to send the wrong disk or a malfunctioning one to the printer), and that everything looks okay.

If submitting camera-ready, check hard copy carefully, verify all information and instructions.

## PUTTING CATEGORY TITLES ON YOUR COVERS

Once a book is sold into an account, the personnel in the store decide where and how the book gets placed. Putting category titles on the book help employees make their shelving decisions, and will give you a better chance of being in the section specified, but is not a guarantee of such. It is the employees decision where your book gets shelved.

# SUBMITTING THE COVER

The cover should always be submitted as one integral package - with all elements being used together. If you have items such as color separations or bar codes being stripped in separately, make sure they accompany the disk or camera-ready copy. Submitting a cover in stages only asks for trouble, and a smart printer won't even accept it that way. Send it in right, or don't send it in until you have it right.

A black and white printout with written instructions calling out the colors, any special work to be done, or a color proof that shows the cover, must always accompany covers to the printer, no matter how the book is submitted. (If color seps are being submitted separately, be sure to include cropping and placement instructions so the printer knows what to do with them.)

If submitting on disk, along with the disk containing the book's cover files, make sure that you enclose the fonts being used if the printer doesn't have them; any files that contain graphics that may go along with the cover (scanned photo, bar code?); color seps and proofs, if any; and the black and white instruction sheet or color proof.

# COVER BLUES OR CROMALINS

You have one final chance to make changes on your cover, or to correct errors the printer may have made, and that is during the printing process itself. Two to three weeks into the printing process (for jobs that take four-five weeks to print), the printer can prepare either a **blueline** or **blues**, a monochrome blue on white or white on blue rendition of the cover (for reverses) which shows positioning of cover elements, or a **Cromalin** or other equivalent, a high-quality proof which not only shows the elements in position, but is an accurate color proof as well.

You should request at minimum, a blueline of the cover, to safeguard against either your error or the printer's error, though to be really safe, especially if submitting electronically or doing complicated cover work, a Cromalin should be mandatory. Even though you've already proofed the cover before press-time, you may have missed something, or the printer may have made a mistake. The cover is too crucial to the book to take chances. If you have any doubts about how the colors will work out, a Cromalin should be requested. Better safe than sorry.

The printer will bill you for either of these processes if you request them. Prices will vary from printer to printer, with the Cromalin, in all cases, being more expensive. (Sometimes the printer may include these charges as part of the job, though that's not usually the case.)

You should proof the blueline or Cromalin carefully, going over the seven proofing steps for a cover that we outlined above (*Proofing the Cover* section), to make sure that everything is correct and as it should be. Once you sign off that all is well, the printer proceeds and makes the cover and the book. If later, it turned out that the printer had made an error and you didn't catch it on the proof, don't blame the printer - it's your fault. Making sure the proof is accurate is your responsibility.

If mistakes are found, the corrections will be billable to you if they're your mistake, and non-billable, that is, the printer's expense, if the printer is at fault.

# 12. PRODUCTION

## INTRODUCTION

Once the manuscript has been edited and the changes entered in the word processing program, we are ready for **production**, the part of the book-making process where we actually put the book together.

The process of **paging**, making pages, and putting a book together is called **laying out a book**, or simply, doing the **layout.** In the recent past, when typesetting machines were an essential part of the book-making process, *layout* signified the manual cutting of long processed galleys of type into pages. Nowadays, with the age of desktop publishing, layout is mostly done on the computer. The hand need never touch the printed type.

In this chapter, we'll go over all aspects of production, from the design decisions that allow us to reach the proper page count, to the paging and laying out of a book in its final form. We discuss how to expand the page count of a book (so that we can justify a more expensive list price), and conversely, how to reduce a page count (to either fit into a 16 or 32 page signature, or simply, to reduce the cost of printing).

We also go over the three sections of a book - front, back and body text, how to work with a raw page count, how to do book planning and chapterization, how to properly proof a book to ensure that it is ready for press, and how to submit your book to the printer as either camera-ready art or electronically on computer disk.

Let's begin with the initial planning and the thinking involved in taking a plain word processing file and transforming it into a book.

# ORIENTATION - THE THINKING

We originally planned the ideal page count and dimensions for our book back when we made the decision to publish. Now our challenge is to translate the edited manuscript from the word processing program along with accompanying graphics, if any, into a book containing the number of pages originally planned. Sometimes, everything will fall perfectly into the ideal page count; usually though, we'll need to do a little tinkering to make it work.

The first step in the production process is to get an idea of the number of pages in the book. Then, looking at the various options available to us, we'll make the final design decisions so that we can bring the book in at the economical 32 page signatures we discussed earlier, or next best, in 16 page multiples close to our ideal page count.

Let's first look at the organization of a book and how it breaks up into the three distinct sections.

# THE THREE SECTIONS OF A BOOK

For ease of organization, I divide a book into three distinct sections; the *Front Pages*, the *Back Pages* and the *Body Text*.

The main body of a book, from the introduction all the way through to the final word in the manuscript is called the **body text**. The complete text of the author's written work, less back and front matter, falls within this section, which depending upon the length of the final book, will usually consist of more than 90% or 95% of its pages.

The other two sections, the *front pages* and the *back pages* are the pages on either end of the text where we can add or subtract pages as desired or needed to fill the book out to the proper 16 or 32 page signatures.

We'll now look at each section in greater detail.

# FRONT PAGES

The **front pages** consist of all the pages that go *before* the Introduction page, which marks the true beginning of a book. These pages can include the Half-Title, Title and Copyright pages, About the Author, the

Table of Contents, Dedication, Epigraph, Frontispiece, List of Illustrations, Foreword, and Preface if any.

When putting together the front pages, we have the option of choosing from among the above options, and thus increasing or decreasing the number of pages used. In the **tight front pages**, we use the bare minimum of space before the table of contents, the title page and the copyright page. In the **standard front pages**, we employ the *doubler*, the half (bastard) and full title pages, plus a dedication and copyright page before the contents. And in the **loose front pages**, we work hard to fill pages. In addition to the contents, which we'll try to stretch out, we use the doubler, plus other creative and blank pages.

The title page in a book always goes on the right side of the page (odd-numbered page) with the copyright page always being on the verso - back side of that page (an even-numbered page). Thus, if page 3 is the title page, then page 4 should be the copyright page.

## Other Front Page Options

There are different page configurations and other ideas you can use. For example, we can place the *About the Author* on a right hand page, or along with the dedication or copyright information on a left hand page, or we can even place it on the back pages, which many publishers do. Acknowledgments can be added, or a left or right hand page can feature an **epigraph**, a quotation which sets a tone for the book.

To add even more pages to a loose front pages design, there are various other options available. The table of contents can be extended by adding subheads, stretching the type with more leading, adding returns between chapter titles or making the type larger. A list of illustrations, if appropriate, can add some pages as well.

Check out other books for ideas and configurations you can use.

## Preface, Foreword

The **preface**, introductory remarks made by the author typically about why or how they wrote the book, and the **foreword**, preparatory and generally exalting remarks by a person usually distinguished in the field or well-known, are sections that can also be used. Both go before the introduction.

# FRONT PAGE DESIGN CONFIGURATIONS

**Tight Front Pages**

1. Title Page
2. Copyright Page
3- Table of Contents
4. Blank
INTRODUCTION, then *Body Text*

**Standard Front Pages**

1. Half-Title Page
2. Dedication (Optional - About the Author, Acknowledgment)
3. Full Title Page
4. Copyright Page
5 - Table of Contents
6. Blank
INTRODUCTION, then *Body Text*

**Loose Front Pages**

1. Blurbs or Sell Copy
2. Blank
3. Half-Title Page
4. Blank
5- Full Title Page
6. Copyright Page with Dedication
7. Table of Contents
8. Blank
9. Filler Book Title, Section Title or Quote
10. Blank
PREFACE, OR FORWARD if any
INTRODUCTION, then *Body Text*

**Very Loose Front Pages**

1. Blurbs or Sell Copy
2. Blank
3. Dedication (can reverse 3 and 4)
4. About the Author
5. Half -Title Page
6. Blank
7. Full Title Page
8. Copyright Page
9. Table of Contents
10. Blank
11. Filler Book Title, Section Title or Quote
12. Blank
PREFACE, OR FORWARD if any
INTRODUCTION, then *Body Text*

I don't like prefaces, for it gets in the way of my first chapter, which attempts to get the readers excited about the book. If anything, I'll rearrange the material somewhere into the first or second chapters (or later) if it's sufficiently interesting. Otherwise, I just edit it right out. Forewords can have their purpose, but it better be a good purpose as far as I'm concerned, because again, I want to sell books. If the foreword (not *forward*) helps sell my book, I'll use it.

## BACK PAGES

The last pages of a book, the **back pages**, begins where the body text has ended, and includes indices, glossaries, appendices, footnotes, addenda, blank pages, advertisements, and the like, pages where a different style may apply than that used in the main body.

Like the front pages, the back pages are an excellent area to fill out a signature if more pages are needed. It is also the ideal place for you to run in-house advertisements of related products you sell, or even to accept advertising from another company. For example, in my gaming books, I advertise products that my readers will be interested in. A chess book might carry ads for other chess books, and a video poker book might advertise more advanced strategies on video poker, and even computer games.

You'll often see books whose last pages are either blank or have "NOTES" written on top of the page. All the publisher is doing here is filling out pages to make his 16 or 32 page signature. If the book needs three more pages to complete a signature, the publisher simply inserts the word "NOTES" on those three pages rather than leaving them blank. This is a strategy you can also use if need be.

If you find that you're tight on space and need to reduce the number of overall pages in the book, there are various strategies that can be pursued. For one, you can reduce the point size and/or leading in the type for end matter such as indices, appendices and glossaries. You can also omit certain house ads if any, or perhaps cut out some of the end matter if it is not integral to the book.

On the other hand, if you need to add pages, increasing the point size and leading of end matter will accomplish the task. Similarly, designing the pages in a looser format will increase the page count. Here's a great place to advertise some of your other books and products and perhaps alert readers to upcoming titles.

## THE BODY TEXT

The main work in expanding or reducing the page count is done in the body text, where small changes in our design get magnified over the course of many pages to produce large changes in the page count. Design changes here can easily add or delete more than 50 pages on larger page counts without hurting the final look of your book.

It's all a question of fitting in the manuscript into a specified number of pages. Either we run a **tight design**, and reduce the number of pages to fit our needs, or a **loose design**, where we expand the number of pages, or we alter the page count altogether because we have too much or too little material in the manuscript to fit the desired page count.

We have three distinct sections in which to work our design magic and make the page count work. Most likely, we'll be able to adjust the book exactly to the 32 page signature that most benefits the project. But if not, we can get the book to the next best signature and maintain the integrity of the book at the price point we're shooting for.

To know the changes we may need to reach the desired page count takes knowledge of the number of raw pages, but that can't be evaluated until the manuscript is transformed into the final book page. Let's look at that now.

## SETTING UP THE BOOK

The first step in making a book is to transfer the manuscript from the word processing program into a publishing program. This allows you to get your first look at the rough page count. Before anything else though, make sure that the publishing program is set up for the correct size of the book you're doing. The margins for the white space and text size must be correct for this size book.

If you assign margins for the wrong book size, you'll probably need to re-layout the entire book later on when the error is discovered. So you need to be super careful that the margins are correct. (Refer to the

Text Margins chart in the Book Design chapter for this discussion.) It is a good idea to confirm that the right size book has been set-up by putting in the crop marks (see below), printing out a page, and measuring the physical area of the page.

## SAFETY TIP

*Always* back-up your work on a consistent basis and keep copies not only at your workplace, but at a separate location. Should your files be thrown away by accident, damaged or stolen, you'll have protected yourself. If you have not kept copies and the files are no longer available, the amount of work lost might be staggering, and even irreplaceable.

## Crop Marks

This is as good a time as any to set up **crop marks**, the lines, crosses, or other symbols, used to indicate the printing area of the page. These marks are set just outside the area to be printed on a page and let the printer (and yourself) know the "live" surface of the page.

If your book is a 5 1/2 by 8 1/2 for example, then these marks will enclose an area exactly that size. Crop marks can be set up on your computer so that the camera-ready copy or the electronic page includes them. If you don't set crop marks or indicate the live area of the page in a descriptive form, the printer will determine this area according to his best judgment. However, it's preferable that the decision on how a page gets cropped is made by you, the publisher, along the dimensions *you* have in mind, rather than blindly by your printer.

Crop marks can be placed on your computer page by using the line tool in your publishing program and marking off the live area in the master page of your documents as the illustration shows. If you're laying out pages manually without the use of a computer, the crop marks can be drawn by hand outside the live area on the page. If an entire book will be manually layed out this way, then you should make one master page showing the crop marks and have the rest of the layout pages printed from this master. This avoids marking off each page by hand.

Following is an example of what crop marks looks like.

# CROP MARKS

These crop marks show the live area for 4 1/4 x 6 3/4 book.

BOOK SIZE BEFORE TRIM

# WORKING WITH THE BOOK FILES

There are different ways to treat your book on a publishing program and you'll have to find the method that suits you best, or that is easiest for the publishing program you're working with.

You can work with the entire book on one file, or you may want to break it down into one file for each chapter or section of the book. There are advantages and disadvantages to each method, and these are dependent on the size of the book you're working with and how comfortable you feel approaching this particular book. We'll discuss each in turn.

## Working with One File

The advantage to working with one file is that *you're only working with one file*. For smaller books, and books without too much variation from chapter to chapter, this may be the preferable way to go. Any type of change that is desired and that applies to the entire book is easily executed.

The disadvantage of working with just one computer file for an entire book is that this file, especially on a large book, may often prove unwieldy in terms of memory size or page count. Also, since everything is on one file, features such as running heads that are common from page to page, must be the same throughout the book. If the running head information is identical from chapter to chapter, or if no running heads are used, then this is no problem.

## Working with Multiple Files

The advantage to working with individual chapter files is that you have more flexibility in making changes to each chapter. What you do to one page in the chapter, like a running chapter header (type running across the top of each page) for example, can apply to all the pages in that chapter, and not to any other chapter. If you did the book as one file, that flexibility is removed.

The disadvantage of working with many files *is that you must work with many files*. If some type of common change is desired, such as a font, subhead size, name, whatever, you can't just do one search and replace.

You'll need to navigate through each file with the search and replace function to effect these changes.

## Conclusion

For the initial transfer into the publishing program, it's probably best to work with one master file. It gives you the advantage of making all the design changes throughout the book at one time. If any adjustments in margins or type are needed to get within the preferred signature count or for design preferences, these changes are easy, for only one file is being worked on.

After these changes are made, and you have a good handle on the book, then you can break the file down into smaller chapter files if desired. Generally, with larger books or file sizes, you'll want to use chapter files, while with smaller books, say under 128 pages, you may find that one file will work fine. It's on a case by case basis - with experience, you'll find the method that best suits the particular book you're working on.

# TRANSFERING INTO THE PUBLISHING PROGRAM - THE ROUGH PAGE COUNT

We'll assume you've made all your edits already in the word processing program. Now, transfer the book file into the publishing program so that we can get to work laying out the book.* If you haven't already done so, assign the type styles, point size, justification and leading you've assigned to this particular book.

At this point, we now have a good idea about the number of raw pages in the book. It's right there on the publishing program. We call this the **rough page count**. The rough page count is only the raw insides of the body text without compensation made for any margin or type changes we may make. It also doesn't take into account the extra pages that chapterizing, inserting graphics, and front and back sections will add to the book. This we'll look at shortly.

The number of pages we'll gain or lose by making these adjustments is a function of how many pages we're shooting for. If we need a tight

*In Pagemaker, use the *Place* command.

# APPROXIMATING FINAL PAGE COUNT FROM MANUSCRIPT
## Manual Calculations

To figure your rough page count by manual calculations, you must first know the approximate number of words you have in the raw manuscript or on disk, and then, how many words will fit on a full page in the finished book.

Approximating words in the manuscript is easy. Simply count the words in 10 consecutive typical lines of type, and divide by 10 to get average words per line. Next, count the lines on a typical page. Multiplying the average words per line by the average lines per page gives you the average words per page in the manuscript. Multiply that number by the number of pages in the manuscript gives you an approximation of the total number of words.

If the book is on disk, your word processing program probably has a word count feature which will give you an exact count without any guesswork at all.

If you're working with a pre-designed page for the final book, a sample printed page can be estimated for number of words it will contain according to the same estimation techniques we discussed above. If, for example, there's an average of 350 words per page in your design, divide that number into the total number of words in the original manuscript and you'll have a rough page count.

Thus, if there's an estimated 50,000 words in the original, dividing that number by 350 gives you a *rough page count* of 143 pages. It's a rough page count, because you must adjust for all the other pages that make up a book. Front pages, back pages, chapter and page design, and illustrations will add to these 143 rough pages.

As we'll see later on, we can loosen or tighten these rough pages to achieve a more desirable page count for the particular book we're doing.

design set-up to reduce the overall page count, we'll plan our design accordingly, while if we have extra pages we need to add, we'll adjust for this as well.

If wholesale changes are needed in the document while in the publishing program, there are features that allow us to select all the type and make the adjustments in one fell swoop. For example, if we change all the type from 12 point to 11 point to reduce the number of pages in the book, a simple computer command in the program will get this done. On a 400 page rough page count, this will take approximately 40 pages off the total.

# WORKING WITH THE ROUGH PAGE COUNT

Easy calculations allow us to plan the tightness or looseness of the design once we have our rough page count. When we add the front and back page estimates, and extra pages for illustrations and chapter design, we'll have a good idea of what we need to do to bring in a book at the optimal page count.

Let's say that we have a rough page count of 100 pages after transferring the manuscript into the publishing program.

Let's go step by step over the process of planning the book's page count.

### 1. Start with the Rough Pages
We start with a rough page count. We get this after transferring the book from the word processing document into our publishing program. In this example, it's 100 pages.

### 2. Add the Essential Front and Back Pages
Our next step is to add the pages we know must go into the book, the essential front and back pages.

In the front section, we pick up four must-have pages; in order, the Title Page, Copyright Page, and either a one page Table of Contents (and blank page) or two page contents. Keep in mind that the Table of Contents must be on a right hand page. While you don't necessarily need any back pages, let's say that for this particular book you'll be using two pages to advertise your other products.

That gives us six essential pages. If the table of contents is longer or you use a doubler (a half-title or bastard page *and* a title page), we'll add more essential pages to the count. For now, let's assume the bare minimum; four front pages and two back pages.

We now have a rough page count of 106 pages, six front and back pages, plus 100 rough count body text pages.

## 3. Add Graphic Pages
We now add illustrations and graphics, if any. Let's say we have four full page graphics (charts, illustrations or photos), and four half page graphics. The four full page graphics and four half page graphics (two pages) added together, gives us six more pages. If there are no illustrations or graphics, then no pages are added.

We now have a total of 112 rough pages.

## 4. Add Chapter Pages
And now for the chapters. In a typical design, each time a chapter is started on a new page, more space and ultimately, more pages are added to a book. The chapter head itself and the white margin above in addition to the blank space at the end of the previous chapter can add up quickly. Let's look at an example.

Let's figure that each chapter will start on a new page, left or right, however it falls, and that the chapter head will begin 1/4 the way down the page. And since, on average, we'll gain 1/2 page for the blank space at the end of every chapter (sometimes less and sometimes more), these 12 chapters will add about eight pages to the rough total.

This is an estimate only, though a decent one, for we're averaging out and making assumptions for each chapter. How the chapters actually fall may be different. To do an exact count, we'll need to *chapterize* the book. This we'll sometimes do to get a more accurate page count. (We'll go over this later.) If chapters run one after another, without a new page being started to signify the chapter, then no pages will be added in this step. Usually though, most books are designed with the chapter starting on a new page - as we're doing in this example - and thus, extra pages will be added when done this way.

The eight chaptered pages added to the 112 previous gives us a total of 120 rough pages.

## 5. Assess the Situation

We take 120 pages and assess the situation. If our goal is a 128 page book, we can easily fill out the eight extra pages between the various aspects of our design; front pages, back pages, looseness or tightness of layout, and variances in chapter design.

If we want to expand the page count to squeeze out 144 or 160 pages, we might use a larger point size and bigger margins, or the other techniques we'll discuss later. Or perhaps we'll want to design the book tight, and keep it at 112 pages for savings on the printing. In this case, we may use smaller margins (getting more words on a page), keep the chapter and page design tight, and/or run a smaller point size or leading.

If we find, like in the above example (assuming we're doing a 128 page book), that we're fairly close to our ideal page count, then the next step is to **chapterize** the book, divide the book into distinct chapters. If we find, on the other hand, that we're significantly off the desirable final page count, then we'll need to use some book planning methods to get the book close. And then we'll chapterize the book, and do the layout.

The following page shows an example of how we would put together a rough page count.

# BOOK PLANNING - LOOSE OR TIGHT

If the rough page count is not close to our desired or ideal final page count, then we need to do some design adjustments to get the page count close so we can chapterize the book. It is here where we make the decisions of what to do to get near the final ideal page count, and if it is not possible, what that adjusted new page count will be.

Our design decisions, of course, are driven by the needs of the book, and the amount of material we need to fit into a required page count.

Let's go over all the ways you can alter your rough page count to gain pages or lose pages.

## ROUGH PAGE COUNT WORKSHEET

**Rough Pages, Body Text**          **217 pages**
*Type in Times, 11 point,*
*normal leading.*

**Front Pages**                     **8 pages**
*Doubler (four pages) 1-4,*
*Contents 5-7, blank 8.*

**Back Pages**                      **2 pages**
*Various House Ads.*

**Illustrations and Graphics**      **7 pages**
*Four full page photos,*
*six half-page illustrations.*

**Chapter Gain**                    **9 pages**
*Twelve chapters mulitplied by*
*1/4 page lead-in - three pages,*
*plus half page average gain at*
*end of every chapter by 12 -*
*six pages, equals a gain of*
*nine pages.*

**TOTAL**                           **243 pages**

The goal for this book is 256 pages, so at a rough count of 243 pages, the count is close and the book can be layed out without further adjustment at this time. With 13 pages of leeway, the book could be layed out loosely.

If the goal instead was 224 pages, major adjustments would be needed, and we would consider bringing the type down to 10 point. That would probably reduce the rough pages body text to around 200 pages. With a tight layout, we could come in at 224 pages.

If the book needed to be 320 pages, we would consider using 12 point type instead, and possibly switching to a wider typestyle. This could easily get us near or in the 270 page area on the body text, and with other adjustments, discussed later, we would have little problem making the book 320 pages.

# EXPANDING A BOOK'S PAGE COUNT

Following are 17 ways to increase the size of the rough page count. In addition to these methods, you can also ask the writer to supply more writing in the form of a glossary, an index, or other material.

## 1. ADD APPENDICES, GLOSSARY, INDEX, AND/OR EXPAND THEIR DESIGN

Adding extra material in these back pages has the added benefit of making the book more valuable to potential buyers by providing them with more material of relevant interest and thus, more sales. However, this is dependent on the author's willingness to submit more material and the ease with which he or she may gather such materials. A book that provides better source references (depending upon the type of book of course) can have an advantage over one without such material.

## 2. LOOSER FRONT PAGES

We can expand the front page section by employing either a loose or very loose front page design. Beginning with the *doubler* adds two quick pages, and from there, within reason, we can add pages as needed.

## 3. ENLARGE TABLE OF CONTENTS

You can perhaps take a one page table of contents and stretch it to three pages, or three pages to four or five, and follow up with a blank page. You do this with a looser contents design (more spacing between lines) or a more detailed contents.

## 4. LOOSEN CHAPTER HEAD DESIGN

**a. Chapter Heads Further Down on Page** - Start the chapter head three-fourths or half way down as opposed to the top of the page. If there are lots of chapters, you gain lots of pages.

**b. Chapter Heads on Page By Themselves** - Chapter heads on their own page are not only classy-looking but they eat up pages.

**c. Chapter Heads Always on Right Side** - You gain additional pages when the last page of the previous chapter ends up on the right side, thus leaving the subsequent left-handed page blank.

**d. Chapter Heads Always on Right Side Isolated Page** - Same as above, only the back side of the page is blank as well.

## 5. INCREASE POINT SIZE

Enlarge your point size from 10 point, to say 11 point, and the net result will be an additional 10% thickness in your page count, more with added creativity.

## 6. INCREASE LEADING

Ditto above. Take leading from say 10 point to 11 point, and you're adding a quick 10%+ to your page count, more depending upon overall design.

## 7. INCREASE MARGINS

Increasing the outside white space in the margins, thus reducing the width and length of your text, can add a bonanza of pages to the book. Fewer words will fit per line (the width), fewer lines will fit per page (the length), and in all probability, you'll have a nicer looking page. Added white space always adds class to a page so don't be afraid to be generous here if necessary, especially with fiction, poetry and art books.

## 8. CHANGE PARAGRAPH STYLE (AND/OR LEADING BETWEEN PARAGRAPHS)

If your book is set up as an indent-only paragraph without an extra return after each paragraph, convert the style to an extra return style (such as this book's style) and remove the indents. The addition of all these returns adds lots of pages to the book. For even more page gain, leave the indent in as well, or add extra leading between the paragraph returns, or both.

## 9. INCREASE FIRST LINE INDENT

If you've set the book up as a first line indent and want to maintain that style, you can increase the indent size. This technique won't add many pages but may prove effective on longer books if only a few pages are needed and the added space is compatible with the design.

## 10. ADD GRAPHICS
**a.** Adding illustrations, charts, photographs and the like makes a book more interesting and easier to read by breaking up the text. And of course, each graphic adds to the page count.
**b.** Use graphics on right hand pages and insert a blank page on the backs of these pages.

## 11. ADD MORE PARAGRAPHS
Breaking out long paragraphs into shorter paragraphs will add more lines to the book, and thus, more pages. It will also make the book easier to read.

## 12. CHANGE TYPESTYLE TO ONE RUNNING LARGER
Typestyles can run larger like Eurostyle or smaller like Times Roman. Using a clean but larger typeface will add more pages than using a smaller one. Run out sample pages of text in various typestyles to see not only which looks best for your book, but additionally, which best fits your needs.

## 13. INCREASE SPACE BETWEEN LETTERS, OR ENLARGE WIDTH OF TYPE
You can increase the spacing between the letters in a word, or alternately, enlarge the width of the type from 100% (normal) to 110%. Expanding type reduces the number of words that will fit on a line, and thus increases the page count in a book. Do not use this technique if readability is affected negatively. It's not the best of options in the list, but is shown as a possibility that may work for you.

## 14. OVERALL "LOOSER" DESIGN
Your overall page design using many of the above techniques can be "loosened" out for an easier feel. For example, rather than getting creative to cram a table onto a particular page, you'll spread out the design and run the table on a following page.

## 15. ADD MORE CHAPTERS
I always like more chapters for easier reference in how-to's, and for greater break-up in fiction, though of course in the latter, the creative aspect is king. By using our chapter design techniques discussed earlier, each chapter adds additional pages to increase the page count.

## 16. ADD MORE SUBHEADS

Subheads break up a page nicely for ease of reading, with the added benefit in this case, of added lines, and eventually, more pages.

## 17. PRINT ON BULKIER PAPER

This is technically not a way to fill up the page count, but if the **bulk** of the final book, the thickness, is a consideration, which it probably is, than you can make adjustments by printing on thicker paper.

The type of paper used in the printing process makes a huge difference in the final thickness of a book. Ask your printer for a high-bulk or higher weighted paper and let him know that you want your book to be bulkier. While higher-weighted paper, such as going from 50 pound to 60 pound, is almost always more expensive (though perhaps worth it in your case), a bulkier house stock may not be. A phone call to the printer will get you an answer.

## WHAT IF YOU STILL HAVE TOO LITTLE TEXT FOR THE PAGES YOU WANT TO FILL?

You have two basic choices in this instance. You either must reduce the page count of the book a half or full signature, or have the author submit more writing. However, with all the possibilities we detailed above, you should be able to work out the page count you need without too much of a problem.

# REDUCING A BOOK'S PAGE COUNT

Just as we expanded a book's design by the above techniques, we can similarly reduce the page count by doing the opposite. Here's the view from the other side of the fence on each of the 17 items for expanding a page, with sometimes, but not always, the opposite advice.

## 1. EDIT DOWN THE BACK PAGES OR REDUCE THE POINT SIZE OF THE BACK PAGE TYPE

**a. Edit Down** - Editing down extra materials in the appendices, glossary, index and other back pages can slim a book down as long as these supporting materials are not important to the book.

**b. Reduce Point Size** - Or alternately, reduce the type sizes of the back pages.

## 2. DO TIGHT FRONT PAGES
Stick to the bare minimum necessary and don't use a doubler.

## 3. REDUCE TABLE OF CONTENTS
Since the table of contents is an important sales feature, think twice before reducing pages from this section.

## 4. TIGHTEN CHAPTER HEAD DESIGN
**a. Chapter Heads Further Up on Page** - Start the chapter head near or at the top of the page as opposed to 1/4 or 1/3 the way down. If there are lots of chapters, you gain lots of pages.

**b. Chapter Heads Never on a Page By Themselves** - Takes up too much space.

**c. Chapter Heads on Left or Right Side** - Chapters need not be on right hand pages. Let them fall where they may.

**d. Chapter Heads Following Text on Same Page as Last Chapter** - For maximum savings of space, start the chapter a few returns after where the last chapter ends, even if on the same page. I layed out my first book this way, and 10 printings later, the book still looks good, and still sells.

**e. Reduce the Point Size of the Chapter Heads**

## 5. DECREASE POINT SIZE
Reducing your point size from 12 point, to 11 or 10 point reduces the overall space by approximately 10% each time and still provides a readable text. This is the best way to reduce the page count.

## 6. DECREASE LEADING
Ditto above. Taking leading down one half point or one full point reduces the overall page count by an approximate 5-10% and possibly more depending upon overall design.

## 7. DECREASE MARGINS
Decreasing the size of the margins increases the number of words per line and the number of lines per page thus reducing the overall page

count. This is a major way to lose pages. However, keep in mind the minimum three pica rule (with four picas preferable) for white outside margin.

## 8. DECREASE PARAGRAPH SPACING/ CHANGE TO FIRST LINE INDENT

If your book is set up with an extra return after each paragraph shorten the leading between those returns. This will reduce some pages, though not many. Even better, change to a first line indent with no returns between paragraphs, and you'll enjoy a major savings in pages.

## 9. INCREASE FIRST LINE INDENT

If you've set the book up as a first line indent, reducing the indent size may not change the page count unless you've set it up with larger indents than normal (more than 1/4 inch - 1 1/2 picas). Even then, it may not reduce many pages, if any.

## 10. REDUCING GRAPHICS

**a.** Reduce the number of graphics only if they don't really add to the book. *Never* sacrifice good graphics if these graphics improve the book. Either trim the fat elsewhere, or go up a half signature in pages.
**b.** Don't insert blank pages following graphics.

## 11. COMBINE PARAGRAPHS TOGETHER

Only consider combining paragraphs in isolated instances, where perhaps you may gain a page. Good design comes first, and should never take a back seat to page considerations.

## 12. CHANGE TYPESTYLE TO ONE RUNNING SMALLER

Changing to a smaller face like Times Roman will get many more words per page than a face such as Eurostyle or Helvetica. Run out sample pages of text in various typestyles to see not only which looks best for your book, but additionally, which best fit your needs. Big page savings can be gained here.

## 13. REDUCE SPACE BETWEEN LETTERS, OR REDUCE WIDTH OF TYPE

You can decrease the spacing between the letters in a word, or alternately, reduce the width of the type from 100% (normal) to 90%. This will greatly increase the number of words that will fit on a line and thus significantly decrease the page count in a book. Don't even consider using this technique if the readability of the type is affected negatively. I have used width reduction successfully in catalogues, but I would think twice about doing the same for a book.

### 14. OVERALL TIGHTER DESIGN
Your overall page design using many of the above techniques can be tightened for page savings. Be parsimonious in the layout of every page and you'll gain a few pages.

### 15. REDUCE THE NUMBER OF CHAPTERS
I always like more chapters for easier reference, so I would be hesitant in recommending fewer chapters, even though there are often savings to be had in the page count.

### 16. REDUCE THE NUMBER OF SUBHEADS
Ditto above. I'm big on subheads for a cleaner read in appropriate books. If possible, don't sacrifice here.

### 17. PRINT ON THINNER PAPER
This is technically not a way to reduce the page count, but if the bulk of the book needs to be thinner, than adjustments can be made by using thinner paper. Ask your printer for a low-bulk or thinner weight paper - and let him know that you want a thinner book. You may even enjoy savings on the job.

### WHAT IF YOU STILL CANNOT FIT THE PAGES INTO THE SPACE ALLOTED?
You have two basic choices. You either must expand the book an extra half or full signature (or more), or edit the book down to fit.

# FIRST TEST OF PAGE
To be absolutely safe that everything is as you think it should be, you must print out a sample page before you get too far into a book's layout. Of greatest importance, you want to make sure that the proper margins have been set outside your text area. For example, if you're doing a 6 x 9 inch book, you want your text area no wider than five inches.

This leaves a total margin of one inch - six picas for the width, an area of one half inch, or three picas, on either side of the text area. You'll also need to make sure that enough room is left for the length. If you miscalculate on the margin area, you risk having to re-layout the entire book.

The purpose of this sample printout is to also check the look and design of your page to make sure it's pleasing to your eye, and that your typefaces and sizes are correct.

# CHAPTERIZING A BOOK

Chapterizing is an accurate way to get an exact final page count before actually laying out a book.

Chapterizing is only done once we know the particulars of the design - the margins, type style, point size, and leading - and have the book close to the ideal page count. Chapterizing gives us an exact final page count so that when we go page by page and layout the book, we know exactly how many pages we can afford to add or lose during the entire process.

For example, if we have chapterized a book and our page count is 318 pages with a final page count goal of a 320 page book, we know we have two pages to give during the layout. But if our final page count is 320 pages, and we're at the bare minimum in our front and back pages (that is, there's not fat to trim here), then we know we cannot have a chapter extend out even one extra page without losing that page in another chapter, or else the book gets brought out to 321 pages - and that's one page over our 320 page signature count.

That's why it's always good to chapterize before laying out a book. We see exactly what room we have to work with in the layout, and know what we can and cannot do in terms of adding or losing pages.

## How to Chapterize

Going back to steps three and four earlier (in the working with the rough page count - see summary on the following page), we add the graphics to the page count, and make a preliminary chapter design for each of the chapters.

---

**ROUGH PAGE COUNT SUMMARY**
1. Start with the Rough Pages
2. Add the Essential Front and Back Pages
3. Add Graphic Pages
4. Add Chapter Pages
5. Assess the Situation

---

This shouldn't take too long since we're not actually laying out pages, just figuring chapters as a whole. Keep in mind that the Table of Contents and the Introduction should begin on right hand pages. If necessary, the left-handed facing pages preceding these chapters can be left blank.

As an example, let's use a standard chapter design where each chapter begins on a new page, and the chapter head comes down a little so the text begins 1/4 of the page down. We now count up the pages that the text will consume for that chapter.

For example, if a chapter contains eight and 3/4 pages, and we extend the chapter head down so that 1/4 of a page more is taken up, we have 9 pages filled. If this chapter also has three 1/2 page graphics, then the final page total is 10 full pages plus 1/2 page, or 11 pages.

It wouldn't matter if only four lines extended onto the last page. Since we're beginning new chapters on a fresh page, 10 pages plus whatever fraction, be it two lines or 30 lines, makes 11 pages. And that is the total for this chapter - 11 pages.

## Adding Up the Chapter Count

We now add up the totals for each chapter in the book. Let's say we have seven chapters in the book with the following page counts; 3, 17, 30, 25, 25, 31, 19. Adding up the these numbers, we get 150 pages. That gives us an exact page count for all the pages in the body text.

Let's say we're shooting for an even signature of 160 pages. We have 150 pages, and need 10 more pages to make 160.

When we actually layout the book, we'll likely end up at those 150 pages for the body text. Sometimes there's a surprise of a page or two lost or gained when the dust settles, but that's no big deal either, for we've already made design decisions previously to get to this close signature count. That was the whole point of the rough body count and adjustments.

We can adjust the front or back pages, or our chapter design again if need be, to get the extra 10 pages or so that we'll need to make the page count.

We're close enough right now to know that the book is going to fit just as planned with just a little more tinkering. We can add pages by loosening up the page design, changing the chapter style, adding more illustrations, making the final adjustments in the front and back pages after the book is layed out, or effecting any of the other techniques we discussed.

## ADDING UP THE CHAPTER COUNT

| | |
|---|---|
| Chapter One | 3 |
| Chapter Two | 17 |
| Chapter Three | 30 |
| Chapter Four | 25 |
| Chapter Five | 25 |
| Chapter Six | 31 |
| Chapter Seven | 19 |
| **Total Chapter Count** | **150 pages** |

## MANUAL CHAPTERIZING ESTIMATION

Here's a way to estimate the number of pages in a book when there are many graphics involved.

First, we estimate the number of words per chapter. For example, if the first manuscript chapter has an approximate total of 2,900 words, and your final book page holds 350 words, than this first book chapter will contain 8 full pages and one partial page (about 1/3) - that's nine pages. Add graphics, if any, and you'll have an exact count for this chapter. For example, if there are three half page graphics, add 1 1/2 to 8 1/3 for a total of 10 pages - nine full pages and one partial. Since this design starts each new chapter on a new page, 10 is our page count for the chapter.

If the chapter heads took up half a page (including white space above for design), than we have to add 1/2 page to the 1 1/2 and 8 1/3, for a total of 10 full pages and one partial, or a grand total of 11 pages.

Do this for each chapter, and you'll get an exact count for the body of the work, and will know how much room we have to play with on your front and back pages. Do we go loose or tight? The chapter estimation shown above will provide us with enough answers to make this determination.

# LAYING OUT A BOOK

With the book chapterized and close to or exactly at our final page count, we're ready for the final step, getting the book laid out. With all the text tied together in our publishing files, layout will be easy, and you'll be surprised at how fast everything goes.*

Starting from the first page in the *body text*, we set up our chapter head a certain amount of space down from the top margin, according to the design decisions we've made. Similarly, with an appropriate space left below the chapter head, we begin laying out the text. Working with the publishing program, this is easy to do. It's just a matter of one return, a few returns, or more, whatever we've decided on as our look.

*If layout is done by hand, the same principles of making pages apply except that the galley strips will be cut and pasted down by hand. This is more tedious work since the text on each page must be measured for appropriate length and positioned properly on the page. You'll also need to individually paste down page numbers and any other items that would appear on the final printed page.

We now let the text flow until the bottom margin of that page, continue onto the next page, and then the next page and so on. We make pages one by one this way, in consecutive order, making sure the top and bottom margins are consistent from page to page, and that room for graphics is made and left available where appropriate.

For example, if a full page graphic goes on page 14, then the preceding text on page 13 continues to page 15, with page 14 left vacant. (The graphic can either be inserted manually onto a camera-ready page later on, or scanned onto the file and placed on that page.) If only a half page graphic goes on page 14, then the type will continue from page 13, to half of page 14 (making sure there's room not only for the graphic, but for some white space to *breathe* the page), and then to page 15, to 16, to 17, and so on.

We continue making pages in this manner, running text from the top margin to the bottom margin, and leaving sufficient space for charts, drawings or photos, if any, until the end of the chapter. Then we begin the new chapter, consistent with the way the last chapter began, with the chapter head positioned in its appropriate place on the page.

Each page gets laid out in succession, until all the chapters in the book have been completely paged. With all pages laid out in the body text, we now add the final back and front pages we need to finish out the book at our signature count.

And *voila*! It's proof time, the last step before the printer sees your book.

---

## PRODUCTION SUMMARY

- Start with rough page count
- Add essential front and back pages
- Add graphic pages
- Add chapter spacing
- Assess situation
- Make adjustments in design to fit situation
- Chapterize book
- Layout the book, make final adjustments
- Proof the book carefully

## LAYOUT BASICS

- The table of contents and the introduction should always start on a right-hand (odd-numbered) page. If necessary, leave the preceding (facing) or following left-handed pages blank, or both.

- Odd-numbered pages go on the right hand side, and even-numbered pages on the left.

- Where there are subheads, make sure text follows subsequent to the heading *on the same page*. Don't leave a subhead hanging alone on a page.

- Where there are charts, illustrations, tables and photos, leave room for the entire image to fit on one page.

- Ideally, text should run consistently along the top and bottom margins from one page to the next, but that won't always be possible. When one of the margins must be shortened, which will sometimes happen due to the placement of graphics, it's best to shorten the bottom margin and to keep the top margin consistent.

- When chapters start on a new page, omit the running headers.

- Always leave the minimum three pica (1/2 inch) white space margins on all four sides of the text.

- Keep typestyles consistent throughout the book. For example, if one type of heading is 14 point bold, all like headings should be the same.

# ORGANIZATIONAL PAGE

As the book nears completion, I find that an organizational page works wonders for saving time and outlining the exact steps needed to finish the book. This page lists the chapters in the book, their current page count and page numbers, the individual pages that comprise the front and back pages, plus a listing of illustrations, photos and other artwork used and needing to be placed.

As each remaining page or section is completed, I check off or cross out the item. Check by check, as items get completed, the visual accomplishments of my list psychologically encourages and keeps me moving in the right direction. And it also clearly organizes the exact work remaining for the book to get ready for press.

Following is an example of an organizational page.

# ORGANIZATIONAL PAGE

## Chapter Count

| | |
|---|---|
| Half-title page | 1 |
| Dedication page | 2 |
| Title page | 3 |
| Copyright page | 4 |
| Contents | 5-7 |
| Blank | 8 |
| Introduction | 9 |
| Blank | 10 |
| Chapter 2 | 11-17 |
| Chapter 3 | 18-41 |
| Chapter 4 | 42-80 |
| Chapter 5 | 81-127 |
| Chapter 6 | 128-142 |
| Chapter 7 | 143-158 |
| Back Pages | 159-160 |

## To Be Completed

*Complete table of contents*

*~~Do title page and half-title page~~*

*insert illustrations on:*

*~~page 17-18~~*

*28 (reduce to 50% at copy shop)*

*37*

*~~156~~*

*~~Verify organization name and numbers on 266~~*

*re-check introduction*

*add two back pages to make 32 page signature*

*~~a. write a one page house ad~~*

*b. do order form*

*~~separate photo for front cover~~*

*insert bar code on back cover*

**As each item is completed, it is checked off or crossed out**

## SOME THOUGHTS ON DESIGN

The basics of good design are easy, but you would be surprised at the number of books by small and major publishers alike which defy good design, and are either unattractive, somewhat unreadable, or a combination of the two.

You should never allow a book to go to press if the design is weak. Sometimes you get off on the wrong track with a book, and by the time the book is almost ready for press, you realize you just didn't do a good job with the layout. That happens. What to do? In my eyes, there are no two ways about it; you must re-do the layout and get it done right.

If quality, respect and success are part of your vision, you should never put a book to press if you feel it is sub-par in its design. With the ease in which books can be manipulated on the computer, there's no excuse not to rework a book that may not have been done right the first time.

# PROOFING

Proofing a book is the last thing we do before we send a book to the printer, and a step that should never be taken lightly. The chance for error is high when you're dealing with the many elements necessary to put a book to press and the last minute pressure inherent at press-time, but if the proper steps are taken during the proofing stage, you can assure yourself of a virtually mistake-free printing.

Being extra careful in proofing guarantees that your book will appear as you want it to appear. Not doing the extra steps necessary to properly proof a book almost guarantees the opposite, that one of the many little or greater horrors possible may occur.

When a book is submitted to a printer, you must not *think* the book is ready, you must *know* the book is ready.

## Preparation for Proofing

You must have a complete hard copy of the book printed out and assembled in the correct page order before the book is submitted to a printer, and this hard copy must be up-to-date. If any changes other than very minor ones were made to a page, *that page must be reprinted*.

If you're submitting the book on disk, the hard copy serves not only as proof for yourself, but also, as a proof for the printer. If instead, you're submitting the book as camera-ready copy, then that very same camera-ready copy will serve as your proof.

With the *complete* and *up-to-date* hard copy in hand, go through the following 11 proof steps carefully:

## 1. ORIGINAL MANUSCRIPT CHECK

Compare the final version of the book with the original and edited manuscript submitted by the author to make sure that the finished book version is complete and accurate.

## 2. THE BODY TEXT CHECK

Reread the book just one more time to make sure that the writing and presentation flows freely, *and is right*. This is the final check to catch grammatical and spelling errors.

## 3. CHAPTER CHECK

Check each chapter against itself and the previous one to make sure that the page numbers are in the correct sequential order. For example, if the previous chapter ended on page 161, the following chapter should begin on page 162.

Also, verify that the chapter heads, running heads, and subheads are consistent throughout the book, and that all pages that should be in the chapter are actually there.

## 4. TABLE OF CONTENTS CHECK

Check to see that all chapters have been listed, that their titles and subheads (if you list these) match what is actually listed on the pages, that the chapters are in the correct order, and that the accompanying page numbers match.

You do this by physically checking each chapter page against what is written in the Table of Contents.

## 5. GRAPHICS CHECK

If you're submitting camera-ready copy for pages with graphics such as charts, illustrations, and photos, check to see that each one is in place and hasn't been lost in the shuffle. If you have a list of these in your book, or on an organizational page (good idea), go over each graphic, one by one, to make sure they are already included.

Since graphics are typically one of the last things you'll paste-down on camera-ready copy, this proofing step is an important safeguard

If halftones or other graphics are being inserted by the printer, make sure their placement on the page is indicated and that instructions are clearly given as to which graphic goes on what page. If the printer is doing halftones or separations, re-check that the correct reduction is given.

## 6. STYLE CHECK
Do a random check that typefaces and sizes, running headers, chart headings, and general style is consistent throughout.

## 7. FRONT PAGES CHECK
Verify that the copyright notice (year and author), ISBN, and Library of Congress Number are in place and correct *for this book*. Also, on the copyright page, check that permissions for photos (cover and inside) and reprinted items are credited. If doing a new edition, check that the new ISBN and Library of Congress numbers (not the previous ones) are in place on the copyright page.

Check that the title, author's name and publishing company are listed properly on the title page, that the author's dedication is listed and correct, that the preface, if any, is proofed.

## 8. BACK PAGES CHECK
Verify that back page items, if any, are correct and in place. Cross-check items such as in-house ads, appendices, indices and glossaries.

## 9. PAGE CHECK
If the book is say 160 pages, physically check to see that each page is there and in order. Page one should be followed by page two, then by page three, and so on, right down to the very last page in the book. All blank pages should be identified by an actual blank page being placed

into the camera-ready copy, and if submitting on disk, in the hard copy.

If submitting on disk, recheck to see that *every* file needed is in place and on the disk going to the printer, and that those files contain every page in the book. With a hard copy printed, this step is easily done.

## 10. THE ONCE-OVER

This final check, the **once-over**, or **final proof**, is a critical safeguard to catch anything you've previously missed. The once-over, is the last look at either the camera ready copy or hard copy accompanying the disk, and is the final look you give the book *after* you've done all the other proofing steps and think the book is 100% ready.

I don't care how rushed you are, always take the time to do this one extra step. *Never put a book to press without doing a once-over.*

If you are looking for something in particular, for example, checking chapter heads, skimming for stylistic inconsistencies, checking order of page numbers, or whatever, than you're not ready for the once-over. The final proof is to be done without distractions or particular purpose other than giving an overall undistracted look at the book before it goes into the irrevocable printing process. Do not combine or substitute the once-over with any other proofing step.

The process of a once-over is simple, but you must concentrate when doing this. Starting from page one on either your hard copy (accompanying the disk) or your camera-ready copy - and make sure the book is in numerical order - turn each page one at a time and look at the page. You're not looking for anything in particular - you're just looking.

You never know what you'll find. You may find text out of place, a page missing, the wrong author listed, a page you had thought changed or replaced wasn't - who knows? The once-over can catch these problems. I have caught so many important things over the years in my once-overs, mistakes that would seriously hurt a book's integrity or correctness, that I never skimp on this step.

If submitting camera-ready, make sure the copy is absolutely clean, for the camera will print what it sees.

The final once-over allows you to *know* the book is ready to go. This way, what gets printed, is exactly what you expected.

## 11. AUTHOR PROOF

If possible, the author should see a finished copy of the galleys before it goes to press to protect against any errors inadvertently made in book production. This is not a necessary step in the proofing process, but has the obvious advantages of allowing the number one expert on the book, the author, to give it a once over.

### TYPOS AND PERFECTION

Perfection is difficult to achieve with any book. A **typo** (a mis-spelled word) or two or more may be found in the text or the cover even, you may find an inconsistency in the design - there's lots of little things you may discover after the book has been printed and it's too late.

You should do careful proofing and attempt to publish a perfect book, but if some typos sneak through anyway - no big deal, it happens. You'll make your little mistakes here and there and readers will notice them. But if you put out a good product overall, that will get noticed more than anything else, and your readership will be happy.

On my very first book printing, the spine type was aligned in the wrong direction and all pages numbers on the right were even-numbered (and odd numbers on the left) - perhaps the only book in the store like that. It was unusual. (Technically, mixing up the odd and even pages wasn't a mistake - I just didn't know any different at the time.) However, I did enough things right and the book has been a best-seller for me. It went through nine printings like that. Until the latest edition, in 1993, *Winning Casino Blackjack for the Non-Counter* had even numbered pages on the right and odd-numbered pages on the left. I actually miss that quirky look to the book.

And why not give your book a little personality. A little fun and personality to your book won't hurt sales. Who said there was a mistake? *We like it that way.*

And if you do enough things right - and that's the name of the game with success - there's always another printing to fix your errors and improve the design. Don't overworry about producing the perfect book - it won't always happen. But get as close as you can to making that great book and with enough important things done right - you'll have books that will sell.

# GOING TO PRESS

There are two basic ways a book can be submitted; as **camera-ready art**, books submitted as original hard copy from which the printer will make film, and **electronically**, either on computer disk or through a modem. Books can also be submitted on film, which can be generated from either of the two methods above by a supply house, but this work is probably best done by the printer for his own specifications.

The superior method for most books will be electronic submission, for the savings over camera-ready art will be huge if you don't own your own equipment, and the quality of going direct from disk to film avoids the one extra generation created in camera-ready art.

If you do own a print quality printer, camera-ready submission is a good choice also, for the quality here is excellent as well, and not an issue for most books. Also, there are times you'll want to submit camera-ready copy to get a faster printing schedule or possibly savings over electronic submission - check with your printer on both these issues - and it's nice to have that flexibility without the expense and trouble of using an output service.

We'll look at each option in turn.

## SUBMITTING CAMERA-READY ART

The traditional method of submitting books, camera-ready art, requires that your artwork be of sufficient quality to ensure a good reproduction in the printing process. This minimum quality level of quality for camera-ready art is called **print quality**, and is defined as at least 1,000 **DPI** (dots per inch).

Giving your printer quality camera-ready output is a must. Do not expect to use your home 300 or 600 DPI printer as the final copy to give your printer no matter what any computer salesperson might tell you. 300 or 600 DPI output is great for booklets, reports and correspondence, and certainly a huge improvement over the dot matrix printers, but not good enough for a professional looking book.

To get this quality of type, you'll either need to purchase a printer good enough to produce print quality output (1000 DPI minimum) or you'll need to use one of the many output shops that can print out your files at a high quality resolution fit for printing.

## Printing at an Output Shop

Prices for print quality output at a professional shop used to vary at prices in the $5-$10 per page range, but with the oost of high quality printers coming down, print-qulity output can probably be had at $1-$2 per page. There are various level of qualities available, going from the bare minimum, 1,000 DPI up to quality as high as 2,400 DPI. Generally, the higher the DPI, the greater the cost per page.

However, for straight text output, 1,000 DPI is all the quality you'll need to produce professional-level type, and there's no reason to pay extra for quality you just don't need.

At old prices of say $7 per page, a 192 page book would have cost $1,344 for the pre-press output if all goes perfectly, but probably more due to some changes that would likely be made. Output at $5 per page would have cost $960. Now, at $1 per page, your cost drops to just $192, or $384 at $2 per page, if you can find an output shop convenient to your area.

However, with everything compatible electronically, it really makes no sense to send the book in any other form but electronically. The quality will be better, the cost will be lower, and simply, that's just the best way to do a book now.

## ELECTRONIC SUBMISSIONS

Books submitted on computer disk or through your modem direct to the printer are called **electronic submissions**. Every printer of note in the last few years has set up an electronic pre-press department which handles all the submissions that come over the computer.

This is the new wave in publishing and printers are starting to gear up their equipment to take advantage of this new technology.

## Submitting on Disk

There's a new department in every modern printer's plant, and that's the **electronic pre-press department**. And I mean, brand new. I would say 1993 really marked the beginning of this new revolution in technology - perhaps a few printers came on line as early as 1992. Electronic pre-press is the new printing technology that allows printers to accept your job on computer disk.

No longer need you submit camera ready copy, mechanicals, or flat art. Books can be submitted on standard storage media such as floppy disks, SyQuest cartridges, Zip disks, Jaz disks, or even by modem direct to the printer. In fact, in the last several years, all books at Cardoza Publishing and Open Road have been submitted electronically on disk. It is the most efficient and cost-effective method to submit books to the printer now.

The printing industry has moved along with the times. No serious printer worth their salt can afford to be without a highly skilled and efficient electronic prepress department. Below, we'll look at some of the more popular storage media being used

---

## Standard Storage Media

All the storage media below are available on Mac and PC platforms.

**Floppy** - The floppy disk holds just under 1.4 megs of information, which is not very much. While some books can be held by a few floppies, many can't, and some of the storage media below will be needed to transform the information to the printer.

**SyQuest Cartridge** - The original SyQuests held 44 megs, a second generation 88 megs, and newer ones have even larger capacities.

**CD ROM** - While the CD ROM holds a very large amount of information and is a great way to store 650 megs of information, the disadvantage to using a CD ROM is that a CD ROM burner is needed to get the information on the disk, and the disk, once written onto, cannot be rewritten with additional or new information, though it can be retrieved at will.

**Zip Disk** - This is the new storage media of choice. Holding almost 100 megs of information, the Zip was a great tool when it came out several years ago and gave publishers an affordable way to both store large amounts of information, and convey that information to printers, service bureaus, and other computers with a Zip drive accessible.

**Jaz Disk** - Following up on their great success with the Zip disk, the Iomega company put out an even larger storage media, the Jaz disk, which hold almost one gig of information.

Since hard copy must accompany any electronic submission, I recommend against sending books by modem. As I mentioned earlier, strange things happen all the time when information is transferred from one computer to another, and thus, there is that absolute need for hard copy to accompany the electronic submission so that the printer has a proof to work with. It would be okay to send an update or correction by modem if the change can be communicated clearly by fax or description on the phone.

When submitting electronically, you must make sure the printer's electronic pre-press department knows what and how you're submitting the job. Indicate the program and its version, the file names, and the fonts used. Also, be clear about any tricky things you've done that the printer should be aware of. And of course, before anything else is done, *make sure your software is compatible with the printers.*

All printers doing electronic pre-press work will have Quark and Pagemaker in appropriate Macintosh and IBM compatible formats so you shouldn't have a problem if these are your programs. If you're using other programs, check to make sure that the printer can deal with your particular software application.

While many printers are current with the most popular software and fonts in their pre-press departments, to be perfectly safe you should call them to verify that they indeed do or don't have the fonts necessary to properly execute your files. If they don't have all the fonts you need, you can either download your work as postscript files, and the job should process without a hitch, or, if you don't know how to make a postscript file on your software, you can supply the fonts along with your job and let the printer deal with it. It's no big deal either way.

In any case, whether supplying fonts or submitting postscript files, you'll need to coordinate with the electronic pre-press department at the printer you'll be working with, and they will let you know the best way to make the process go smoothly.

## Getting the Job to the Printer

If you're not submitting the job electronically, then there's only one way to submit your job to the printer - and that's by next day air with a reliable national delivery service such as UPS, FedEx, USPS Express Mail or other. You're sending original artwork that in most cases would cost you a lot of time and money to replace should the package get lost.

It's very important to see a new book as having a time value. The faster that book gets onto the printing press, the faster it will get printed and shipped to the appropriate warehouses. It is axiomatic that the sooner your book gets into the stores, the sooner it can be making you money. Two more days of sales is probably worth a whole lot more than the extra postage it will cost you for faster service. Add up the numbers. Surely, an extra $10-$15 spent on moving the book into production as fast as possible will be covered in just one day of extra sales, let alone two days, three days, or even one week.

## SEND THE WHOLE JOB AT ONCE

If you want your job done right and you wnat it done without too many hiccups, send the entire job - both text and covers - in one delivery. You leave too much room for error when you send a job out piecemeal.

Do not send your job to the printers in various stages. It's unprofessional and greatly increases the chances for a big screw-up on your book. As a matter of fact, many printers will not even accept your job unless it comes in whole. And these are smart printers.

Don't be under the illusion that sending the first section of an almost finished book will speed up your job. It won't. Printers won't even look at your job until the rest of the book arrives. Printers have found through experience that working on partial jobs causes confusion and problems. They're also aware that a person who sends in jobs this way is probably inexperienced, and that the job will come in so confused and become so problematic, that they would probably be better letting some other printer have the headaches that this job surely will have.

At worst, you may send the cover in separately, as much as one to two weeks after the body text is delivered to the printer, but like everything else, you must coordinate with the printer to see if; one, it will speed up the job, and; two, it is an acceptable way to hand in the print job. If the job is speeded up by either an earlier delivery of the cover or text, and time is of the essence, which it usually is, than it can be acceptable. If the job is not speeded up, or your printer recommends against it, do not submit a book this way.

## GETTING THE BOOK PRINTED

Now that the book is ready for press, we'll need to get it mass-produced at a printing plant. So let's move right on to the next section - *Printing*.

# 13. PRINTING

## INTRODUCTION

Going to press and printing a book is the part of the book-making process where the excitement builds, for once the book comes off that press, your baby has been delivered!

Eventually you'll get to the stage of a book where you have a good idea of how the book is shaping up and are ready to pursue pricing with printers. Unless the printer you'll be using happens to be nearby, there's no need to even meet them or see their plant since, with clear instructions, the whole process can be done by phone and mail.

This section will show you how to get proper quotes from a printer, the buzz words you can use (or understand if the printer springs them on you), and how to explain just what you want in your quote. We'll go over the proper instructions to use when submitting books to a printer, the basics of locating and choosing printers, and all that's involved in dealing with the printing process.

You must use reliable printers when printing your book and that might not always mean the best price. It doesn't mean it won't be the best price also, but remember, the final printed book is your goods and your sales tools, and you'll need the job done right. But there's no worries in this: There's an abundance of excellent printers who'll be able to do your job properly, and these printers are located all over the country and for that matter, all over the world.

Let's begin our discussion with the types of presses used for printing books.

# THE THREE TYPES OF PRINTING PRESSES

There are three basic types of book presses in the printing industry; the **sheetfed**, **web** and **belt** presses. The sheetfed and web presses are commonly found among large printers in the industry, while the belt press, the most sophisticated of the three, will be found in only the very largest of the printers.

There are many configurations of these presses, configured for handling one type of job better than another, but you won't need to know about these differences. You will find it helpful, however, to understand more about these presses, so you understand which press will work best for your book, and what's going on when the printer discusses the type of press they'll be using.

## The Sheetfed Press

Sheetfed presses, as the name implies, print one sheet at a time through the press, making these machines the slowest of the three presses and therefore the most expensive to print books on. These are also the machines that produce the highest quality work.

Sheetfeds are used by the smaller local printers, who cannot afford anywhere near the expenses of owning the faster and larger web and belt press, and by large printers who use them predominately to print the precise color work needed on the covers, while the text itself is done on their faster presses.

Printers doing books wholly on sheetfed presses, due to its slowness, cannot compete price-wise with printers using the web and belt presses that print books at a much faster rate.

The sheetfed is most compatible for small print runs, 2,000-3,000 books or less, high quality color work, and smaller printings of flyers, pamphlets and the like.

## The Web Press

Web presses use giant rolls of paper in their system and print signatures in 32 page counts. They're economical, and certainly the most frequently used of the three types of presses for large book runs. Webs produce good quality work and can cover most of a publisher's needs.

Webs are used predominately in one color work (black ink) though there are web set-ups that can print two color jobs, and even up to six color jobs or more. However, don't be surprised if your quote takes a quantum leap in price for two colors over one. Many printers won't have the type of web needed to handle two color or more jobs, or won't do it on that web if the job demands very precise quality - they'll do the multi-color work on their sheetfeds instead.

If you're used to printing sheetfed jobs with your local printer, you'll be astounded and incredibly pleased at the price savings you'll enjoy printing with a web instead. For the same price you pay for a 3,000 run on a sheetfed you may get a 10,000 run on the web. That's big savings, and I bet savings you wouldn't mind at all.

## The Belt Press

The super-fast modern belt press is a wonder of new technology. It prints, collates, binds and trims, all in-line, so that at the end of the belt, out comes a finished book. Amazing! The only thing the belt doesn't do is print covers - these are done on a sheetfed and fed into the belt.

Belts are great for high quantity runs, 5,000 and up, black text only (no color), but not for high quality work. The belt press is not recommended for books using a lot of small type, under 8 point or less, or for books with halftones - the quality is just not there. However, for straight black and white line text, the belt puts out a good book and will get the job done economically.

Belts presses charge a set-up fee on text and cover to make the belt, a fee that is dropped on reprints where the belt can be reused. However, that reprint savings may be lost if more than 10% of the book is changed - a new belt may be needed.

Belts use signature of 36 pages, not the 32 that's standard with webs. If your book is set-up for a web and you decide to print with a belt at the last minute, remember to adjust your final pages to compensate for the different page count.

The belt, like the web, is an economical press well worth considering.

## HOW A BOOK GETS PRINTED

Here's a quick look at the printing process from your submission to the printer to the final printed book.

Working from either your camera-ready copy or your disk, if the book is an electronic submission, the printer will make negatives of the text and cover. Text and cover will be worked on separately. Metal or plastic plates are made from these negatives on plate-making machines; these are the impressions that will be used on the printing press itself. Some newer technology actually skips the negative process, and takes electronic art right to the plates.

The text and cover get printed separately. The text will be done in signatures, folded on the press, and then collated with other signatures. These signatures will go to the binder where they will be bound together with the cover, and then to a machine that will trim the three open sides.

The finished books will get boxed by hand or machine and placed on pallets ready to ship. The pallet itself will get shrink-wrapped to keep the load from shifting.

In a nutshell, that is what happens to your books.

# GETTING QUOTES

It's best to get quotes from three or four web or belt press printers so you get a range of prices for your job and can see which printers are the most competitive. I don't recommend sheetfed printers for book printings of greater than 3,000 copies as they're just not competitive enough.

Printers can be located through recommendations of other publishers, and advertisements in trade publications and directories. (See *Appendix F* for some resources.) Recommendations from fellow publishers are a great way to find out about a printer's quality and service; price comparisons, of course, can easily be ascertained from the quotes.

On the following page, I've included a list of some of the main book printers in the United States and Canada. I have used many of these printers with varying degrees of satisfaction. Generally, my experiences with these printers have been positive, though in some cases, the opposite has been true. However, it is beyond the scope of this book for me to rate printers or give a stamp of approval or disapproval.

Printers are listed in alphabetical order.

# LIST OF PRINTERS

**Banta Company**, Curtis Reed Plaza, P.O. Box 60, Menasha, WI 54952; (920)751-7771.

**BookCrafters**, 140 Buchanan Street, Chelsea, MI 48118; (734)475-9145.

**Book Mart Press**, 2001 42nd Street, North Bergen, NJ 07047; (201)864-1887.

**Braun-Brumfield**, 100 N. Staebler Rd, P.O. Box 1203, Ann Arbor, MI 48106; (734)662-3291.

**Cushing-Malloy**, 1350 N. Main Street, P.O. Box 8632, Ann Arbor, MI 48107; (734)663-8554.

**Bertelsmith Industry Services,** 28210 N. Avenue Stanford, Valencia, CA 91355; (800)323-3582, (805)257-0584.

---

### SENDING ARTWORK TO A PRINTER

Camera-ready artwork or electronic submissions along with hard copy should be sent to your printer by a *next day* air delivery service with a signature required.

There are two reasons to send your books by this method. First, you want to be sure that your artwork package reaches the printer. Next day air delivery is the most secure way to do this. Second, every day that can be saved in getting your book to the printer is one day faster that your book can get off the press and start selling. That extra $10.00 or so in postage will be a drop in the pocket compared with the amount of money your book will earn for every extra day on the market. Plus, of course, you get to see your book that much faster.

**Malloy Lithographing**, 5411 Jackson Road, P.O. Box 1124, Ann Arbor MI 48106; (800)722-3231, (313)665-6113.

**Maple-Vail Book Manufacturing**, Willow Springs Lane, P.O. Box 2695, York, PA 17405; (717)764-5911.

**Metropole Litho**, 1201 rue Marie-Victorin, St-Bruno-de-Montarville, Quebec, CANADA J3V 6C3; (514)441-1201

**Publishers Press,** 1900 West 2300 South, Salt Lake City, UT 84119; (801)972-6600.

**Quebecor Printing/Fairfield,** 100 N Miller Street, P.O. 717, Fairfield, PA 17320; (717)642-5871. (Formerly Arcata Graphics.)

**RBW Graphic**, 2049 20th Street, P. O. Box 550, Owen Sound, N4K 5R2, Ontario, Canada (519)376-8330.

**R R Donnelley & Sons Company**, 1009 Sloan St., Route 32 West, Crawfordsville, IN 47933; (800)428-0832, fax (765)364-2559.

**Rand McNally & Company**, 8255 N. Central Park Avenue, Skokie, IL 60076; (800)333-0136, (708)673-9100.

**Rose Printing Company**, 2503 Jackson Bluff Road, P.O. Box 5078, Tallahassee, FL 32314; (850)576-4151.

**Thomson-Shore**, 7300 West Joy Rd, Dexter, MI 48130; (734)426-3939.

# CHOOSING A PRINTER

If you haven't worked with a particular printer before, or this is your first time going to press , you will doubtless have some trepidation. Keep in mind, that while there are printer screwups from time to time, your book will most likely be in good hands. Following are the factors you should consider when choosing a printer to manufacture your book.

## Quality Issue

While your two main guidelines in deciding whether to accept a quote from a printer will be quality and price, clearly, the most important concern before anything else is that the printer can produce the quality you need. *Do not work with a printer unless you have complete confidence in his work.* A poorly produced book is of no use to you, no matter the price. Have printers that you're considering send a sample of a book they printed so that you can see their work.

## Price Issue

If you feel secure on the quality issues, then you can think about price. Basically, you want to produce your book as inexpensively as you can, with of course, the appropriate quality levels. Among the bids you receive for your book will be a range of prices, from the lowest to the highest.

You need to match these bids against each other carefully to make sure the printers are bidding on the same exact specs. For example, a printer's price might seem to be $500 higher than a competitor's but that's because he may be quoting 60 pound paper as opposed to the less expensive 50 pound, or 50 pound compared to 35 pound, or he may be quoting estimated freight charges, or film lamination, or even a different page count, where the seemingly less expensive printer is not.

One factor you should keep in mind on the price issue is the location of the printer, and where the books will be shipped. If you'll be shipping to Florida, you might save $200-$500 (or more, or less) by printing in Florida as opposed to California, for example, and you should factor that in to the overall cost of printing the book.

The prices a printer gives you for a job can vary from one month to another according to the economic laws of supply and demand. If a printer is overly busy, there won't be a lot of pressure for him to drop his prices. On the other hand, if work is slow, a printer may give you a better price just so he can keep his shop productive. Generally, printers will be consistent with their prices over time, but keep in mind, printers want your business and will do what they can within their profit structure to get it.

## Turnaround Time

Service can also be an issue. The standard **turnaround time**, the time it takes from receipt of book until the finished book is printed and ready to ship, is 4-5 weeks among the big printers. Perhaps one printer will be a little higher in price, but will offer you a faster turnaround time, say three weeks, to compensate as their advantage.

## Summing Up

So when choosing a printer, you weigh the quality, price (including estimated freight) and turnaround times to find the printer that's best for this job. Again, quality assurance comes first, and after, choose among printers for the best price and service.

# UNDERSTANDING PRINTER'S QUOTES

While each printer's **quote**, or **estimate**, the printed proposal that outlines the job to be done and its price, will contain the same basic information, the presentation of these quotes will often completely vary so you'll have to take some time to understand the quotes given.

There are many items that make up a quote, and to navigate you through the maze of terminology that appears on a typical estimate, we've produced a sample quote on the following page. We'll discuss the significance of each item in the quote, and how they affect you. (Keep in mind that each printers quotation will look different.)

**1.** This is the general information a printer will use to identify the book, publisher and the quote. We see the book title, *The Complete Guide to Successful Publishing,* our publishing company, *Cardoza Publishing,* the estimate # and the date of the quote. When referring to an estimate with a printer, always use the working title of the book that was quoted. We also might add the estimate # and date if we accept the quote on a letter separate from the quote itself.

**2.** On our example, we see "camera ready copy for text and color separated negatives for cover." This shows that the text price is based on camera ready copy - not film and it also assumes we're providing the color separations. If not, the printer will charge for this work. If the book was previously printed and negatives exist, the book would be somewhat cheaper to print (maybe a few hundred dollars) and your quote will reflect this in the price. If the book was previously printed

**3.** The publishing company receiving the quote.

## SAMPLE PRINTER QUOTE

# KRANMAR
# PRINTING COMPANY, HUCKABUCK DRIVE, O'NORTON, CA

*This quote is firm for 30 days except paper which will be billed on the price prevailing at the time of shipment from the paper mill.*

**3** CARDOZA PUBLISHING
132 Hastings Street
Brooklyn, New York 11235

**1** Date: 2-11-96
Estimate #10195

Book Title:
*The Complete Guide to Successful Publishing*

**2** Artwork Supplied:
Camera-ready copy for text
color separated negatives for cover

| | | |
|---|---|---|
| **4** Binding | Perfect Bind | |
| **5** Trim | 6 x 9 | |
| **6** Total Pages | 416 | |
| **7** Spine Bulk | 27/32" | |
| **8** Type Area | 25/32" | |
| **9** Copies | 5m, 7.5M, 10m | |

**10** Text Stock          50# Glattfelter, 500ppi
**11** Ink                      Black, **12** no bleeds
**13** Cover Stock        10 pt. C1S **14**
**15** Cover Ink            4-0-0-4/UV Coating

| **23** QUANTITY: | 7500 | 10000 | 15000 |
|---|---|---|---|
| Prepress | $x,xxx | $x,xxx | $x,xxx |
| Press | $x,xxx | $x,xxx | $x,xxx |
| Text Stock | $x,xxx | $x,xxx | $x,xxx |
| Bind | $x,xxx | $x,xxx | $x,xxx |
| Covers | $x,xxx | $x,xxx | $x,xxx |
| **TOTAL** | **$x,xxx** | **$x,xxx** | **$x,xxx** |
| | | | |
| Less for #45 | $x,xxx | $x,xxx | $x,xxx |
| Add'l for | | | |
| Film Lam | $x,xxx | $x,xxx | $x,xxx |

*ADDITIONALS*
**16** Halftones              $15.00 each,  $20.00 min.
**17** Text Bluelines      .50 per page
Cover Bluelines     $47.00
**18** Cromalin               $137.00
**19** Text Corrections  $9.75 each page, $25.00 min.
**20** Cover Corrections  $19.75 per color

**21** FOB:      O'Norton, CA
**22** Terms:   Net 30 days

with the same printer, the quote may read, "reprint from standing negatives."

If negatives of the book do exist, let the printer know this so they can
estimate the job as such and provide a better price in their quote.

**4.** *Binding* is how the finished book is bound. There are different possibilities ranging from **saddle stitching**, staples put into the side, to
**spiral binding**, the coiled rings you find standard in school notebooks.

If you're publishing books for the general book trade, than you must
have the book **perfect bound**. Perfect bound books have a flat binding
that allow type to be imprinted on the spine. Thus, when a perfect
bound books sits on a shelf, the title and author can be read. Some
printers use a similar process called **adhesive side binding**, which is
basically the same thing, and thus perfectly acceptable.

**5.** *Trim* is the final size of the book after all work is completed. The
first number always indicates the width; the second number, the length.
In this example, the book to be quoted is six inches wide by nine inches
long - 6 x 9.

Though we often refer to books as 5 1/2 x 8 1/2 or 6 x 9, in reality, the
final trim is usually closer to 5 3/8 x 8 3/8 or 5 7/8 x 8 7/8. A sixteenth or eighth of an inch in any direction won't make a bit of difference so don't worry if a printer has a slightly different size trim.

**6.** *Tot. Pages* is quite simply, the total pages in the book. This does not
include the cover. You could theoretically bind a book with a *self-cover*
which means that the cover is the same paper stock as the text, but if
this is a book targeted for sale in bookstores, you need the quality of a
heavier paper stock on your color cover and do not want to do a self-
cover. (The total page count in self-covers *includes* the cover.)

**7.** *Spine Bulk* is the width of the spine area. This alerts you to the final
thickness of the book. Spine bulk takes on greater importance if the
thickness of the book is crucial to your marketing plans. If you feel
you're charging a lot for your page count and need the book "bulked-
up," than the spine bulk is an important item for you. Otherwise, a
little thicker or a little thinner won't matter all that much.

In addition to the page count, spine bulk is affected by the paper stock being used.

**8. *Type Area*** is the printer's maximum suggested area of the type you may print on the spine. Type running any larger may extend over the spine and run onto the front or back cover. This area will typically be 1/16 of an inch less than the spine bulk itself. If this information is not provided on your quote, you'll need to call the printer and ask how much room you have to work with.

**9. *Copies*** shows the quantity of books being quoted. In this instance, I've asked for quotes on runs of 5,000, 7,500 and 10,000. This is often shown as 5M, 7.5M, and 10M - *M* representing 1,000 copies.

**10. *Text Stock*** in this example shows the "weight" of the paper. The most common weight for trade books is 50 pound and that is what I recommend you use for your standard book. Lighter weights are sometimes used for books with larger page counts or for savings, while heavier weights, such as 60 pound, are used to either bulk up a book or for better quality. Even higher weights are used for books reproducing art-quality black and white or color photography or drawings, and typically this paper will be coated as well.

On my thinner books (64 pages), I use 60# paper so the books bulk out enough to be perfect bound. Below 1/8 of an inch is too thin for books to be perfect bound, so I need that extra bulk. On my larger books though, I use 50# paper because it's less expensive.

Printers will often state the brand of paper, the opacity and the color (cream white and blue white). For example, you may see *Glattfelter* or *Finch* being quoted. Until you are really experienced, you won't know one paper brand from another or one opacity from another, and frankly, it doesn't make a hoot of a difference. You ought to be perfectly safe using the printer's house stock. I've been publishing for more than 15 years, have put books to press more than 200 times, and I still don't know one paper brand from another.

Don't get intimidated by all these options - paper brand, weight, color, whatever. It's not important. Go with the 50# house book stock recommended by the printer. If there are choices to be made, let the printer suggest what's best for your book and have samples sent.

**11.** *Ink* is the color of ink you requested. In just about all books, that will be black. If you're printing a color other than black for the text, that color (or colors) will be listed here.

**12.** *Bleeds* refers to the printing of ink right to the edge of the printed page. Unless you're doing a bleed, always leave printers a minimum working space of two picas between the edge of the printed text and the end of the page. This goes for all four margins: right, left, upper and lower. Text bled right to the end of the page requires special handling. Some printing presses cannot even print bleeding pages.

The illustrations following shows one example where a page bleeds and another where the page has white space margins.

## EXAMPLE OF A BLEED

←Heavy black border indicates final book size.

The grey area shows where ink will be printed.
There are no margins in this example - thus, this page *bleeds*.

## EXAMPLE OF A BOOK WITH MARGINS

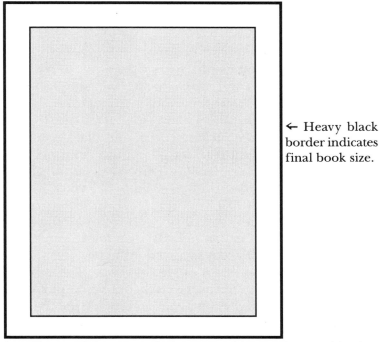

← Heavy black border indicates final book size.

We see margins all around the grey printing area - this page is not a bleed.

**13.** *Cover Stock* refers to the thickness of the cover paper. The standard cover stock is 10 point (10 pt), the thickness quoted here. This is my recommendation. You may get a better deal on 8 point stock, a cheaper and thinner stock which you may find acceptable also. See samples first if you're considering 8 point.

**14.** Covers begin as a blank piece of paper having two sides, and after being printed and folded, four sides. *C1S* (coated one side) indicates that one side of the cover stock, the side used for the outside covers, front and back, is coated. For books meant to be sold through the trade, you should almost always use coated stock to get the best reproduction of your colors. Books sell by their cover. Almost all trade books are printed as C1S.

*C2S* would mean both sides of the unprinted cover stock is coated, and when folded, the inside covers will be coated as well as the outside.

There's probably a good reason for some publishers to go C2S (which is more expensive), but I've never found one for my books. The cover on this quote is for C1S; only the outside covers are coated.

**15.** *Cover Ink* 4-0-0-4 shows how many colors are used on each panel of the cover. The numbers, in order from front to back, indicate, front cover, inside front cover, inside back cover, and back cover. Thus, the book quoted here shows a four-color front cover, no printing inks on the inside two covers, and a four color back cover. If you used the four color process on the outside covers and black printing only on the inside, the line would read 4-1-1-4. A fifth color printed as a "called" color on the outside covers (as opposed to trapping with the process colors) with no inside printing would read 5-0-0-5.

The *U.V. Coating* indicates ultra-violet finish on the cover - a standard protective finish. You can also film laminate, a more expensive process, but one which protects the cover better.

**16.** *Halftones* are the process black and white photographs must go through to be printed. Either you can provide the finished halftones as camera-ready art or on disk, or the printer will shoot them for you and charge you as shown here. You still might incur charges for extra work when you provide your own halftones, but this will be at a lesser price than if the printer had shot them. Check with your printer to see the best and most economical way to submit halftones.

**17.** *Text Bluelines or blues* are the proofs developed by the printer in blue ink - the similar blueprint process used by engineers - that show how the finished insides will look. *Cover blues* will show the representation of the cover in blue ink (no colors). Bluelines give you one last look to make sure the book is as it should look - that the pages are in the right order, and that there are no missing pages or devastating errors. There's usually a charge for blues, but it's minor compared to what your costs are if there's a screw-up in your book.

If your book is produced straight from the disk, *you must have a blueline done*. I've had strange things transpire with what a disk shows on my computer screen, and how it appears on another. I could spin some stories about this. Make no exception to this rule - ever. Insist on a blueline when printing from a disk.

If your book is handed in the traditional way, camera-ready, on artboards, you can get away without blues as long as you've proofed your copy carefully and have worked with this printer before. However, if you haven't worked with this printer before, you must get bluelines. If the printer isn't totally thorough, and you won't know about this with a new printer, pages can flip-flop, or get lost, or marred, or a million other things will go wrong, and it will be a mighty sad day if this happens without getting caught before press-time.

**18.** *Cromalin* is a four color representation of your cover. A Cromalin is actually four transparent plastic sheets, one for each process color - black, yellow, magenta and cyan - laid over one another to give the full color effect much like the actual printing. While the color match won't be perfect, you'll get a very close idea of what the cover will look like.

A Cromalin is money well spent if you haven't seen a four color representation of your cover and should really be mandatory for you due to the importance of the cover - your main sales tool. Alternately, you may get a *color key*, a similar four color proof, or other rendition - depending upon what the printer uses.

**19.** *Text corrections* indicate the amount you'll be charged for each correction the printer must perform *after* the book has been submitted. There's usually a minimum, even if only one correction is done. You should carefully proof your artwork, so you don't add unnecessary expenses to the book.

**20.** *Cover corrections* are corrections made to the cover after the artwork is submitted.

**21.** *FOB* is Freight on Board. Indicates that the buyer pays freight from the shipping point. "FOB O'Norton" means the printer will charge shipping from its O'Norton plant.

**22.** *Terms* states the payment terms for the print job. *Net 30 days* states that the payment is due 30 days after the job is shipped. You may see terms such as half down, half net 30; or if your credit is not yet established, perhaps a request for all money paid before shipping.

**23.** These are the prices quoted for the book as described in this quote.

# HOW TO ACCEPT A PRINTING QUOTE

I like to keep in reasonably close contact with my printer, especially when accepting a quote. It gives me an extra chance to discuss the details concerning the book's printing and make sure I'm in agreement with the printer over exactly what's to be done.

You indicate your official acceptance of a printer's quote by signing a copy of the quote itself (copies are usually provided) and sending that to the printer along with the artwork, and if your credit isn't yet established, a check as well.

However, the book is not officially accepted in the printer's eyes until he actually receives the artwork, so there's no sense in sending the signed quote ahead of time. Send them together, and your book will be in motion.

As a quote often contains several possible options for your book, different print runs, page counts and whatever, you should indicate which options you want with the printing on the quote itself. You can also send a letter in place of the quote stating that the quote for the book is accepted. If a letter is used for acceptance, provide estimate number, date and the particulars (see box below).

---

## FORMAL ACCEPTANCE OF THE JOB

The printer must be clear on the following items and they must be stated in writing on either the accepted estimate or your written acceptance of the job to avoid any confusion.

- The dimensions of the book. This needs to be stated only if several options were on the quote itself.
- The page count.
- Number of books ordered.
- Type and thickness of paper. Generally, the simple instruction of 50 or 60 pound paper will suffice if the job was quoted on house stock, but if you need special paper such as high-bulk, make sure that's 100% clear - in writing - when the job is submitted.
- If special arrangements for a quick turnaround are made, re-state this on your acceptance of the job.

## SAMPLE ACCEPTANCE OF QUOTE

February 11, 1996

I accept your quote, number _____, for the book, <u>The Complete Guide to Successful Publishing</u>, and want a print run of 10,000 copies on 50 pound paper.

---

[Most of the particulars for your book will be in the quote itself, so you don't need to mention every detail in your acceptance of the quote. If several options have been provided on your estimate, indicate the options you are choosing. It's okay to communicate these items to your sales representative verbally, but always confirm this in writing as well. For example, if I was quoted several paper options, my acceptance of the quote might read as follows:]

I accept your quote, number _____, for the book, <u>The Complete Guide to Successful Publishing</u>, and want a print run of 10,000 copies on *50 pound antique white, high-bulk paper.*

---

[If time is an important element in your acceptance of the quote, indicate this factor as well *in writing.*]

I accept your quote, number _____, for the book, <u>The Complete Guide to Successful Publishing</u>, and want a print run of 10,000 copies on 50 pound paper. *The job is due for delivery on February 11, 1996.*

Avery Cardoza
Publisher

# ORDERING THE PRINT RUN

Choosing the number of books you should order from your printer, known as the **print run**, is a tough decision with no set answer that applies across the board. Every publisher's situation is different, and every book is a new situation. The basic issues involved are the amount of money that can be committed, the per unit cost of a book, and the sales (or estimated sales) that can be made on a six-month or yearly basis with the book.

Money, of course, is always the biggest issue. The larger the print run, the more money one must commit to the printing and subsequent inventory. For many publishers, money is tight, and print runs are kept down for cash flow reasons - the less money tied up in books, the more of it can be used to develop other products or to simply keep the business going.

Then there's the aspect of optimizing the print run to bring the cost down to the lowest possible per unit cost. On one hand, we would like to order a large print run to reduce the cost per book. The larger the print run, the less each book costs and the more profit we make on each title. On the other hand, while cost per book goes down the more we print, each additional book adds to the overall print bill. If those extra books don't sell, that's dollars down the drain, money that could be used for other products, or simply taken home as profit. Somewhere in between we have to find the happy minimum.

It all boils down to a determination of just how many books you can sell within a specified time, and how much money you're willing to lay out for this time frame. For established books, you can afford to print more aggressively (more books) as you can estimate future sales with some accuracy. With new books lacking sales history, printing conservatively is definitely the name of the game (fewer books).

Let's look at each situation in turn.

---

### SOME PRICING INSIGHTS

The costs of setting up a press and getting it ready for your job is a major part of the expense in a printing bill. Once the presses are rolling, you're only paying for paper and time. You'll observe on printing estimates how the price of a book goes substantially down in the higher quantities, or for extras, as opposed to the per book charge for the smallest quantity quoted.

---

## Books With a Sales History

On existing books with a sales history, or books that are part of an established series, we have past numbers from which to base our order, and thus can make a reasonably accurate determination of the correct print run. Here, the determination of our print run is based on the amount of money that can be tied up in printed books (as opposed to being available for other products or operating expenses), and thus, how long we'll maintain stock before we need to go back to press.

The general rule of thumb used by many publishers is to print enough books to last six months to one year's worth of estimated sales. You may lean toward the six month inventory formula, as opposed to one year (or two year supplies) if you can't afford to have your cash tied up in warehoused inventory (along with those warehousing bills) while it could be working on other projects. If cash flow is not a current worry, and the book has a sales history you can depend upon, choosing a two year print run will keep cost per book down and long-term profits up.

I like printing large quantities and keeping large inventories on solid backlist performers, because I find it keeps my profits at maximum levels. However, until a book fits this general "solid performer" status, I'll generally opt for a more conservative print run.

## New Books

Of course, estimated sales is not easy to determine when the book is new and we have no similar titles in our house on which to base potential sales. There's no sales history to go by and we must rely on a best-guess basis.

When your initial sales are made in advance (such as with a national exclusive distributor) and you have solid advance numbers to go by, you should order in the range of 25-50% over your advance orders for untested books. For example, if there's an advance order of 2,000 books on a book with no sales history, 2,500-3,000 books should be ordered. If the advance order is 1,000 books, the print run ordered should be in the 1,250-1,500 range. Which number you lean toward in the print run is a function of your confidence in your distribution system and the potential sales of a particular title.

Of course each publisher's situation is different, and you'll want to determine the best print run for your own scenario. Perhaps the above figures are too conservative for you, but in any case, these are determinations you'll have to make.

If there is no distribution network yet set up (perhaps you're a new publisher, or working different types of markets or doing different distribution), and you don't have advance orders, you'll need to be extra careful in ordering your print run. In these instances, where you basically have no clue as to how the market will accept your book, you need to print as lightly as you can until the book can prove itself, or bow out with a minimum of extra costs. Printing small this way will give the book a high per unit cost, but going conservative in this instance is the wise business decision.

Getting stuck with an overly large print bill and books you can't sell due to premature over-ordering is not the best strategy to pursue. Print light and go back to press if you have to.

Runs of 500-2,000 may be appropriate for new books without advance orders, but again, these are decisions you'll have to make based on your *reasonable* expectations.

## General Print Run Strategy

The cardinal rule in any case is to *always choose the conservative print run over the optimistic one*. You can anticipate the market and possible sales all you want, but all the anticipation in the world won't make the book sell any faster. If the book is successful, you can always go back to print, but if the book is not as successful as you hoped, those extra books printed is money down the drain. It's better to go back to press with a successful book and bring the per unit cost of a book down at that point than to throw money away on books you simply can't use. I learned this the hard way.

Several years ago, as part of my gambling line, I came out with the first of my lottery books, *The Basics of Winning Lotto/Lottery,* a book I felt sure would sell like crazy. Lotto and lottery fever was sweeping the country, and I was confident that the book would be a hot seller. Being optimistic by nature, and buoyed by the other sales in my gaming line, I decided to print 25,000 copies, which in hindsight, was foolish. The book *was* successful, but not to the tune of 25,000 copies, nor even half that much. My per copy cost was cheap, but at the same time, I paid for thousands and thousands of books I couldn't use.

My thinking was correct in that the market was there for this book, and that this potential market was huge, but incorrect in that I anticipated something before I had real reason to do so. It is easy to convince yourself that there's definitely going to be big sales, but the real world situation may not go according to plan. Only the acid test - getting the book out to the market - can determine whether the thinking was right. Thus, in ordering print runs, the correct strategy is to plan within *existing* trends in the book market, and not base decisions on scenarios created within one's own head. As I learned, that can lead to waste.

Your overall cash flow and profit as a publisher is always a concern, and therefore, ordering books must be done with due caution and based on realistic expectations.

# THE ACTUAL PRINTING BILL

The final bill you'll get from your printer will probably be 15-25% higher than what you were quoted, so be prepared to take this into account in your overall budgeting and pricing. There are normal extras you'll have with every printing job, and you should be aware of them.

## Overs

For one, it is standard in the printing industry to allow for a maximum of 10% overruns on any print job. There is a certain amount of waste in the process of printing books, thus printers run extra signatures and covers to ensure that they can fill a customer's order. The thinking goes that it's better to overrun a job and make sure the customer has the number of books they need, than underrun the job, and have to go back to press (very expensive for the printer) to make up lost copies if they're really needed.

Thus, if you order 5,000 copies, your actual print total may end up being, say 5,373. You will be charged for these extra 373 copies, or **overs**, at a rate that should be on your quote.

## Shipping

You will also be charged for shipping, typically paid in advance by the printer, which may come out to 5-10% of the total bill, depending upon the book's weight and the distance it travels.

## Extra Work

There may also be charges for extra work performed beyond the scope of the quote, such as last minute changes and corrections done after the job was submitted, work such as trapping for colors, or shooting screens or halftones, that may be billed by the piece or by the hour, and charges for bluelines and cover proofs. These are legitimate charges that the printer will tack onto the total bill.

## Check the Bill

However, you must examine your print bill carefully, for mistakes and overbillings can and do occur. Extra charges sometimes find their way onto the bill that don't belong there. Don't assume that because the printer made an error that they're being dishonest. Many honest mistakes occur. Sometimes the charges may be legitimate, but you just need to have them explained. On the other hand, if there are many charges that don't belong, don't assume that the printer is being honest either - I've had my share of bills from printers where the intent was all too clear, and I let them know about that, sweetly, of course.

In any case, if something doesn't seem right, get your printer on the phone right away and have it explained. If the charge is valid, the printer can explain it to you. If it isn't, the charge will be corrected and removed from the bill.

# MAINTAINING A GOOD PRINTING PRICE

Just because the printer gave you a good price on the first run of your book, doesn't mean they'll match it on the reprint. Sometimes a printer will give you an extra low price to get your job, and make you comfortable with their work, and on the reprint, will raise the price because they figure it's easiest for you to keep the job where it is.

This happens sometimes and it's all part of the game of keeping your printer competitive. It could be a paper price rise that's passed on, and there's not much you can do about it, or it could be because the printer feels they can get a little more for the job, and there's something you can do about it. Simply requote the reprint with several other printers as well, and if you get a better price, you might just let your printer know about it.

Printers do not want to lose your business, so if they know you're serious about keeping them competitive, they'll stay competitive. They know that whoever currently has your work, will most likely get your other work too. They're smart businesspeople. If you get lax about keeping your printer competitive, you may see your prices go steadily up.

# STORING NEGATIVES

Though a printer prepares the negatives for your job, prints the book, and holds onto the negatives, you've paid for those negatives and own them. At any time, you can request that the printer either send those negatives to you, or to another printer of your choice.

However, unless you're going to transfer the job to another printer, you might as well have the current printer store them for you. They'll do this anyway, hoping, just as you do, that there'll be further printings. Most likely, they'll be doing the next job for you.

# PRINTING PROBLEMS

Mistakes do occur during the production and printing process, mistakes that can ruin a book and make it unsaleable. Many of these problems can be fixed without any cost or at reduced cost if you know what to do. We'll try to cover some of the main things that may occur. Let's look at Pre-Press problems first.

## Solutions to Pre-Press Problems
**1. Book is set up with too little margin space.**
If you do make an error in the setup and discover that your margins have less than two picas, 1/3 of an inch, on any of the four sides, you can fix the problem without having to reset the entire book.

Inform the printer of your problem and instruct them to shoot the book at a percentage less than 100% to reduce the overall text area and thus increase the margins. It won't cost you anything extra; it's the same camera shot whether the book is shot at 100% (the normal setting) or a little smaller.

We had this problem recently. My production department set up a text area of just 5 x 8 1/2 inches on a 6 x 9 inch book. While this gave us enough margin on the width, the 1/2 inch *total* top and bottom margin was certainly not enough vertical space.

This was a big goof, but easily fixable. We instructed the printer to shoot the book at 95%, thereby lowering the effective height from 8 1/2 inches (51 picas) to 8 inches (48 picas), and our 10 point type to 9.5 point. This 8 inch height still didn't give me ideal white space margins for the vertical height (I wanted a little more), but the one inch total was certainly workable, as was the smaller point size.

To figure out the reduction necessary, use your proportional wheel or calculator, or have the printer make a suggestion.

**2. Book has too little margin space on one side and too much on the other.**
If you leave too much margin space on the left margin, but not enough on the right margin, or similarly, too much space on the bottom margin but not enough on the top margin, this is easily fixed. The important measurement is that you have enough white space overall on the horizontal or vertical plane.

For example if the page is set-up with five picas on the left margin and only one pica on the right, there's still a total of six picas overall on the horizontal plane, which is sufficient. Just redo the crop marks so that each left and right margin contains three picas, or instruct the printer to make the proper adjustment.

**3. Book is set up with too much margin space.**
Having too much white space isn't necessarily a problem and you may find that you can go ahead with the book "as is" with those extra large margins. I'm a big believer in white space, whether in ads, in covers, or in book margins. Big margins lend class to a book, especially fiction and poetry works.

You can ask the printer to enlarge your copy somewhat, but to do so effectively, your original needs to be of good quality. If your original is only of marginal quality, blowing it up may give you sloppy results. A slight enlargement, say up to 110 % may or may not be a problem. This is a function, however, of the original resolution quality.

Check with your printer if you have any doubts. In any case, extra white or "breathing" space makes a book more readable.

**4. Book has too many pages.**
Let's say you miscounted somehow and ended up with one or two pages over your signature. Obviously you'll need to get rid of pages and the best place to look is in the back pages, with the second best place being the front pages. You cannot alter the middle pages. Removing any page from the interior can leave missing pages, throw off the page count, and screw up both the index and table of contents. See the section on *Reducing a Book's Page Count* in the Production Chapter.

**5. Book has too few pages.**
If your book is already paged and set to go but lacks enough pages to fill the last signature, you can always throw in blank pages before the last page and after the body of the book. You can call the pages "Notes," leave them blank, or get creative. See the section on *Expanding a Book's Page Count* in the Production Chapter.

## Solutions to Printing Problems
Problems can and do occur in the printing process. Good printers do make mistakes, but if it's their fault, they should make good on it by either doing a **pick-up** on the book, that is, reprinting the book at no charge, or by discounting the bill if you can live with the errors.

Printing errors run the gamut of possibilities. A printer might print your cover backwards, print someone else's picture where yours belongs, print a signature upside down, forget to print a page or pages, print your cover out of registration (so that it 's blurry), improperly dry or coat your cover (so that it peels or looks shopworn), etc, etc, etc. These all have happened to me.

I hate waste and will avoid a pick-up if possible, but sometimes there's no choice. If your cover has been compromised, or there is a serious problem with your introduction or table of contents pages, you have to demand a new printing. Your book's success depends on these areas. If the problem is with the interior of the book or the cover, and won't hurt sales, you can ask for compensation from your printer.

How much?

There's no set answer. It's really a case by case basis where the overriding principle is *fairness* - to yourself and your printer. If the problem is really minor, and doesn't affect much, let it ride. If the problem is more than minor, but not catastrophic, settle on something reasonable if it's the printer's error. If the mistake is your fault, don't blame the printer or ask for compensation because none is due - you have to live with the results.

## ADDITIONAL PRINTING INSTRUCTIONS

In addition to the standard instructions we discussed earlier for handling artwork and ordering the print run, you should instruct the printer to stamp or label the boxes in which the books will be packed. Ask the printer to label the boxes in the following manner:

*Please stamp boxes with the following information:*
- Title of Book
- ISBN Number
- # of Copies in the Box
- Weight of Box
- Publisher

Having the preceding information printed or affixed on the boxes helps all people involved in the packing and warehousing of your books to easily identify the book, and ready it for shipping.

## SHIPPING

Shipping from the printer's plant to your distributor's warehouse, your office, or any other location will be arranged by the printer. Larger shipments, those going by the pallet-full, will be sent care of the larger truckers such as Yellow Freight, Roadway, or whoever else the shipper contracts for the work.

Printers can often consolidate book shipments from several publishers going to the same general destination at nice savings. Make sure to ask if there are any consolidated savings you can take advantage of.

Smaller shipments, those by the box, will be sent by carriers such as UPS or RPS, while artwork may be sent by an overnight carriers.

If you have special instructions on any shipment, such as sending books by USPS book rate or any other method, coordinate with your printer. They'll do their best to accommodate your needs.

Shipments made by the printer on your behalf will be charged to you.

## Shipping Instructions

The printer will want to know your shipping instructions as soon as possible after the job is submitted, but you could really wait, if need be, to deliver them to the printer the day before the job is ready. They don't like to do this at the last minute, but if you need the extra time for certain orders, take it.

It's best to submit your shipping instructions in writing (send by fax if at the last minute) to avoid the possible mistakes that can happen verbally.

## Order Extra Covers

You may need extra covers as sales tools for your own and perhaps some of your distributor's sales efforts, and if you do, they should be ordered at the same time your book is ordered. While the presses are rolling, printing extra covers is a minimal expense.

However, should you order those extra covers after the press run, you're talking big time set-up expenses that would probably price you out of the ball park. So be sure to order extra covers, if needed, along with your print run.

# THE BOOK HAS ARRIVED!

About four-five weeks after your book was submitted to the printer, it will be finished and shipped to you. As you open the box, and see the book for the first time, you'll know the big moment has arrived: The culmination of many months of hard work from the author and publisher - the birth of your new book.

Enjoy the moment, break open the champagne, and then get down to the business of sales and distribution. We'll look at that next.

# 14. DISTRIBUTION & SALES

## INTRODUCTION

Distribution is the name of the game. It is everything. The better your distribution network, the more books you're going to sell. No two ways about it: Distribution is the single most important facet of your publishing business. No matter how good of a job you do putting your books together, if you can't reach your potential market, those books won't sell.

You have many choices available; from selling the books yourself (the worst choice in my opinion), to going with an exclusive distributor (the best choice). There are distribution possibilities in between; commissioned sales rep groups, individual sales reps, national and regional wholesalers, jobbers and IDs, and sales based almost wholly on mail order and advertising. Typically, a successful publishing operation will use some combination of the above in getting their books out on the market and making sales.

In this chapter, we'll show just what each one of these distributors does, the kinds of discounts you need to think about when dealing with them, what to expect from their distribution, and just what's involved in the whole process.

The discussion on distribution is not just about getting your books out there, it's about the cost, efficiency, and amount of work involved in doing so as well. We'll start with the basics - self-distribution as opposed to using distribution agents - and then we'll go over the various possibilities in the distribution process and how each can work to support your publishing program.

## Self-Distribution vs. Trade Distribution

When it comes to deciding on a direction in the distribution world, the choice is clear in my opinion - using distributors, sales reps, and wholesalers are a better and more profitable choice for publishers than self-distribution.

Not only will these agents reach the bookstore market more efficiently than you can possibly do through your own efforts, but booksellers would rather buy books from these consolidated sources than directly from smaller publishers. It's not that bookstores aren't supportive of small publishers and their programs - they certainly are, where possible - it's just that they are loathe to order directly from undue multiple sources and deal with the additional hassles, costs, and paperwork involved in buying from smaller accounts. Booksellers will buy direct from smaller publishers, and it is a viable way to sell books, but overall, it's not the best way for you to sell books.

Only large publishing houses, companies such as Random House and Simon & Schuster, can afford their own exclusive sales force and the huge costs involved in paying the salaries, commissions, and expenses. Short of a company this size, the rest of the publishing world needs to rely on distribution channels such as those we'll discuss in this section.

With that in mind, let's start with your best choice, the **National Exclusive Distributors**.

# NATIONAL EXCLUSIVE DISTRIBUTORS

The best way to sell books is through the services of a national exclusive distributor. They'll put your books in touch with countless more buyers than you can ever hope to reach through your own efforts. You'll reach more outlets, make more money, have less headaches, work less, and have more free time to pursue other books, or take long vacations if that's what you wish to do.

The distributor not only has an "in" with buyers and provides services in helping you properly market your book, but if they're good, their reputation is behind every book sold and this will help you sell books. They sell direct to the independent and chain bookstores, to wholesalers, and sometimes to jobbers and specialty stores as well. They demand exclusive trade representation of a publisher's books to the trade, and as long as they do a good job, that's great news for your company.

National exclusive distributors represent independent publishers and differ from other players in the distribution process, such as wholesalers and jobbers, in that they rely on an aggressive sales force to alert and sell bookstores the titles they represent. Their sales force may consist of a network of independent reps threaded throughout the country to cover all geographic zones, a sales force wholly employed by the distributor, or some combination of the two.

Distributors work on a consignment basis, report monthly sales, and typically offer other valuable services including warehousing and order fulfillment. You'll be giving up approximately 60% of the retail price for this relationship, but it's a discount well worth giving. For that price, the exclusive distributors take care of all the work involved in the marketing, distributing, shipping, warehousing, invoicing and collecting of money. They often offer additional services and consultation on the book itself; cover design, editorial objectives, and overall marketing of a line of books. Simply put, your main job is to provide them with good books and cash your checks.

Many publishers new to the distribution game are put off by the 60% discount and figure they can do better than that by themselves. They can't. When you add up all the costs involved in making the original sale, actual order-taking, warehousing, fulfilling, packing, shipping, invoicing, collecting, and bookkeeping, and realize that bookstores and wholesalers need to be given a discount of between 40%-55%, and that you won't make nearly as many sales as a distributor, and won't collect the same percentage of receivables as the distributor (you have less leverage to collect from bad payers - this is a major problem for many small publishers), then you'll find that 60% or so discount is quite fair.

See the *Income From Distribution* section in the *MAKING MONEY* chapter for a further discussion of the discounts.

Sound like it's all advantages, and it is, as long as you have a good distributor. Now the questions are: How do you find a good distributor? How do you know that the distributor will be good for your program? And how do you get your desired distributor to take your books?

Let's look at each one in turn.

## Finding Distributors for Your Books

Doing your own market research for finding qualified distributors, whether large, small or specialized, helps ensure you'll make the best choice and find the most appropriate distribution network for your books.

Whether you're looking for exclusive national distributors, or distributors of any kind, the best way to find good distributors for your products is to go to those locations and retail outlets where either your book would be an appropriate fit or where similar items are sold. Ask to speak to the buyer, manager, or owner, whoever does the buying for that location, and strike up a conversation.

After introducing yourself and the books you're publishing, immediately let the buyer know that you would like to sell your products to him, but through a distributor if possible, so you can reach other like stores in the regional area. Basically, you want to find out which distributors service their account and whom they would recommend for your books.

The buyer will be more than happy to help you out with names and numbers of distributors, or commissioned sales reps they feel give them the best service. He may even request that you sell them direct meanwhile or suggest other ideas that will prove valuable.

Do this market research at all bookstores and appropriate locations you can get to. For example, if your book is about vitamin therapy, approach not only the local bookstores in your area, but the health food and metaphysical bookstores as well.

Take good notes and add up the opinions until you have a good feel of who is good and who is less good. Ideally, you would like these opinions to come from bookstores in several cities, but practically speaking, this is often not possible.

I generally find that three or four stores gets the job done for me, or in the case of an airport gift shop, or perhaps local convenience stores, there will usually be only one distributor, and he will have an exclusive on the placement of books there.

## Contacting Distributors

Once you have a list of possible distributors, get out your pad and pencil and start calling. Find out the person who handles new accounts and get the ball rolling.

Introduce yourself and your company and *briefly* outline what your books are about and why they'll be solid sellers. The distributor will have some basic questions to see if your publishing program is a good fit, but basically, there's not much that could be said until they see an actual sample of your book or books and can judge for themselves. Get the quick pitch in, but don't overdo it. Talk is cheap at this stage. They need to see some action, your books.

You'll have to send out samples of your book or books (make sure your covers are good or you will not be taken seriously) along with a strong cover letter telling them how essential your book is, and the need it fills in the marketplace. *Sell* your book. Don't be shy, hold nothing back - all cannons firing.

## What Do Distributors Want to Hear?

Why your book will sell. Period. They couldn't care less if your book covered the true second coming of the Messiah, if it was a guaranteed cure to cancer, or if it was one of my lotto books going to make you a millionaire. They only care - bottom line - that the book will move off their shelves and sell. That's their business.

If you can't convince a distributor that your book will be bought, then there's no reason they should carry it.

Well then, how do you show the distributor that your book will be bought?

## Sales Technique

When you get your buyer on the phone, don't waste anyone's time. For maximum effectiveness, get to the point and stick to the point. Here's how my call may go.

The buyer says "Hello, this is Vicenzo Martelli." I come back as follows.

"Hello Vicenzo, my name is Avery Cardoza, I'm with Cardoza Publishing in New York. We've just published a book called, *The New Way to Fish*, and I think it's a perfect fit for your market. It's 120 pages, trade size, 5 1/2 x 8 1/2, lists for $8.95, and basically, addresses... (briefly describe the book's specific appeal to its audience, how it's unique, and let the conversation ride from there).

This gets the message across sweet and simple. There are other ways to sell, and other approaches to use, but don't try them in front of me. I don't want to hear about the weather, your back or your golf game. I've trained a lot of salespeople through my direct mail advertising company, my magazine, and of course, my book publishing businesses, and I've always found that the most effective approach is the most direct. Here's who I am, who I'm with, what I've got, what it's good for, and how it will be successful. And take it from there.

Tell the buyer what you've got and how it's going to benefit them. Small talk is okay *after* the basic pitch, if you're comfortable with that style and it's appropriate, but don't start out a conversation with, "How's the weather" - please! Get to the point and make the conversation relevant before bringing in a more personal basis to the conversation.

## Following Up
A few days after your book has arrived, get on the phone and call the buyer. If he or she is busy, call back later, and if he hasn't had the chance to look at the book yet, find out when he will and call back again. Be persistent. If you don't follow-up, he or she may turn down your book just because they didn't get around to either looking at it carefully, or as silly as this sounds, calling you back. The buyers are busy, and may like your book, but may not have time to deal with it. I've turned down books I've liked and wanted to publish just because I got too busy and never made that one simple phone call.

Do not expect the buyer to read your book and don't ask him if he did. If you're really curious despite this advice, I'll answer the question for you. *No, it wasn't read.* Buyer's don't have the time.

Buyers judge your book just like a browser judges a book in the bookstore. *They will look at your cover* and make a snap judgment based upon its quality. The buyer will also peruse the contents of your book rapidly to see the quality of the presentation and writing, and this will have some weight. However, it's the bottom line marketability of that book that the buyer is interested in. And it is the cover (and overall presentation of the book), the price, and the subject matter that will be the biggest factors in the decision.

*You cover will quite likely make or break this deal.* I emphasize over and over in this book the importance of the cover. In marketing your book, that's what it's all about. Of course, the quality of the book itself counts, the list price compared to perceived value, and what they think they can do with your book. They're all factors. But the cover is king.

# CHOOSING YOUR DISTRIBUTOR OR SALES REP

You not only want to answer their questions about your books and plans, but want to ask some as well. Get a sense of this distributor's size, what their vision is, and how you might fit into their plans.

## ASKING QUESTIONS TO POTENTIAL DISTRIBUTORS

You should find out about the following information:

- How many accounts do they service, and how do they service them?

- What makes them better than their competitors? (Find out who the competitors are and call them as well).

- How many sales can they make? (Keep in mind that there is really no way they can answer this question, but the way they respond will give you significant information to mull over.)

- What kinds of publishers and books do they distribute?

- On the financial side, you'll have a bunch of questions?
  - What percentage is paid for each sale?
  - How they report sales, when they pay for them?
  - Who pays shipping?
  - How are returns handled?
  - What extra charges are there to do business with them?
  - Do they warehouse books - is there a charge for this?
  - Do they do fulfillment of your own orders (to non-bookstore accounts for example?

## Choosing a National Distributor

Your particular publishing program will have various degrees of appeal to each distributor approached, and in turn, each distributor will have their own strengths and weaknesses for your program. Some will match up for you better than others, so you'll have to weigh your options and make your own carefully formed judgments.

Before deciding on a distributor, you must check their reputation with bookstores whom they serve and with the publishers they represent. You want to feel certain that the distributor does a good job, is reputable, pays their bills, and, also important, is in good financial condition. You don't want to get left holding the bag if your distributor suddenly goes out of business as happened several years ago to some publishers when a distributor called Kampmann went kaput and their publishers got burned.

Get a range of views on distributors you're considering by checking *at least* three publishers represented by them so that when your decision is made, it's an educated one, a decision you feel comfortable with. If at all possible, try to visit the distributor as well. There is no better way to get a sense of a company than to actually see their offices.

## Big or Little?

Hopefully by this point, you've narrowed down your possibilities to two good prospects; the big distributor and the small distributor. The classic choice. What to do? Both distributors sound good, but only one can be chosen. There's a lot to be said for each one's advantages and disadvantages, and you really need to take a long, hard look since so much rides on this decision.

The big distributor offers a powerful sales presence and large line of books, with the risk of getting lost in the shuffle. The small distributor, on the other hand, lacks the presence and market power of the bigger competitor, but offers extra enthusiasm and personal care.

Of utmost importance in your decision is that your book program, of whatever size, is important to the distributor. I would not seriously consider anyone that didn't make the right noises about my books. The distributor doesn't have to feel that they're the good lord's gift to publishing, but they certainly better feel enthusiastic about my books and like what my program is about. If you don't get that feel from a distributor, take your books elsewhere.

If the big distributor likes what you have, but you don't get the feeling from your conversations that they feel it's important to them, or that they're excited about your books, they're probably the wrong choice. You want to hear the exciting things they'll do with your books, the sales they'll make, the markets they'll reach. Lacking this, this distributor doesn't sound good for you - I would go with the smaller one who does care about your books.

It doesn't matter how big or how many stores a distributor might reach; if they're not going to push your books, all that power won't do you any good. If the big distributor, on the other hand, makes a big pitch for your books, you've got to feel secure that you won't get lost in their program. And, if the answer is positive, that the big boy can get your books out there and you're comfortable with the organization, than that's certainly the way to go. Bigger is better under these conditions - there's no doubt about it. If they won't push your program though, than smaller is better.

It's really a tough decision whether to go big or little, and the only way to come up with the correct decision is to go ask a lot of questions and do a good job with your research. Call other publishers they represent, get a better feel of the distributor's strengths and weaknesses, and how well they pay.

## List of National Exclusive Distributors

On the following page, I have listed the main national exclusive distributors in the United States, along with their contact information. There are other distributors available; check the *American Wholesalers and Distributors Directory*, the *Literary Market Place*, or the *Book Publishing Resource Guide* for more listings. See *Appendix F: Recommended Resources*, for more information.

When contacting distributors, it's always best to make contact first on the phone before sending your books and sales materials. Identify yourself as a publisher and ask for either the acquisitions department or the person who handles new publisher accounts.

The national exclusive distributors listed below employ an active national sales force to sell their publishers books into the general book trade. When discussing your books with a potential distributor, you want to get a sense of their enthusiasm for your line and whether it would be a good fit with their overall program.

We've listed the distributors in alphabetical order.

**Associated Publishers Group,** 1501 County Hospital Road, Nashville, TN 37218; (800)635-0204, (615)254-2450, fax (615)254-2408.

**Associated Publishers Group,** 3356 Coffey Lane, Santa Rosa CA 95403; (707)542-5400, fax (707)542-5444.

**Consortium Book Sales & Distribution,** 1045 Westgate Drive, Suite 90, Saint Paul, MN 55114; (800)283-3572, (612)221-9035, fax (612)221-0124.

**Independent Publishers Group,** 814 N. Franklin St., Chicago, IL 60610; (800)888-4741, (312)337-0747, fax (312)337-5985.

**Login Publishers Consortium,** 1436 West Randolph Street, Chicago, IL 60607; (800)626-4330, (312)432-7650, fax (312)733-3107, (800)334-3892.

**National Book Network,** PO Box 190, 15200 NBN Way B, Blue ridge Summit, PA 17214; (800)462-6420, fax (800)338-4550.

**Publishers Distribution Services,** 6893 Sullivan Road, Grawn, MI 49637; (800)345-0096, (616)276-5196, fax (800)950-9793, (616)276-5197.

**Publishers Resources,** 1224 Heil Quaker Blvd., La Vergne, TN 37086; (800)937-5557, fax (800)774-6733.

**Publishers Group West,** 1700 4th St., Berkeley, CA 94710; (800) 788-3123, fax (510) 528-3444.

**SCB Distributors,** 15608 S. New Century Drive, Gardena, CA 90248; (800)729-6423, fax (310)532-7001.

**Small Press Distribution,** 1341 7th Ave., Berkeley, CA 94210; (800)869-7553, (510)524-1668, fax (510)524-0852.

**The Talman Company,** 89 5th Ave. Suite 802, New York, NY 10003; (800)537-8894, (212)352-1770, fax (212)352-1772.

# INDEPENDENT SALES REPS

There's a vast network of independent sales reps and sales rep groups whose sole purpose is to gather a good line of titles, much as a distributor would do, and sell those books into accounts in their territory. The key concern in choosing sales reps, as in distributors, is to find ones who are enthusiastic about your books and who have a good reputation in the trade. Many large and small publishers use the services of independent reps and it's certainly a valid option to consider.

Independent sales reps differ from distributors in that they're only responsible for the sales. The publisher handles all else: shipping, billing, warehousing - all the business things that would be done in a national distribution relationship. The reps may carry as many as 50 lines of books from various publishers which is a lot of books, or as few as 10 lines or less.

The sales reps make their money on commissions, the more they sell, the more they make. The standard commission is 10% of net for bookstore sales and 5% of net for wholesalers and chains. Net is defined as a percentage of the invoice amount from the publisher. Some groups pay a higher percentage, some lower. Returns and non-paying accounts are credited against sales - if you don't get paid on a sale, neither does the rep. Payment is expected by the reps 30-90 days after the close of the month in which books were shipped, not when the order itself is taken.

Like distributors, sales reps expect exclusivity in the trade on accounts sold in their area, and expect credit on sales whether the sale is made by them or by you. Their sales area is their domain, and they expect to be supported in their efforts - that is, not to have the rug pulled out on them in the area they represent you in. While trade accounts include bookstores, they do not typically include libraries, gift shops, individual sales, and special sales you may make outside the book trade.

Reps spend the majority of their time on the road and are generally reachable only in the evenings, or by leaving messages on their machines. They're out selling your books and earning their money. (If you can find them consistently, then you've got a rep who's not selling your books and you better find one who *will* work.) Important accounts may be seen 2-3 times a year, while less important accounts, smaller bookstores, may be seen but once in the cycle. Additionally, the rep may make numerous phone calls to keep in touch with his or her accounts.

Independent reps and rep groups use the covers of your books as their main sales tools. The actual books themselves are too bulky to carry around on their sales calls, especially when you consider how many books they may be representing.

With basically only your cover and the title of your book to make that initial splash, and a time-span of perhaps between 30 seconds and a minute or more, you get a feel how crucial the cover is to the success of your book.

## US REP SALES TERRITORIES

Traditionally, the United States is divided into six book-selling territories;

**New England:** Connecticut, Maine, Massachusetts, New Hampshire, Rhode Island, Vermont.

**Mid-Atlantic:** Delaware, District of Columbia, Maryland, New York, New Jersey, Pennsylvania.

**Southeast:** Alabama, Florida, Georgia, Mississippi, North Carolina, South Carolina, Tennessee, Virginia.

**Southwest:** Arkansas, Louisiana, Oklahoma, Texas.

**Midwest:** Illinois, Indiana, Iowa, Kansas, Kentucky, Michigan, Minnesota, Missouri, Nebraska, North Dakota, Ohio, South Dakota, West Virginia, Wisconsin.

**West:** Alaska, Arizona, California, Colorado, Hawaii, Idaho, Montana, Nevada, New Mexico, Oregon, Utah, Washington, Wyoming.

While there are many benefits from a sales rep relationship, in particular, getting (hopefully) excellent distribution and having a team of skilled professionals sell your books into the trade, there are shortcomings as well.

Your bookkeeping, accounts receivable and shipping staff will be kept busy. Each bookstore that is sold must be invoiced, must be shipped, and must be reminded to pay if their bill becomes outstanding. When payments are received, bookkeeping must enter the check and the credit on the account. Multiply these operations by each sale made, and you're running a labor intensive business. You'll also deal with 3-10% of your bills not getting paid, and with cash-flow problems as bookstores hold payments for 60 days, 90 days and longer. Being small means you have less leverage in collecting money, and may be at the bottom of the totem pole when bookstores pay their bills. Welcome to the business world!

If a national distributor doesn't fit your plans, and you can hook up with good reps and rep groups, they're a great way to reach bookstore accounts you'd have no other way of selling.

## Finding Rep Groups

One of your best sources for reps is the reps trade organization itself. The **NAIPR** (National Association of Independent Publishers Representatives) puts out a free directory of their membership, and a useful book, also free, entitled *Selling on Commission*.
**NAIPR**, 45 Wayside Inn Rd., Framingham, MA 01701; (508)877-5328, fax (508)788-0208.

Ask around the bookstores in your area for recommendations of reps and rep groups. Take a consensus, see who gets recommended and contact the best choices. Also check LMP under the listing "US Book Distributors & Sales Representatives" for a listing of sales reps and their territories. Classified ads in *Publishers Weekly* and *American Bookseller Magazines* (check libraries or bookstores) should lead to good contacts as well.

The annual ABA extravaganza every Memorial Day weekend, now held in Chicago, is a great place to hook up with reps as well. There are bulletin boards where you can post notices to attract reps to your line, or find reps looking to find lines.

## Computerizing Operations

If you go the route of rep groups, or start to develop a larger, more complicated operation, you'll need to computerize to stay efficient. We've listed two companies that sell software targeted to the book trade. (See Appendix D for brief reviews on these products.)

**PIIGS**, Upper Access Inc., P. O. Box 457, Hinesburg, VT 05461; (800)356-9315, fax (802)482-3125.
**Cat's Pajamas,** 1253 Highway 20, Anacortes, WA 98221; (800)827-2287, (360)293-8372.

# LARGE PUBLISHERS AS DISTRIBUTORS

Some of the larger publishers also serve as distributors and will pick up other publisher's titles for distribution. You can look into this possibility for your books and see if the match is good. For example, in 1997, we moved our line away from a large distributor who started ignoring our needs, and went with a mid-size publisher where our line was more important to their overall program. Our new distributor was able to represent us much better to the trade.

A big advantage of using a large publisher as your distributor (as opposed to going solo) is the clout they carry in the marketplace. A larger publisher with a solid line will have excellent standing with independents and chains and can get a friendly ear on new titles they bring with them to sell. And, as compared to a small publisher selling books on their own and possibly being at the bottom of the totem pole when it comes to getting paid, the big publisher enjoys a lot more leverage. Few stores can afford to be without the best-sellers and the bread and butter backlist titles of the big publishers. And this means they'll pay their bills a lot more readily than otherwise.

One fear I would have with large publishers is that my books would play second fiddle to their in-house line and not get the proper attention. But that is the same fear I would have with any large distributors who can just as easily lose your line as a big publisher could. Thus, you'll need to do careful research when choosing distributors. You want your potential distributor to say the right things, have a good reputation, and come with good recommendations from other publishers doing business with them.

Check the *Book Publishing Resource Guide* and *LMP* for listings of publishers who distribute for other publishers.

# WHOLESALERS

Wholesalers basically serve as a one stop shopping center for independent bookstores, chains and libraries. They stock a huge variety of titles from a wide range of publishers. Bookstores count on wholesalers for rapid service and a place where one phone call can fill all their ordering needs.

Wholesalers don't typically use a sales force to promote sales, and instead, are *passive* sellers - they rely on their catalogues, warehouse displays and microfiche as their main sales tools. They are basically order takers, filling demand as opposed to creating it. Creating this demand is the job of the publisher.

Wholesalers provide an attractive alternative to direct ordering from publishers or distributors by providing faster service to their bookstore accounts, typically filling orders within a day, while publishers may take weeks or even months to get an order out. Also, by consolidating orders, there's only one collective charge for shipping and one account to do the billing. Ordering books from a multitude of sources adds up to extra shipping costs and lots of paperwork for bookstores who have to deal with an umpteen number of publishers.

Wholesalers often supply other services in the form of advertising vehicles to help publishers reach their primary markets. They may sell advertising space in their catalogues or trade magazines, provide direct mailing or telemarketing services to their customers, or even a phone update service to alert buyers of new titles.

**Plus sales**, which is really a term retailers use more than wholesalers, is one way wholesalers might actively sell a title. When retail customers call to place an order the order taker may also suggest other titles - hence the term, *plus sales*. Wholesalers will charge an advertising fee for this service, which, depending upon the book, may or may not work well. Plus sales work well for hot titles and books that buyers already know about, generally because the books have had publicity, but may not be as effective as an introduction for new titles.

# National Wholesalers

**Ingram** and **Baker & Taylor** are the two biggest national wholesalers. The third largest, **Golden-Lee**, has bowed out of the picture. A large chunk of the book business goes through these two giants. They service nearly every bookstore in the country, and are important cogs in the wheel of the book industry. Keep in mind that these wholesalers do much of their business by filling demand, not creating it.

It will be up to your book to generate its own demand, whether through reviews in the major trade periodicals, which are very important for certain titles, in-store promotions, or just simply good packaging and audience targeting, what we do with our books at Cardoza and Open Road.

To have your titles considered for distribution, you'll need to send a sample book, or if you publish a line of books, several of the better books, along with a cover letter explaining your market strategy and how bookstores and individuals will find out about your books, or simply, why they will sell.

The national wholesalers generally ask for a 55% discount, 90 days net, with all books being returnable. We'll look at each wholesaler in turn.

**Ingram Book Company**, c/o Book Acquisitions, One Ingram Blvd., LaVergne TN 37086; (800)937-8222. Ingram is not only the largest national book wholesaler in the country, they're also a giant in video and software distribution as well. If nothing else, you should try to establish an account with Ingram as virtually every bookstore in the country orders books through them.

Ingram supplies the trade from their seven warehouses, located in Walnut City (California), Fort Wayne (Indiana), Avon (Connecticut), LaVergne (Tennessee), Denver (Colorado), (Petersburg) Virginia, and their newest location, Roseburg (Oregon). Central buying is from the main office located in LaVergne, Tennessee. They're known for having a huge selection of titles (over 275,000 titles) and fast service provided from their various geographical warehouses. Most of their book sales are to the bookstore market, but they service libraries as well.

**Baker & Taylor Books**, Attn: New Publisher Contact, 50 Kirby Ave.,

Summerville, NJ 08876; (908)218-0400. Baker & Taylor's national headquarters in Charlotte, North Carolina, is supported by its four warehouses in Momence (Illinois), Commerce (Georgia), Somerville (New Jersey), and Reno (Nevada). While B & T does most of their sales to the library and school market, they do service many bookstores, and take pride in their very large data base of more than 20,000 publishers. They are the largest library wholesaler in the United States and can supply virtually any book in print - more than 1,500,000 active books are in their database.

## Regional Wholesalers

The regional wholesalers buy at a 50%-55% discount on a consignment basis. Since the book industry works on returns, it doesn't matter whether the books are sold on consignment or are actual sales with return privileges. Either way turns out the same.

While most of the regional wholesalers do ship nationally, we've listed them as regional wholesalers since they are strongest in their geographical location. They typically service bookstores, libraries and schools, with many of these wholesalers now stocking multi-media titles in addition to books.

Following is a selected list of regional wholesalers you might want to contact. (Toll-free 800 numbers are not listed since these are generally reserved for order-taking.)

**American Wholesale Books**, P.O. Box 219, Industrial Park, Florence, AL 35630; (205)766-3789, fax (205)764-2511. Wholesales general interest titles to the South while slowly expanding into the Northeast.

**Bookazine**, 75 Hook Road, Bayonne, NJ 07002; (800)221-8112, (201)339-7777, fax (201)339-7778. Ships books and multi-media mostly to East Coast accounts. Carries over 60,000 titles, 20,000 of which are juvenile.

**Bookmen**, 525 North 3rd Street, Minneapolis, MN 55401; (800)328-8411, (612)359-5757, fax (612)359-5727. Services the North-Central (Upper Midwest) United States. Over 50,000 titles in stock.

**Bookpeople**, 7900 Edgewater Drive, Oakland, CA 94621; (800)999-4650, (510)632-4700, fax (510)632-1281. The largest small press wholesaler,

they're very strong with specialty stores. Bookpeople buys on consignment from more than 3,000 publishers, stocks 30,000 titles and publishes thick catalogues twice a year. They're strongest in California and
both sides of the Pacific Rim (Asia and North America).

**Booksource**, 1230 Macklind Avenue, St. Louis, MO 63110; (800)444-
0435, (314)647-0600. Services the Midwest.

**The distributors**, 702 S. Michigan, South Bend, IN 46601; (800)348-
5200, (219)232-8500. The distributors (they use the small "d") is a general trade wholesaler with accounts mostly in the Midwest.

**LTC Group**, 1436 W Randooph, Chicago, IL 60607; (800)243-0138,
fax (800)334-3892. Specializes in carrying small and independent publishers. They sell mostly to alternative stores in the Eastern US. Their
accounts include feminist, gay, political, Afro-American, and literary
stores.

**Koen Book Distributors**, 10 Twosome Drive, Moorestown, NJ 08057;
(800)257-8481, (609)235-4444. Operates East of the Mississippi. Has
about 2,000 accounts. Mails every Friday to their accounts using themes
such as Black History Month or Children's Books to promote their
catalogue.

**L-S Distributors**, 130 East Grand Ave, South San Francisco, CA 94080;
(800)654-7040, (650)873-2094, fax (650)873-4222. Regional wholesaler
to Northern California based in the San Francisco area. Stocks over
30,000 books.

**Koen Pacific Distributors**, 18249 Olympic Ave. S., Tukwila, WA 98188;
(800)444-7323, (206)575-7544, fax (206)575-7444. Regional wholesaler
to the Northwest region buys from publishers on consignment and
stocks close to 20,000 titles. The Koen group in New Jersey recently
expanded to the Northwest and purchased the phone number from
the now-defunct Pacific Pipeline.

**Partners Book Distributing**, 2325 Jarco Dr., Holt, MI 48842; (800)336-
3137, (517)694-3205, (517)694-0617. Wholesales predominantly to Great
Lakes region. Specializes in books about Great Lakes area, native and
black American books, and children's titles.

**Richardson's Books**, 2014 Lou Ellen Lane, Houston, TX 77018; (800)392-8562, (713)688-2244, fax (713)688-8420. Wholesales general interest titles to Texas and the surrounding region.

**Southern Books**, 5154 NW 165th Street, Hialeah, FL 33014; (800)966-7323, (305)624-4545, fax (305)621-0425. Regional wholesaler in the Florida region, stocks more than 15,000 titles.

## Some Specialty Wholesalers & Distributors

**Alpenbooks**, 3616 South Road C1, Mukilteo WA 98275; (425)290-8587, fax (425)290-9461. Sells their line of outdoor-related books, videos and maps to outdoor-oriented outlets .

**Christian Book Distributors**, P.O. Box 7000, 140 Summit Street, Peabody, MA 01960; (978)532-5300, fax (978)977-5010. Specializes in religious books and videos.

**De Vorss & Company**, P.O. Box 550, Marina Del Rey, CA 90294; (800)843-5743, (800)331-4719 - in California, (213)870-7478, fax (310)821-6290. Distributes (and publishes) new age, spiritual, occult, self-help, inspirational books. Carries more than 4,000 books, plus audio and interactive software.

**Gale Research Company**, 835 Penobscot Building, Detroit, MI 48226; (800)877-4253, (800)414-5043. Distributes (and publishes) general reference books.

**Homestead Book Company**, 6101 22nd Ave. N.W., Seattle WA; 98107; (800)426-6777, (206)782-4532, fax (206)784-9328. Specializes in alternative lifestyle and pop culture books.

**J A Majors Company**, 1851 Diplomat Drive, Dallas, TX 75234; (800)633-1851, (972)247-2929, fax (972)888-4800. Specializes in scientific and medical books from more than 200 publishers. Stocks over 30,000 titles.

**Motorbooks International**, PO Box 1, Osceola, WI 54020; (800)458-0454, (715)294-3345, fax (715)294-4448. Specializes in books and transportation-related titles.

**Nacscorp**, 528 E. Lorain St., Oberlin, OH 44074; (800)321-3883, fax (800)344-5059. Wholesaler of academic and trade books, audio and software products, servicing college and university bookstores across the country.

**New Leaf Distributing**, 401 Thornton Rd., Lithia Springs, GA 30122; (800)326-2665, fax (800)326-1066. Largest wholesaler of new age, spiritual, and metaphysical books, videocassettes and audio tapes.

**Samuel French Trade,** 7623 Sunset Blvd., Hollywood, CA 90046; (213) 876-0570, fax (213) 876-6822. Distributes theatre, film, performing arts.

**Samuel Weiser**, Box 612 York Beach, ME 03910; (800)423-7087, (207)363-4393, fax (207)363-5799. Distributes alternative, new age, esoterica, self-help books. Warehouses over 3,000 titles.

**Spring Arbor Distributors**, 10885 Textile Road, Belleville, MI 48111; (800)395-5599, (313)481-0900, fax (800)395-2682. Largest wholesaler of religious books to Christian outlets. Stocks more than 70,000 items.

# JOBBERS

**Jobbers**, sometimes known as **rack jobbers**, or **ID's** (Independent Distributors), service book racks in non-traditional book outlets such as supermarkets, drug stores, airports, convenience stores, grocery stores and supermarkets, and the like. The jobbers have exclusive control over what books are placed on the shelves in these locations. Their job is to place the books on these shelves that they think will sell best.

The majority of books placed by the jobbers will be mass-market bestsellers, strong selling regional and special interest books, and other books with strong sales potential for the area. Typically, the jobbers have a limited number of spots to place their goods, so they pay careful attention to stocking and placing the books that will be most popular for the location.

Newspapers and magazines make up the majority of a jobbers business, perhaps as high as 90%. Books may account for the other 10% of their business, but that 10% will be important to them. The actual ratio will vary from one location to another.

Rack jobbers deal almost exclusively with mass market sized books, 4 1/4 x 6 3/4, for these are the books that fit onto their racks. Larger sized titles, trade paper (5 1/2 x 8 1/2) and over, are too big for these racks, and may only fit in a few of the rack jobbers outlets. Thus, to talk turkey with a jobber, you'll pretty much need to be discussing mass market-sized titles.

Most jobber's territories are confined to one-city or one-region businesses and they typically operate and often will be the only choice in an area. They demand exclusivity with their accounts, and generally need a 50% discount. You may get bargained down to 55%, but go no lower than that. You'll be expected to pick up shipping, but again, that's part of the negotiating process.

You can find jobbers either through the LMP's directories or by asking any news shop or airport gift shop in the area who receives their books, magazines and newspapers. If you're passing through an airport, drop in on one of the gift shop/newsstands and get the buyer's number.

The two biggest jobbers, with operations across the country were Aramark and Anderson News. However, Anderson News took over Aramark and is now the single largest jobber with no competitors anywhere near the size of this giant operation. Their local agencies stretch right across the country, operate on a semi-autonomous basis, and do their own buying. National headquarters can make recommendations as well, but typically, the local operations will be run locally.

**Anderson News**, *National Office*: PO Box 36003, Knoxville, TN 37931; (423)670-7575, fax (423)470-7388. *Regional Offices*: Contact individually for appropriate books. Anderson is the largest jobber of them all, and owns more than 70 agencies nationwide. In addition to gobbling up Western Merchandisers several years back, Anderson grew yet bigger again by acquiring rival Aramark.

## Stripping Covers

Best-sellers (and other paperbacks), the bread and butter of the jobbers book market, routinely get **stripped**, have their covers removed, when returned to the warehouse. The stripping process occurs daily and in large numbers as the jobber constantly refigures and restocks their racks with the current best titles. The stripped books get destroyed and the covers themselves are returned to the publisher for credit.

If you ever get a chance to visit an ID's warehouse, ask to see their paper shredder, and you will have an eye-opening experience. The number of books stripped weekly and then mulched in their machines (then sold to paper recyclers) is astounding.

While stripping covers is an accepted part of the wholesaling business among large publishers who can afford this waste, it being cheaper to strip than ship and process paperwork on these books, you can insist that your covers not be stripped if your books come back as returns. Your agreement with the wholesaler should state that the covers are *not stripable*, that the books must be returned in saleable condition.

# WHAT HAPPENS IF YOU HAVE TROUBLE GETTING A DISTRIBUTOR?

Not too many things come easy in life, and it's quite possible you'll put your book together, and buyers will not be convinced that it will sell enough to warrant the shelf space. You make the good arguments about your market, and why this book will appeal to them and be bought, but bottom line, you can't get a distributor, sales rep group, chain store, or whatever, that you like.

Don't give up. The sale can be made, but you'll have to prove your book first by establishing a track record of sales so that you can go back to the buyers with some success stories and make a more convincing argument.

Start small and build. Sell it locally or wherever you can get the book placed. Do some local promotions and get some attention directed to the book. Take small success stories back to the buyers, and if they still don't buy, keep on building your sales. With hard work, your business will grow, and barriers will fall. There are lots of places to sell your books, and if you do a good job in producing your book, by following all the steps outlined in this book, success and acceptance will follow.

# DISTRIBUTING YOUR FIRST BOOK

If you're a new publisher, with no track record, or even an established one with a good sales history, distributors will need to see copies of your book before any serious discussions can take place.

Theory and talk may be interesting, but until an *actual* book is seen, nobody will know the type of work you do, what your books will look like, and most important of all, how they'll sell. All the talk in the world about how wonderful your book will be won't mean anything unless they can see a book. Show me, they'll say.

Thus, if you're new to publishing, simply showing a book cover will generally not open doors into the distribution outlets. You'll need to actually produce and print the book, and send a physical copy to the buyer to get the ball rolling. A great advance cover can generate interest, but if the publisher has no track record, the investment of actually printing the book may have to be made.

## GIVING AWAY FREE COPIES TO BUYERS

While you won't need to give away many copies to enhance your success in selling books, in many situations sample books are a necessity of making sales and getting your books promoted. Don't be shy about sending free samples of books to distributors who can set you up with many stores in their network. The more distributors that see your books, the greater the chances are that one of them will pick up your books for distribution.

Free samples should not be sent to individual bookstores or locations that would only be buying a few books at a time. A catalogue or sample cover would be sufficient in this instance. If the bookstore is a buying office for a chain, than I would definitely consider them as I would a distributor, and send the full product.

# SALES & SELF-DISTRIBUTION

Self-distribution can take many forms; from complete self-distribution where you attempt to reach the trade directly through your own efforts and fill all orders, to self-distribution where you enlist the services of wholesalers to help fill orders, to self-distribution where you make sales in addition to the efforts made on your behalf by wholesalers, distributors, sales reps and the like.

The first case, complete self-distribution, is the least preferable way to get your books into the marketplace for the reasons we discussed earlier.* Sometimes it may be the only way to go if your publications are not appropriate for the general book trade (non-book and specialized reports, certain "gifty" books, specialty publications, pricey reference works and such), or if your books initially are not gaining acceptance into the regular book channels. In these instances, direct efforts through advertising, direct mail, catalogues, telemarketing, and personal efforts are the keys to success. And if the books are appropriate for the book market and are done well, perseverance will eventually pay off with some acceptance into the general trade.

In the second case, when you opt to distribute your titles without the aid of sales rep groups and distributors, you should enlist the services of the wholesalers to help keep stores supplied. While bookstores may be supportive of publishers efforts to do their own distribution, they will often prefer to consolidate orders through a wholesaler rather than deal with a multitude of sources for their reorders.

You may not want to give up the extra discount necessary to sell through wholesalers, but if you want to make the maximum amount of sales possible, you'll find that discount well-worth giving. Wholesalers are a necessary and integral part of the book business and trying to get around their services is like shooting yourself in the foot.

Even if you're using distributors, sales reps, and wholesalers, you'll still be selling books direct to individuals (from advertising or promotions), and possibly to retail stores, wholesalers and IDs who may be outside your distributor's or sales rep's network. Below, we'll discuss establishing terms of doing business to serve these markets.

## Setting Your Terms & Discount Schedule

If you sell books outside a distribution network, you'll need to have a discount schedule and a set of terms available for your prospective buyers. On the following page is a sample trade discount schedule:

*Besides the limited distribution and greater costs of sales, you are reminded that a large drawback of self-distribution is the lack of leverage in collecting money. Many self-distributed publishers report long delays in getting paid for their books, and a costly percentage of invoices that don't get paid at all. It's one thing to sell books; it's another thing to get paid for them.

## SAMPLE DISCOUNT SCHEDULE & TERMS

Terms are net 30 days for approved accounts, FOB our warehouse; bills past 60 days payable at 1 1/2% finance charge per month. Books may be returned for credit not less than 90 days nor after 12 months from original invoice. Titles may be mixed to enjoy discount.

| Books | Discount |
|-------|----------|
| 1-4 | 20% |
| 5-9 | 40% |
| 10-49 | 42% |
| 50-99 | 43% |
| 100-249 | 44% |
| 250-499 | 46% |
| 500-999 | 48% |
| 1000+ | 50% |

Notice the return clause which restricts a store from returning books until *after* 90 days. This is to make sure that bookstores ordering your books give them an honest sales effort before returning them.

You should employ a different trade discount when selling to libraries as they do not resell their books. For libraries ordering one or two books, I would charge full price (no discount); and for libraries ordering three or more titles, I would provide a 20% discount.

## How to Put Together Your Catalogue

If the vast majority of your business goes through a distributor who has his own sales catalogue, I recommend you keep your catalogue costs to an absolute minimum. A simple printout on attractive paper detailing your books will work for your other accounts.

On the other hand, if a primary market is getting your book into bookstores using *your* catalogue (and not the distributor's) as a sales tool, or if you intend extensive marketing to individuals or outside markets directly, then the catalogue is an important marketing tool. And when your catalogue is the primary sales tool, using color and maintaining a high quality piece are important - *they will help sell your books*. The catalogue becomes your cover, so to speak, the piece by which your books are judged.

However, if your main dealings are with distributors, and not the individual or bookstore buyer, than your catalogue takes on less importance. It is your work, your books, that will do all the talking, and not your catalogue. The distributor couldn't care less if your catalogue was an award-winning art project by Picasso, or a black and white listing of titles - as long as your books sell. The book itself is your sales piece. The main purpose of your catalogue is to show distributors and buyers a concise listing of your line of books. All the color in the world won't sell your book if the book doesn't sell itself.

Until we began developing the direct marketing side for our gambling line, Cardoza Publishing never had the need for a catalogue that was any more sophisticated than a basic list of our books because our distributor did all the retail sales. But the minute we pursued the individual through mail order, we put money into a glossy, four-color catalogue - with immediate benefits.

## Mail Order Sales

**Mail order sales**, sales solicited through advertising and filled by mail, typically solicited through one's own catalogue, classifieds, or ads in other media, is a great way to make money in publishing. There is no middleman to split profits with (as in a distributor or retail store) since all orders come direct to you. For many publishers, almost the entirety of their business is done through mail order sales.

Mail order generally works best for informational-based books and reports, the same how-to type books that will work well for us in the bookstores, but many other types of books can be marketed successfully this way. As with everything else, targeting your audience is key.

But there's one major difference in the winning formula. To make money selling how-to books through mail order, especially if your predominant strategy is mail order sales, you need to make the products *more expensive* to make money. For many items, the price point should certainly be at least $25, though $50 would be better. Add up all the expenses of buying lists, advertising, shipping, printing, fulfillment of orders, and overhead, and you'll see the need for a higher price point than one would think about in a bookstore item.

While in regular trade publishing, a lot of what we're selling is our presentation; in mail order, the key product we're selling is *information*, and the presentation is not quite as important. We're not selling mail order items by their cover, but instead, by our descriptions of the product.

You do, however, want to do at least an adequate job so your customer feels he or she is getting good value on their purchase. People will pay good money for good information, and will buy your information at higher prices if the perceived value is there. This is in contrast to a bookstore, where readers won't pay as much for information, perceived value being judged on a smaller dollar basis.

The key to successful mail order sales - just like in bookstore sales - is targeting your audience. To be successful, you'll need to advertise in the places where your target audience can be reached, and if you buy mailing lists, as many do, you want them to be good lists with real names. You'll also want to provide this audience with the information most useful to their needs.

You can get lists from mailing list companies, from other companies in the same field who are selling their customer's names, or from a list you've generated yourself. However, before doing any substantial mailing to a list you've bought, test it out with a smaller mailing. There are many bogus lists on the market, and you want to make sure you've got live wires and not deadbeats on the list.

A complete discussion of mail order strategies is beyond the scope of this book, and worthy of its own dedicated text, so if you'll be doing serious mail order sales, you'll want to buy some of the excellent books available.

## Toll-Free 800 Numbers & Credit Cards

If a significant portion of your business will be based on selling to customers directly, you may want to consider setting up an 800 number, but of course, you'll need to be set up with a credit card account so that orders can be taken. Otherwise, a toll-free 800 number won't do you much good. You'll also need to have your phones manned to accept these orders.

Alternatively, you can hire a service that will process toll free orders and credit card accounts, but at a hefty charge.

Without doubt, toll free numbers improve sales. The easier you make it for your customer to order, the more they will order. This is a long-standing truism in the mail order business and one you should always keep in mind.

To establish your own toll free 800 number, you can contact the various long distance phone companies in your area to see which ones will best suit your purposes. To arrange for credit card service, contact your local bank for information or referrals.

# AREAS TO GET EXTRA SALES

Besides the trade book markets as we've covered earlier, there are many more markets to sell your books and increase your business.

I'll detail a few below.

## Specialty, Premium & Incentive Sales

There are many markets beyond the book and library trade - incentives, promotional tie-ins and premiums, specialty stores, and more. With creative lead finding, and a lot of letter sending and follow-up phone calls, you'll be opening doors to sales that could be in the thousands or tens of thousands range.

The main key to success here is simply doing a lot of leg work and letting the various companies associated with the type of book you're doing know that the books you've produced exist, and may be good for their own marketing efforts.

Let's say, for example, that you're publishing books on cat care, or raising happy and obedient dogs. You're ignoring a wonderful market for your books if you didn't let the pet stores know about it. Go into a few pet stores, tell them about your book and find out which of their distributors would be appropriate to contact for the book and would do the best job in distributing it. Or sell them direct. Find out how you can contact other pet stores. Perhaps there's an association of sorts, or an important convention.

And how about cat and dog food makers? A good promotion for them might be, *"Buy two cans of our cat chow and get a free book"*. Sell the companies on ideas that use your book. If your book can make them money, they'll listen. Cat litter companies and pet grooming supply companies are good possibilities as well.

Contact magazines catering to the pet market. Your book may be great for subscription drives, or for a mail order book shop in the back of their magazine. At the very least, you can probably trade articles about pet care for ad space, or sell them the article straight-out.

Make time to find sales in this very lucrative market.

## Selling to the Wholesale Clubs

The big consumer wholesale clubs such as Price-Costco and Sam's, venues which feature huge warehouses of food, household and other consumer goods, are great markets for selling books as well - if you can make a sale into these accounts. While you can sometimes sell directly to the central offices, a good portion of the book buying goes through a company called **Advanced Marketing Services** (AMS). It's worth contacting them to see if your book is a good fit with their customer base.

**Advanced Marketing Services**, 5880 Oberlin Drive, Suite 400, San Diego, CA 92121; (619)457-2500, fax (619)452-2237.

## Catalog Sales

Here's a great way to increase your book sales and procure a steady stream of additional revenues. Catalog companies have highly targeted and excellent mail lists, not to mention a loyal audience, and they're always looking for new products to sell to their customers.

Many catalogues carry books, but even if they don't and your book seems a good fit with their audience, you've got another outlet to sell your books.

## Selling to Book Clubs

Deals with book clubs are a nice way to supplement income from a book, but the typical deal, which is not generous, may leave you wondering whether it's even worth selling to a book club at all. Overall, you'll have to judge for yourself based on the particulars of the deal offered. Some deals may be viewed as marginal, while others may come in as windfalls.

Here's how the typical book club deal works. Royalties, generally no higher than 10%, are based on a percentage of the club's selling price. Their club price will be discounted from the publishers list by as much as 10-30%, sometimes more. For example, if your book normally lists for $20, and the book club sells it for $15, you'll receive 75¢ if a 5% royalty is being paid, and $1.50 if the figure is 10%. They will usually pay a non-refundable advance against royalties. The more you negotiate, of course, the better.

The funds paid from book club sales are typically split 50-50 between the publisher and the author according to the standard clause in many author contracts.

Book clubs either print your books from supplied negatives or tack on an order to your overall print run. If the book club orders from your own print run, they will try to negotiate a deal to cover the cost of their part of the printing. In the case of some of the smaller clubs, they may simply order finished books outright. In addition to the printing costs (which they expect you not to make money on), the book club will pay the royalty as discussed above.

Larger book clubs such as Book-of the-Month Club and Literary Guild will demand exclusivity, which shouldn't present any problem considering the number of books they will move (tons!), but be careful giving that exclusivity to smaller clubs who may not move that many. If a smaller book club won't be selling all that many books, you might make non-exclusivity a condition of the contract.

When trying for sales to book clubs, as with all else, target your book to clubs that may have an interest in your title. For example, don't send a reference book to a club specializing in outdoor sports. Follow up the sending of your manuscript or book with phone calls to the proper editor so they *know* who you and your book are. Persistence gives you the best chances of success.

The major book clubs will want to see your manuscript at least eight weeks *before* publication, preferably even earlier, while smaller clubs may be content to see the finished work. All in all, you have over 200 book clubs as potential sales for your books. A listing of book clubs can be found in the very useful LMP.

## Remainder Dealers

There comes a time in some book's lives, when they've outlived their time and need to go to the book graveyard. That is, they either no longer sell, were bombs to begin with, they were supplanted by new editions, or some of the other myriad reasons a book just is no longer needed or wanted in the general trade.

Well, there's another market out there for these books, one more place you can get money for your books - and that's the remainder dealers, the last resort option for disposing of your books. **Remainder dealers** buy closeouts, overstocked books and titles that are not moving well for pennies on the dollar and then resell these books, also at huge savings, to stores which pass these savings on once again to the consumer. You ever wondered where those 99¢ for-any-book stores were getting their books? Wonder no more.

Remaindering is a great way to move old merchandise out and get cash for it. You can offer your books to several dealers, and take the best offer you receive. Every fall, CIROBE (Chicago International Remainder and Overstock Book Exposition) holds their annual fair in Chicago. Call (312)404-8357 for futher information.

Following is a selected list of remainder dealers.

**Book Sales, Inc.** 114 Northfield Avenue, Edison, NJ 08837; (732)225-0530, fax (732)225-2257.

**Booksmith Promotional Company**, 100 Patterson Plank Road, Jersey City, NJ 07307; (201)659-2768, (718)782-0405, fax (201)659-3631.

**Camex International**, 535 Fifth Avenue, NY, NY 10017; (212)682-8400, fax (212)808-4669.

**Daedalus Books**, PO Box 9132, Hyattsville, MD 20781; (800)395-2665, (301)779-4102, fax (800)866-5578. Buys literary, scholarly, trade remainders.

**Edward R. Hamilton**, Falls Village, CT 06031. Buys general books, send letter listing titles and basic information.

**Marboro Books** (Barnes and Noble), One Pond Road, Rockleigh, NJ 07647, (800)The-book, fax (201)767-6638.

**Publishers Overstock Unlimited**, 149 Madison Ave. Suite 610, New York, NY 10016, (800)736-7336, (212)481-0055, fax (212)213-6074.

**S & L Sales**, 2165 Industrial Boulevard, Waycross, GA 31503, (800)243-3699, (912)283-0210, fax (800)736-7329.

**W.G.P Distributors**, 551 W. Lanchester Avenue, Suite 209, Haverford, PA 19041; (610)525-9957, fax (610) 525-3014.

# THE BOOK MARKET

### US Book Chains and Independents

The 1990's marks a big trend toward the chain and chain superstore, with many smaller and independent book stores getting squeezed out. The **superstore** is a bookstore stocking an inventory of more than 75,000 titles and with more than 10,000 square feet of retail space. In other words, it is very, very big, more than 3-4 times the size of an average book store.

Bigger seems to be better in the 90's, and though some publishers may get hurt by the resultant loss of independents and their supportive small press buys, they also get helped by the fact that the superstores carry many more titles than smaller stores.

The big three books chains, **Barnes and Noble** (B. Dalton, Bookstop, Bookstar, Doubleday, Scribners), **Waldenbooks/Borders** (Brentanos, Readers Market), and **Crown**, accounted for about 40-50% of the market in the mid-90's. However, as the trend toward the domination of the book business by the chains and the squeezing out of the independents and smaller chains continues, this percentage grows higher each year. In addition, a substantial part of **Ingram** and **Baker & Taylor**'s business, the two giant national wholesalers, is in book replenishment to these chain stores as well (they also service smaller chains and independents) making their share of the book market well over 50%.

The next largest bookstore chain, **Books-A-Million**, is expanding rapidly and is often considered part of the "big four." See the discussion in Appendix E for a bigger discussion of the book chain retailers.

If your books are not bought centrally at the chains, it doesn't mean sales can't be made into them. Often, the local branches of the chain stores can make independent buys as can the regional managers, so don't overlook these potential ways to get your book out into the market. If at first a chain store won't buy your book centrally, you can always build on a base of good sales at the local or regional chain level, and go back to the central office with news of your books being bought at their stores and at other chains and independents. If you're not represented by an exclusive distributor or sales rep, you'll want to contact the chain stores yourself. See *Appendix E* for address and contact numbers for some of the chain stores.

Though under pressure from the chains, independents still represent a good part of the market and are important stores to reach.

While there are more than 25,000 outlets selling books, only about 10,000 of these locations could be considered bookstores. Somewhat over 5,000 of these outlets are general trade book stores holding stocks of more than 10,000 books while the remainder of these 25,000 locations include stores which sell books but which wouldn't be considered bookstores such as specialty sellers (Christian, New Age and the like), newsstands, and retail and chain stores which sell books as a sideline.

**Canadian Book Chains**
The two main book chains in Canada, SmithBooks/Classic Bookshops (about 175 stores) and Coles Book Stores (about 250 stores) agreed on a merger in late 1994 to become one big chain. In May 1995, the buyout of Coles Book Stores by SmithBooks became effective. The new entity is called Chapters. See *Appendix E* for address and contact numbers.

---

### SELLING SEASON

There are two main selling seasons for books; **spring**, where sales traditionally begin after the first week in January, and **fall**, with sales beginning in earnest Memorial Day weekend, when the yearly book gala, the ABA, convenes in Chicago. There's an additional, smaller selling season, **winter**, which begins around late September.

# TARGETING THE LIBRARY MARKET

The library market has different needs and requirements from the book trade. For one thing, libraries are more interested in the quality of a book and the versatility it may add to their collection, than necessarily the sales potential of that book. After all, the library is not in the business of reselling books, but rather to serve the public's need, as best these needs can be determined.

Another difference is in the quality. Where we economize in our approach in producing for the general book trade, for certain types of books targeted to the library market, a more expensive quality version (using acid-free paper and hardbound) might be preferable, especially if it's a reference book that will be well-thumbed.

Libraries will buy lesser-priced paperbacks targeted toward the general trade as well, even more so now that they're faced with tighter budgets than in the past.

Getting your books reviewed in the main trade journals is the best way to generate library sales, many of which can go through Ingram and Baker & Taylor, direct, or even through Quality and Unique, the two library distributors we'll speak about next.

## Library Distributors

The following two library distributors, Quality Books and Unique Books, are library distributors who do a good job getting small- to medium-sized publisher's books into the library market. They employ a sales force who call on libraries across the US and Canada, and actively seek new books they can add to their list.

Books are sold on a consignment basis, with flexible payment schedules offered by both. You can choose to sell them books at a 55% discount off list, net 90 days, or 60% off list net 60 days. Statements are delivered at the beginning of each month like clockwork, along with payments for past sales.

Quality and Unique only take new books, and when a book is printed, they'll need sample covers (Quality - 22, Unique - 20) for their salespeople to use in their presentations, so make sure to order extra covers with your print run. They have simple forms they ask to be filled out in advance of a book's publication.

Quality and Unique also offer Cataloging in Publication (CIP) registration as a separate service for publishers who cannot obtain this on their own. Following is the contact information for each company.

**Quality Books**, 1003 West Pines Road, Oregon, IL 61061; (800)323-4241, (815)732-4450, fax (815)732-4499.

**Unique Books**, 4230 Grove Avenue, Gurnee, IL 60031; (800)533-5446, (708)623-9171, fax (708)623-7238.

## LIBRARY-QUALITY BOOKS

While libraries will purchase books they deem to be valuable for their collection, the following items will be of particular value if the books themselves, such as reference books, are targeted toward the library market itself.

## Library of Congress Number, ISBN, LC Number

These are essential data to include in a book of any nature. See the *Getting Official* chapter for information on getting these numbers.

## Index

To give your book the best chance of success and make your work valuable to libraries, many librarians insist that your book include an index. Indices are certainly not necessary for fiction or poetry books, but if you've produced a reference book, that work will be viewed as suspect if no index is included.

If the table of contents is extremely detailed, you may be able to get away without an index for certain types of books. For libraries, however, an index is an index, and the inclusion of one in a book where it's appropriate will increase the saleability of your book to them and is thus recommended.

## Acid Free Paper

Library buyers consider it important that a book is printed on acid free paper. The book will last much longer than one printed on standard book papers and thus, is really a better buy for librarians thinking of long term value.

Older books and newspapers printed on standard paper crumble with age and must be trashed when the disintegration becomes advanced. One buyer told me of newspapers from 50 years ago that had to be brought out, literally, in plastic bags full of decayed pieces. He said that on many of their books there was but one more handling left before they had to be destroyed.

## SOME INDEXING BASICS

- Main headings should be relevant, and directed at the audience. Avoid the term "ferrous oxide" for a lay audience on manufacturing and use "iron." Similarly, for a technical audience, "nitrous oxide" is preferable to "laughing gas".
- More than 6 or 7 page references under a heading should be broken down into subheadings. Similarly, more than 6 or 7 subheadings should be broken down into more headings when appropriate.
- Subheadings should contain the most important word first. "Herds, and the leadership of dominant bull" should be "Herds, dominant bull leader".
- Avoid unnecessary words, articles and prepositions in headings and subheadings. Keep the index concise.
- Double and triple list (*double post* and *triple post*) important headings. "Books: fiction" and "Fiction books" increases usefulness of an index.
- Use the indicative reference "see" when appropriate to help direct reader to term used similarly, on the same topics, and for more related information. For example, "Republican China, *see* **Taiwan**". "Riverboat excursions" *see* **boat trips.** "Chain Stores", *see also names of individual chain stores.*
- Headings and subheadings should be easily distinguished from text and from each other.
- Index should be appropriate for the type of book done. While fiction and poetry books have no need for indexes, reference books, on the other extreme, should have voluminous indexes.
- Index listings stretching across two pages should be followed by the word "(continued)" in parenthesis on the top line of the new page, as in "Printing *(continued)*".

# SELLING TO THE ACADEMIC MARKET

Many academic publishers sell by the **short discount**, a discount of 20% to the trade and 30% to wholesalers. Most of these sales are made outside the regular retail market (where stores generally expect at least a 40% discount) into an audience that is a "captive audience" - students have to buy the book if it's required class reading. To sell to the academic market, requires a lot of sales effort, and of course, the appropriate books.

# 15. MARKETING
## (Advertising & Publicity)

### INTRODUCTION

While some books will sell by virtue of simply being on a shelf, other types of books which may not sell themselves, such as fiction, *need* that extra push if the book is to come to the public's attention and sell enough copies to be considered successful.

There are two basic ways of marketing a book. There's **publicity**, where a book is advanced to the various review media, the author makes appearances to bring attention to the book (such as book signings), or the publisher sets up or joins an event for the same purpose; and **advertising**, where the publisher pays for actual ad space in print, broadcast and other media.

The main purpose of publicity and advertising is to bring a book to the public's attention; to let them know that a book exists and that it may be of interest to them. In general, the more attention a book gets, the more units it is likely to sell. And that of course, is a subject we're interested in - selling books.

In this chapter, we'll go over the basics of getting publicity for your books: How to write a press release and cover letter, where to send them, and how to maximize your chances of getting reviewed; and where to send advance galleys so that reviews can be obtained prior to publication. We also go over the various forms of advertising, and the best way to inform the public about your books.

With that in mind, let's start with publicity, the springboard of success for many books.

# PUBLICITY - GETTING REVIEWS

For some publishers, publicity is the catalyst from which a good portion of their books get sold. Getting publicity in the right venues can lead to hundreds or even thousands of book sales, and can even launch a book onto the best-seller lists. Publicity leads to many other sales as well. Reviews might catch the eyes of subsidiary rights buyers, of other reviewers looking for a good story, or even of talk show hosts looking for an exciting guest.

Book reviews influence people at all levels of the book chain, from buyers stocking library systems and bookstores, to the average consumer looking for a good book to read. In the case of library buyers, a book review, especially a favorable one, brings a book to their attention, and quite possibly leads to an order. For consumers, if a review piques enough interest in a book, it may send them running to a store to purchase it. At the retail level, at the bookstore, extra stock is needed to supply the created demand as consumers come in looking for a book they saw reviewed.

In fact, in all these cases, this review may be the only way that all these people even know that the book exists. Bottom line: A lot of sales get generated from the right review in the right media outlet.

The big publicity machines of the major publishers help churn out best-selling book after best-selling book. While smaller publishers normally can't command the type of attention afforded the major players, they too sometimes score with big hits, and they can certainly be successful in moving their regular titles even if they don't become best-sellers. It's all a matter of effort and persistence.

But not everything has to be a big hit to be successful. Many publishers get some nice publicity going, and move significant numbers of books. And once the books get noticed by the public and the bookstore, they develop sea legs and keep on selling. This success leads to other successes by the same author and publisher.

Time-wise, there are two basic phases in the promotion process: pre-publication reviews and post-publication reviews. Before we move on, let's define the ill-understood concept of the publication date.

# PUBLICATION DATE/SHIP DATE

The **publication date** or **pub date** is the date a book is *announced* as being officially published, not the date a book comes off the press. Typically, the publication date is announced as being six weeks to two months after the ship date, enough time so that a book can get into the stores and be available to the general public for purchase. Keep in mind that publicity is worthless if the book is not available for purchase in the stores.

The **ship date** is the date the books come off the press and are ready to ship. Don't use your ship date as your publication date.

# PRE-PUBLICATION REVIEWS

The pre-publication reviews, reviews that occur *before* a book's publication date, are among the most important reviews a book can get and often lead to very significant sales. The major review publications, which we'll cover in this section, will only review books before a book is printed and available to the general market. To get reviewed in these media, you'll have to submit your work in the proper format.

## How to Submit Pre-Publication Books

There are two generally accepted forms for submitting books before their publication - page proofs and galleys. Manuscripts are sometimes accepted as well, but these are typically accepted only in cases where there is a major author involved, such as a Steven King or Leon Uris, or when a major publishing house is pushing an important title. For the average publisher though, page proofs and galleys are the generally accepted form of submission. We'll look at each below.

A **page proof** is a rough unbound copy of the book as it will appear when published, except that it is typically output on standard 8 1/2 x 11 paper as opposed to the cut and bound size of the book itself. If this proof is bound, it will be called a **bound page proof**. A page proof should be almost fully edited and be in the approximate layout that it will appear when printed. It may be missing the table of contents, index, illustrations and other matter of that type.

**Galleys** used to indicate the long uncut strips that came out of the typesetting process. The revolution in computer publishing technology has changed the meaning of the term. A galley, which is also known as a **bound galley** or **reader's proof**, is a *bound* copy of your book put together before the actual book is printed. Thus, your bound galley should have a plain cover imprinted with the name of the book, the author, and your publishing company. Don't produce the galley with the final cover, for then it will look like the real McCoy (and actually be the real thing) and won't get reviewed. Galleys can be produced either at your local copy shop, or through specialized short run printers who can provide a fast turnaround and low price.

Galleys and page proofs must be in presentable reading form before they are submitted to the appropriate media. *Presentable* means that the galleys are fully written (partial manuscripts will not even be considered for review), edited properly, and in clean form. It is generally acceptable to submit the proof without an index, as long as the galley or page proof indicates that an index will be used (this is very important). It is also acceptable to submit galleys whose illustrations are not yet in place as long as these images are not integral to the galley and the book can properly be judged.

Don't jeopardize a good book's review chances by submitting a galley or page proof in an unedited or unacceptable state. If time permits, do the little extra things that make a book stronger so that readers get the absolute best pre-publication look. Reviewers always stress that the better the form in which a book is presented (bound galleys always being better), the better chance it has of being reviewed.

## Along With the Page Proof or Galley

A one page cover letter that provides an overview of the book in a few lines and lists the author's credentials (if particularly relevant or interesting) should accompany the galley or page proof. If the author had been reviewed by that publication previously with an earlier book, include that as well.

The standard book information (see following page) *must* either be printed on the galley itself, or affixed with glue or an adhesive that will stay. Do not include this information on a loose piece of paper slid into or included separately - it will get lost and it can cost you a potential review.

## Standard Book Announcement Information

The following items must be printed on the cover letter *and* galley itself (for pre-publication reviews) and on the press release (for post-publication reviews): name of book, publication date (not shipping date), author, price, binding, ISBN, number of pages, illustrations if any, distributor, publisher name, address and phone, and contact name and phone number.

---

**THE COMPLETE GUIDE TO SUCCESSFUL PUBLISHING**

Author: Avery Cardoza
Publication Date: January 15, 1999
Price: $19.95, trade paperback, 6 x 9
ISBN: 0940685-94-9, 432 pages, diagrams, charts, illustrations

Published by Cardoza Publishing, 132 Hastings Street, Brooklyn, NY 11235
Distributed by Carol Publishing Group, Ingram Books, Baker & Taylor
Contact: Rose Sally (718)743-5229

---

## Where to Send Galleys - Trade Publications

The publications listed below should be sent bound galleys or page proofs 90 days or more before publication date unless otherwise noted. Books *must* be addressed to the appropriate review editor for your book to get reviewed, so make sure to call each publication to learn the full name and correct spelling of the review editor. With the large volume of books being received, you must make sure your book reaches the proper reviewer. (We've avoided listing names that might become outdated due to an editor having changed positions.)

The three most important media in this group are Publishers Weekly, Library Journal and Kirkus Reviews. Do not overlook the others though, they can be important as well. A full pre-publication campaign by a big house may include as many as 40-50 sources. In addition to five or so trade publications, you may include the top 10 or 20 newspapers, and 20 or more magazines that may be appropriate.

For a more modest and less costly campaign, you may restrict the galleys to the five or 10 key media you feel are most likely to review your book.

**Booklist,** c/o American Library Association, 50 East Huron St., Chicago, IL 60611, (800)545-2433 ext.5723. Booklist requires one advanced copy 15 weeks in advance. More than 30,000 libraries subscribe to this important review source. Upon review, Booklist will send one *tear sheet*, literally, the torn-out printed review from the actual publication, to the publisher.

**Kirkus Reviews**, 200 Park Avenue South, New York, NY 10003, (212) 777-4554, Fax (212)979-1352 ext. 10. General information calls won't be returned, so write or fax for info. Kirkus prefers galleys 4-5 months prior to publication. They will review from manuscript - timing being more important than form. Kirkus specializes in fiction and also reviews general interest non-fiction such as biography and history. They don't do how-to's, poetry, reference. Books should be addressed to one of the three editors; Children's, Fiction and Non-Fiction.

**Library Journal**, 245 W. 17th St, New York, NY 10011, (212) 463-6818, This is one of the three main reviewer journals in the industry and could mean thousands of sales should your book get reviewed. Library Journal reviews books in terms of their value to the library market.

**Publishers Weekly**, *Forecasts*, 245 West 17th Street, New York, NY 10011, (212)645-0067. This highly respected weekly publication is the main voice of the book industry. If you can get reviewed in any one publication, this is the one you'd want. Publisher's Weekly is read by library buyers, bookstore buyers, subsidiary buyers, other reviewers, and pretty much everyone else important in the industry.

**School Library Journal,** 245 W. 17th St., New York, NY 10011, (212) 463-6759. Only if your book is for school-aged children, kindergarten - 12th grade.

**Small Press**, 121 E. Front St. Traverse City, MI 49684, (616)933-0445, fax (616)933-0448. This excellent publication reviews books both before publication or after, when the book is completed. Enclose self-addressed stamped post card with review copy and they'll let you know if and when your book is up for review.

## Where to Send Galleys - Newspapers

The newspapers listed in this section represent the top 10 book buying metropolitan areas - Los Angeles, New York, Chicago, Boston, Washington D.C., Philadelphia, San Francisco, Seattle, San Jose and San Diego - along with some national circulation papers. While these newspapers generally accept the finished book, they vastly prefer bound galleys or bound page proofs 90 days or more before publication date; 120 days would be even better.

Books should be addressed to the appropriate review editor - call to verify appropriate editor; or send care of Book Review Editor. As before, we've avoided listing names that might become outdated due to an editor having changed positions.

**Boston Globe**, P.O. Box 2378, Boston, MA 02107; (617)929-2800, fax (617)929-2813.

**Chicago Tribune Books**, 435 N. Michigan Avenue, Room 400, Chicago, IL 60611; (312)222-4125, fax (312)222-8604.

**Los Angeles Times Book Review**, Times Mirror Square, Los Angeles, CA 90053; (213)237-7778, fax (213)237-4712.

**New York Newsday**, 2 Park Avenue 6th floor, New York, NY 10016; (212)251-6624.

**New York Times Daily Book Review,** 229 W.43rd St., Third Floor, New York, NY 10036. (212)556-1234.

**New York Times Sunday Book Review**, 229 W. 43rd St., Eighth Floor, New York, NY 10036; (212)556-1234.

**Philadelphia Inquirer,** 400 N. Broad St, Philadelphia, PA 19101; (215)854-5616, fax (215)854-2531.

**San Diego Union**, P.O. Box 191, San Diego, CA 92112; (619)293-1321, fax (619)293-2432.

**San Francisco Chronicle Book Review,** 901 Mission Street, San Francisco, CA 94103; (415)777-8439, fax (415)957-8737.

**San Jose Mercury News,** 750 Ridder Park Dr., San Jose, CA 95190; (408)920-5825, fax (408)271-3786.

**Seattle Times**, Box 70, Seattle, WA 98111; (206)464-2357, fax (206)464-2239.

**USA Today,** 1000 Wilson Blvd., Arlington, VA 22229; (703)276-3475.

**Wall Street Journal,** 200 Liberty St., New York, NY 10281; (212)416-2503, fax (212)416-2658.

**Washington Post Book World**, 1150 15th Street, N.W. Washington, DC 20071; (202)334-7882, fax (202)334-5059.

## Where to Send Galleys - Magazines

We've listed a few book review magazines that you'll want to keep on your publicity list. While these publications prefer galleys (be sure to follow up with the printed book), they'll also accept the finished book.

**The Bloomsbury Review,** Attn: Editor, 1028 Bannock Street, 80204, Denver, CO 80201; (303)863-0406. This respected publication prefers galleys, except on art-intensive titles where the finished book is better.

**Book Page**, 2501 21st Ave. South #5, Nashville, TN 37212; (615)292-8926, fax (615) 292-8294.

**The Book Reader**, 245 Mt. Hermon Road, #256, Scotts Valley, CA 95066; (408)475-3412.

**Hungry Mind Review**, 1648 Grand Ave., St. Paul, MN 55105; (612)699-2610. Reviews predominately literary fiction, nonfiction and poetry.

**New York Review of Books**, Attn: Editor, 1755 Broadway 5th floor,New York, NY 10019; (212)757-8070.

**San Francisco Review of Books,** 126 South Park, San Francisco, CA 94107; (415)575-1450. They review general trade non-fiction and literary titles; how-to books are generally not reviewed.

**Voice Literary Supplement,** 842 Broadway, New York, NY 10003; (212)475-3300. This widely read and respected publication has been part of the literary scene for many years. Galleys are preferred.

## Where to Send Galleys - Other Publications

There's also mass circulation magazines such as Time, Newsweek, and People, who do few book reviews (though a review in any of these would be a bonanza), smaller special interest magazines (hunt these up in your local magazine shop), and smaller newspapers, magazines and publications which may review your book as galleys. Since each galley costs money to print and mail, send them only to publications that are likely to give your book a serious look. Typically, this description would not include a Time or Newsweek, and if your book is a local-oriented book on a Texas hummingbird, it may not be appropriate for a paper such as the Boston Globe. You can also send out the finished book instead as part of your post-publication campaign.

## Where to Send Galleys - Book Clubs

Book clubs, such as the Book-of-the-Month Club and Literary Guild, are a good source for potential sales (see *Distribution and Sales* chapter), and you may want to send them galleys if your book seems appropriate. You can also try clubs specialized for your market. See the Literary Market Place for a thorough listing of book clubs.

# POST-PUBLICATION REVIEWS

Once a book has been completed and is off the press, you're ready to begin the next phase of the publicity campaign. Now it's time to send out the **review copies**, copies of the actual printed book. As with every other phase of the book publishing process, you want to target your audience and send review copies only to the media that is most likely to review it. For example, don't send adult-oriented books to a media targeted toward children, or a hip-hop dance book to a fishing magazine. You must target your list carefully for each book sent out for review costs money. In addition to the cost of printing the book, there are packaging materials, postage, and setup costs to do the accompanying publicity pieces, and of course, the cost of your time or whoever you pay to do the mailing.

When all is said and done, you may have $3-$5 invested in each mailing piece that includes a book, plus the costs of the follow-up phone calls. However, this effort is generally worth it if you do a good job targeting your audience. While not all media will review your book, some portion of them will, and those reviews will generate sales and help make your book a success. Depending upon how aggressive you want to get, and the amount of money budgeted toward promotion, you may send as few as 10 copies to highly targeted media, or as many as 100, 300, or even 600 review copies, as some of the major publishers do.

While you could send a sample book to all likely book reviewing media, you'll incur a great expense in doing so. A wiser course is to send books only to the review sources you deem most important. And to the less important sources, you could send a flyer asking them to request a free copy if the book is of interest to them. When requests subsequently follow, a copy of the book could then be sent.

Don't overlook magazines for which your author's book holds special interest, local and regional media - local news is always interesting - and the whole range of news-starved media that's always looking for news items to print. Newspapers and magazines have lots of space they need to fill, while television, radio and cable have plenty of air time looking for filler. If you present them with something interesting, they might provide you with some free publicity in return.

Also, all publications that were sent galleys should now be mailed the final printed book. Often, the final review will be based upon the printed publication being received (though the reviewing was actually done earlier), and for publications that didn't review the book earlier, the printed book may reinforce the earlier mailing and secure the review.

To generate these reviews, a publicity package must be put together. Let's see what that involves.

## The Publicity Package

The publicity package consists of a news or press release, a cover or pitch letter, and for the more promising review prospects, a sample book as well. Additionally, if there have been other reviews of note, especially in prominent trade media, enclose a copy of them as well, or an excerpt. The more "legitimacy" your book has, the more likely it is to get reviewed.

# The Cover or Pitch Letter

The **cover** or **pitch letter** is a one page letter - no more - whose main purpose is to solicit reviews and interviews. A strong pitch letter presents an unusual, provocative or fascinating angle or hook in a book, something that makes that book newsworthy or interesting to the audience of the media addressed, and basically, makes a compelling case that the book or author should be reviewed or interviewed.

If the book is timely or the author controversial, either of which can spark debate, or there are fascinating issues or subjects that will intrigue an audience, these should be emphasized. Be sure to point out the particular qualifications of the author for this book, and ask for the book to get reviewed (or for the author to get interviewed).

Basically, the pitch letter should be interesting and concise, and should address some basic questions. Why is this book interesting or unique? How will readers benefit from this book? What need or issue does the book address?

The following page shows a sample cover letter.

---

### MARKETING TIP

If the main market for your book is a bookstore or retail location, make sure that your books are *already* available in these locations before you do any advertising and promotion, otherwise your efforts will be a waste of money and effort if there's no place for the consumer to act upon their buying impulse.

---

### TIPS ON GETTING MORE REVIEWS

Reviews are worth their weight in gold, and you want to give yourself every chance to obtain them for your books. Not every media target will review your book, but a certain percentage of them will. It's a numbers game - the more copies sent out for review, the more reviews you'll get. The other key to getting reviewed is following up; call or write a few days after the book should have been received. See if the book has been received, or if additional information is needed. This extra attention (keep the conversation brief - reviewers are generally busy) definitely helps your review chances.

## SAMPLE COVER LETTER

# CARDOZA PUBLISHING

East Coast Office: 132 Hastings Street, Brooklyn, New York 11235
**Phone (718)743-5229 · Fax (718)743-8284**

---

<u>For more information, please contact:</u>
Julian Silberstang:
Phone (619)794-0401
Fax (619)794-0402.

The dream of being published and even better, starting your own publishing company, is now possible thanks to a new book, **THE COMPLETE GUIDE TO SUCCESSFUL PUBLISHING**.

Written by Avery Cardoza, best-selling author, and owner of two book publishing companies, (totaling more than 100 books in print and 5,000,000 copies sold), and a new multi-media software publishing firm, this step-by-step guide shows beginning and established publishers how to successfully produce professional-looking books that not only look good, but sell in the open market.

Differing from previous attempts on self-publishing by authors who skimmed over many crucial basics necessary to be successful, or incredibly, did not even self-publish their book, Cardoza culls 15 years of experience into a book that leaves nothing to chance. From raw idea to finished book, 432 pages show readers how to:
- develop marketable ideas into books
- find authors and negotiate contracts
- establish, run, and increase profits in a publishing company
- design the inside text and cover
- chapterize and layout a book
- find distributors and get them to carry your book
- identify a target audience and successfully market books
- succeed in fiction and non-fiction publishing
- expand a publishing company into a large enterprise
- and much more...

For the first time, all the necessary ingredients of publishing books in the *real* world are under one cover, and that book is now in your hands.

**<u>The Complete Guide to Successful Publishing</u>**
Author: Avery Cardoza
Publication Date: January 15, 1999
Price: $19.95
ISBN: 0940685-43-4,
Trade paperback, 6 x 9, 432 pages; includes charts, illustrations.
*Distributed by:* Carol Publishing Group, Ingram Books, Baker & Taylor
*Published by:* Cardoza Publishing, 132 Hastings Street, Brooklyn, NY 11235

# The News or Press Release

The **news release** or **press release** is a one or two page flyer whose purpose is to immediately create interest in a book or its author by being provocative or intriguing in some form. A good news release should provide a brief overview of the book and its author, elicit curiosity, raise an interesting question, bring up a fascinating challenge, or somehow tie the book in with current day concerns or issues. Most of all, the news release should grab the reviewer, and make him or her want to read the book, or interview the author.

A good news release is a stand-alone news item that can be taken word for word and used as a review, which many publications just might do. Keep in mind that reviewers use news releases as the main source material for their reviews, and often, their reviews will either paraphrase the news release or use them verbatim.

Reviewers are generally overloaded with work, and rely on good press releases to help them decide if they'll actually review a book. A good press release not only sells the reviewer on the interesting nature of a book and its news value, but takes the burden away from them having to write the full review. Thus, you want to make your news release *interesting*.

It's best to focus on the subject itself, and then to show how the book gives a new or more interesting angle or answer to that issue. One paragraph should highlight the author's relevant credentials and his motivation in doing the book (if interesting), and bring out the human interest side of the story. If the book is in a crowded field, a few lines should stress why this book is so different or superior to similar books.

The news release should contain the standard book announcement information we presented earlier at either the top or bottom of the page. Also at the top should be the words, "*For Immediate Release*." Next comes the title of the book in big letters, any interesting quotes, and finally, the news release itself.

When the flyer is two pages, the word "more" or "continued" should be at the bottom to alert the reader that there is more. The following page shows a sample news release.

# NEWS RELEASE

## CARDOZA PUBLISHING

East Coast Office: 132 Hastings Street, Brooklyn, New York 11235

**Phone (718)743-5229 · Fax (718)743-8284**

### FOR IMMEDIATE RELEASE

<u>For more information, please contact:</u>
Julian Silberstang:
Phone (619)794-0401 • Fax (619)794-0402

### Dreams Really Can Come True!

You have a great book you or a friend has written and want published? You want to own your own business and live out the American dream? Why not!

The dream of being published and even better, starting and owning one's own publishing company, can now come true, thanks not only to the computer age, but to a new book, **THE COMPLETE GUIDE TO SUCCESSFUL PUBLISHING**. This 416 page comprehensive guide shows beginning and established publishers the steps necessary to not only design and produce professional-looking books, but to be successful in getting them sold and distributed.

Differing from all previous attempts on this subject by authors who incredibly, either did not self-publish their book, or who completely ignored or skimmed over the most important process of all - transforming a manuscript into a finished book - Cardoza shows how to publish books in the *real* world. Step-by-step, in sections spanning more than 100 pages, Cardoza shows with numerous examples, how to take raw manuscripts and transform them into professional-looking books that will sell.

In the most complete and definitive book ever written on the subject, readers learn how to find and develop ideas; set up the business from the ground up; design and layout a book; find authors, work contracts and negotiate deals; get books distributed; expand a publishing company into a large enterprise; and much more.

Cardoza is the owner of two book publishing companies, *Cardoza Publishing* and *Open Road Publishing*, and publisher of more than 100 books with total sales exceeding 5,000,000 books sold. *Cardoza Publishing* (1981) is the world's foremost publisher of gaming and gambling books; *Open Road Publishing*, with 20 travel guides published in its first 18 months, is an up and coming player in worldwide travel guides. Cardoza is also a best-selling author of more than 15 books.

Avery Cardoza knows more about publishing, designing, writing and selling books, and the business of making it all happen, than just about anyone. In addition to his two book publishing companies, and his high-tech software development firm, *Cardoza Entertainment*, Cardoza has founded, owned and operated, two direct mail sales companies, a typesetting and graphics business, a dining club, and a four color lifestyle magazine. This book took Cardoza more than two years to write and has restricted him to writing just four other books, publishing 25 titles, and starting just one company during this time.

**THE COMPLETE GUIDE TO SUCCESSFUL PUBLISHING**, published by Cardoza Publishing, sells for just $19.95, and will be available October 1995 in stores nationwide.

## Following Up

Persistence is one of the most *important* facets of getting your book reviewed. Once your book is sent out for review, follow-up with calls, with notes and with calls again. The more you work at trying to get your book reviewed, the better chance it will get done.

## Other Review Sources

In addition to the many newspapers, magazines and broadcast media that may be appropriate for your book, here's a few other sources that may be appropriate for your book.

**Choice**, 100 Riverview Center, Middletown CT 06457; (203)347-6933. Choice is the main reviewing source for undergraduate library buyers and serves as an advisor on the titles most appropriate to stock. They review reference books, scholarly monographs and other material suitable for undergraduate libraries. Books aimed at the general public such as self-improvement and general fiction are not reviewed. Choice accepts only the finished book for review. Having an index is not necessary for getting a review, but that fact will be noted in their review.

**Horn Book Magazine**, 11 Beacon St. Suite 1000, Boston, MA 02108; (617)227-1555. Reviews children's, young adult books. Send galleys or finished books.

**Small Press Review,** Dustbooks, P.O. Box 100, Paradise, CA 95967; (800)477-6110, (530) 877-6110. (Not to be confused with Small Press.) This monthly, small circulation magazine, reviews small press books and magazines. They generally review from the finished book only.

# BOOK SIGNINGS/BOOK READINGS

Events like book signings and book readings at local stores help launch interest in a book and promote sales. There's nothing like personal contact with an author to get readers interested in an author's book (assuming the author has interesting things to say!). Book signings and readings present such a forum. The personal touch of having a book signed is a thrill for most and gives the work that much more value to its reader.

# ADVERTISING

Since we're concentrating on aspects of successful publishing *for the general book trade*, much of what could be said about advertising, which could fill up a volume or two on its own merit, is beyond the scope of this book. However, we will address advertising strategies that affect many publishers and try to give you a handle on what advertising can or cannot do for your company.

The main purpose of **advertising**, buying space in one of various media to promote an item, is to call attention to one's book and to generate sales. With operating and profit margins typically being tight for most publishers, dollars spent in marketing must be cost-effective. Money spent to reach the consumer or bookstore must generate enough sales, either in the short term or the long term, to bring sufficient return on the investment.

For publishers targeting books to the general book trade, advertising through consumer publications or through media directed at the trade, will generally not be cost-effective. Advertising rates are costly, and unless one has a solid line of established titles in a particular category and runs a general coordinated campaign to create greater recognition and market position in that area, an advertising strategy may not be worthwhile. Advertising just a few titles to the general trade or in general circulation newspapers and magazines will not usually pay off. The money spent in these mass vehicles will come right out of profits with the general result being that much less comes back in as a direct result of these efforts than what is spent going out.

For most publishers competing in the general market, the best advertising is simply getting the books on the shelves where they can be seen, and sending out more review copies in a solid promotion campaign as discussed above. Book reviews and author appearances in the media is a far more effective way to sell books than advertising, and is considerably less expensive. There are exceptions, of course, and everything must be looked at on a case by case basis, but in general, you'll find that advertising just a few titles will not pay.

One problem with advertising with a general ad in a newspaper is that you're reaching a broad spectrum of people, most of whom may not be appropriate for your type of book. This is akin to advertising a local Florida-based business that only services Florida in a national publication. You're being charged for the whole country in the advertising rates, but really, you're only interested in the Florida population. Thus, you're not buying cost-effective advertising.

You can also pursue the strategy of advertising to the trade through the industry journals, but this type of strategy is aimed more at increasing recognition within the trade as opposed to directly going after the consumer. While this is certainly a strategy you may want to pursue at some point, that point often means having an established line that needs to position itself better in the marketplace.

Meanwhile, though, you'll find your marketing efforts more effectively achieved by concentrating efforts in the book promotion arena - sending out books for review and following up with phone calls and notes to move that process along. Success here will increase sales *and* recognition in the trade.

Not that advertising can't be an effective strategy. It can be, but again, for most general trade publishers, this extra money spent may not translate to enough sales. Like any other issue in running a business, spending money on advertising is an issue of cost-effectiveness. Where it is effective, it should be pursued, and where it is not effective, the money should be saved for other aspects of the business.

Let's look at a general strategy that can be effective - selling directly to the consumer.

## Advertising Directly to the Consumer

Advertising does pay and in fact is crucial when your main publishing and marketing strategy is to sell to the consumer directly, outside of the standard book channels. These types of marketing efforts generally work well because you're selling directly to your target audience, and you receive the full list price of your item - there is no middleman involved as there would be going through retail channels.

The two main print strategies, classified or display ads in target magazines and mailings to specialized lists often pull well because you're targeting your audience directly. There is also direct solicitations through other media such as radio, television, or computer, strategies that can work effectively if the audience can be isolated. And the good thing about these forms of direct response advertising is that cost effectiveness can easily be ascertained. The responses can get tracked by adding a box number to the address, such as "Box 5" or to "Mr. Smith's attention" or whatever, and thus income and costs for each ad are easily compared.

See the *Distribution and Sales* chapter for a more in-depth discussion of reaching the consumer through direct sales efforts.

## Word of Mouth Advertising

**Word of mouth advertising**, satisfied readers who pass the good word on about a product, is the best advertising of all - and it's free. Word of mouth advertising generates the good word about your books through it's own dynamics - the more people who read your books, the greater the word of mouth will be generated. Just like with a movie, as enthralled moviegoers recommend a movie they've seen, book lovers pass the good word on for books they've enjoyed.

With good books, the ever-widening circle of recommendations spreads, and gives a book a life of its own. Once your book gets established in the marketplace, word of mouth will often take over and give the book sea legs to keep on going.

## Co-op Advertising

**Cooperative advertising**, when an advertising space is shared and paid for by two or more parties, is often used in the publishing business by a combination of bookstores, publishers and distributors to mutual benefit. It is a great way for the advertisers to increase their exposure at a lesser cost than if they advertised alone.

A publisher may get together with his distributor to push a title in one of the trade magazines, or with a bookstore to run a promotion or book signing in their bookstore. Or all three may combine on the idea, with everybody getting exposure. There are other variations on the theme as well.

Co-op advertising is a fairly common practice, so if you'll be advertising your books in various media, you may want to check around and see if you can find some partners to share in the benefits and cost.

Let's move on and talk about the brass tacks of running a business.

# 16. RUNNING THE BUSINESS

## INTRODUCTION

Once a book has been produced, the business takes on a different nature; inventory must be kept, books have to be packed and shipped, accounts have to be set-up and billed, moneys have to get collected, and a bank book needs to be kept. In short, there's a business to run.

In this section, we'll go over all the basics of running a publishing business. You'll learn how to take orders, set up accounts, invoice customers and increase the size of orders; how to pack books into a box, properly seal that box, and protect those books during shipping; the best way to ship small packages and book cartons through the various shipping services available to you; how to ship important documents that cannot afford to be lost; and fulfillment and storage options you'll need to be aware of.

That's the order-taking and shipping. But there's the money aspect of running a company, and we'll look at these issues in this chapter. We go over the essentials of collecting money from accounts and giving credit to new and existing customers. Basic recordkeeping and simple tax preparation is covered as well. Basically, by the time you finish this chapter, you'll have the rudiments necessary to run the business part of the publishing company.

But without orders, there's no business to run, so let's get right to the basics; taking orders, checking references, invoicing, and collecting your money.

# TAKING ORDERS

Initially, most orders from trade accounts will come in by phone so that the terms of doing business can be established and agreed upon. Most first-time accounts want to ascertain prices and product availability through this first contact, and want to find the best way of doing business with your company. It is generally after an account is already established, and the buyer knows your product and company better, that trade orders will come in by mail or through the fax.

## The Order

When orders are called in from trade accounts, there's some basic information that should be taken down. First of all, unless you're dealing with the company a long time, it's good to verify the *shipping address* and *billing address*, plus their contact *phone number*. It would be disheartening to have an order and not be able to fulfill it due to sloppy order-taking.

In addition to the order itself, which should be written legibly, take the *name of the person placing the order*, and the *PO#*, the *purchase order number*, the number companies assign to their purchases. If the company doesn't assign PO numbers to their orders, you can use that day's date as a reference, or just ignore it altogether. If it's not used by the company making the order, there's no real reason you'll need it.

For new accounts, you may want to ask for *references* as well. If they're an established bookstore and especially a wholesaler or distributor, we go by the trust system at our business here. If they're not in the book trade, we require payment in advance of the first order, especially for new mail order operations (who typically don't stay in business very long). How you handle a new account though, will be up to you.

---

## PHONE ORDERS CHART

The basic information to be taken in a phone order
- shipping address
- billing address
- phone number
- name of the person placing the order
- purchase order number
- the order itself

---

## KEEPING GOOD NOTES

Keep good notes when talking with buyers so that key points are recorded where you can find them again. If a buyer is strong with certain types of books and weak with others, that's important information to detail. You should take notes during the conversation, and immediately after if there are good points you didn't get time to write down.

After many buyers and phone calls, you'll tend to forget who was who, or exactly what transpired. Good notes take care of that problem.

You want to keep track of what marketing tips they shared, who they sell to, how best to reach their market and other pertinent shop talk. But that's not the only thing I keep track of. I also jot down notes on personal things we discussed and make it a point to remember (at the least through my notes) what we've discussed in the past, especially things that concern their personal lives. A good personal relationship with a buyer makes doing business with them a whole lot more satisfying. Remembering things you spoke about with them keeps that personal touch and is always appreciated.

## Setting Up Accounts

As orders start coming in, accounts will have to be set up with the various retailers, wholesalers, and distributors you'll be working with. For best organization, each account should be assigned a separate folder containing copies of their purchase orders, and a history of their sales and payments. These account folders should be filed alphabetically for quick reference.

Orders can be taken **prepaid**, where the books are paid for in advance of shipment, or on **credit**, where the books are shipped in anticipation of payment at a specified date - the usual condition of sales for trade accounts. In the latter case, when credit is given, the account will be invoiced (see below).

Bookstore and retail accounts are typically given terms of **net 30 days**, or more simply, **net 30**, that is, money is due 30 days after the books are shipped. Deals with wholesalers and distributors are made on a case by case basis, with terms stretching to net 90 depending upon the account. More then net 90 shouldn't be extended domestically, though you may stretch those payments past net 90 for overseas distributors.

I have found that distributors and wholesalers are good for their money, though in some cases, that may be a long time coming. Just because you have a bill that says net 90, doesn't mean that's when your bill will get paid. Many wholesalers are notorious for being late-payers, and that's one of the problems of self-distribution. Cash flow can become a problem, and you have little leverage to force an account to pay their bills when they're due. Retail accounts are generally good with paying their bills, but you'll also get a fair share who not only will pay late, or very late, but won't pay at all.

But that's part of doing business. There's always a certain amount of receipts you'll have to write off, in the 3%-10% range, and a certain percentage of receipts that will be delayed in coming.

If you do everything on a pre-payment or cash only basis, you won't have a problem with any bills not being paid, but you also won't make many sales. The book business is run on a credit system, and many accounts expect to get their books net 30. If that is not offered, they may not buy at all as a matter of principle since credit terms are probably offered by everyone else they buy from.

## Checking Credit References
It is often standard business practice to request three credit references when you're doing business with someone for the first time. While this is probably a good practice, I'm not sure how much trouble you'll save yourself checking credits. Taking credit references won't necessarily get all your accounts to pay their bill.

A bad payer or "deadbeat" can easily come up with three good credit references, and that won't stop them from stiffing you on your bills. However, there is some value to taking credit references as it may weed out some bad credit risks, and since many people in business check credit religiously, you'll want to establish your own policies carefully.

## Invoicing Orders
All orders taken that are not prepaid, that is, are ordered on credit, will have to be **billed** or **invoiced**, given a written statement of monies owed for the products ordered. You can buy standard three part invoices in your stationery store, or have them custom printed with your company's name, phone, address or other pertinent information. There are com-

puter programs that will do this as well.

The standard invoice contains the following information:

---

# STANDARD INVOICE

### BASIC INFORMATION AT THE TOP
- Your company name, address and phone
- Company name, address and phone
- PO# (purchase order number)
- Buyer's Name
- Terms of Sale (net how many days?)

### ITEMS ORDERED INFORMATION
- Item ordered, quantity, list price, total
  (for each book separately)
- Ship Date (date when books shipped)

### IN THE TOTALS COLUMNS
- Gross Sale (total cost of order before discount)
- Discount (the dollar amount discounted)
- Sub-Total (cost of order after discount)
- Shipping (shipping charges)
- Amount Due or Total (sub-total plus shipping
  - amount to be paid)

---

# BILLING TIP

Always get your billing done either immediately after shipping, or within 1-2 days of the shipping, that is, pretty much immediately. The longer you wait to bill, the longer you'll wait for your money, and the greater chance you have of forgetting to bill altogether. Bills that aren't sent generally don't get paid.

**INVOICE EXAMPLE**

# CARDOZA PUBLISHING

*The World's Foremost Publisher of Games and Gambling Books*

132 Hastings Street, Brooklyn, New York 11235, Phone (718)743-5229 • Fax (718)743-8284

**SOLD TO:** Gravy Train Distributing
91 Berk Trade Avenue
Irving City, NY

**SHIP DATE:** February 30,1996
**PO#:** 384
**ORDERED BY: Mr. Black**
**TERMS:** 40% discount, Net 30

| QNTY | TITLE | PRICE | TOTAL |
|---|---|---|---|
| | **$5.95 POCKET SIZE  (4 1/4 X 6 3/4)** | | |
| 10 | Beat the Odds | $5.95 | 59.50 |
| | Las Vegas Guide | $5.95 | |
| | Winner's Playbook | $5.95 | |
| | Winning Casino Play | $5.95 | |
| | **$6.95-$19.95 TRADE SIZE** | | |
| | Backgammon for Winners | $6.95 | |
| | Beginning Chess Play | $8.95 | |
| 10 | Caro's Fundamental Secrets of Winning Poker | $9.95 | 99.50 |
| | Casino Craps for the Winner | $6.95 | |
| | Complete Guide to Winning Keno | $12.95 | |
| 10 | Complete Guide to Winning Hold'Em Poker | $14.95 | 149.50 |
| | How to Play Winning Poker | $6.95 | |
| 10 | How to Win At Gambling | $12.95 | 129.50 |
| | How to Win At Horseracing  (Hardcover $19.95) | $9.95 | |
| | How to Win At Sports Betting | $8.95 | |
| | Las Vegas Guide (Trade Edition) | $12.95 | |
| 10 | Silberstang's Encyclopedia of Games and Gambling | $17.95 | 179.50 |
| | Winner's Guide to Greyhound Racing | $7.95 | |
| | Winning Blackjack for the Serious Player | $9.95 | |
| | Winning Bridge Play | $9.95 | |
| | Winning Casino Blackjack for the Non-Counter | $6.95 | |
| 10 | Winning Chess Openings | $8.95 | 89.50 |
| | Winning Craps for the Serious Player | $9.95 | |
| 10 | Winning Lotto/Lottery for Everyday Players | $9.95 | 99.50 |
| | Winning Poker for the Serious Player | $9.95 | |
| | **PUBLISHING AND WORD TITLES** | | |
| 20 | Complete Guide to Successful Publishing | $19.95 | 399.00 |
| 30 | Ultimate Word Challenges (Rare, Strange & Fascinating Word Quizzes) | $7.95 | 238.50 |
| 120 | Gross Sale | | $1,440.00 |
| | Less Discount | | $ 577.60 |
| | Sub-Total | | $ 866.40 |
| | Plus Shipping | | $ 25.17 |
| | Amount Due | | $ 891.57 |

## Collecting Money

If the account has been delinquent beyond their due date for payment, you should send them a **past due notice**, a copy of their bill showing the amount owed. If the account is more than 30 days late, you should follow-up with a phone call to either the buyer or the accounts payable department, whichever is the more appropriate for the account, to try and get that bill paid.

When the buyer is responsible for approving payments, he or she is the appropriate person to call; and when the accounts payable department is responsible, the call should be shifted in their direction. On smaller accounts, you may need to deal with the manager or owner; on larger accounts it may be the bookkeeper. After dealing with companies for a while, you'll get to know who pulls the strings for bills to be paid.

If the bill is still not paid two weeks later, another past due bill should be sent. These notices remind the accounts that you haven't forgotten them and puts some pressure on them to catch up with their bills.

You should be firm in your insistence on being paid, but not overbearing or obnoxious as you don't want to lose an account over personality conflicts.

## Increasing Orders

While you have the buyer on the phone, you should use the opportunity to sell them other titles not included in their order. Since you have a live ear on the other hand who obviously likes your books, let them know about others that may sell well for them.

Our general manager, Barbara, never lets a buyer get off the phone without getting them to try a new book they haven't bought before, or at least trying to make that sale. If they call 12 times in the same day (or more likely Barbara has made those 12 calls), Barbara will try them 12 times for that extra sale.

The result of this persistence? Buyers respect the effort, enjoy the battle they know is coming, and purchase more books.

### Selling to Individuals

As opposed to trade accounts where credit is given, sales to individuals should always be on a **COD**, cash on delivery, or prepaid basis, with appropriate shipping charges added. Unless the individual ordering is trying to pull a fast one, credit will not be expected. If an individual insists on credit, ship the books only if you don't feel like getting paid, for that's what will happen.

You should add $2-$4 for the first books ordered, with a lesser amount for each additional book thereafter to cover postage and handling.

## FULFILLMENT

There are companies that will provide **fulfillment** services, keep stock of a publisher's titles, and send orders out on their behalf.

It's best if you can fill your own orders, but if you're not equipped to warehouse and ship sufficient books, you'll need to hire a company that is set up for this. Fulfillment companies can be found around the country, and they don't necessarily need to be anywhere physically close to your office.

What is important with fulfillment companies is that they provide fast service on your orders, and at a reasonable price. You can find listings of fulfillment companies in the LMP, and can also call your distributor or fellow publishers for recommendations.

## STORAGE

If you don't have enough room for storage where your office or home is located, you can store books with your distributor (inquire as to their arrangements), at the printer's (for a price), or with a private fulfillment company which will store and fulfill your books for a fee. Or you can rent your own storage unit nearby.

If you're storing your own books, try to keep them away from damp areas, such as a musty cellar, so the books don't get damp and musty themselves and ruined.

# PACKING BOXES

Boxes must be packed tightly, and the box securely taped to avoid damages during shipping, but before anything else, you'll need to get the right size box. Your first resource is the boxes your books come shipped in from the printer. They're sturdy, made for shipping, and of course, fit your books. Additional boxes and sizes can be purchased from stationery and packing supply houses, and from the many mail order companies who will eventually find you - in abundance.

While you can get away with using any box at all to ship your books in, provided it's a good box, you may decide that a little extra money may provide a little extra class. Though you could theoretically ship your books in a Tampon or Waldbaums cardboard box, your operation may look a little better mailing those books in a more appropriate carton.

## PACKING MATERIALS NEEDED

All the following materials are easily found in stationery, general merchandise stores, mail order companies, and the like.
• Packing Tape and Dispenser
• Thick Magic Marker
• Packing Slip Pouches (and packing slips)
• Straight Edge or Scissors for Opening Boxes
• Mailing Labels
• Packing Materials (newspaper, styrofoam popcorn, or bubble paper)

## How to Pack a Box

The spines of perfect bound and hardcover books are slightly thicker than the opposite, non-bound end, so you'll want to reverse the spine direction of every five or ten books when packing them in a box. Placing a pile of paperback books spine-side together puts stress on the weak side and can cause bending in the middle of the book due to lack of support. Try doing this and you'll see what I'm talking about.

You can pile books in a box until almost up to the top, but make sure there's space between the top of the books and the top flaps. However, under no circumstances should books ever be packed right to the top or even until they go over the top; the top books will get damaged during transit with this kind of packing.

Sometimes you'll fill only half the box, other times you may get close to the top, and still other times, you'll find it necessary to make a second box because the number of books in the order are a few too many to fit into one box alone.

Packing material should be tightly packed in the empty spaces of the box so that when the top and side flaps of the box are closed over the top opening, the books are firmly kept in place. Books that aren't tightly packed will shift during shipment causing scruffed covers or worse, bent and damaged books.

Good packing materials include flat styrofoam sheets, **popcorn** - styrofoam bubbles, bubble paper, and newspaper and/or butcher block paper. (If you do use newspaper, make sure that clean paper, or flat styrofoam sheets are between it and the books, otherwise you risk the very real possibility of having the ink rub off on the books and damaging them.)

Popcorn or styrofoam sheets are preferable, because of their lighter weight compared to other materials such as paper. Less weight, of course, cuts down on the costs of shipping. On the other hand, while cardboard will protect the books equally well, it also adds a lot of weight, and thus, is used less often.

## Taping the Box

After closing the lids tightly over the packing material, making sure the whole package holds firmly in place, run a single strip of tape down the middle of the box to close the two top flaps in place and to cover and protect the seam in between. Begin the tape at least four inches down from the top, on the side, continue it all the way over and across the center top and down at least four inches along the opposite side from where the taping started.

Your tape should be at least two inches wide and of commercial quality. Good quality tape is readily available. Buy plenty. You'll be using it all the time. Do not use masking tape or the thin, 1/2 inch clear tape used around the house. They're not strong enough and will not keep your package closed.

In addition to the long strip running down the center part of the box, it's a good idea to place smaller strips, on either side of the main strip, and on both edges of the box - that's four more strips, albeit smaller ones. Each strip should start four inches below the top and continue for four inches above the top. This tape provides more security and is worth the extra effort. On smaller boxes, the one central strip will be more than enough. Make sure the bottom of the box is secure as well.

Do not tape one slice right over another. It will make your box weaker, not stronger. If you want extra protection, run extra tape up the sides of the main strip as discussed above.

Be aware that the tape on boxes stored for a long period of time has a tendency to dry up and withdraw from its surface. If the tape looks suspect in any way on your boxes, take no chances, re-secure the box so you know it will be fine during transit.

## Other Items on the Box

Besides the basics of your destination address and your own return address - standards for any shipment - the box should contain a packing slip and a packing slip pouch. The packing slip pouch is used to enclose a **packing slip**, an important document that lists the complete materials enclosed in the shipment .

The packing slip is not an invoice and thus should not contain the discount and final billing information. The invoice itself should be sent by separate mail.

Only one packing slip is needed per shipment, even if that shipment includes 10 boxes, or is just one box. If there is more than one box in a shipment, each box should be numbered by hand on the top corner of the box itself showing how many boxes are going out in the shipment, and which numbered box this is in the group.

For example, if three boxes are going to the same destination, one box (it doesn't matter which one, though generally it's the one with the packing slip) gets marked 1/3, indicating the first box of three being sent, and the other two boxes are marked 2/3 and 3/3 respectively. This method lets the receiving party know if all boxes expected actually arrived. If there's just one box going, the box is numbered 1/1.

# SHIPPING

Shipping your orders is a relatively easy part of the business, but must be done correctly to assure a minimum amount of problems.

The standard means of shipping orders is through the either the services of *UPS* (*United Parcel Service*) or through the *USPS (United States Postal Service)*, or simply put, the *postal service*. There are other services as well that may work for you.

Below, we'll talk about the advantages and disadvantages of using UPS compared to the postal service.

## Shipping Packages with UPS

For shipping boxes, UPS is clearly the best way to move your merchandise around the country. UPS is reliable, and very important for your business, all their deliveries are signed for upon receipt. If a customer claims that their shipment didn't arrive, which happens periodically, we simply have UPS trace the shipment, show the signature, and the problem is solved. Finger-pointing, bad feelings, and the cost of shipping free merchandise is all avoided. (Shipments sometimes get lost internally at a company due to misplacement of a packing slip or the shipment itself.)

The confirmed shipments are a big advantage UPS enjoys over the postal service and why they are the carrier of choice for business. The postal service has no idea if a particular package arrives at a destination, and has no accountability if it doesn't. UPS, on the other hand, can track your order down, and verify its whereabouts.

UPS automatically insures all packages up to $100, so if a package gets lost, you can get compensated. (Additional insurance is available for all shipments.)

Best of all, UPS will pick up your orders. If you ship orders on a regular basis, or have an order consisting of 10 boxes, the convenience of their pick-up service is a godsend in time. For a weekly service fee of $6 if more than $50 is shipped, and $8 if shipments total less than $50, UPS will send a truck every day to pick up your packages. The UPS pick-up charge is the same whether you send one box or twenty. To save on pick-up charges, you may want to hold packages a few days for the following week where you can combine them with other orders going out. If you only ship infrequently, you can also bring your packages to one of their centers (call them for information).

You can sign up with UPS as a regular customer if you do enough shipping, and they will automatically come every day. Call customer accounts at **(800)742-5877** for information on signing up and receiving deliveries.

UPS does not deliver to P.O. boxes (post office boxes), so make sure your destination has a street address. Also, phone numbers are helpful so that if there's any problem on the delivery end, UPS can call to fix the confusion and make the delivery.

UPS breaks the United States down into eight zones, one through eight, and charges for shipping based on the weight and the number of zones it crosses. In addition to their standard service, UPS offers three day, two day, overnight services, and even same day; each faster method, respectively, is more expensive. UPS also offers international service.

## Shipping Boxes with the Postal Service (USPS)

**Fourth class mail**, also called **book rate**, is the best way to ship books through the postal service. It enjoys a lower rate than first class, and overall, is a pretty good value. On long-distance shipping, fourth class is less expensive than competitors such as UPS.

While price can be an advantage for shipping books through the postal service, the lack of a pick-up service, and the fact that boxes are not signed for upon receipt are significant disadvantages. Boxes are sometimes left out in front of people's doors in residential deliveries, open season if someone happens to come by and wants some merchandise, or prone to a book-ruining rain. Delivery time is not particularly fast either - usually two to three weeks - sometimes faster, sometimes slower

The major inconvenience of having to take every package mailed to the local station and waiting on line to process the shipment is generally not worth any savings you may get, unless your particular postal station is efficient and mostly line-free. Otherwise, it takes time, time, time, especially in certain stations where the experience can be an adventure. (I won't mention our local station in Brooklyn.) And if you have several packages of size, you'll have to deal with the logistics of carrying them in as well. Good luck.

The postal service price schedule on shipping boxes is based solely on their weight. A 12 pound package going from New York City to Poughkeepsie, NY, 75 miles or so north, costs the same as one going from New York to San Francisco, about a 3,000 mile hike. UPS, on the other hand, will charge a lot more for the longer distance, San Francisco, than for the New York to Poughkeepsie delivery. Thus, you'll generally find the post office an economical and less expensive way to go on long distance shipping.

For international shipments, the post office has excellent rates for shipping. Books can be sent either surface or air. A surface shipment, which goes by boat, takes longer to reach its destination than a package going by air. Spend a few minutes at the post office and have them explain your overseas shipping options. At the same time, pick up their current rate charts for shipping.

## Shipping Individual Books

Books shipped by the ones, two and threes, that is smaller orders that can be packaged in envelopes, are safely sent through the regular US postal service as either priority mail or book rate. Book rate is cheaper, but takes longer to arrive - perhaps 10 days or so depending upon location. Priority mail, once heavily promoted as two day service, but in fact standard first class type service, will generally take a few days, though sometimes it can take up to a week or more to get delivered.

Pick up the latest first class/priority mail rate charts at the post office and keep them handy. You'll find priority mail an efficient and cost-effective way to send a lot of your mail. You'll see that priority mail over 11 ounces and up to two pounds is the same $3.00 rate, so once you're over the 11 ounce weight, your package should be sent using the priority rate as opposed to first class. Otherwise, you're needlessly paying extra postage. The nice thing about priority mail is that you not only get free cardboard envelopes or plastic mailers from the post office, and the discount mentioned above, but the package itself looks impressive, and your customer will feel that he or she has received special service.

The post office almost always gets their mail to the location addressed, and you should have almost no problems using this service. I know that now and again things do get lost, but that is the rare occasion. America's business works perfectly fine through the postal system with a minimum of problems.

## Packing Individual Books

The preferred way of packing small orders of books is in a padded mailing envelope. Padded envelopes keep books well protected and prone to a minimum of damage during shipping. The disadvantage of these bulkier envelopes is the extra cost in purchasing them, 25-75¢ each depending upon their size and the place purchased, and the extra postage needed to pay for the heavier package.

Padded envelopes can be fastened by either stapling at the ends, or taping them securely shut with packing tape, or both.

Alternately, you can use the Priority Mail packaging and shipping if your books fit. It's a pretty good value - it's free. There's also standard mailing envelopes at a cost of 5¢-25¢ or so per envelope (they come in various sizes) but this type of packaging may not protect your books sufficiently. On some thinner books however, if the books are packaged tightly, these envelopes might do the job well enough and save you money.

Mailing envelopes, whether plain, manila, or padded, come in a variety of sizes, and can be found at stationery and general merchandise stores. They can also be purchased through the many mail order companies that specialize in selling office supply products.

---

# PIGGYBACKING ORDERS

When orders are shipped, they should be "**piggybacked**" with your catalogue or advertisements for other related products you carry. Since you're
already paying for the postage, adding a sales flyer or catalogue with
your books (piggybacking), gives you advertising with no postage costs.

---

## Stamps or Meters

Many companies use metering machines to apply postage to their mailings to take advantage of savings in time and ease of use. One disadvantage with the postage machines that may be inconvenient is that
once postage is affixed, it must go out that same day. This can be a
problem if you like to prepare mail in advance, or would hold particular mailings until checks cleared or whatever. In any case, I like stamps
better.

If you do use stamps, make sure to affix them securely. When using
more expensive postage, such as priority mail or Express Mail stamps,
or stamps adding up to values over several dollars, I suggest you put
clear or scotch tape over one half of the stamps, the top half or bottom
half, to make sure they stay on the package. Though the post office
frowns on this, I can tell you from personal experience that your stamps
will stay on the package this way. We got tired of having expensive
packages coming back from lack of postage when our stamps, somehow, fell off. (The lower denomination stamps didn't seem to have this
problem.)

## Shipping Items You Resell

We stock many items that we purchase from outside suppliers and resell to our customers as part of our mail order business, and find that
the most secure way and ultimately the least expensive was shipping
UPS.

We found that too many of our packages were not reaching their destination for whatever reason, and we were reshipping items already sent.
I don't know if they got lost in the post office, if they were delivered to
the wrong address and the person never passed them along to their

neighbor, or the person simply denied getting it and wanted another one for free.

Whatever the reason, we found it best to use UPS so that our more expensive items got *signed for* upon receipt. This way, everybody remained happy in the process. We avoided unhappy customers that didn't receive their packages, and we remained happy because we knew they received their packages.

## Shipping to Libraries
Shipping books to libraries can go by a cheaper service, **library rate**, through the postal service. Once you start getting orders from libraries, you should check with your local post office for the current rates and requirements so you can apply the savings.

# SENDING IMPORTANT DOCUMENTS
Never, ever send *irreplaceable* documents, or documents that are time sensitive, by the regular mails. Though the postal service is a reliable carrier, heaven forbid if an original piece of artwork, an original slide or slides, or some document that cannot be replaced gets lost in the shuffle. You're in big trouble and there's not a thing that you can do about getting it back or being compensated for the loss.

When a package must get to its destination, you must use a service that requires a signature for delivery. For overnight and rush shipments, use either the postal service's **Express Mail Overnight Delivery**, **UPS Red Label** (overnight delivery), **UPS Blue Label** (two day delivery), **UPS Standard**, **Federal Express Priority** (overnight by 11am next business day) or **Standard** (by afternoon next business day), **Airborne Express** or other reliable delivery service. All these methods of sending documents require a signature for receipt of delivery and are kept track of by sophisticated computer systems.

The USPS Express Mail Overnight Delivery service is not as good as the others for if a package is lost or delayed, as happened to us once, their tracking and problem solving is a royal headache. When one of our packages got lost, we had to go down to the post office itself to straighten out the situation. UPS and Federal Express, on the other hand, can handle and solve all problems by phone and instantly track your package's whereabouts - which is a big advantage in using their services. The USPS, however, does offer the advantage of Saturday and Sunday delivery at no extra charge.

UPS and Federal Express will pick up for a charge while the Post Office will not. However, USPS Overnight packages can be dropped off at designated boxes provided the correct postage is affixed, and of course can be dropped off at the post office itself. UPS and Federal Express have designated pick-up areas, and drop boxes in addition to their offices - call for the ones nearest to you.

The post office also has registered and certified mail delivery services, but these can only be done at the post office itself.

**Contact Information:**

| | |
|---|---|
| Airborne Express | **(800)247-2676** |
| FedEx (Federal Express) | **(800)238-5355** |
| United Parcel Service (UPS) | **(800)742-5877** |
| United States Postal Service (USPS) | **(800)222-1811** |

# A NOTE ON BOOKKEEPING

Unless you decide to sell direct to bookstores and end up with hundreds or even thousands of accounts, there is no reason to computerize your bookkeeping. All the bookkeeping can be done easily in your check register as you would with your personal account.

When a check is written, enter it into the debit side, and when a check is received, enter it into the credit side. I know the tendency nowadays is to computerize everything to make things easy, but with the bookkeeping being so easy for many publishers in this business, all that computerization does is create more work.

Each account should have their own file, with the invoices and other pertinent information stored within. There should also be a dedicated sheet detailing each sale made and its date, the debit amount, and when that is paid, the date of its being paid. This keeps each account tightly organized, and allows credit and debit information to be easily accessed.

## Preparing the Accounting & Taxes

At the end of every accounting period, quarterly as a corporation, yearly as a single proprietorship or partnership, you'll need to get your figures together so that the taxes can be figured out.

Take a sheet of paper and list the following classifications as shown below in the *Accounting Classifications* box. Now, go through your checkbook listing the amount of each check written in the appropriate column until all checks that have been written are entered. For example, if $1,000 has been paid to your printer, $200 to your separation house, and $75 for your phone, you would list $1,000 in the *book printing* column, $200 in *pre-press*, and $75 under *utilities*.

Now add up the totals in each column. Besides being ready for the tax man, you'll have a capsulation of your expenses and can see what really went on during the business year.

Below is a list of classifications you may find helpful.

---

### ACCOUNTING CLASSIFICATIONS

1. Commissions/Employee Costs
2. Royalties
3. Pre-Press
4. Book Printing
5. Other Printing
6. Shipping (UPS & USPS)
7. Telephone and Fax
8. Office Supplies
9. Books & Publications
10. Computer Equipment
11. Advertising
12. Accountant
13. Petty Cash
14. Refunds
15. Travel and Entertainment
16. Petty Cash
17. Office Furniture
18. Utilities (Gas, Phone, Electric)
19. Warehousing

You'd probably be best advised to let an accountant handle your taxes, especially if you're a corporation, so that you best comply with the tax law and enjoy the maximum savings allowable.

# WAREHOUSING

The ideal situation for the small- to medium-sized publisher is an arrangement with a distribution company. Along with the other benefits discussed earlier, there is the bonus that your distributor will warehouse a portion of your titles for you, and most likely will do some fulfillment of your outside orders as well.

You'll still want to keep a portion of your book inventory in your own warehouse so that your own accounts can be serviced in-house with a minimum of expenses. If you have access to a basement, you can store a portion of your books there without added costs, or if self-storage units are convenient, rent in these locations is quite reasonable. When I first started my business in Santa Cruz, California, back in 1981, I kept my books in storage units there for the first three years before I moved them into a garage, then into a spacious house, and finally, in 1987, into our own regional warehouses.

## Outside Warehousing

Your company may be in a position where there is either no room in the office for warehousing (or living quarters if you operate your business from home), no arrangement with a distributor to hold your titles, or no easy access to other alternatives we discussed earlier.

There are two viable alternatives in this situation.

You can either store the books with your printer, or you can hire a company which specializes in storage and fulfillment. Check listings in the Literary Market Place (LMP) for further information on companies if you have need for a fulfillment/storage company to warehouse your books.

# RESALE NUMBER

You also want to file for a **tax resale number** with your county or state. This allows you to claim exemption on taxes for items you buy or manufacture that will be resold again later. Thus, costs that go into the manufacture of your books, such as the pre-press costs and the actual printing, are exempt from sales tax.

Using a resale number won't be much of an issue anyway for goods bought out-of-state, since currently, out-of-state purchases are non-taxable.

# 17. MAKING MONEY

## INTRODUCTION

Starting a publishing company offers the ambitious entrepreneur a greater return for less risk than most any other business. With $10,000 or less, even as little as $5,000 or less, a marketable, professional-looking book can be published with the potential to earn many, many times the original investment. If enough things are done right, that original investment can be parlayed into a small publishing empire.

Making money in publishing, like any other business, not only requires effort and market-sense, but also, careful examination of the costs and pricing structure of the books. In this chapter, we'll take a brief look at these elements that make up pricing books and the profit structure, and not only show the various costs associated with publishing and how to minimize them, but also, how to increase income and improve the bottom line. In other words, lots of good stuff.

We'll also discuss the concepts of establishing and expanding a line of books, expanding into new lines, and risk-taking with books that have a chance to go big.

With that in mind, let's talk money.

## TYPICAL PUBLISHING COSTS

Following is a brief discussion of the typical expenses that will give you an idea of where the money goes in the publishing business, and some ways these costs can be minimized. Note that many of these expenses would be part of any business, regardless of the product or service offered.

## Production & Printing Costs

By far, the biggest expense for smaller publishing houses is the costs of printing books. This can be as high as 50% of the total company expenses or even upwards of 75% in some cases. As a company grows in size, the proportion of the print bill compared to the overall expenses will fall, and in many cases will be supplanted by other expenses such as employees costs. However, regardless of the size company, print bills will remain a major cost.

We can divide overall production costs into *pre-press* costs and *printing* costs.

**Pre-press costs** include data entry, layout, halftones, separations, design, illustrations and all other costs related to the production itself and getting the book ready for the printer. These one-time-only costs, also known as **production costs**, are not incurred on reprints.

**Printing costs** are the sum total of any costs that make up the printing *including* the cost of shipping these books to their final destination regardless of whether that destination is a distributor, warehouse, drop ship location, or any combination of the above.

On future printings, called **reprints**, the overall costs of getting a book printed will drop, and thus, allow you to have a higher profit margin. For one thing, the production costs disappear. These expenses drop out entirely - they were taken care of on the first printing. On the printing end, there are savings as well since the printer already has made the negatives and plates. The amount of savings for a second printing vary from situation to situation, and depend somewhat on the extra work the printer did in getting your job print-ready the first time. Generally though, there should be some savings from the printer on the reprint.

So not only does a reprint show that your book is selling and is successful, but the lower expenses of the printing allows you to increase your profit margin.

## Employee Costs

Employee expenses, typically one of the major costs associated with a small business, are greatly minimized in small publishing operations, and can even be non-existent when you're the CC&B (chief cook and bottle washer) of your own start-up company.

As a company gets larger however, employee costs go up. More people are needed for the various tasks of getting books ready for press, marketing them to the media, and handling all the things that need handling by a growing business. But these increased costs are good. More employees signifies more business, and more people doing the work you were previously doing.

To grow a business, you need to delegate so that you can focus your energies on the big decisions and the parts of the business that afford you the maximum profit. Delegating responsibilities is one of the most difficult adjustments an owner must make, but a necessary one if the business is to grow.

## Rent

Start-up and smaller publishing operations can not only minimize the costs or renting an office, they can eliminate them altogether. A small publishing business of a few people doesn't take up all that much room and can easily be operated from one's home.

A slightly larger outfit, say three or four employees and up, probably needs to command an office space, but even there, the rent can be minimized by obtaining a lower rent space than retail would need. Location is unimportant in book publishing - it's what the publishing house does, not where it's located that determines its success.

## Author Costs

Royalties are a necessary expense in publishing, and is a cost you want to have as high as possible. The more royalties you pay, the more books you are selling.

## Set-Up Costs

In the *Getting Started* chapter we discussed the basics start-up costs; computer equipment, word processing and publishing software, and fax (refer there for further discussion). Once these initial expenses are outlaid, these costs are not reincurred until future technology convinces you that an upgrade is desirable. Meanwhile, the costs of this equipment can be spread out over the many books you'll be publishing.

## Marketing

Depending upon how you promote your books, there will be marketing costs associated with your business. A lot of the marketing will express itself in postage, shipping, printing, phone and time costs. However, as we discussed in the marketing section, these extra costs will generally translate into profits.

## Warehousing & Fulfillment

If the warehousing services of a distributor are not used, and you don't have the storage space in your office or home, you'll need to rent outside warehouse space to store your books. You can hire out a friend's or family's garage or basement space, a mini-storage facility, or if your needs are large, a professional warehousing company that specializes in book storage for publishers. If you're doing self-distribution, you may even hire a fulfillment house to both warehouse your books and fulfill orders.

## Postage and Shipping

The greater this expense, either the better your business is doing, the harder you're trying, or most likely, both. In any case, you want to keep busy using the mails, to promote your books, get new distributors, increase your mail orders, and whatever else, overall, that helps you generate and expand your business.

## Additional Costs

You'll have a host of other costs standard to any business; telephone and utilities, office supplies, copying and small print, and all the other expenses that fit under the category of miscellaneous.

# THE LIST/PRINT RATIO & PROFITS

In the *Initial Marketing and the Decision to Publish* chapter, we talked about setting the list price of a book in relation to the ideal price for the audience being targeted and for its best positioning in the market. We also discussed list price in relation to the price you'll need to charge based on the costs of production and putting a book together. We're going to continue that discussion here and introduce some concepts that are important to consider when pricing your book.

To insure that a book *can be profitable*, you must charge enough to not only cover your expenses but leave yourself room for profits. In publishing, a handy formula for measuring this capability is the List/Print ratio.

Basically put, the **List/Print** ratio is the ratio between the list or retail price of the book, and the costs of producing and printing the book. For example, if a book costs $2.00 each to produce and print, and $9.95 is the list price on the book, then the list/print ratio is 5-1 ($9.95/$2.00). If $15.95 was charged for that same book, then the list/print ration is 8-1 ($15.95/$2.00). In both cases we rounded out to the nearest dollar.

(It's always better to use the 5¢-off price as in $5.95 or $10.95 in discussing list price. Psychologically, $5.95 sounds much cheaper and is a more effective selling price than $6.00, and $10.95 appears to be much cheaper than $11.00.)

At a minimum, we want the list price of a book to be five times the cost of production divided by the number of books printed. That is, we want a list/print ratio of 5-1 at an absolute minimum, though this is really on the low side. A ratio of 6-1 would be better, with a list/print ratio of 8-1 or higher, being more ideal.

This margin takes into account several things. First, if you're going through national exclusive distribution channels, which I strongly recommend, you'll get only 40% of the list price of the book. Second, you have to foot a print bill and pay for the production expenses to get it to that printer. Third, in addition to having the costs of paying the author's royalty, shipping, storing, and fulfilling the orders, and covering all your overhead, there's also down-the-road costs of damaged books and books you just can't sell from the print run. And one more thing. You have to consider the fact that your company must make profits for all these risks.

Pricing yourself below a 5-1 spread - and I personally consider that spread low - gives you margins that are just too tight. For example, if a book costs you $2.50 to print and you charge only $10.00 (a 4/1 spread), but receive $4.00 from your distributor (40% of the retail price - a fairly standard arrangement), then you have just $1.50 left over. If the author is paid 70¢ of that - a 7% royalty - you now have a margin of 80¢. When you consider all the other costs involved in making those books and running your company, that 80¢ margin is simply not enough to make money. In fact, if you value all the other expenses that go into the making of the book, that 4/1 ratio and the 80¢ left over point out that you'll be losing money on this book - even if you sell out the print run.

Using the same $10.00 list price as above with a 6-1 list/print ratio - your printing in this example costs you $1.65 per book - presents a whole different picture. Subtracting the $1.65 printing costs and the 70¢ royalty from the $4.00 received from the distributor, leaves $1.65 as a preliminary margin. Now that's a whole lot more room to work with than the 80¢ in the example above.

Let's go over a full example to see how the list/print ratio works. Let's say a book costs you $4,500 to print, and the pre-production (really pre-printing) costs - production, cover design, some halftones and sepa-rations - cost $500. Thus, our production totals $5,000. If 5,000 books are printed, than we have a cost per book of $1.00. Based on the list/print ratio, at a bare, bare minimum, the retail price should be $5.00 per book, actually $4.95, while $5.95 would be better, and $6.95 better still. If the book can command $9.95 out in the market, a 10-1 ratio, that would be much better again.

Let's say instead that we printed only 3,000 copies with the same $5,000 production totals. Now, our price per book is $1.67. With these num-bers we can't list the book for $4.95 or even $6.95. The book will be priced as a losing proposition, our list/print is simply not high enough. If we charge $9.95 instead, meeting a marketing mandate to keep the book under a $10.00 list price, we get a 6-1 list/print ratio while still maintaining a profitable outlook. And ideally, we would like to get even more than that. But that comes back to marketing decisions and the list price this book will bear for the targeted market.

Basically, we're always trying to set a balance between what we would like to charge as a list price, a higher list price, and what we need to charge, perhaps a lower list price, so the book can be competitive.

The key to making this whole formula work, is to keep production and printing costs down as much as possible. Smaller publishers with a line of books already accepted into the marketplace and steady sales, can reprint books at a lower per-unit cost and do larger print runs on books they know are going to sell because a ready market has already been built for their books. And larger companies, by the same token, can build off their successes and do larger print runs on lines that have already broken the ground and attracted a following.

Keep in mind, that sometimes, on certain books, your pre-press costs may be particularly high, and consequently, there's no way to achieve an ideal list/print ratio on a first run. (As we discussed earlier, you sometimes need to print conservatively on the first run and thus will have a higher print price per book.) However, on reprints, all these pre-press prices drop out, and that, along with the printing getting a little cheaper, allows you to gain back the margins you couldn't achieve on the first printing, and maintain a higher print/list ratio. And there-fore, make more profits.

## More on the 8-1 List/Print Ratio

When possible, you should aim to get the list/print ratio in the 8-1 range or higher. The 8-1 ratio gives you enough built-in margins to be able to afford marketing and promotion, or just simply, to make more money for your efforts. Thus, if a book costs $1.25 to produce, then ideally, you want to list it at $9.95. If the same book costs $1.75, than you would like to get $13.95 (8-1), though at that price point level, you can probably go $14.95 (almost 9-1).

If your marketing sense tells you that the book really needs to retail under $10.00, than maybe you list it at $9.95 (just under 6-1), and on the reprint, with the book already set up, and overall production and printing dropping 50¢ per unit to $1.25, that $9.95 list price nets you an 8-1 list/print ratio.

# WAYS TO INCREASE PROFITS

Following are seven ways that will increase your **net profits** in your business.

## 1. INCREASE THE LIST PRICE

By increasing the list price of a book, you can increase the net percentage received for each book sold. A raise from $8.95 to $9.95 may not reduce sales, but most certainly will increase profits. Of course, raising the list price of a book is a marketing decision that must be thought out carefully. You don't want to price your book out of the marketplace. But then again, you don't want to underprice yourself either.

## 2. REDUCE PRODUCTION COSTS

By lowering the cost of production and printing, or a combination of the two, you can increase the net percentage received for each book sold. Reducing the cost per book can include doing a larger print run and bringing down per unit cost, reducing pre-press expenses, or getting more competitive pricing from printers on your jobs. If you find that you end up paying many extras on your print bill that could have been avoided, look at ways to reduce those costs by being more efficient, or submitting the job differently.

## 3. PAY A SMALLER ROYALTY

Net percentage can be increased by either paying less of a royalty, writing the book yourself, or paying author by the work done - on a strict pay per page or per job basis. Keep in mind however, that your author deserves to share in fair profits, and that he or she shouldn't be cut too tight.

## 4. INCREASE ADDITIONAL REVENUE SALES

Increase net percentage by selling related items to customers through the back of the book (starting your own mail order sales division) or selling advertising space to increase revenue. Also, by increasing the percentage of sales to buyers where no discounts at all are given - direct sales to customers - the overall profit picture improves.

## 5. MAKE HIGHER PERCENTAGE SALES

Increase overall net percentage by making more sales to outlets such as libraries, stores and non-conflicting distributors (you don't want to compete with your distributor who most likely has an exclusive), situations where there's less of a discount, and you receive more per book. Also, reexamine your discount schedule, and if any of your discounts are out of line, try to negotiate them back towards a standard level.

## 6. REDUCE OVERHEAD

Examine your expenses every six months, and see where the fat lies. To do this properly, you'll need to summarize all the checks you've issued and payments you've made into totals for their category, and list them on one page. With everything black and white like this, you'll have a good idea of what's going on, and most likely will be surprised as well.

Don't worry if bad money decisions, such as a bad advertisement or a purchase that was wasteful, are revealed. Mistakes are part of doing business and learning. With a proper list/print ratio, your business will be able to afford the inevitable decisions that don't work out and cost the company some money.

## 7. SELL MORE BOOKS, FIND NEW ACCOUNTS

Spend a few hours each week concentrating on finding new outlets where you can sell more books. With books, the possibilities for sales are almost endless. The more you work at getting new accounts, the more you'll get.

# INCOME FROM DISTRIBUTION

In this section, we'll look at the net income numbers assuming that you use a national distributor to get your books into the market. There are two basic payment structures that distributors use to pay a publisher; payment as a straight percentage of list price, or payment based on their net sales. We'll look at each one.

## Payment as Straight Percentage of List Price

Some distributors might base their payments to publishers as a straight percentage of the list price. When structured this way, the average payment received by the publisher will be around the 40% of the list price mark.

The rest of the 60% would break up as follows; 42-50% would be the margin given to the retailer or distributor, with the rest, 10-18%, kept by the distributor for their expenses and profits.

As we discussed in our distribution chapter, when everything is taken into account, this is a very fair arrangement for the publisher.

## LIST PRICE AND NET PRICE

**List Price** - The price listed on the book's cover - the official price of the book. Also called the **Retail Price**.

**Net price** - the amount received by the vender. In the case of a distributor, it's the amount they receive *after* the bookstore has taken their discount. In the case of the publisher, it's the *amount received*, after the distributor has taken its cut.

## Payment Based on Net Sales

The other payment structure, payments being based on a percentage of net sales, works as follows. We'll say your distributor, we'll call them ABC, pays publishers 76% of the **net price**, the price they receive from their bookstores and distributors, for each book sold.

ABC sells books to all sorts of accounts; individual bookstores, university stores, chain stores, library distributors, wholesalers, book distributors and the like. Depending upon the number of books bought and the type of account, ABC's discount to the account might be anywhere from 44% to 50% per title, with most books sold in the 47-48% range.

We'll assume a $10.00 list price book to make the math easy to follow. At a 50% discount, ABC will receive $5.00 for the $10.00 book; at 48% discount, ABC will receive $5.20 for the same book; and at a 44% discount, they'll receive $5.60. These discounted totals, $5.00, $5.20 and $5.60 are the *net price* - the amount received by ABC after the discount is given to their accounts. The publisher will receive 76% of that amount - that number is the publisher's net. The following chart shows the publisher's net as a percentage of the original list price.

### PAYMENT AFTER THE 24% DISTRIBUTOR SHARE

| Discount | 44% | 45% | 46% | 47% | 48% | 49% | 50% |
|---|---|---|---|---|---|---|---|
| ABC Net | 56% | 55% | 54% | 53% | 52% | 51% | 50% |
| Publisher Net (at 76%) | 43% | 42% | 41% | 40% | 39% | 39% | 38% |

**Discount** is the discount given to accounts; **ABC Net** is the amount received by the distributor; **Publishers Net** represents 76% of ABC's Net expressed in relation to the original list price.

The previous chart shows the percentage of list price we'll get based on the discounts ABC gives its customers. For example, if ABC gives a 48% discount to its customer, we'll end up with only 39% of the list price. If our book lists at $6.95, we'll receive payment of $2.71 for that book - that's 39% of list.

Averaging out the various discounts ABC allows its customers, we find that we'll get an average 39% of List Price for each book sold if the percentage paid by our distributor is based on 76% of net sales. Our net income based on list price then, will be 39% in this example, and that is the numbers we must use to estimate our profit structure. These numbers can change up or down a few percentage points if instead we're paid 75% or 77% of net price, or if the average discount given to the retailers, is higher or lower.

Here's a chart that shows what we'll get for various priced books with our 39% average net:

| 39% AVERAGE NET | | | | |
|---|---|---|---|---|
| **List Price** | $6.95 | $8.95 | $9.95 | $12.95 | $14.95 |
| **Net Price** | $2.71 | $3.49 | $3.88 | $5.05 | $5.83 |

If you're working with a distributor who does base their payments on a net arrangement, you should run through the numbers every six months or so to get a sense of how your profit structure is working out.

Let's move on now and look at some concepts in expanding your business.

# ESTABLISHING A LINE

Establishing and solidifying a line of books is the key to maximizing profits and expanding your business. The basic strategy in establishing a line is to build success upon success.

Once you've scored with one title, and distributors and bookstores are making money selling that book, they'll be eager to buy similar books from your company. Now it's time to pounce on the opportunity and stake out your turf. Come back with another book in the same field and then another and develop your line. These books are easy sales for you to make into the book trade (and the public who bought or heard about the first book) for now your work is known.

If you follow the same principles that made the first book successful, then there's no reason the second book shouldn't be successful. And the third. They're not automatic, but if you do your work well, they're not that far away from being automatic either. You've developed a successful formula that the public is buying. Stick with that formula, and success should stick with you. When I see a book I like, I search out more books by that author or publisher. They've established a level of quality and reputation in my eyes, and I want to buy more of their work. And I'm no different than anyone else out there in this regard.

After my first gaming book, *Winning Casino Blackjack for the Non-Counter,* was successful, my following book, on craps, published six months later - sticking with the casino gambling line - was readily bought by the book trade. They had already made money on my first book, and had expectations, which were met, that they would make money on this book too. From that point, developing my line was easy because I had a ready market. My books were proven sellers.

I increased and expanded my line, laterally adding gaming books such as chess and bridge, to my gambling line until at the time of this writing, I now showed a line of 50 titles on gaming and gambling. In 1993, I parlayed that success by starting **Open Road Publishing** with a partner and developing a line of travel guides. All this came from the tiny seed of carefully constructing my first book, and when it hit, aggressively pursuing my niche market into more books, more shelf space, and more profit for my company, and the distributors and bookstores who carried these books.

## Keeping Within Your Strengths or Creating New Strengths

Developing a line is your first order of business. Once this is established, then, and only then, should you expand your base of strength and expand into new areas, or even better, into parallel areas that are not a far stretch from your original line. Diverting your energies into new ventures before your original line is established can weaken your existing program, and possibly, cause distributors and bookstores to question the validity of your entire program itself.

For example, if your company, *Tennis Pros*, has established a reputation for publishing tennis books, and you decide to take on a how-to woodworking book, *Basic Woodworking Today*, your distributor may have trouble convincing buyers that the *Tennis Pros*, or *the people who publish Tennis Pros*, have the credentials to enter into the woodworking line.

The question might arise, "What do the tennis people know about woodworking?" You can answer questions of this nature, the same way you answered the questions "Who are these tennis people?" on your first book - by producing quality books. You just need to be aware of perceptions when crossing into new lines, and being able to adequately deal with them.

Of course, moving from one line into another is certainly possible. You can move successfully from tennis to woodworking and then on to camping books. Expansion *should* be part of your program - just make sure the timing is right for your particular circumstances. If you're working with a distributor, coordinate with them for the best way to introduce your new line of titles.

Having the time, energy and manpower to develop a new line and get it rolling is a key consideration also when pondering expansion. Timing and readiness is all-important. You're no longer plugging a book into your system of automatic sales. The pro shops, sports stores, tennis magazines and other specialty customers who were a steady buyers of the tennis titles and bought everything you published are not appropriate outlets of your woodworking line, regardless of the respect they may have for your books. They'll have no interest at all in stocking *Basic Woodworking Today*.

Thus, you'll have to pursue a list of accounts interested in woodworking books. If you don't have the time at this juncture in your business, or if the new line diverts too much energy from what you're already good at, expansion is a bad idea. You're better off putting the time into improving the tennis (or related) books - getting more accounts, developing new titles, and improving existing sales.

## Developing a New Line

As a publisher, you'll be brimming with ideas about new books and possibilities, with many of these ideas for books being outside your established specialty.

If you follow the suggestions we've outlined in this book, you have a good chance at success with any book you publish, but keep in mind that success in one line does not necessarily carry over into other lines; you'll have to work hard to get your new line established.

When starting a line, begin with the book that has the best chance of being successful. Other books that you may like better on a personal level should wait until your flagship book, the one that is the strongest title, can get the new line established.

# EXTRA MONEY ON THE BACK PAGES

There's extra money waiting to be harvested on the last few pages of your book, a source of free advertising for your other books and products that can increase the business your book generates. The back pages are a great place to develop a small mail order bookshelf for extra income or a good place to advertise other products you publish in the same field.

We know one very important thing about a consumer who buys your book - they have concretely established that they are interested in the subject matter of the book they purchased. And if they bought once and enjoyed what they purchased, they're quite likely to buy again. All they need is the chance to do so. So why not do a service for your customer and provide them with opportunities to get more items of similar interest from your publishing house?

There are lots of possibilities here for further sales. From developing special advanced reports targeted to the market if you're publishing how-to books, to providing fishing gear for fishing books, or clothing for exercise and dance books, you've got a range of possibilities that may work. You've developed a relationship with your reader as he or she goes through your book, and if they're happy with the approach you've taken and trust your work, they'll be interested in pursuing more advanced information with your company, or other items of quality.

When a reader enjoys a book by a certain author, or a book on a certain subject, typically, they wand to read more and more. For me, it's a gift to find an author I really like, and I'll buy everything I can get my hands on by that same author. Similarly, if the subject is how-to or non-fiction, the same principles apply. People fascinated by the JFK conspiracy theories eat up every new book written on the subject, while baseball fans will devour books on baseball, and people into Danielle Steele for example, can't wait until her new books show.

That's the nature of the marketplace, and in one of those rare freaks of life, the logic in it actually makes sense. Whatever you publish, don't be afraid to let the reader know you have other items for sale, or that these items are found in their local bookstore.

## Doing the Order Form

To achieve the most from your free advertising space, you have to make it easy for the reader to act on your offers. And that means having an order form and even better, a toll-free 800 number with the ability to take credit cards to go along with it (if the 800 number makes sense in your situation). Providing the reader with these easy-to-use forms of ordering will maximize potential sales. Clip-out coupons also work great.

The order form must contain several basics; the price of the item, the cost of shipping, and how the reader can take advantage of your offer - that is, your address - where the money gets sent.

The following page shows a sample order form. Notice that it includes the ordering address and phone - very important.

# TAKING CHANCES IN PUBLISHING
# - Going for the Downs

Now and then an exciting book may roll across your desk, one offering excellent potential profits, but one which requires a great deal more investment than you're accustomed to. If the book's possibilities intrigue you though, you should give the project some thought, some very careful thought. I would consider a project of this nature only under the following conditions:

## SAMPLE ORDER FORM

## CARDOZA PUBLISHING
### ORDER FORM

For U.S. and Canada, please include $3.00 postage and handling for the first books ordered, and 50¢ for each additional item. Other countries, double these amounts. Orders outside USA, send money order payable in US dollars on US bank only.

Name _____

Address _____

City _____ State _____ Zip _____

| Quantity | Your Order | Price |
|----------|------------|-------|
|          |            |       |
|          |            |       |
|          |            |       |
|          |            |       |
|          |            |       |

Make checks payable to
**Cardoza Publishing**
**132 Hastings Street**
**Brooklyn, NY 11235**
**(718)743-5229**

| | |
|---|---|
| Subtotal | |
| Postage and Handling | |
| NY residents add 8.25% | |
| **Total** | |

**1.** Stick with your strengths. This is not always true, but it usually is. Specialization that brings success to one in his or her own limited field, often doesn't carry over when that person steps outside their own waters. There are a million examples of this. For example, there are professional poker players who make tens and even hundreds of thousands of dollars playing poker, but end up flat broke as gamblers.

Why? These players move away from their strengths and blow their winnings on other gambles such as sports betting, craps or the horses, games they either don't have the skills to beat, or simply, that cannot be beaten.

What are your strengths? Better figure them out, before you move forward.

**2.** Kick the idea around with your family and friends. They know you and can give you good outside advice. You don't have to listen to the advice, but you should hear it.

**3.** Make sure you can afford the downside risk if the book flops. Don't jeopardize your entire business and all your hard-earned success over one project. If you do, you're a fool.

**4.** If you're going to do this special book, do it right. Don't kill the book because you got cheap on the promotion or on the design if that's what the book requires to be successful. Half-assing an ambitious project is a sure way to doom it. Thus, do it right, or don't do it at all.

**5.** If you feel the book is too risky, stop right there. *The book is too risky.* Go with your head, not your emotions.

**6.** Talk about the book with your distributor. Their input is vital. If they're pessimistic about the product, you should probably reconsider.

**7.** If you're sticking your neck out somewhat, make sure the potential rewards are there. Don't take what you consider a big chance if the upside is only okay. If the risk is substantial, the upside must be tremendous - or don't do it.

## MAKING MONEY WITH NEW EDITIONS

If an original title you've published does well, and you're able to sell through or nearly through your print run, you have the opportunity to reprint the book with substantial improvements *and* possibly substantial sales. The advantage of the new edition is that it allows you to present the book as if it was a new book, and thus reap the benefit of a nice sell-in. Sell-ins give books a giant boost that could amount to six months or more of sales in a single go.

As long as a reprint must be done, if changes are substantial, you may want to announce the book as a new edition - with a new ISBN and Library of Congress Number, and updated text.

This, as opposed to a reprint where no announcement is made, and the book simply gets reprinted (perhaps with some changes if needed) and plugged into your pipeline without any ado.

Once your book is established in the trade as a book with a positive sales history, then you have a marketable commodity. The book has already proven itself where it counts - in the marketplace, and buyers will be anxious to rebuy the book as a new edition.

## Improving Your New Edition or New Printing

To maximize the potential sales of your book in the marketplace requires a constant reassessment of your book's interior and cover design. There's always room for improvement in a books' design, and it is the smart publisher who realizes this and constantly strives to make that improvement.

One of my titles, *Beat the Odds*, a mass-market sized paperback covering five gambling games, went through five different book covers on five different printings before I finally was pleased enough with the result and let the cover ride two printings in a row, a record for the book.

In one sense, this is lunacy (and it is), but on the other hand, I felt that the book had much more potential than what it had already shown and I wanted to get the book to the level of sales I felt it belonged. Its sales improved cover by cover, but I knew sales could be better. (You probably would too if you saw how bad the previous cover was - I really had done an awful job.) Well, you might ask, why didn't I do it right the first time, or at least the second time? Good question.

Publishing is a learning process with lots of trial and error, and it is the successful publisher who will move forward through it all and realize that a better job can be done, and then do it. If you're always slapping yourself on the back for the wonderful job you're doing, you'll gain dexterity in your arm, but you'll never improve your books. But if you constantly reassess your work, and look at your books from an honest and open vantage point, as best you can, you'll see ways to produce a better book, and will be able to improve your sales.

Will I change the cover again? Probably, but only slightly if I do. The book is now one of my distributors top 30 best-selling titles, and I'm a big believer in the maxim, "If it ain't broke, don't fix it." If something is working near its full potential, or at a level that is its full potential, then don't play with a successful formula. Of course, it's hard to know what the full sales potential of any book is, but if you feel you're close, don't mess with success.

Always keep your eyes open for improvement. There's always one more thing you can do to help your book's sales or improve its quality. Do that one more thing, time and again, and you'll find that success will have a hard time denying you it's satisfaction.

# 18. MULTIMEDIA PUBLISHING

## INTRODUCTION

This section is just a brief overview of the processes involved in producing multimedia software products for the retail market. It is by no means inclusive since a full book would need to be devoted to properly cover all aspects of the business. However, this introductory chapter will give you an overview of the realities and some of the processes involved in software publishing.

### Staying Timely and Predicting the Marketplace

In developing and publishing multimedia titles, it is absolutely mandatory that you stay up to date with the times. Computer technology is dynamic, and what is in vogue now, may be and probably will be outdated in six to twelve months. With some game products, that shelf life may be as little as three months. That's it! Outdated methods of operation may work in other fields, but in the software industry, if you don't run with the herd, you're not going to be a player.

When I formed Cardoza Entertainment in late 1995, the Pentium 60 computers were just making headway into the market, Windows for the PC was not yet a standard, DOS was the typical platform, and almost all games were delivered on floppy disks.

We were ready to do our game design and had some decisions to make. Of most importance, what platform would we develop the game for–DOS, Windows? Additionally, would we gear the game for delivery on a floppy disk, or the up and coming CD ROM formats? These were important decisions, and had we made the wrong calls, our project would have been doomed from the start. To borrow a term from the game of poker, *we would be drawing dead* (betting on a future card that could not possibly beat the stronger hand of an opponent no matter what card was drawn). That is, regardless of how well we proceeded along, the project would be doomed to failure because we were working in a media that was going to be outdated.

At the time, knowing little about the field, I asked lots of questions of publishers, developers, potential future distributors who I was trying to interest in our game, and anyone else who had working knowledge of the software business. I did a lot of listening to figure out what was going on in the market and where things were headed. While there was much disagreement among players in the know, a central theme seemed to emerge: "DOS is dead." (This now antiquated operating system for the IBM and compatibles required programming-like action to operate, and for the average Joe, was way too complicated. Macintosh already had the issue solved with their easy-to-use point and click system, but they dropped the ball, and allowed the IBM and compatibles to dominate the market and push the Mac platform to near extinction.)

A new platform was emerging, one that would catapult Bill Gates into a billionaire and revolutionize not only the computer industry, but have far-reaching effects throughout society and the way the world operated as well. Windows was the great revolution that propelled the entire software industry into a new age. With windows anyone with an IBM or compatible was easily able to operate a computer and tap into the vast resources and power of these machines. The IBM-compatible world finally had an answer to the Macintosh. The computer revolution *really* was born. Hardware and software sales skyrocketed.

By the time *Avery Cardoza's Casino* came out, in early 1997, Windows had replaced DOS as the standard operating system, and completely dominated the marketplace. Times had really changed. You couldn't even talk to a distributor unless your product was not only Windows-based but delivered on a CD ROM as well. Products delivered on a floppy disk were just about history. If we told the retail marketplace that our game operated in a DOS environment, we would have been laughed out of their office. Actually, that's not true. We never would have gotten into anyone's office to even talk to them about what we had.

The point of all this? The marketplace had completely changed in the two year span from the start of our development to our product release. Had we not been savvy to the changes occurring in the marketplace, and consequently made the wrong decisions (which undoubtedly many other developers and publishers did) we would have been two years and one million dollars sorrier. It would be like releasing a record collection while CD's are the music industry's standard, or a fancy buggy cart when autos were already the rage. We would be delivering old technology into a new marketplace. Not good.

What's happened since then? Plenty. Pentium 60's became outdated within six months of our inception as did their successors six months later. P60's (pentium 60's) were followed by P75's, P90's, and P120's. The first group of upgraded machines for our staff, the P120's (to replace our older P60's) were state of the art when we upgraded. Six months later, my programmers were complaining again about the antiquity of their machines. We upgraded again to twin processing P200's, and now these are old machines. P300's, then P400's, then the next generation of machines will be on their way. What is a screaming hardware system as I write this paragraph will be outdated by the time you read this, probably by two generations. And before I get to updating this book, even those machines will be dinosaurs.

Further changes since I opened doors in 1995 were that the CD ROM became a standard component on every Mac and IBM compatible computer made, as were the Windows operating systems for the IBM compatibles. First generation CD ROM's went to double speed, 4X, 6X, 8X, 12X, and 24X. Email, which was a foreign concept to most people in 1995 and 1996, became the new medium of communication for business and personal use. The same with the internet. Going on-line is now *de rigeur*. Times are changing fast with the technology and equipment, and to be successful, you'll need to change along with it.

## THE SEVEN PERILS OF MULTIMEDIA PUBLISHING

Developing and publishing computer software is one of the most difficult businesses one can find and I would not recommend this venture for the average person. There are many hurdles to overcome to become successful in this field, and these hurdles are not easy. From finding a skilled and reliable staff, to funding a business with a bottomless pit, to getting distribution and then getting paid, the entire process can be nightmarish at times. In this section, I am going to outline the various perils involved in getting through it all, and well, if that doesn't scare you, welcome to the lion's den.

## 1. Financing

Developing and publishing software is flat out expensive. Whether it's your money, and you'll need a lot of it, or someone else's, and you'll still need a lot of it, the bills will pile up fast. Skilled programmers and artists are pricy, computer equipment must be updated during the course of the project, and there are more et ceteras than you will be able to plan for. A lot more.

Your best guess for what the project will cost will not nearly be enough money. Software projects are notorious for being delayed and concomitantly, running over budget. The delays run amok in every software company regardless of the skill set of the players, the size of the company, or the number of people thrown at the project. Delays are simply a fact of life in the software business and virtually every company and project experiences them.

Our first project, *Avery Cardoza's Casino,* ran fifteen months behind schedule, and our current project at the time of this writing, the development of an online casino, is already late and we're still in the design stage! Even the behemoth itself, Microsoft, which has more money and access to more talent, runs into massive delays every time they release a new version of Windows.

The point is, not only do you need to count on delays, *budget them in*. If your production team gives you a date, even guarantees a date for delivery, don't hold your breath. Get them off the stack of bibles they're swearing on, and relieve them from their promise: it's not going to happen. Expect at least several months in delays, perhaps a year or more on a large project.

## 2. Skilled Staff

Money and delays are just the start of your worries. You also have to hire a competent staff that has the ability to plan out and complete the project. This is where the real fun begins.

**a. Hiring an Art Department:** Here's the good news: The skills of an artist are easy to judge. You simply look at their work, and if you like their work, you know what you'll be getting. If you don't like the work you see, you keep looking until you find the artist or artists who has the style appropriate to what the project needs. The work speaks for itself. Of course, you also want to make sure they can work in the basic art programs that will be needed.

**b. Hiring the Programming Team:** Here's the bad news: The difficulty in hiring and working with programmers is that you can never really see what they're doing until the project is well under way, if not complete. You could conceivably hire an incompetent or insufficiently skilled programmer and not find out that he's not up to the task until the project is handed over for testing! You may be in big trouble if the programmer can't work out the "bugs," glitches or "gotchas" that plague the program and interfere with its proper functioning.

Maybe the news isn't quite as bad, and the bugs *can* be worked out, except that it will take "two months" to do, says the programmers. Two months more of payroll and expenses will be the cost if it takes only two months (which it won't) and if they can even do it (probably, but there are no guarantees).

Even if you find out somehow, halfway through a project, say in the six to 12 months time frame, that your programmer isn't up to the task, you may need to start from scratch if he did nothing worth building on. And then you have to find another programmer and go through the same doubts again. Or perhaps he can't get along with you or the other staff and quits. Or the programmer simply quits midway through the project because it is not interesting to him. *Anything can happen.*

### 3. Post-Release Gotcha

Hopefully you have tested your product well for functionality *and* on a wide variety of hardware configurations, at least enough so that you can release the product with confidence. But you never really know until the consumers get hold of the product and you're under "live" testing. That's the acid test.

It has happened, and can happen to you, that your program has such major problems that the entire run has to be recalled from the trade.

Not only are you out all your manufacturing costs and marketing expenses (more on that later), but if you're a first time player, you may have signed your death warrant in the trade. It's hard enough to get a product on the shelves. If you crash and burn on your first opportunity, you and your very expensive project may be history.

## 4. Retail and Distribution

Not enough potholes yet? The beat goes on. Let's say you get through the above "tests" and get your product finished. And believe me, it won't be easy. Programmers and artists can be a cranky and creative bunch, and that means things will not go smoothly. But let's say you've successfully plowed through the problems and are ready to get distributed.

Well, now you're thrown in with the piranhas. The distributors in this business will eat you alive if they can and the retailers will be in the feeding frenzy as well. Whatever meat the retailers can't pick off your bones as **MDF's** (Market Development Funds), fees charged by retailers just to get onto their shelves, the distributors will get through **rebates**, a percentage taken off the top of every sale, and **coops**, cooperative advertising done theoretically to promote your product (a huge profit center to them with little benefit to you from the money spent).

Distributors will use every bit of leverage they have to get you to sign one-sided, blatantly unfair agreements, that with a little luck, will leave you with enough scraps to make dinner with. You'll need to fight tooth and nail to get an agreement to a fair level, and to do so, you'll need to have your own leverage, and you'll need to be tough. It won't be pretty. Without a product that gives you leverage, you'll be negotiating on uneven terms.

But let me not pick on the distributors too much, for the publishers, who can also act as distributors, can be even worse. When I was negotiating with publishers for distribution deals, I was incredulous at the clauses they had the nerve to include. Overall, these contracts were so obnoxious that I told them to simply shove their contracts up their hinterlands, and far. When my lawyer looked at one of the contracts I actually signed, he asked me, "How can you sign such a piece of paper?" I replied, "You should have seen the contract before the changes were inserted." He shook his head in disbelief when I showed him clauses that some companies tried to pass over on me. The contract I signed wasn't ideal, but it was workable. Bottom line, you have to eat a little dirt to get into this business, but hopefully, not too much of it. *

* By contrast, in the book business, I have never been handed anything but a fair contract from a distributor.

Are we having fun yet?

## 5. Packaging and Product

If your product is not unique, interesting enough, or properly priced, and your product doesn't bring out that message clearly, you may not even have to worry about battling distributors over your contract - you'll be sunk before you even had a chance to swim. As with books, and even more so in this field, the product often sells by the cover. With a lousy cover, the odds are good you won't even get a chance for consumers to be under underwhelmed by it–retail won't even pick it up to begin with. Hello Titanic.

Big hint: Spend the extra money to make a better box. You must make software retail packaging compelling and exciting, or baby, y'all not coming back now, y'hear?

## 6. The Product Must Sell

If you've made the right decisions, created a good product, and made a sizzling box, hopefully everything will fall in as it should at retail: consumers will be wowed enough by the product to buy enough numbers to generate reorders in the trade and create a market for your product. And hopefully, the product will receive reviews in the proper media will help push sales.

At this stage, you're now on the cusp of success as long as enough sales are made to justify the money and efforts that have gone into the product.

On to the next step.

## 7. Getting Paid

Let's say you've worked out a reasonable arrangement with some distributors, you arrange your manufacturing and shipping, your product meets with approval and some excitement at distribution and retail, and you have shipped a product into the marketplace that will not be recalled or and trigger massive returns. All is going well.

Now, you must get paid. Making sales is one thing, getting the greens for it is another. Distributors take their dear sweet time paying the bills, and when you do get payments, they may be a lot less than you were hoping for. When you see the deductions that will come off your check from MDF's, co-ops, returns that were or weren't made, marketing allowances, and whatever else that may show up, you'll get the full picture of what I mean about the software business being tough. If you're not on top of your accounts and checking the validity of your deductions, you'll be swallowed whole.

A typical payment schedule may be net 60, though in reality, payments may come a lot closer to net 90, net 120, or more, depending upon your leverage, the distributor, and how the distributor is doing from a cash flow perspective. Some distributors have payment terms unaffectionately known as "net never." In any case, you'll need to aggressively stay on top of the distributors to get payments close to what was agreed.

## Wrapping Up the Seven Perils

I haven't covered all the gory details but you get the idea: This business is not for the meek and weak of heart. When you enter the software business, you're entering a very high risk enterprise that demands a certain amount of toughness to survive. You've been warned.

That's the down side. Now to the positive side of the coin.

## The Good News

The good news is that if you can navigate through the trenches and treacherous waters of development, complete a product, and get it through distribution and onto the shelves, you'll not only find that sales can be very substantial, but you'll get a high dollar price for your products.

For example, our first CD ROM game, with a suggested price of $39.95 retail, was bringing in about $29.00 wholesale (actually closer to $26-$27 after some built-in deductions). That's a healthy markup by general retail standards. As a comparison, in the book industry, a book marked as $14.95 retail will fetch me back roughly $6.00 after distribution and retail have taken their cuts. Not bad, but a far cry less than I get selling CD ROM's.

Once you've been successful with a product, you will have created a market hungry for anything else you can put out on a similar theme, assuming the same level of quality is maintained.

# THE TYPES OF PLAYERS IN MULTIMEDIA

There are various roles played in the production and distribution of multimedia titles, and this section will give you a brief overview of these roles. Unlike the book trade, where there are roughly two types of basic entities, the book publisher and the distributor, the software trade has a whole set of partial entities in between. We'll look at these below.

## Developers

A developer programs and produces the final product that will be mass-produced. There are development houses which do nothing but provide game titles to larger publishers on contract. Developers will often work for several publishers at a time if they are large enough, or sometimes will concentrate most of their work for an individual house that they have a good relationship with. Typically, development companies will be paid according to a milestone schedule. The first milestone will be the contract and the last milestone may be the final version of the product or its actual delivery onto the marketplace. In between, other milestones will be marked for each stage of the project that is completed.

In addition to the money paid for development of the project, which may be an outright payment, an advance against royalties, or some combination of the two, will be royalties based on sales. Developers, like other players in the business, have a tough road to hoe, as the production of a project is no easy feat.

Developers are developers because they don't want to take the risks associated with publishing, or can't afford to take the risks. This way, they get paid for their work, and if a project goes well, can gather tidy profits if one of their projects hits it big.

## Publishers

Publishers bear the risk of bringing a project to market, paying for the development costs, and getting the product onto the shelves. This distribution occurs either through their own in-house efforts or those of a hired sales force, affiliate label relationship, or distributor. With costs being what they are, publishers are at enormous risk in this business, and cannot afford too many mistakes.

While Cardoza Entertainment is both a developer and distributor, though all our development is for our own publishing efforts, there are players who simply act as publishers, and leave the majority the development headaches to the developers.

## Hybrid Publisher-Developer Relationships

The enormous expenses of developing a game and bringing a product to market makes it difficult for start-ups, developers, and underfinanced publishers to take on the full role and risks of the publisher. As a result, the void between wanting to be a full-on publisher with all the rewards if the product line is a success, and the straight developer with just a 10-15% cut or so, has created many hybrid relationships that don't fit in strictly with either type of role.

There are many degrees of this relationship depending upon the amount of risk a developer is willing to take on. For example, if the developer agrees to design and pay for the packaging and initial marketing, two very large bills, he will get a larger share of the pie than if he just produces the product but takes none of the publishing risks. The more risks that are taken in the form of monetary outlays, the larger the cut a developer will get.

These "hybrids" are usually found in some form of an affiliated label relationship and we'll look at that and the distribution channels now.

# RETAIL AND DISTRIBUTIONS
## Affiliated Labels (AL)

Many of the larger publishers have set up affiliated label programs to not only augment their income, but to increase their presence in the retail trade. Taking on additional products that are developed elsewhere is typically an important part of a large publisher's product line, and indeed, many of a large publisher's biggest hits are produced out of house.

At the heart of the AL program is the distribution the big publisher offers, for in software, as in books, getting the product onto retail shelves is the lifeline to being successful. Additionally, the large financial resources of the larger players allows the smaller players to play the game when the two sides can strike a deal. The small player produces the product, the big player gets it to market and nurtures it there.

The AL relationships can take on many forms, particularly when a new publisher is strapped for cash, and certainly when the company is a development house. These can range from the straight affiliated label deal where the larger publisher acts as a strict distributor and the AL client is responsible for delivering the completed product in its packaging and paying for the marketing, to one of the hybrids discussed earlier, where the larger publisher takes on some of those functions also.

When the AL publisher client takes on all the risk, the standard arrangement is to keep 75-80% of the wholesale receipts, with the larger publisher getting the other 20-25% for distribution fees. When the client takes on less of these risks, the larger publisher, of course, will get a much larger share of the receipts according to a program they have developed.

Most of the larger publishers have active affiliated label deals. Some companies that have affiliate label programs are Electronic Arts, Interplay, Maxis, and Brodurbund. You might want to check on medium size or even smaller companies as well as a way to enter the market.

## Sales Force

When you act as your own publisher, you will need an experienced sales force to get your product in front of the retailers. Unless you're very well funded and have enough products to justify hiring your own sales force, the best choice is to work with an outside sales force, a group of professionals that will represent several lines to the trade. This is the route I chose, and in my case, it worked out great.

The sales forces' job is to get your product in front of the buyers, and get these buyers to commit to a certain amount of units. Typically, this entails a commitment on your part to do marketing with the retailer, for the buyer to agree to carry your product. The MDF's, marker development funds, required to launch a product can easily exceed $100,000. Get used to the large sums of money asked of you, because you'll need to spend the dough to get shelf space. That is a reality in this industry.

Once an order is firmed up by your sales force, it will now get funneled, usually at the retailers request, through a particular distributor that either they have a preferred relationship with, or the one that cuts them the best deal.

It is essential that the sales force you use has experience and contacts in the trade. Personal and business relationships are extremely important in this industry. Calling in a good salesperson with no experience to present your product to the retail buyers will lead to disaster–don't even think about this as an option.

Keep in mind that the sales force acts only as an order taker, but at the same time, don't underestimate the value of a good sales force. They are the lifeline of your money.

I've only listed one sales force below, Tri Synergy, because it is the only one I would recommend. They've done a terrific job with my products and saved me tons of money by negotiating good deals on my behalf. With such a stellar performance, I could not even mention any other organization in the same breath, let alone the same page. This is not to say that other organizations won't do a good job as well. But I cannot believe any sales organization would have done even half the job of Try Synergy.

To get in touch with Tri-Synergy, contact Tamra Nestler at Tamranest@aol.com, (972)307-1799.

## Distributors

The majority of product that sits on the retailers shelf gets there through the hands of the various distributors that handle the trade. If you are being distributed by a larger publisher under an affiliated label arrangement, that publisher will already have contracts and relationships in place and will fit your product in under those agreements. However, if you are using the services of an independent sales force, you will need to establish those arrangements yourself, since in this case, you will be the one supplying the distributors with stock.

Multiple distributors will be needed to supply the trade, a topic we'll discuss below in a little more depth. Below is a list of some of the software distributors that are players in the industry. Each company has its own submission process, and you'll need to contact them individually to see how it applies to your product.

## Distributor List

Following is a short list of multimedia software distributors that service retail accounts. I have not listed contact names or the retailers with whom they have special relationships as everything in this industry is so mercurial that such a list would be out of date by the time this book came off the press.

As I've mentioned elsewhere, dealing with distributors is not easy, so the listing of any company below is not an endorsement of any type, just a listing so you know who you may need to contact to get your products out on the market.

**Beamscope Canada,** 33 West Beaver Creek Road, Richmonc Hill, Ontario L4B 1L8; (905)763-3000, (800)268-5535, fax (201)763-3001.

**GT Interactive,** 16 East 40th Street, New York, NY 10016; (212)726-6500, fax (212)679-6850.

**Ingram Micro,** 1600 E. St. Andrew Place, P.O. Box 25125, Santa Ana, CA 92799-5125; (714)566-1000.

**Merisel Inc,** 200 Continental Blvd., P.O. Box 984, El Segundo, CA 90245-0984, (310)615-3080.

MULTIMEDIA PUBLISHING

**Micro Central,** POB 1009/8998, Rte 18N, Old Bridge, NJ 08857; (908)360-0300, fax (908)360-1369.

**Navarre,** 7400 49th Avenue North, New Hope, MN 55428; (612)535-8333, fax (612)533-2156.

**Tech Data**, 5350 TechData Dr., Clearwater, FL 33760; (800)237-8931, fax (727)538-7876.

## Distributors and Exclusivity

While going too deeply into any aspect of the contract is beyond the scope of this book, (and such a conversation belongs with your council anyway), one warning you'll need to take heed of: Do *not* sign any contract giving a distributor an exclusive on getting your project into the trade. No one distributor has close relationships with all the important accounts you would like to get into. You will need multiple distributors.

Retailers have certain distributors they will work with, and certain ones they won't. To effectively cover the whole market, you'll need a relationship with at least two or three distributors (that's at least two or three negotiations–have fun). So avoid letting any distributor box you into any type of exclusive deal, or affix penalties in the contract for working with their competitors.

This warning applies only to regular distributors whose business is solely in acting as a reselling agent to retail, not to affiliate label relationships where a publisher also acts as a distributor. In an affiliate label relationship, an exclusive arrangement would be appropriate as that company would be the one sales voice of your products to the various distributors and retailers.

## The Retailer

Almost all software products sold in large volume get sold through the retail channel. Major software vendors like Comp USA, Electronics Boutique, Best Buy, and others, can move a lot of product, and it will be important for you to establish relationships with as many of these important retailers as possible.

As with distribution, if you're under an affiliate label relationship, these arrangements will be taken care of already. But if you're going solo as an independent publisher, you'll need to make sales arrangements with each retailer individually, and that is best handled through an experienced sales force.

Keep in mind as you prepare to get your product into the software retail channel that shelf space is at a premium, and you'll need to pay to play by supporting the retail channel with various marketing programs. We'll look at these MDF's next.

## Market Development Funds (MDF)

While the costs of getting onto the shelves can be high, with a successful product, it's actually not too bad compared to other industries. I would say the high cost entry (retail MDF's) but low markup model in software distribution is preferable to the book industry, the caveat being that your product would need to be successful. The industry has evolved so that retail takes very little markup, and to stay afloat, they ask for market development funds to help support the product.

When you average all things together, the low markup compared to the weighty entrance fee in the form of MDF's, the bottom line comes out favorable for the pubilsher-that is, only if your product sells well. However, if your product is not successful, and relatively few sales are generated, these MDF's will be a painful pill to swallow.

## Retail List

Some of the major retailers in software are CompUSA, Elek-Tek, Hastings, Egghead, Babbages, Best Buy, Computer City, Staples, Office Max, Office Depot, Costco, Target, Walmart, BJ's Wholesale, and Sam's Club.

## SALES AND DISTRIBUTION AS A PUBLISHER

To get your product out to market, you will need to use the services of a professional organization. You have two basic choices here. You can go it alone as I did, using your own identity and hiring the services of a professional sales force, or you can go under the auspices of a larger publisher such as Electronic Arts, Maxis, or Interplay, and sign what is called an Affiliated Label, or AL deal.

When it came time for me to get my product distributed, I thought long and hard about working through a large publisher as opposed to using a sales force. It's a tough decision that every new publisher must decide upon. On one hand, the AL program offers stability and the advantages of riding on the back of a large player, while using one's own sales force offers greater control and higher profits–if they can get the job done for you.

In my case, I chose going through a sales organization and it couldn't have worked out better. My title, *Avery Cardoza's Casino*, became a best-seller, and the product launched our company, Cardoza Entertainment, into a certain recognition in the trade, a recognition which helped us with our second title, *Avery Cardoza's 100 Slots*, and that will help us with any future titles.

The main advantage of a sales force, if you get a good one, is that the costs of getting out into the channel is much less than working with a AL deal. The typical sales force would ask for 10% of your sales as commission compared to 20-25% of the affiliated label deals. Note that these numbers are approximates and may vary by a few percentage points. The actual deal you sculpt will be a function of how strong your product is, what the current market conditions are for products, and how badly the sales force or AL label wants to have your product in its stable. This difference between 10% and 25% is significant and will add up to a ton of money over the short run and many tons in the long run if things work out for you. For Cardoza Entertainment, the difference was astronomical and allowed us to be in a financial position we never could have reached going through an AL relationship.

Another important advantage, if you work with the right sales force, is that your product will get a lot of personal attention and there is nothing as critical as this for the success of your product and your company. A third advantage that I would consider important, is that using a sales force allows you to promote your brand identity since it's not subjugated under big labels' auspices. If your product sells well, forging your own identity is a good thing.

You want to make sure that the agreement with your sales force is for a long term basis, and not just for the launch of the product. I would recommend against using any sales force whose approach was just to launch your product for the first three months then leave you to your own methods. I thought then, and still think now, that you need to have your sales force tied in with your long term interests because that also ties them into your success. They then have a stake in the big picture. Working with distribution and retail is rough and you need a representative to hold your interests and help fight your fights out there. My sales force had my long range interests at heart and fought battles to get my MDF's down that an organization with a shorter vision never would have even contested. After all, it's not their money, why should they care?. Thus, they helped me reduce requested MDF funds to lower amounts.

On the other hand, the AL labels offer some good things as well. A well-known publisher pushing your product should harness immediate acceptance of your product into the marketplace and rapid widespread distribution into the channel. That's the theory. If you do sign an AL deal, however, you need to feel confident that this company will push your product as if its their own and not let it get lost in the shuffle of their big mix, particularly their own product line. While they will always assure you otherwise, make sure you get the right feelings on this. Talking to other AL partners will be one step in that direction.

I have never worked with an AL deal, going independent right from the beginning, but the fear of getting lost in the shuffle along with settling for a smaller piece of the pie were the two largest negatives I had to making such an arrangement. To be sure, some AL deals have worked out great for certain publishers, but by the same token, some have not. The same could be said for going independent. My sense is that an AL deal would have worked great for my product line, and in fact I had a deal in place for a while (losing that deal when my product fell too far behind schedule), but the way things turned out, gong with the sales force was the right decision for us–and in a big way.

One advantage to working with an AL label that was impressed upon me by the larger publishers with whom I was negotiating was that they have a lot more leverage to collect money for products sold compared to being an independent with just one product. This is undoubtedly true as leverage is important in this industry. A publisher with modest sales will have trouble getting the proper attention from the payable department. We have much stronger than modest sales at Cardoza

Entertainment, and we have our own battles getting paid, but the money does make it to us, albeit, not without going through a process akin to extracting teeth, and not on time. And while this is a process that is never smooth, it is manageable and not overwhelming.

I wonder if I wouldn't have the same struggles getting my payments from the AL deals. It's possible that the large publishers don't go through the same struggles I do getting paid, I don't know, but I suspect they do But since my game is successful, my main distributors have been responsive with the payments, if sometimes a little slow. But hey, this is the software business. On the other hand, my lesser distributors, some of whom are very large, have ran the gamut from practicing less than wholesome business practices to put it kindly, to being outright crooks.

In any case, getting money from retail and distribution is notoriously slow in the software channels, and that's what you'll have to deal with. If you have a good product, they will pay, especially if you threaten to stop shipping until they catch up with payments. (That gentle nudge works wonders sometimes.) Just don't expect payments to come the day they're due.

In making the decision on how you'll enter the market, hopefully, you'll be faced with a couple of good choices. I cannot steer you one way or the other because everyone has their unique situation. You'll need to weigh out those options on your own. It's a very tough decision. However, if you can't figure it out intellectually, which will probably be the case, my best advice is to go with your instincts and the organization your are most comfortable with. That will be probably end up being the right choice.

# THE DEVELOPMENT TEAM

The basics of a development team consists of artists, programmers, and a producer-designer. On a small project, or one operating by the shoestring, there may be only one programmer, one artist, and an individual that functions as the designer, drawing up the production plans. Often, the designer will double as the producer, the person who coordinates the development, or that same person may even be the programmer.

On larger projects, two, three, or even dozens of programmers, artists, and various producers and other creative types may be employed to get the job done.

## The Roles of The Staff

Producing a multimedia product requires a highly skilled staff proficient in the technologies and techniques requisite to make a product compatible with the majority of machines. The three types of roles that form the heart of a production team are the producer, the programmers, and the artists. Other employees will be needed as well to run a successful development, particularly the non-development people that help run the business end or assist one of the three core positions.

However, we will concentrate our discussion here on the three positions that form the core of the actual development. We will also give a brief look at the technical writer's role as well as that of the associate producer.

## Producer

The development of a multimedia project requires close teamwork among the creative staff as well a leader to push the whole process forward toward its completion. In a nutshell, this is the job of the multimedia producer. Using a design document as a guideline, the producer's responsibility is to liaison between the various creative people and make sure each department achieves its' objectives. He or she will work closely with the artists to achieve the right look and feel of the product, the visual aspect of the product that the user will see, as well as supervising the programming staff, to see that the objectives of the design are achieved.

From the technical standpoint, the producer should have some knowledge of programming limitations and constraints, or at least the ability to understand them when they are explained by his engineers so that on-the-fly decision can be made as the project progresses.

Ultimately, it is the producer's job to make sure the project gets completed.

## Programmers

The programming team is responsible to create code that can read by the computer and allow the software being written to function according to the design specs created for the project. The final code must be able handle all aspects of the game, from allowing it to load up onto various types of hardware configurations, to all the screen changes, audio, logic flow, and other aspects of the program. This is not a trivial task, in fact, the programmers, in many ways, are the most important members of the team.

When there is more than one programmer involved, the team will need a leader to direct the flow and assignment of the work. This position is called the lead programmer (or sometimes lead engineer). The lead programmer will set the tone of the development, determine the overall architecture of the system to be used, and assign and supervise the individual duties of each member of the team.

## The Art Department

The art department, which could consist of one artist, or a bank of them, gives the project the visual look as it will appear to the consumer. Their work, in essence, showcases the entire project. Most of the artwork created in games now are created in 3D programs such as Studio Max, though 2D art and other graphic programs such as Photoshop, Corel Draw, and Illustrator, still play a vital role in development.

One thing to keep in mind when hiring artists: Even if you're producing games on the PC platform, the artist can work on Macintoshes or the PC. For example, in the games we produce, we create many of the images we use in Photoshop on the Mac, and using this excellent program called Debabalizer, convert them over to a format that will be used on the PC.

## Technical Writer

The technical writer's job is creating the official documentation that will be used as the master print from which to develop the project. Sometimes, this individual will be the programmer himself, especially in small companies. To do this properly, the technical writer will need to coordinate with all facets of the team, particularly the designer and the programmers.

## Associate Producer/Audio Engineer

Another development role is the associate producer position, an individual whose job is to take on other responsibilities that may not fall directly into the shoulders of the producer, programmer, and artist, or to assist them in various projects. For example, our associate producer was responsible for synching up the sound to the animations in our game, as well as configuring the install program so that it functioned according to our needs.

# DEVELOPMENT AND PLANNING

Inadequate planning is a blueprint for disaster in software development. As in constructing a building, work cannot proceed properly until the entire structure is planned out. There really is very little difference between software development and construction as regards planning. Both need architects to plan out the loads each structure will carry, how the inner mechanisms will function, and how the whole thing will be put together. That is why, in software development, programmers will often refer to themselves as engineers, and indeed they are.

Having only a ballpark idea of the project to be completed will add months, if not more than a year, to your project. If you don't know what you're trying to do, and *not* having a carefully detailed plan is not knowing what you're trying to do, means you're heading for a undefined goal. There's nothing programmers hate worse than this because the whole structure of their program is a balance and intercommunication of the various parts.

Altering the plan or adding a new part that wasn't planned for will not only throw off the whole structure, but frustrate the programmers who have to rebuild parts of the engine they're creating. Going back to the building analogy, if you change the lobby structure, or the shape of the building midstream, you have affected the entire project, with likely major consequences. It is no different in a software project. Changing a project mid-stream is called by programmers, "trying to hit a moving target."

In dollars and cents, this means you'll be spending a fortune trying to figure out what you're doing. You want to avoid this, and the way to do so is by drawing up the proper plans before any actual coding begins.

Let's look at the nature of those plans now.

## The Design Documents

Before any actual coding should be commenced, two very important documents must be created. The first to be written is the **design document**, that spells out, step-by-step, and scene-by-scene in fine detail, every screen and functionality of the product to be created. It is the blueprint by which the programmers will understand the job they have to do and the product to be produced. This document must be well thought out and complete in every aspect. Anything less, as we discussed earlier, will cost a fortune down the road.

The second key document, the **technical design document (TDD)**, is created by the programmers using the design document as a guideline, showing how they will attack the various problems and approach the issues.

## Pricing Your Product

As opposed to the book industry, where the publisher sets a retail price and prints that price right on the book, the software industry works according to a completely different model, or "paragon," to use the most hackneyed expression in the industry. You don't actually set the retail price of your product; in fact, it is illegal to do so! A landmark case of several years back involving a major retailer deemed such practices in this industry as actual price fixing.

In other words, you cannot tell a retailer how to price a product in their stores. In fact some buyers will get very touchy if this issue is addressed. This is why you'll never see pre-priced prices on retail software boxes as in the book industry. Issue prices will always be stickered by the retailers themselves.

You can however, set your wholesale price, and working forwards, target it toward achieving the desired retail price in the main sales channels. There is a whole strategy involved in this which will be influenced by current market conditions, and I would refer you to your sales organization and distributors to work this out. Roughly speaking though, a product being aimed for a $29.95 retail price point should be wholesaled to the distributors for around $19-$20.

Typical price points you will see and should aim for products under $50 retail, depending upon your product, will be $9.95, $12.95, $14.95, $19.95, $29.95, $39.95, and $49.95. I personally don't believe in the validity of $24.95, $34.95, and $44.95. I could be wrong here, but my thinking says that if you're going to shoot for $34.95, get the extra wholesale money and go for the full $39.95. I don't think sales will be affected greatly.

The same applies for the $24.95 and $44.95 prices. Go up, and take the extra few bucks. Again, this is my opinion, and I would suggest you give those mid-priced price points serious consideration if that appears to be a good option to you.

## Manufacturing a Game

Once your product has been finished and fully tested, you create a **gold disk**, the final version of the program on a CD ROM that will go to manufacturing. The gold disk is not actually gold or gold in color, it is simply the term used to denote the complete and final version. However, with all the money, time, and effort sunk into a software product, the term "gold" is certainly fitting.

The gold disk will need to be sent to a manufacturing outfit to get replicated. Other pieces that will be part of your final package will be a **jewel case**, the plastic housing that holds the CD ROM, or a paper or Tyvek sleeve, less sturdy but cheaper, an instruction manual for the game, and of course, a flashy box to display and house the package. Most games are **shrink-wrapped**, a see-through plastic wrapped around the product to protect the box against wear, tear and customers with slippery fingers. In our games, we chose to forego the shrink-wrapping so that the holographic foils we used could have their full effect, and instead, sealed the box on two ends.

Additional pieces that may be required as part of the package are inner supports to make the box feel sturdier or to hold the components in a tighter fit.

Before putting your box together, check out other packaging in the software stores to see what ideas and techniques they have used that may work for your product.

# UPC Code

To sell your product into the market, you will need to obtain a UPC Code from the Uniform Code Council. The UPC code must get printed on the box according to the mandated guidelines so that it can be scanned at retail when a sale is made. Without a UPC code you will not be able to sell to anyone. The contact information for the Uniform Code Council is shown below.

Uniform Code Council
8163 Old Yankee Street, Suite J
Dayton, OH 45458
(513)435-3870

To actually produce a UPC Code, you'll need to have a program that can generate bar codes, or have one produced by companies that specialize in making the bar codes. For more information on this, see the discussion on bar codes for the book industry beginning on page 100.

The UPC code is comprised of 12 digits. The UPC code for our first game, *Avery Cardoza's Casino*, is 6 31728 77777 8. The first digit is called the number system character and denotes the type of category in this system. Regular UPC codes will begin with a 0, 6, or 7. The first six digits identify the publisher. Thus, 6 31728 is the identifier for Cardoza Entertainment.

The following set of five digits are an arbitrary set of numbers chosen by the publisher to identify his product. Any five numbers from 0-9 can be chosen as long as that exact number has not been used previously by the publisher. For a product to be uniquely identified, it must have its own unique identifying number. I chose to use all sevens, 77777, since 7 is considered a lucky number for many gamblers. I could have chosen 77100, which I did on my second game, *Avery Cardoza's 100 Slots*, the numbers 99999 or 03475, or any set at all.

The final digit is a check character that is derived from the first 11 numbers according to the algorithm shown on the following page. We'll use the UPC code from our third game, *Avery Cardoza's Video Poker*, to show how this works.

The first 11 numbers are 6 31728 52200. Again, the first six numbers identify Cardoza Entertainment, and the next five is what I chose to represent my product.

1. First add all the odd number positions. These are underlined below: 6 31728 52200 - These add up to **16**.

2. Multiply this number by three. This becomes **48**.

3. Now add up all the even number positions. These are underlined below:

6 31728 52200 - These add up to **20**.

4. Add steps two and three. 48 + 20 = **68**.

5. The number that can be added to step four, such to produce a multiple of 10, will be the check character. In the above example, **2**, would be the check character. (68 + 2 = 70.) Some other examples: If the number had been 45, "5" would be the check charter. 63 would be "7," and 51 would be "9." In our example though, **2** was the check digit.

The complete UPC number for *Avery Cardoza's Video Poker* is thus, 6 31728 52200 2.

As you see, creating a UPC code is not all that difficult.

## ESRB Rating

A large segment of the software industry is submitting products to the Entertainment Software Review Board, the ESRB, an organization that reviews software for content and applies ratings to the final product. The final rating given can be affixed to the box using one of the icons the board supplies on floppy.

**Entertainment Software Rating Board,** 845 Third Avenue, New York, NY 10022; (212)759-0700, fax (212)759-2223.

# ESTABLISHING YOUR DOMAIN SITE

It is now commonplace for publishing companies to register their site online. To see if a site is available, type in the address you want and see if it is taken. If the internet address is already being used, you'll have to try another combination until the one you like is available. Then you should apply to Internic to register your site.

For example, before we reserved our site, we went to www.cardozapub.com, saw that it was free, and contacted Internic to nail down the address.

Here is Internic's contact information for reserving your web address:

Apply to Internic online at domreg@internic.net
You can also write, call, or fax:

**Network Solutions**, P.O. Box 17304, Baltimore, MD 21297-0524, Phone (703)742-4777, Fax: (703)318-9125

Once you have your web address, you'll want to design a site that presents the information and look you'll want to convey to the public. In the software review section we discuss a few applications that may be helpful tools for designing your site.

## Hosting Your Site

Unless you're willing to dedicate a computer to hosting your site and paying for the bandwidth requirements that site will need, you'll do what many businesses do–have your site hosted by your local ISP (Internet Service Provider). For most businesses, this is the easiest and most cost-effective way to get your site going.

# 19. FINAL THOUGHTS

We've covered a lot of ground in this book; from inception to finished product and marketing. Hopefully I've answered enough questions and provided you with enough information to move you along the road to successful publishing. Now it's up to you.

Publishing has been good to me and with some hard work on your part, it can be good to you too. As with anything else, hard work and dedication coupled with making sound decisions can bring you success. Positive thinking backed by positive actions and persistence can build dreams. If your dream is the freedom to express yourself through your books, be your own boss, and become financially free through the success of your own efforts, publishing can be that road to the dream.

I wish you success and good skill, for it is skill in the long run, and not luck, that will make your opportunities golden.

Write and tell me about your success stories -

*Avery Cardoza*


Cardoza Publishing
132 Hastings Street
Brooklyn, New York 11235

# 20. GLOSSARY

**ABA** - American Booksellers Association. The association of booksellers which hosts the book convention every Memorial Day weekend.

**ABI - Advanced Book Information** form. The ABI gets filed with Bowker and gets the book listed in *Books in Print* and *Forthcoming Books in Print*.

**Accounts Payable** - Money owed by a business from merchandise already bought but not yet paid for.

**Accounts Receivable** - Money owed to a business from merchandise already sold but not yet paid for.

**Acid Free Paper** - Special paper printed without acid for long-lasting life.

**Across the Grain** - See **Cross Grain**.

**Adhesive Binding -** A hardcover binding that affixes the insides to the hardcover by using glue.

**Advance** - The amount of money paid to the author before publication of his book as an advance against future royalty payments.

**ALA** - American Library Association.

**All Caps -** See **Caps**.

**Anthology** - A collection of writings by one or more authors.

**Antique Finish** - Paper with a relatively rougher finish.

**Appendix** - Supplementary material printed in the back of a book.

**Artwork** - Technically speaking, artwork is the images other than type that are used to accompany text, though it is often used to indicate the physical boards that make up camera-ready copy and that also include the text itself.

**Author** - A writer who has written a book.

**BACKLIST** - Books that are in print and still being sold. This is opposed to *front list* or new books.

**Back Order** - Books that are *on order*, but can't yet be filled due to no available inventory.

**Back Pages** - The last pages of a book, begins where the body text has ended, and includes indexes, glossaries, appendices, footnotes, addendum, blank pages and advertisements.

**Bar Code** - The coding system of bars that gets printed on the back cover and now universally used in the book industry to automate ordering and inventory systems and to identify books. The Bookland EAN is the bar code used for books.

**Bastard Title** - See **Half Title.**

**Belt Press** - A type of printing press that automated almost the entire book making process on one machine.

**Best-Seller** - A top-selling book, or one which makes a listing of such.

**Bibliography** - A listing of references used by the author as part of his or her research in doing a book.

**Bill of Lading (B/L)** - Paperwork attached to a shipment which details the contents of the shipment. Also called a **Packing Slip.**

**Binding** - The process of affixing pages together into one bound book.

**Black** - One of the four process colors. The standard color of text in a book.

**Black and White** - The standard printing process for text, black ink on white paper. Also, refers to black and white (non-color) photos.

**Bleed** - When the image area of a book prints right to the edge of the page, and thus is said to *bleed* off the edge of the page. Covers not printed in white are always bleeds. Also refers to type or color that appears fuzzy or blurred because either the printing is out of registration or the ink has expanded outside of the intended area.

**Blind Embossing** - An effect produced by stamping or imprinting an image on a blank surface without using ink.

**Blowup** - An enlargement.

**Blueline** - A proof sheet of a book made from the negatives and revealed in bluish ink, that shows exactly how the pages or cover will look when printed. Also known as **blues, proofs, Dylux proofs, vans,** and **silverprints.**

**Blues - See Blueline.**

**Blurbs** - Praiseworthy reviews of your book or author, given in appropriate abbreviated form.

**Body Type** - The main body of a book, from the introduction all the way through to the final word in the manuscript. Does not include matter in the front or back pages.

**Bold** - Type that is made darker and heavier than the standard type. Also called **Boldface.**

**Boldface (BF)** - Type that has been made bold. See above.

**Book** - A bound publication of 49 or more pages that is not a periodical.

**Bookland EAN/5** - The bar code symbol used for books in the book trade.

**Book Packager** - An outside company or individual which is hired to transform a manuscript into camera-ready copy ready for the printer, thus, book production not done in-house.

**Book Rate** - A special United States postal classification for sending books. Also called **fourth class,** or **fourth class book rate.**

**Bullet** - A round dot · used to call out text or items in a list.

**Bulk, Bulking-out** - Used to indicate the thickness of a book.

**C1** - The front cover.

**C2** - The inside front cover.

**C3** - The inside back cover.

**C4** - The back cover.

**C1S** - Coated One Side. Paper coated on one side only.

**C2S** - Coated Two Sides. Paper coated on both sides.

**Camera-ready** - The final artwork, including type and graphics, that's ready to be reproduced in the final book process - *ready for the camera*.

**Caps** - Short for capitalization. Type which is all in upper face. Also known as **All Caps**.

**Carton** - A shipping container for books, almost always made of cardboard..

**Case Bound** - A hardbound title.

**Centered** - Text which is centered in the middle of an imaginary vertical margin line, or looking at it differently, is equidistant from the left and right margins.

**Certified Mail** - Mail sent through the United States Postal Service which is signed for and considered legal certification of receipt.

**Chapter** - A distinct division in a book, usually, but not always, begun on a new page.

**Chapter Design** - The design used in making chapters.

**Chapter Headings** - Titles used to indicate and announce a chapter. Usually set in a different style than the text that makes up the chapter itself.

**Chaptering** - The process of dividing a book into chapters.

**CIP** - Cataloging in Publication. The bibliographic information supplied by the Library of Congress that is printed on the copyright page.

**Clip Art** - Generic (not custom) graphics that can be "clipped out" and used for illustrative purposes in a book. Generally denotes inferior quality graphics.

**Clipping Service** - Service that scours nationwide periodicals and clips out mentions of one's book or articles of interest for clients.

**Clothbound** - Hardbound title.

**CMYK** - The four process colors, Black, Process Yellow, Process Cyan, and Process Magenta.

**Coated Paper** - Paper that is treated or coated so that the finish is reflective or shiny. Opposed to a matte or uncoated stock.

**COD** - Cash on Delivery. A term for delivering items on the condition that they're paid for upon receipt.

**Collating** - A gathering together of sheets or signatures into a predetermined order.

**Color Correction** - The "correcting" or improvement of color.

**Color Key** - A type of color proof.

**Color Proofs** - A color reproduction used as a proof before the actual printing is undertaken.

**Color Separation** - The process of separating a color slide or print into four negatives, Black, Process Yellow, Process Magenta and Process Cyan, for the purpose of printing. Also known as **Separations**, **Color Seps** or **Seps**.

**Comb Binding** - A continuous spiral-shaped plastic binding inserted through punched holes. Used for book such as cookbooks which need to lie flat when opened.

**Condensed Type** - Type which has been narrowed or *condensed*, less than its normal width.

**Confirming Proof** - A proof sent for inspection - no approval is required, and work on the job will continue to proceed.

**Content Edit** - An edit checking the flow of the text, its contents, and its organization. Also called an **Overview Edit**.

**Co-op Advertising** - Advertising whose costs are shared by two or more benefiting groups; such as in publishers and distributors, or publishers and retail stores.

**Copy Edit** - A technical edit specifically covering grammar, punctuation, spelling, and the like.

**Copyright** - The legal protection afforded to intellectual rights such as written and published works.

**Copyright Notice** - Notice printed on the copyright page that by law protects the copyright holder.

**Corner Marks** - See **Crop Marks**.

**COSMEP** - The Committee of Small Magazine Editors and Publishers. A west coast-based trade organization.

**Cover Comp** - A color reproduction of a cover done before the actual cover is produced.

**CPU** - Central Processing Unit. The computer's main operating system and brain.

**Credit Memo** - A memo indicating that an account has a credit, or balance to its favor.

**Cromalin** - A type of color proof.

**Crop** - To trim an image on any or all of its four sides (top, bottom, left side, right side) to fit a specified area.

**Crop Marks** - The lines, crosses, or other symbols, used to indicate the printing area of the page. Also known as **Corner Marks**.

**Cross Grain** - Printing term used for printing the paper against the grain.

**Cross Gutter** - An image that prints across the gutter, the inside margins of the book.

**DATA ENTRY** - The entering of information, such as a manuscript, into the computer.

**DBA** - Doing Business As. A sole proprietor or partnership operating a business in a name other than their own.

**Deadline** - The date at which point a job must be finished.

**Deboss** - Depressed printing (below the paper surface) made with a blank die.

**Decorative Type** - A stylized font used for creating a look such as a logo; type specifically designed for this purpose.

**Delete** - To take out, remove.

**Design Edit** - An edit where the main purpose is to make preliminary design decisions.

**Desktop Publishing** - Book design, layout and production done on a computer - *from one's desktop*.

**Die-Cut** - A printed piece where holes have been cut out.

**Direct Mail** - Mail sent directly to prospective customers to solicit orders.

**Distributor** - In the book business, anyone who buys from the publishers or other distributors and resells to retail accounts.

**Doubler** - The term for two title pages. Also, term used for two of anything such as a two book order, or a second pancake eaten. Used only by cool and hip publishers or those pretending to be such.

**Drop Shipment** - An order shipped to an address by a manufacturer or publisher which is different than that which appears on the invoice.

**Drop-Out** - Images that don't reproduce from the original image - usually planned that way.

**Dummy** - A representative mock-up of a book, including all the pages, made up to show what the printed book would look like.

**Dump** - A display used for merchandise and books in retail outlets.

**Duotone** - A two-color halftone reproduction made from a one color original.

**Dust Jacket** - The paper sleeve that covers and protects hardbound books. Also known as **Dust Cover**.

**EDITING** - The changing of a book's written contents intended to improve the final result, or fit into a required format.

**Edition** - A printing of a book whose contents are announced or presented as being new; not to be confused with a new printing.

**Electronic Pre-Press** - The department at a print shop that processes electronic submissions.

**Electronic Submissions** - Books submitted on electronic media, either on disk or by modem.

**El-hi** - Publishing term for books intended primarily for the elementary and high school market.

**Em (space)** - The typographic term for a small unit of space, approximately the width of the letter "m".

**Embossing** - Raised printing made with a blank die over a printed surface as opposed to *blind embossing* which is done on a blank surface.

**En (space)** - The typographic term for a small unit of space, approximately half the width of an em space.

**Enlargement** - To increase or enlarge in size; an image that has been so enlarged.

**Epigraph** - A quotation printed in the front pages which sets a tone for a book.

**Epilogue** - Additional text inserted at the end of a book, which brings the reader more up-to-date on the subject matter or author.

**Errata Sheet** - Sheet inserted to a book after its printing to note and correct errors within the text.

**Estimate** - The quote for a printing proposal. Also **Quote**.

**Extended Type** - Type which has been widened or *extended*, beyond its normal width.

**FACE** - See **Typestyle**

**Face-out** - Books displayed with the front cover out. As opposed to *spine-out*.

**Facing Pages** - Two pages, that when a book is opened, face outward together.

**F & G's** - Folded and Gathered Sheets. The unbound signatures of a book.

**Film Lamination** - Thin but relatively durable plastic coating used to protect a paperback cover after printing.

**Final Proof** - See **Once-Over**.

**First Edition** - The first edition of a book, regardless of which printing; for collectors, it means the first printing of the first edition.

**First Printing** - The first printing of the first edition of a book.

**First Serial Rights** - The rights to serialize a book before the publication date. Opposed to Second Serial Rights which occur *after* the publication date.

**Flat** - A composite of negatives or positives on a flat surface which is ready for the plate-making process.

**Flat Pay** - Hiring an author for a set amount of money to do a book; as opposed to royalties. Also called **Work for Hire**.

**Flush Left** - Type that is flushed in a line along a left margin with the right side being ragged, or uneven. Also called **ragged right**.

**Flush Right** - Type that is flushed in a line along a right margin with the left side being ragged, or uneven. Also called **ragged left**.

**FOB** - Free on Board. Indicates that the buyer pays freight from the shipping point.

**Font** - A complete set of type in a particular typeface.

**Foreign Rights** - Rights granted so that a book can be published in other countries.

**Foreword** - Preparatory and generally praising remarks that get printed before the introduction. Usually done by an individual either distinguished in the field or well-known.

**Four Color Process** - The color printing process of using magenta, cyan, yellow and black to produce a wide range of colors.

**Four-Up** - Term for printing four identical pages or images on one sheet so that when cut, there are four copies.

**FPO** - For Proof Only. Lower resolution scan or image not meant for final printing.

**Freight Forwarder** - An individual or company who combines shipments from various parties to send to a common destination.

**Frontispiece** - A graphic, usually a photo, that faces the title page.

**Front list** - Books that are new titles. This is opposed to *backlist* titles, books that are no longer new, but in print and selling.

**Front Pages** - The pages in a book that precede the introduction.

**Fulfillment** - Term used to denote the packing and shipping of an order by a company other than the one that took the original order; also used to indicate the packing and shipping of an order by anyone.

**Full Page Graphic** - A graphic that occupies a full page in a book.

**GALLEY** - In typesetting, the long strips of type that come out of the processor; now, more commonly used for the pre-publication copies sent to authors for a final proof or to reviewers for review.

**Ganging**, **Gang Run** - The practice of combining more than one job or more than one copy of a particular job together to economize on printing.

**General Book Trade** - A term to denote books sold through the general book stores and the business conducted in those stores.

**Genre** - A specific category of books.

**Ghosting** - Reducing (or heightening) color density in a photo; used for effect.

**Glossary** - A listing of definitions relevant to the work; generally found in the back pages.

**Glossy** - A photograph with a shiny or glossy finish, as opposed to a matte or "flat" finish.

**Going to Press** - Sending the book to the printer for reproduction.

**Graphics** - The non-type items - drawings, illustrations and photos - that are used to enhance a book.

**Gutter** - The inside margins of a book, those along the spine.

**HAIRLINE** - Very thin line.

**Half Title** - The front page in which the title prints by itself and which precedes the complete title page. Also known as a **Bastard Title**.

**Halftone** - A dot pattern used to reproduce photographs and make them suitable for black and white printing; photographs are sometime loosely referred to as *halftones*.

**Hard Copy** - An actual printout of the book.

**Hardbound** - See **Hard Cover**.

**Hard Cover** - A book bound in a hard cover. Also called **Casebound**.

**Headings** - Text used to lead off and announce a passage of text.

**Headline Type** - The typeface used for headings of any kind; type specifically designed for headings.

**High Bulk Paper** - Paper that is thicker than normal. Makes fatter books.

**High Resolution** - Print quality, used in reference to output of various types.

**House Sheet** -A standard sheet of paper stocked by a printer.

**IBM COMPATIBLE** - One of two commonly used computer systems. Represents all computer systems which are compatible with the IBM DOS or Windows operating systems.

**ID (Independent Distributor)** - See **Jobber**.

**ISBN Number** - International Standard Book Number. An identification number code uniquely assigned to every book.

**Illustrations** - Drawings, photographs or artwork used to enhance a book.

**Image** - The drawings, photographs, artwork, type or page which is to be reproduced.

**Image Area** - The actual area of a book that will be reproduced.

**Imprint** - The name of the publishing company on the title page.

**Indent** - To set in type so that is further from the margin than the rest of the type to which it belongs.

**Index** - An alphabetical listing of subjects, names, places and other relevant matter, with relevant page location, and often found in the back of a book.

**In-House** - Functions performed within the company and not hired out.

**In Print** - A book still available for sale. Opposed to being *Out of Print*.

**Inside Delivery** - Delivery which is brought inside, as opposed to sidewalk delivery.

**Inventory** - The stock that is on-hand and available for sale.

**Invoice** - A written statement of monies owed for product ordered.

**Italic** - Type with the letters *slanted*.

**JACKET** - The cover of a book.

**Jiffy Bag** - Padded bag used to ship books and protect them from damage during transit.

**Jobber** - A type of distributor who services book racks in supermarkets, drug stores, airports, convenience stores and the like and who have mostly exclusive control over what books are placed on these racks. Also called a **Rack Jobber** or **ID (Independent Distributor)**.

**Justify** - To align type on both left and right sides.

**KERNING** - To reduce or properly align the space between letters in a word.

**Key Area** - The essential area in an image which cannot be cropped.

**Knock Out** - To eliminate the background from an image.

**LAMINATE** - To lay a clear see-through coating over a printed piece for extra protection.

**Lamination** - See **Film Lamination**.

**Layout** - The process of paging and putting together a book either manually, or on the computer.

**Leaders** - Dots, dashes, periods or other like characters used to fill a space and lead the eye. Often used between a chapter listing and the page number in a table of contents.

**Leading** - The space between line of type, measured from the bottom of one line to the bottom of the line above (or below), or in the jargon of the graphics industry, from *baseline* to *baseline*.

**Library of Congress** - The national library serving the U.S. Congress and located in Washington, D.C.

**Library of Congress Catalog Card Number** - The number assigned by the Library of Congress to identify books for their records.

**Library Rate** - A less expensive USPS mailing classification used for mailing to libraries.

**Limited Edition** - A special edition of a small print run; often signed and numbered.

**Line Art** - Artwork that can be shot with the rest of the type - it does not require special camera work to be reproduced.

**Line Drawing** - See **Line Art**.

**List Price** - The retail price, the price which is listed on the book.

**LMP** - Literary Market Place. The directory of the book publishing industry.

**Logo** - The symbol or identifying mark used by an individual, an organization, or a business.

**Loose Design** - Design intended to provide a lot of white space or increase the number of pages.

**Low Bulk Paper** - Paper which is relatively thin and won't "bulk-up" a book.

**Lower Case (LC)** - Small letters - not capitalized.

**MACINTOSH** - One of two generally used computer systems.

**Mail Order** - Sales solicited through advertising and filled by mail.

**Make-ready** - Printing term for getting the press ready for printing.

**Manual Paste-Up** - See **Paste-Up**.

**Manuscript** - The author's book in typewritten form, or that same version on disk.

**Margins** - The space between the outside of the text and the edge of the page. There are four margins; left, right, top and bottom.

**Mass Market Paperbacks** - Best-seller type books which are targeted to racks such as are found in convenience stores and airports.

**Mass-market Size** - Books that are approximately 4 1/4 by 6 3/4 inches (sometimes 4 x 7) in size.

**Matchprint** - A type of color proof.

**Mechanicals** - Camera-ready black and white artwork; when used for covers or color work, the black and white artwork with instructions for color placements.

**Media** - The medium of communications including radio, television, print, and electronic (computer) used for mass exposure.

**NEGATIVE** - The film made in which the original copy shot is reversed, and used for printing; clear or white areas become black, and dark areas become white.

**New Edition** - A revised edition of a book. See **Revised Edition**.

**Newsprint** - The inexpensive paper that newspapers are printed on.

**News Release** - A one or two page release used for promotion.

**Niche Publishing** - Publishing books in a narrow field.
**Non-Repro Blue** - Blue ink which will not reproduce when shot on camera.
**Non-Returnable** - Books that may not be returned for credit, they're a final sale.

**OCR** - Optimal Character Recognition. Font used for ISBN in bar codes; also a device that can read this language.
**Once-Over** - The final proof after all other proofing steps have been done. Also called the **Final Proof**.
**One-Up** - Term for printing one page on a sheet (as opposed to two or more).
**Opacity** - The quality of paper that allows light to come through.
**Opaque** - To eliminate an unwanted part of negative by painting or "opaquing" the area so that the part covered doesn't print; also, blocking out all light.
**Original** or **Original Image** - The original or best copy of an image from which reproductions will be made.
**Orphan**- The first line of a paragraph which is "orphaned" alone at the bottom of a page, and continues on the following page.
**Out of Print** - A book no longer available for sale. Opposed to being *In Print*.
**Out of Register** - Print that has shifted during printing creating a blurring effect, that is, a misprint.
**Overlay** - A transparent sheet placed over another to indicate a second or additional colors.
**Overprinting** - When one type or element prints over another. Usually done for effect; the term *overprinting* could also signify a printing error.
**Overrun** - A print run more than the amount ordered.
**Overview Edit** - See **Content Edit**.

**PACKING SLIP** - Paperwork that accompanies a shipment and states the merchandise within. Also called a **Bill of Lading (B/L)**.
**Page** - A single side of paper within a publication.
**Page Design** - The design used in making pages.
**Page Margins** - The space between the outside of the printed text and/or graphics area, both length and width, and the physical end of the page.
**Page Numbers** - The numbers that run consecutively throughout a book, one per page, and mark the page.
**Page Proof** - A proof of a single page.
**Pagination** - See **Paging**.
**Paging** - The process of breaking a book up into pages. Also known as **Pagination.**
**Pallet** - A wooden crate used to ship and store cases of books.
**Pantone Matching System (PMS)** - A standard and acceptable system for indicating colors in the printing process. The PMS book works with process colors in exact percentages and shows hundreds of combinations on both coated and uncoated stocks.

**Paperback** - See **Paperbound**.

**Paperbound** - A book bound in paper; *opposed to hardbound*. Also called **paperback**.

**Paragraph Design** - The design used for paragraph style.

**Parcel Post** - A United States Post Office classification for the cheapest rate of overseas shipping.

**Paste-up** - The manual placement of artwork or text on a page; to layout a book by hand, literally "pasting" (waxing, glue stick, tape or other means of affixing) artwork or type onto the original to be reproduced.

**Perfect Binding** - The standard binding where the finished books have a flat or "squared" spine and are bound by glue.

**Perforate** - To pierce holes in a page so that they're easily removed.

**Periodical** - A publication such as a magazine, issued at regular intervals.

**Permissions** - Authorization to use material that is copyrighted by another.

**Photostat** - See **Stat**.

**Photocopy** - A copy made on a copying machine.

**Phototypesetting** - Type set on a phototypesetter (typesetter) machine. More commonly referred to as **Typesetting**.

**Pica** - Unit of measurement used in graphics. These are six picas to an inch.

**Pica Rule** - A ruler that measures in the finer increments of points and picas.

**Pickup** - Printing term for reprinting a book at no charge to the customer due to a printer's mistake.

**Plate** - The material used in printing, usually metal or plastic, which holds the printed image during the printing.

**PMS** - See **Pantone Matching System**.

**Point** - Unit of measurement used in graphics. These are 12 points to a pica, 72 points to an inch.

**PO#** - Purchase Order Number. The number used to identify an order.

**Positive** - Reverse of the negative.

**PPI** - Pages per Inch. Measurement used for the thickness of paper. The higher the PPI, that is, the more pages that fit per inch, the thinner the paper, and consequently, the thinner the book.

**Preface** - An introductory section to the book written by the author usually about why or how they wrote the book.

**Prep** - Work done to prepare a book or the press for printing.

**Prepaid** - When the item ordered is paid before manufacture or delivery.

**Pre-press** - Work done to get the book ready for press.

**Pre-publication** - Before publication.

**Premium** - A book given away as part of a promotion.

**Press Kit** - An assemblage of promotional materials used to promote a book, an event, or an author, and sent to the media.

**Press Release** - See **News Release**.

**Press Run** - See **Print Run**.

**Printer** - A company which manufactures books.

**Printing Date** - The date when the books are off the press and ready to be shipped.

**Print Quote** - See **Quote**.

**Print Run** - The number of books printed or ordered.

**Priority Mail** - USPS rate classification for mail sent.

**Print Quality** - Type that is at least 1,000 DPI; artwork (including type) which is of sufficient quality to be reproduced at a professional quality level.

**Pro Number** - The tracking number that's assigned to freight so that it can be tracked and identified during shipping.

**Process Colors** - The four colors, Black, Process Yellow, Process Cyan, and Process Magenta. Also known as **CMYK**.

**Process Cyan** - Bright, light blue. One of the four process colors.

**Process Magenta** - Bright pink. One of the four process colors.

**Process Yellow** - Bright yellow. One of the four process colors.

**Proof** - To go over and make sure copy is correct. Also, the copy used for this purpose.

**Proofing** - The last stage in the pre-press process where all information is verified to be right and ready for press.

**Proofreader** - The person who proofs galleys to make sure everything is correct.

**Proofreader's Marks** - The marks used by a proofreader to indicate changes.

**Proportional Wheel** - A round, thin plastic device using one wheel set atop another, that is used to figure the enlargement or reduction of images. Also known as a **Reduction Wheel**.

**Proposal** - A proposed idea for a book.

**Publication Date** - A date set, usually 4-6 weeks *after* printing, that is used for the official publication of the book.

**Public Domain** - Material which is no longer protected by copyright and which is available for all to use.

**Publicist** - Individual or company in the business of promoting people or products.

**Publisher** - The person or company, depending upon how the term is used, responsible for the entire process of making books, from finding the talent and overseeing the writing, editing and production, to the final printing and marketing. When the term is used to signify the company, as in a **publishing house** or **publishing company**, then it includes the financing of the books as well.

**Publishing Program** - A software program specifically designed for laying out and publishing books.

**Purchase Order** - An order to buy books.

**QUADTONE** - A four color halftone reproduction made from a one color original.

**Quality Control** - Department at a printers which oversees the entire printing process to keep standards high; the term to denote the process of insuring high quality.

**Quality Paperback** - See **Trade Paperback**.

**Query Letter** - The initial inquiry by an author or agent to see if a publisher is interested in a proposed project.

**Quote** - A bid on the printing of a book.


**RACK JOBBER** - See **Jobber**.

**RPS** - Roadway Package Service, a book shipper.

**Ragged Left** - see **Flush Right**

**Ragged Right** - See **Flush Left**

**Ream** - A stock of paper, usually 500 sheets.

**Recto** - A right-hand side of the page.

**Recycled Paper** - Paper that has previously been used.

**Reduction** - To reduce in size; an image that has been so reduced.

**Reduction Wheel** - See **Proportional Wheel**.

**Register** - To align properly.

**Registration Marks** - The marks used to perfectly align separations and other registration-sensitive materials.

**Remainder** - To heavily discount a book at a fraction of the normal discount for the purpose of discontinuing an edition and clearing out the stock.

**Reprint** - A further printing done.

**Reproduction Size** - The final size after an image has been enlarged or reduced.

**Retouch** - To "touch up" a photo, and render it better.

**Returns** - Books that come back to the publisher or publishers agent due to being damaged or insufficient sellers.

**Reverse** - Printing everything that's white as black, and everything that's black as white.

**Review** - A critical evaluation of a book.

**Review Copy** - A free copy given away to be reviewed.

**Revised Edition** - A previously published book that has been updated, expanded or revised, and is being presented as such.

**Rough Page Count** - The process of getting a rough idea of the number of pages in a book; that number itself.

**Royalty** - The percentage paid to the author for each book sold.

**Rubylith** - Red see-through plastic used to mark additional colors or screens.

**Rules** - Graphic term for lines.

**Runaround** - Text that follows the outline of a graphic.

**Running Foot** - Printing that runs consistently from one page to another below the main text and hence, *runs* along the foot of the book.

**Running Head** - Printing that runs consistently from one page to another above the main text and hence, *runs* along the head of the book.
**Running Large** - The printed characters of a typeface print larger than a standard point size.
**Running Small** - The printed characters of a typeface print smaller than a standard point size.

**SADDLE-STITCH** - Form of binding using staples in spine.
**Sales Rep** - Salespeople who do not work for any one publisher, but instead, are independent and represent multiple publishers to the book trade for a commission.
**Sales Rep Groups** - A group of sales reps.
**Sans Serif Type** - Type face without flourishes and hooks.
**SASE** - Self-Addressed, Stamped Envelope. The standard method for prospective authors to submit unsolicited manuscripts and queries.
**Scaling** - To measure out, reduce or enlarge.
**Score** - To crease a paper so that it will fold easily on that indentation.
**Screens** - a. Dot patterns of various percentages that tone down a solid color to appear as shades of that color on the printed page - gives the appearance of extra colors. Also known as **Tints**. b. Also, the acetate of various dot patterns placed over film to reproduce halftones (black and white photos) in the pre-press process.
**Scuffing** - Rub-off or surface damage to a cover.
**Second Serial Rights** - The rights to serialize a book after the publication date. Opposed to First Serial Rights which occur *before* the publication date.
**Self-Cover** - A book whose cover is printed on the same stock as the inside text.
**Separations** - See **Color Separations.**
**Serialize** - To publish a book in successive installments.
**Serif Type** - Type face with flourishes and hooks.
**Sheet-Fed Press** - The highest quality press which prints paper one sheet at a time.
**Short Rate Discount** - A discount less than 40%. Used when selling to schools - typically a 20% discount.
**Short Run** - A print run that is small, whether measured in the hundreds of copies, or less than 3,000 copies.
**Shrink Wrap** - To enclose within a see-through plastic wrap. Usually used to protect a book, group of books or pallet of books from damage during shipping; sometimes used to prevent customers from reading a publication while on shelf.
**Signature** - A large printed sheet, that when folded forms a section of the book, usually 32 pages, though can be smaller quantities divisible by four on other presses.

**Silverprint** - See **Blueline.**

**Simultaneous Edition** - The printing of both a hardcover and softcover edition at the same time.

**Sizing** - To measure an image and specify its final size.

**Skid** - A pallet of cartons.

**Slip Case** - A decorative box used to hold more than one title - usually open at one end only.

**Small Caps** - Type where all the letters are capitalized, but the first letter of the capitalized word is LARGER THAN THE SUCCEEDING LETTERS.

**Smyth Sewing** - A type of hardcover binding where the signatures are first sewn together and then glued.

**Softcover** - Book printed with standard paper cover.

**Software** - Programs designed to run with computers.

**SOP** - Standard Operating Procedure.

**Spec** - To assign attributes to type such as point size, leading, color, etc. A diminutive of *specify* or *specification*.

**Spine** - The binding on the side of the book.

**Spine-out** - Books displayed with the spine showing. As opposed to *face-out.*

**Spiral Binding** - A continuous spiral-shaped wire binding inserted through punched holes such as are used in school notebooks.

**Stamping** - Printing, usually on a cover, which has been impressed or "stamped" on.

**Stat** - A high quality photographic reproduction done on a stat camera. Also known as a **Photostat**.

**Stat Camera** -A machine that photographically reproduces images and makes stats.

**Statement, Statement of Account** - An official document showing the current state of affairs in an account, whether money is due or there is credit, and its recent history.

**Step and Repeat** - Printing method of re-shooting the same image.

**Stet** - Editor's mark for *no change* - used when a previous editing instruction is to be disregarded.

**Stock** - Inventory.

**STOP** - Single Title Order Plan. A method of payment-with-order used by bookstores for single orders.

**Straight Edge** - A surface with a straight, uncurved edge, such as a ruler.

**Straight Line** - Printing term used to indicate that the camera-ready text needs no special treatment and can be shot with one negative; thus the book is only text and straight line drawings - it has no screens, halftones or separations.

**Straight Line Drawings** - Drawings consisting of artwork that needs no special treatment and can be shot as a negative along with the rest of the text.

**Strip In** - Graphic or printing term for inserting one element within another. In printing, one might strip in a negative as a correction.

**Stripping** - Printing term for the assembling of negatives or positives on a flat surface, usually paper or plastic, in preparation for plate-making.

**Subhead, Subheading** - A lesser heading.

**Subsidiary Rights** - Additional rights, such as foreign or serial, to publish a book in a different form.

**Subsidy Press** - See **Vanity Publisher**.


**TAB** - A preset automatic spacing used in data processing.

**Table of Contents** - The listing of chapters (and sometimes additional descriptive information) found in the front of a book.

**Table of Illustrations** - The listing of illustrations and charts found in the front of a book.

**Tear Sheet** - A clipping from a printed newspaper or magazine used as proof an ad was run.

**Terms** - The conditions of doing business. In printing, it's the payment terms; in bookselling, it's the discount schedule, payment terms, and return policy.

**Text Paper** - The paper used for the text pages as opposed to the cover.

**Text Type** - The sentences, paragraphs, and charts that make up a book; a typeface good for both text and headlines.

**Tight Design** - Design intended to restrict the amount of white space and decrease the number of pages.

**Tints** - Dot patterns of various percentages that tone down a solid color and appear as shades on the printed page.

**Tissue Overlay** - A thin overlay made from see-through tissue paper to indicate printing instructions.

**Title** - The name of the book.

**Title Page** - The page in the front of the book.

**Trade Size** - Books that are 5 1/2 x 8 1/2 or 6 x 9 inches in size.

**Trade Paperbacks** - Any book targeted to the book trade regardless of size.

**Trap** - To set up a printed inked area so that further inks can be printed over it to form a new color.

**Trim** - To cut the book at the bindery. Also refers to **Trim Size**.

**Trim Size** - The finished size of the book after the binder has trimmed the edges.

**Tripler** - See **Doubler** and add one. Never used.

**Tritone** - A three color halftone reproduction made from a one color original.

**Two-Up** - Term for printing three identical pages or images on one sheet so that when cut, there are three copies.

**Turnaround Time** - the time it takes from receipt of book until the finished book is printed and ready to ship.

**Two-Up** - Term for printing two identical pages or images on one sheet so that when cut, there are two copies.

**Type** - The characters comprising the alphabet, numbers and special characters that make up printed text; non-graphic elements; also, the written text in a book.
**Type Face** - See **Typestyles**.
**Type Family** - See **Typestyles**.
**Typesetting** - See **Phototypesetting**.
**Typestyles** - The families of similar types that are designed as a group. Also called **Typefaces, Faces** or a **Type Family**.
**Typo** - Short for typographic error. A misspelling or mistake in the text.
**Typography** - Type design.

**U/L** -See **Upper and Lower Case**.
**UPS** - United Parcel Service. Private shipping and overnight service.
**UV Coating -** Ultra-violet coating.
**Uncoated Paper** - Untreated or matte paper stock.
**Uncut Pages** - Pages in a printed book which have not been trimmed at the bindery.
**Underline** - A line that runs <u>under</u> the text.
**Underrun** - A print run less than the amount ordered.
**Unit Cost** - The cost to produce each item.
**Upper and Lower** - See **Upper and Lower Case**.
**Upper Case (UC)** - Where a letter or letters are capitalized.
**Upper and Lower Case** - Type with letters capitalized according to standard punctuation. Abbreviated as U/L.
**USPS** - United State Postal Service.

**VANITY PUBLISHER** - A company which edits, designs, manufactures, "promotes" and "distributes" finished books for pay by authors. Vanity publishing is generally not considered "legitimate" publishing.
**Vans** - See **Blueline**.
**Varnish** - Coating used to protect a cover.
**Velo-Bind** - A binding process that punches holes in the material to be bound, and affixes two long strips of plastic outside the holes to hold them together within flexible and colored plastic covers.
**Vendor** - A seller.
**Verso** - A left-hand sided page.

**WASHUP** - The cleaning of the ink rollers at press.
**Waxer** - Machine that melts wax and affixes it to the back of copy for paste-up.
**Web Press** - A type of printing press that uses huge rolls of paper and can be configured in various units.
**Weight (of paper)** - The weight of the press paper measured in hundred-weights. Fifty pound paper is a standard weight.

**White-out** - To opaque, or obliterate by "whiting-over" the surface.

**Wholesaler** - Type of distributor which stocks titles from a multitude of publishers and serves as a one-stop shopping outlet for their trade accounts.

**Widow** - The last line of a paragraph standing alone at the top of a new page.

**With the Grain** - A printing term used for printing with the grain of the paper.

**Word of Mouth** - The advertising generated by satisfied readers telling their friends and acquaintances about a book they've read.

**Word Processing Program** - A software program specifically designed for entering and manipulating text.

**Working Title** - The preliminary title for a book.

**X-ACTO KNIFE** - A pen-shaped metal tool with an interchangeable sharp metal blade for a point used to hand cut galleys, film, and other items.

**Z** - The last letter in the alphabet.

# APPENDIX A

## SAMPLE AUTHOR CONTRACT

The following contract is provided as an example only of the language that a contract with an author might contain. You may want to consult with a lawyer before formulating your own contract.

This agreement dated _____ between **Successful Publishing Inc.**, hereinafter called the **Publisher**, and _____, hereinafter called the **Author**, and residing at: _____; citizen of _____, concerning the book tentatively titled _____, and hereinafter called the **Work**.

### 1. MANUSCRIPT

The Author shall deliver to the Publisher on or before _____, the completed manuscript on computer disk and one hard copy; plus all related materials such as maps and illustrations, including any necessary permissions for the reproduction of copyrighted materials (incurred at the author's expense). The manuscript and related materials shall be sufficient to fill a ____ page book.

If the manuscript is not submitted on computer disk, any charges accrued to input manuscript onto disk will be charged against the Author's royalties.

### 2. COPYRIGHT

The Publisher shall copyright the Work in the name of the Author in the United States and other countries as it may deem expedient.

### 3. PUBLISHING RIGHTS

The Author hereby grants and assigns to the Publisher, during the full term of copyright of the Work, and all renewals and extensions of copyright, the exclusive right to publish, sell and license the Work in the English language and all other languages throughout the world.

## 4. ADVANCE
The Publisher shall pay the Author as an advance against earnings under this agreement: $_____ as follows:

a. $_____ upon signing of this agreement
b. $_____ upon delivery of final acceptable manuscript

## 5. ROYALTIES
The Publisher shall pay the Author the following royalties on sales (less returns):

**a.** Sales of **paperback** (trade and/or mass market) in the United States;
    5% of the retail price for all copies sold

**b.** Sales of **hardcover** (if applicable) in the United States;
    7.5% of the retail price for all copies sold

**c.** Sales of paperback and hardcover **outside the United States**
    50% of the normal royalty price for all copies sold
No royalty shall be paid on free copies furnished to the Author, or on copies used for review, sample, or other similar purposes, or for copies returned. On sales of a special edition at a reduced price, or on sales of the regular edition at reduced prices for special use, a royalty of 5% of the gross price obtained shall be paid. If the Publisher shall sell copies of the Work at less than the manufacturing cost (which it shall not do prior to one year after publication of the Work), no royalty shall be paid.

## 6. SPECIAL SALES
The Publisher shall have the exclusive right, at the Publisher's option, either to license rights of publication or sell copies of the Work to a book club. If rights are so licensed, the Publisher agrees to pay to the author 50% of the Publisher's net receipts after deduction of the costs of any necessary manufacture, freight or other expenses arising from such a sale. For regular edition copies sold to a book club, the Publisher agrees to pay the Author 50% of the royalty paid by the book club to the Publisher.

The Author grants to the Publisher the exclusive right to license subsidiary rights in the Work and agrees that the net proceeds received from the license of such subsidiary rights shall be divided equally between the Author and the Publisher.

## 7. AUTHOR'S COPIES
The Publisher agrees to furnish the Author with 7 free copies of the Work on softcover editions and 5 free copies on hardcover editions.

The Author may purchase further copies of the Work at a 43% discount off list. No royalties shall be paid on such sales. The Author is permitted to buy books from the Publisher for the purpose of selling them for a profit, in effect, acting as a distributor or direct sales agent but only under the condition that these sales as distributor or agent must be approved in writing by the Publisher. However, under no condition may these sales impede sales by the Publisher or constitute direct competition.

## 8. ACCOUNTING and ROYALTY PAYMENT

The Publisher agrees to render biannual statements of account due 60 days after the half has ended. January-June and July-December are the biannual periods.

Royalty payments are due biannually and are due 90 days after the half has ended.

## 9. AUTHOR'S WARRANTY

The Author represents and warrants that he is the sole author and proprietor of the Work and has full power to make this agreement and grant; that the Work has not been published previously in book form; that it contains nothing of an obscene, libelous, injurious or unlawful nature, and that the Work will not infringe upon any copyright, propriety right, or other right. The Author agrees to indemnify and hold harmless the Publisher from and against any and all suits, claims, damages, and liabilities, based on or in respect of any violation or alleged violation of such whether actual or claimed. The control of the defense of any action against the Publisher in respect of the Work shall be exercised jointly by the Publisher and the Author but at the expense of the Author.

In the event that the Author does not meet the agreed upon deadlines, the Publisher has the right to either extend the deadline or at his discretion, demand an immediate return of any moneys advanced whereupon the Author must return said advance within 10 days of receipt of such request.

## 10. GUARANTEE TO PUBLISH

The Publisher agrees to publish the Work within 12 months of acceptance of the complete and satisfactory manuscript. If the manuscript is not complete and satisfactory or no mutually agreeable definition of "complete and satisfactory" can be reached between Author and Publisher, this Agreement shall be terminated and the Author shall return all moneys advanced out of his first earnings from any agreement reached for this Work with another publisher.

## 11. REVERSION OF RIGHTS

In the event that there is no edition of the Work in print and no contract or license in existence for the publication of any reprint or for the use of the Work in any manner, then the Author may demand in writing at any time the reassignment to himself of all rights granted under this agreement. In such event, the Publisher shall have six months during which it may make arrangements for printing or other use of the Work or may submit other evidence of anticipated earnings from the Work, and upon satisfactory evidence of such, this agreement shall continue. If however, at the end of six months, the Publisher shall not have made any such arrangement or submitted such evidence, all rights hereby granted to the Publisher shall revert to the Author.

## 12. ASSIGNMENT

The provision of this agreement shall apply to and bind the heirs, successors, executors, administrators and assigns of the Author and the Publisher. This agreement as a whole may be assigned by either party upon due notice being given in writing to the other party.

## 13. NON-COMPETITION CLAUSE

The Author agrees that during the continuance of this Agreement, he will not write, publish, print, or cause to be written, printed or published, any altered version of the Work, or in any way become interested is such version or in any book that is competitive or might interfere with or reduce the sales of the Work covered by this Agreement.

## 14. OTHER

This agreement shall be construed in accordance with the laws of the State of New York.

THE AUTHOR _____

**Address** _____

**Social Security Number** _____

SUCCESSFUL PUBLISHING _____

**Address** _____

_____

408

# APPENDIX B
## LIST OF US STATE ABBREVIATIONS

| | | | | |
|---|---|---|---|---|
| AL | Alabama | MT | Montana |
| AK | Alaska | NE | Nebraska |
| AZ | Arizona | NV | Nevada |
| AR | Arkansas | NH | New Hampshire |
| CA | California | NJ | New Jersey |
| CO | Colorado | NM | New Mexico |
| CT | Connecticut | NY | New York |
| DE | Delaware | NC | North Carolina |
| DC | District of Colombia | ND | North Dakota |
| FL | Florida | OH | Ohio |
| GA | Georgia | OK | Oklahoma |
| HI | Hawaii | OR | Oregon |
| ID | Idaho | PA | Pennsylvania |
| IL | Illinois | PR | Puerto Rico |
| IN | Indiana | RI | Rhode Island |
| IA | Iowa | SC | South Carolina |
| KS | Kansas | SD | South Dakota |
| KY | Kentucky | TN | Tennessee |
| LA | Louisiana | TX | Texas |
| MA | Massachusetts | UT | Utah |
| MD | Maryland | VA | Virginia |
| ME | Maine | VT | Vermont |
| MI | Michigan | WA | Washington |
| MN | Minnesota | WV | West Virginia |
| MS | Mississippi | WI | Wisconsin |
| MO | Missouri | WY | Wyoming |

# APPENDIX C
## POINT SIZE CHART

**4 POINT TO 72 POINT**

Ee4
Ee5
Ee6
Ee7
Ee8
Ee9
Ee10
Ee11
Ee12
Ee13
Ee14
Ee15
Ee16
Ee17
Ee18
Ee19
Ee20
Ee21
Ee22
Ee23

Ee24
Ee25
Ee26
Ee27
Ee30
Ee32
Ee34
Ee36
Ee38
Ee40

Ee42
Ee48
Ee54
Ee60
Ee66
Ee72

# APPENDIX D

## SOFTWARE REVIEW

## ESSENTIAL PROGRAMS

The two basic type of software programs you'll need to publish professional looking books are a word processing program and a publishing program. Other types of programs, which can certainly prove helpful depending upon the work you're doing, will also be briefly reviewed in this chapter so that you can be in tune with other software that can expand your capabilities.

I have kept my recommendations to mainstream products that are widely used by professionals so that compatibility with writers, printers, and production houses shouldn't be an issue. All programs, unless otherwise mentioned, are available for both the Macintosh and IBM formats.

### A. Recommended Word Processing Programs

**Microsoft Word**
This is the class of the word processing programs and a real pleasure to work with. Incredible features, ease-of-use and popularity in the industry, make Microsoft Word the program of choice. I highly recommend this program. Microsoft, One Microsoft Way, Redmond, WA 98052. (425)882-8080.

**Word Perfect**
This widely used word processing program has lost ground in recent years to Microsoft Word. Published by Corel Corporation, 1600 Carling Avenue, Ottawa, Ontario, Canada K1Z 8R7. (613)728-3733.

# B. Recommended Publishing Programs

The following programs can be used to create the pages in your book and lay it out ready for press. They include a multitude of features, pretty much everything you'll need to get your books ready for press. Each subsequent version of these programs gets updated with even more features and capabilities. The programs also have extensive capabilites for doing the covers as well, and as such, are a complete tool for the self-publisher. These programs are widely used.

### Adobe Pagemaker

Pagemaker is an excellent program for laying out and producing text - perhaps the best of the three software programs reviewed here for this purpose. Making pages and creating simple graphics are a breeze. Updates and recent improvements have made Pagemaker more powerful than ever and give users HTML capabilities so that web pages can be created for one's site.

While some artists feel that Pagemaker is not quite as good as Quark for doing covers, Adobe has made major changes to the program and it is better than ever. Regardless, Pagemaker is still excellent for this purpose - in fact, we do all our book covers in this program.

From Adobe Systems, 1585 Charleston Road, Mountain View, CA 94309. (800)411-8657.

### QuarkXpress

While not as good as Pagemaker for creating the inside text in a book (though still effective), QuarkXpress is preferred by designers for doing covers and color work. Originally available on the Macintosh only, now has a IBM compatible version.

From Quark, 1800 Grant Street, Denver, CO 80203. (303)894-8888.

### Ventura Publisher

Though not as popular among professionals as is Quark or Pagemaker, Ventura Publisher is still widely used and will get the job done. Available only on the IBM platform.

Published by Corel Corporation, 1600 Carling Avenue, Ottawa, Ontario, Canada K1Z 8R7. (613)728-3733.

# USEFUL PROGRAMS

The following programs are not essential starter software for book publishing, but later on, you may find these tools quite useful. Following is a quick preview of some excellent software programs. Unless otherwise mentioned, these programs are available for both Macintosh and IBM compatibles.

### Adobe Photoshop

A mind-boggling program that allows you to take scanned photographic images and do virtually anything with them. Photoshop is also used extensively to create original artwork. This software is beyond belief and is *the* program of choice among professionals.

To properly run Photoshop, you'll need a minimum of 32 megabytes of RAM for at least reasonable performance, though at least 64 megabytes of RAM is preferable. If you're working with large complicated images, even more RAM may be preferable. These memory requirements will go up as each succeeding generation of operating systems gets developed, and possibly, as the Aldus engineers program even more features in succeeding updates and revisions of the Photoshop product.

If you get any graphics program, and can afford the memory needed to run Photoshop properly, this is the program to get. From Adobe Systems, 1585 Charleston Road, Mountain View, CA 94309. (800)411-8657.

### Adobe Illustrator

An excellent program for creating original logos, drawings, and images of all types, Adobe Illustrator is a staple for artists looking to create professional computer illustration. Illustrator allows you to import virtually any printable image or document created from any program - or scanned images - and manipulate their form, color, texture and other properties with the many tools provided for manipulating and shaping images. Also includes text-handling capabilities such as tabs, spell-checker, search and replace fonts, rows/columns, punctuation and more.

Adobe Systems, 1585 Charleston Road, Mountain View, CA 94309. (800)411-8657.

**Adobe Premier**
Now that the book industry is getting more closely related to electronic media, you'll definitely want to be aware of this program. Premier is a powerful and versatile digital video editing program for creating multimedia presentations. In a sense, you create your own movie-like presentations; add or subtract frames to create terrific presentations, product demos, and animations by using preset or customizable options.

If nothing else, you'll have great fun with this product. Published by Adobe Systems, 1585 Charleston Road, Mountain View, CA 94309. (800)411-8657.

**Corel Draw**
A graphic design program used by many designers and artists. Published by Corel Corporation, 1600 Carling Avenue, Ottawa, Ontario, Canada K1Z 8R7. (613)728-3733.

**MacBarcoda Professional**
This super-simple program creates print-ready Bar Codes on the Macintosh. Enter just the ISBN and price, MacBarcoda does the rest. Creates EAN, UPC, and more than 150 other bar codes. Their latest version allows you to make virtually any type of bar code in whatever color combination you like. MacBarcoda is available at: (800)289-0993, (978)462-0993.

**Microsoft Excel**
This marvelous spreadsheet and number-crunching program has more capablilities than you can possibly use. Excel can be used for a variety of useful tasks including automating sales reports and analyses. At Cardoza Publishing we've set up Excel to generate royalty reports, six months sales statements, vendor totals, book summaries, and profit analyses. Since Excel is not specifically made for publishers (like the programs listed below), you'll need to do a bit of programming to setup your systems.

Published by Microsoft, One Microsoft Way, Redmond, WA 98052. (425)882-8080.

# PUBLISHER ACCOUNTING PROGRAMS

Following are a two excellent choices for automating your sales, commissions, and accounting records.

### Cat's Pajamas - MiniCat System

Specializing in custom computer systems for publishers for more than 20 years, the Cat's Pajamas software, and the more basic version, the MiniCat, gives publishers and distributors, both large and small, the ability to organize and run their business smoothly.

The MiniCat gives users all the major features of the full Cat's Pajamas, with royalty reporting, fulfillment systems, inventory and warehousing controls, order processing, returns processing, customer service, marketing tools, mailing list management, and more. There is a lot of depth to this program, and the many features will be greatly appreciated when your business gets to the stage where organization is key.

The purchase price of $6,500 for the MiniCat includes training, documentation, and some phone support. While this is a serious investment, it is an overall excellent value for keeping you on top of your business.

This software is available from 1253 Highway 20, Anacortes, WA 98221; (800)827-2287, (360)293-8372.

### PIIGS

PIIGS™ (Publisher's Invoice and Information Generating System) is currently designed as a single-user program for small publishers. It handles a wide variety of tasks, from backorders, inventory maintenance, and sales reports, to royalties and commissions. Companies needing simultaneous multiple-user access to a system will not find the PIIGS program appropriate to their needs.

While this book was going to press, the publishers of PIIGS stated that the release of both the Macintosh and Windows platforms of the program were imminent. DOS version 2.2 was the only one available as this book was going to press. A demo version to test the software is available for $25, fully refundable if returned within 30 days or deductible if the full program is purchased. Published by Upper Access Inc., P. O. Box 457, Hinesburg, VT 05461; (800)356-9315.

# SOFTWARE REVIEW SECTION

The software programs reviewed in this section are important tools used by many software developers. This list is not meant to be inclusive of everything you need, just a sampling of some top professional software, with a little more emphasis on graphics tools.

### Photoshop
This excellent program is an integral tool for many software companies. See the book section for an expanded review.

### Debabilizer
Debabilizer is simply an indispensible and essential program for software companies. Converting bit-mapped images graphics between formats and platforms on Macintosh, Dos, Windows, Silicon Graphics, Sun Microsystems, and other platforms is just one of the many great features this program offers software developers.

Debabilizer also fully automates a multitude of time-consuming tasks including automatic batch processing, color reductions and scaling, palette creation and manipulation, and a host of other functions. For example, images that are created in thousands or millions of colors can be reduced to a preset 256 color palette or the program can be set to create its own optimal 256 color palette.

Equilibrium Technologies, 475 Gate Five Road, Suite 225, Sausalito, CA 94965. (415)332-4343.

### Director Multimedia Studio
A whiz-bang multimedia package that not only includes Director, but xRes, Extreme 3D, *and* SoundEdit (Macintosh) and Sound Forge XP (Windows). Director is a tremendous authoring tool for creating movie-like sequences and comes with a database of graphics, sounds, color palettes, and Lingo scripts for writing routines. xRes comes with a vast array of tools to allows you to create original artwork in all styles or to manipulate photographic images. Extreme 3D is a powerful 3D program, and the sound programs allows you to synchronize, manipulate, and digitize audio for your multimedia applications. Shockwave is a program for delivering multimedia onto the internet.

With this great bundle, you can create 2D and 3D graphics and animations, link them up to audio tracks, and direct the whole ensemble into a tightly knit multimedia project for everything from corporate presentations to interactive advertising and even CD titles. You'll get all the authoring tools you need to combine all sound, animations, 2D and 3D art into presentations that can be used on your web pages as well!

The Director Multimedia Studio is highly recommended - this is really a terrific product. Macromedia, 600 Townsend Street, San Francisco, CA 94103. (800)288-9576.

### 3D Studio Max

This is a professional tool used by artists to create sophisticated 3D effects and images used in simulations, games, and even movies. You'll need to devote months of study and practice to create even a fraction of the effects and images this unbelievable program allows you to do. The possibilities of Max are virtually limitless. This sophisticated tool will assure any skilled user a job in the multimedia industry.

Kinetics Incorporated, 642 Harrison Street, San Francisco, CA 94107. (415)547-2000.

# WEB PUBLISHING SOFTWARE

There are many programs available for web publishing. Below, I've reviewed two Adobe products that can be used by laymen (that is, there is no need to know HTML coding or be a super computer geek to get the job done), and two professional web building tools from Allaire for experienced webmasters.

### Adobe PageMill

Another fine Adobe product that allows users to create functional and elegant designs for their web pages and get their business up on the net. PageMill also includes a limited edition of Photoshop (Photoshop LE), plus a stock library of animations, sounds, and images which can be used to enhance the site being created.

Adobe Systems, 1585 Charleston Road, Mountain View, CA 94309. (800)411-8657.

**Adobe SiteMill**
SiteMill is a more sophisticated version of PageMill that allows novice web masters and designers to automatically maintain integrated links throughout a site no matter the size. Using icons and easy drag and drop connections, you can move text, images, and links directly onto a Web page, and apply HTML formats without the hassle of typing HTML code.

SiteMill is an effective tool for overall Web site management since it keeps all pages throughout a site linked and unbroken, no matter how many updates and edits are made to the site. From Adobe Systems, 1585 Charleston Road, Mountain View, CA 94309. (800)411-8657.

**Cold Fusion Studio**
The list of companies using ColdFusion as the application tool to build their web sites is a who's who of companies and shows the power of this superb software. From AT&T, official government sectors, and NASA, to our own companies, Cold Fusion provides the power for companies big and small to use the vast resources of the web and build a state-of-the-art site.

There are many professional tools available in Cold Fusion for the experienced or programming-oriented webmaster. From Allaire Corporation, One Alewife, Cambridge, MA 02140. (617)761-2000.

**Homesite**
For building great web pages, Allaire's HomeSite gives webmasters a full range of authoring, HTML editing, and page management tools to allow developers to build and manage their sites. Intuitive WYSIWYN (what you see is what you need) interface, and an extensive library of wizards allows for a precise control of layout and design. By Allaire Corporation, One Alewife, Cambridge, MA 02140. (617)761-2000.

# APPENDIX E

## US AND CANADIAN BOOK CHAIN LISTINGS

### US BOOK CHAINS

The retail book trade has experienced tremendous upheavals in the 1990's with the steady disappearance not only of the independent book stores, but the questionable viability of both medium size chains and large chains that simply cannot compete profitably in this new era.

The days of the local hip bookstop and the strong community bookstore are fast disappearing, much to the chagrin of many book purists. The heavyweights, particularly Barnes and Noble, are deeply capitalized, pursue an aggressive marketing strategy, and cannot afford losses for years if need be, while the indies just can't handle losses for too long.

It boils down to the fact that there are fewer and fewer places to sell books. In a nutshell, if you don't get well represented into the Barnes and Noble and Borders Group chains, you'll be picking from a minority of the book trade and simply won't get widespread distribution into the general book trade.

To give you an idea of how fast this trend is occurring, the last edition of this book, just three years ago, contained listings for several chains whose status is greatly changed. Encore Books (now part of the Lauriet Group, who at the time of this writing is under bankruptcy protection), Krochs and Brentanos, and Taylor's, the latter two of which have met their maker, are obviously places whose door can no longer be knocked upon. Three chains have been removed from our list.

On this dwindling and small list, two chains, Crown and Lauriet's, were under bankruptcy protection as this edition was being written, and a third, Musicland, was not as healthy as they would like.

The chains are listed in alphabetical order.

(Since Little Professor franchisees are privately owned, and buying is not centrally done, we have not included them on this list.)

**Barnes and Noble** (B. Dalton, Bookstop, Bookstar, Doubleday, Scribners), 122 5th Avenue, NY, NY 10011; (212)633-3300. B & N is the largest and most powerful player in the book trade. They've invested heavily in the superstore concept.

**Books-A-Million**, 402 Industrial Lane, Birmingham, AL 35211; (205)942-3737. At press time, this Southern-based chain appeared healthy.

**Borders/Waldenbooks** (Brentanos, Readers Market), 5451 South State Road, Ann Arbor, MI 48108; (313)995-726. One of the two big players in retail books, the Borders Group Inc. company, like B & N, is publicly traded.

**Crown Books**, 3300 75th Avenue, Landover, MD 20785; (301)731-1200. At press time, Crown had filed for bankruptcy protection. Whether they emerge stronger from their travails, get submerged or incorporated into a different umbrella, or say bye-bye altogether remains to be seen.

**Lauriet/Royal Discount/Encore,** 10 Pequot Way, Canton, MA 02021; (617)828-8300. This regional chain has taken a beating and, at the time of this writing, is under bankruptcy protection.

**MusicLand** (On Cue and Media Play), P. O. Box 1245, Minneapolis, MN 55440; (612)932-7700. At the time of this writing, word has it that this chain is struggling.

**Tower Books and Records**, 2601 Delmonte Street, Bldg C, West Sacramento, CA 95691; (916)373-2500. Tower appears to still be a player.

## CANADIAN BOOK CHAINS

Chapters, 40 Ronson Drive, Etobicoke, Ontario, Canada. (416)243-3138. In May 1995, the two large Canadian bookstore chains, Coles Book Stores, about 230 stores (they also owned The Book Company, about 20 stores), and SmithBooks, about 175 stores (they also own Classic), officially merged into one large chain. Now the new company, called Chapters, is the only big player in the Canadian market.

Chapters has trimmed down the mall-based Coles and SmithBooks stores to a few hundred outlets total, while investing heavily into the Chapters superstores.

## INTERNET SALES

Book-selling on the internet is starting to become big business. The first company to establish a major presence in this new market was Amazon.com. Not to be outdone, the retail giant Barnes and Noble got into the game as well.

Featuring easy-to-use and extensive search engines, discounted prices, an enormouse selection of titles, and a simple method of ordering books without ever having to leave one's deck, these two sites are making big inroads in the way books are being purchased.

Check out the sites:
Amazon.com: www.amazon.com
Barnes and Noble: barnesandnoble.com

While these sites may not account for a large number of titles sold per publisher, the increased usage of the internet as a medium to buy books could very well change that.

You can also set up your own web site to sell your books, but be fore-warned that the costs of doing so may only make it worthwhile for certain publishers, in particular, publishers with a highly targeted audience.

# APPENDIX F

## RECOMMENDED RESOURCES

The publications listed in this section are important wells of information and knowledge that can benefit your publishing business. Any tool that helps you produce a better product, sell more books, or in any way improve your knowledge about publishing, is worth considering for your library. A mere $10, $20 or even $150 or more spent on knowledge that will earn you money is dirt cheap in my bayou, and a great investment. If $200 spent will help you find a way to sell $1,000 worth of books, you've got yourself a good deal.

Keep in mind that there are many other valuable resources available beyond which I've mentioned in this short list.

### Directories and Periodicals

The first three listings, the *Literary Market Place, American Book Trade Directory,* and *American Wholesalers and Distributors Directory*, cost more than $150 to purchase. If this is beyond your budget, you can generally access these references at your local library.

**Literary Market Place (LMP)**, R.R. Bowker, 121 Chanlon Road, New Providence Road, NJ 07974. Phone (908)464-6800. An important reference tool for publishers, the LMP contains listings of printers, wholesalers, distributors, reviewers, associations, literary agents, book clubs, subsidiary rights contacts and much more. An invaluable resource. The international version of the LMP, *International Literary Market Place*, also available at Bowker, provides the contact and information you'll need to sell rights and distribute your books overseas.

**American Book Trade Directory**, R.R. Bowker, 121 Chanlon Road, New Providence, NJ 07974. Phone (800)521-8110. Lists 27,000+ U.S. and Canadian retail and antiquarian booksellers, 1,500+ - wholesalers, distributors, and jobbers, plus numerous contacts in the foreign book trade.

**American Wholesalers and Distributors Directory**, Gale Research, P. O. Box 33477, Detroit, MI 48232. Phone (800)877-GALE. Thorough guide lists more than 28,000 wholesalers and distributors at local, regional and national levels.

**Publishers Weekly**, 249 West 17th Street, New York, NY 10011, (212)645-0067. Published weekly, the magazine of the book trade has improved it's content in the last few years becoming both more interesting and more relevant to the independent publisher. A subscription to PW is worthwhile to keep yourself abreast of the trends, the news, and the general climate of the publishing business.

**Small Press**, Kymbolde Way, Wakefield, RI 02879, (401)789-0074. This is the best magazine for independent publishers. A subscription here is well worth the money. Published quarterly, every issue contains at least two or three relevant articles targeted toward the self-publisher.

## Newsletters

**Book Marketing Update**, Open Horizons, P.O. Box 205, Fairfield, IA 52556; (800)796-6130. Edited and published by John Kremer, this terrific newsletter is definitely recommended. $60 year.

**Publishing Poynters**, P.O. Box 4232, Santa Barbara, CA 93140; (800)PARAPUB. Dan Poynter, author of *The Self-Publishing Manual*, publishes a free monthly newsletter packed with lots of great tips.

**Publishers Marketing Association Newsletter**, 2401 Pacific Coast Highway #102, Hermosa Beach, CA 90254, (310)372-2732. $80 annual fee includes excellent 48 page monthly newsletter.

**SPAN**, P.O. Box 1306, 425 Cedar Street, Buena Vista, CO 81211. Phone (719)395-4790. $95 annual membership fee includes informative monthly newsletter loaded with good ideas.

# Books Related to Publishing

**1001 Ways to Market Your Books** by John Kremer (Open Horizons). Kremer does very thorough work. Your money is will go a long way with this tremendous publication. His strengths are showing you how to find new channels of distribution and suggesting endless numbers of money-making ideas. A must-buy. Also by Kremer, the useful *Book Marketing Made Easier*, and the excellent and highly recommended *Mail Order Selling Made Easier*. (Ad-Lib Publications.) This latter book is especially recommended.

**The Complete Guide to Self-Publishing** by Tom and Marilyn Ross (Writer's Digest Books). Though it's a book about self-publishing by authors who don't self publish it, this an excellent book with lots of good information.

**The Self-Publishing Manual** by Dan Poynter (Para Publishing). As opposed to other publishing books you might find, Poynter has self-published this book and others, and done so quite successfully. There's information here that will help you.

**Book Publishing Resource Guide** by Marie Kieffer (Ad-Lib Publications). Valuable directory of key contacts for marketing and promoting books. Includes distributors of all types, book clubs, bookstore chains, mail order catalogs, book reviewers, and much more.

**Tested Advertising Methods** by John Caples (Prentice-Hall). A classic guide to writing ad copy that sells. Excellent book.

**The Unabashed Self-Promoter's Guide** by Jeffrey Lant (Jeffrey Lant Associates). Tons of essential information on promoting authors, books, events and more.

*See pages 102-104 for other resources.*

# BOOK SECTION INDEX

**Aachen Bold, 118**
ABA Convention, 105, 276
ABI forms, 98
About the Author, 198, 199, 200
Academic market, 300
Acid free paper, 298-299
Accounting, 337-338, 414
Accounts, setting up, 321-322
Adhesive binding, 246
Adobe Illustrator, 412
Adobe Pagemaker, 411
Adobe Pagemill, 416
Adobe Photoshop, 412
Adobe Premier, 413
Adobe SiteMill, 417
Advanced Book Information (ABI), 98
Advanced Marketing Services, 292
Advances, 76-77
Advertising, 315-318
   co-op, 318
   direct to the consumer, 317-318
   word of mouth, 318
Airborne Express, 335-336
ALA Convention, 105
Alpenbooks, 282
Amazon.com, 420
American Booksellers Association (ABA), 105
*American Bookseller Magazine, 276*
*American Book Trade Directory, 422*
American Library Association (ALA), 105
American Wholesale Books, 280
*American Wholesalers and Distributors Directory, 272, 422*
Anderson News, 284
Appendix, 201, 212, 215
Atrium Publishers Group, 273
Audience, 48-52
   addressing, 49, 52, 81, 290
   identify, 48-51
   target, 48-50, 81
Author, *see* Writer

***Backgammon for Winners, 93***
Back pages, 198, 201-202, 208-209, 215, 227, 353-354
Baker and Taylor Books, 279-280, 295
Banta Company, 241

Bar code, 100-102
   Bookland Ean, 100-101
   UPC, 101-102
Barnes and Noble, 295, 419, 420
*Basics of Winning Chess, The,* 55-57
*Basics of Winning Lotto/Lottery, The,* 256
*Basics of Winning Series, The,* 86, 93
*Basics of Winning Slots, The, 52*
*Beat the Odds, 357*
Belt press, 239-240
Bern Convention, 99
Bill/Billing, 40, 322-324
Binding, 82-83, 246
   comb bound, 83, 88
   hardbound, 83, 87-88
      adhesive, 88, 246
      smythe-sown, 88
   paperbound, 83-86
   perfect bound, 83-86, 246
   saddle-stitching, 83, 89, 216
   spiral bound, 83, 88, 246
   velo-binding, 83, 89
Bleed, 136, 248
*Bloomsbury Review, The,* 308
Blueline, 195, 250-251
Blues - *see* Blueline.
Blurbs, 62, 200
Body text, 198, 202, 227
Bold, 127, 142-143
Book, 26, 67
   budget, 42-43
   dimensions, 82-83
   edit, 27
   files, 205-206
   idea, 26, 67
   paperback, 83-86
   place to buy, 71-73
   plan and design, 27
   price, 51, 81
   production, 27
   selling features, 51-63
   setting up, 202-204
Bookazine, 280
Book chains, 295-296, 418-420
   Canadian, 296, 420
   U.S., 295-296, 418-419
Book clubs, 292-294, 309

BookCrafters, 241
Book design, 51, 62,116-148, 226
　　concepts, 138-143
　　standard, 137-138
Book Industry Study Group, 101
Bookkeeping, 336-338, 414
Book layout, 222-224
Bookland Ean bar code *see* Bar code
*Booklist*, 306
Book market, 295-297
*Book Marketing Update*, 422
Book Mart Press, 241
Bookmen, 280
Book-of-the-Month Club, 293, 309
*Book Page*, 308
Bookpeople, 280
Book planning, loose or tight, 210-218
*Book Publishing Resource Guide*, 272, 423
Book Rate
*Book Reader, The*, 308
Book Sales Inc., 294
Book signings/Book readings, 315
Books-A-Million, 296, 419
*Books in Print,* 96, 98, 102
Booksmith Promotional Company, 294
Booksource, 281
*Borders/Waldenbooks, 419*
*Boston Globe*, 307
Bound galley, *see* Galley
Bound page proof, 303
Braun-Brumfield, 241
Break-even, 41-42, 45-46
Budget, first book, 42-45

**C1S (Coated one side), 249**
C2S (Coated two sides), 249-250
Camera-ready, 190-191, 231-232
Camex International, 294
Canadian Booksellers Convention, 105
Catalogue,
　　how to put togerther, 288-289
　　sales, 292
Cat's Pajamas, 277, 414
CD ROM, 233
Centered, 129-130
Chapter
　　chaptering, 110
　　check, 227
　　count, 220-221
　　design, 130-137, 214, 216
　　headings, 119, 136-137, 212-213
　　pages, 209-210
　　sample, 68
　　size, 137
Chapterizing, 210, 219-222

Chapters, 296, 420
Cheltenham, 124
Children's books, , 32, 103, 113, 116, 119,
　　124, 179
*Chicago Tribune Books*, 307
Choice, 315
Christian Book Distributors, 282
CIP (Cataloging in Publication) - *see* Library of
　　Congress
CIROBE, 294
Clothbound, *see* Hardcover
CMYK, 175
Cold Fusion Studio, 417
Coles Book Stores, 296
Collecting money, 325
Color keys, 187, 251
Color separation, 162-163
Comb binding, 83, 88
Company
　　establish, 26, 32-34
　　list of, 103
　　name, 31-32
　　setting up, 31-46
　　start-up costs, 40-41
Competition, 47, 68, 92
*Complete Guide to Self-Publishing, The*
　　(Ross), 423
Comps, 185-190
Computer design techniques, 143-147
Computer equipment, 35-38
　　buying, 37
　　hardware, 37-38
　　IBM compatible, 37-38
　　Macintosh, 37-38
　　set-up, 36-39
Consortium Book Sales and Distribution, 273,
*Contemporary Authors*, 104
Contract
　　advances, 76-77
　　flat pay, 77
　　negotiating, 76-79
　　provisions, 78
　　royalties, 76-79
　　sample contract, 404-407
　　signing, 78
Co-op advertising, 318
Copy edit, 109, 111-112
Copyright, 99-100
Copyright page, 198, 199, 200, 208
Corel Draw, 413
Corporation, 32-33
Courier, 126
Cover, 51-55, 166-196
　　black, 179-180
　　black and white, 177-178

blues, 195
color, 175, 178-183
comps, 185-190
copy, 53-54, 173-174
costs, 43-45, 177-178
Cromalin, 195-196
designer, 183-184
ink, 250
instruction sheet, 192-193
making on disc, 192-193
making with mechanicals, 191-192
production, 166-196
proofing, 194
protecting, 184-185
reverse, 179
sales, 167-175
setting up, 181-183
submitting, 195
Cover design, 52, 54, 166-196
principles, 169-173
Cover letter, 311-313
Cover stock, 249
Credit card account, 290-291
Cromalin, 163, 195-196, 251
Crop marks, 203-204
Cropping, 155-159
Crown Books, 295, 387
*Cumulative Book Index*, 103
Cushing-Malloy, 241

**Daedalus Books, 294**
DBA (Doing Business As), 34
Debabilizer, 415
Decorative type, 118
Dedication, 199, 200
Delta Lithograph, 241
Design, *see* book design, chapter design,
        cover design, page design, spine
        design, type design
Design concepts, 138-143
Design edit, 112-113
Desktop publishing, 35
Design, loose or tight, 214, 218
DeVorss and Company, 282
*Director, Multimedia, 415*
*Directory of Poetry Publishers*, 103
*Directory of Printers*, 240
Discount schedule, 287-288
Distribution, 264-290
income from, 348-350
self, 265
trade, 265
Distributors, 265-270
contacting, 268

choosing, 270-274
finding, 267-268
large publishers as, 277-278
library, 297-298
national exclusive, 265-270
Distributors, The, 281
Documents, sending *see* Shipping
Doubler, 199, 212, 216
DPI (dots per inch), 231
Duotone, 163-164

**Editing, 27, 109-114**
communicating, 113-114
content, 109-111
copy, 109, 111-112
design, 109, 112-113
entering, 114
Edward R. Hamilton, 295
Electronic submissions, *see* Submissions
Endorsements, 174
Epigraph, 199
Equipment and Materials, 34-39
Establishing a line, 350-353
Establishing a publishing company, 31-34
Estimate, *see* Quote
Exacto cutting knife, 151

***F and W Publications*, 103**
Fax machine, 40
Federal Express, 235, 335-336
Fiction books, 23-24, 51, 54, 67, 71, 74-75,
        116, 173, 213, 260, 298, 299
table of contents, 55
Fictional genre books, 26
Fictitious Business Name Statement, 34
Film lamination, 184-185
Final proof, *see* Once-over
First impression, 51
Flat pay, 77
Floppy Disk, 233
Flush left (ragged right), 129-130
Flush right (ragged left), 129-130
FOB (Freight on Board), 251
Font, 186
Foreword, 199-201
*Forthcoming Books in Print*, 98, 102
Fotel/GGX, 101, 102
Four color process, 175-177
FPO (For Proof Only), 188
Front pages, 198-201, 208-209, 212, 216,
        228
Frontispiece, 199
Fulfillment, 326, 343

**Gale Research Company, 282**
Galley (bound galley or page proof), 35-36,
   303-309
   sending, 305-309, 315
     book clubs, 309
     magazines, 308-309
     newspapers, 307-308
     other publications, 309, 315
     trade publications, 305-307
Garamond, 124
GGX Associates, 101-102
Glossary, 201, 212
Goal setting, 21
Graphics, 142, 164-165, 209, 214, 217
   check, 227-228
   manually inserting, 164-165
   tools, 151-153

**Haddon Craftsmen, 242**
Half title, 198
Halftone, 160-162, 250
Hand waxer, 151
Hardbound, 83, 87-88
Hardcover, *see* Hardbound
Hardware, *see* Computer
Headings, 119, 139-141
Headline type, 118
Helvetica, 122-123, 125, 145-147
Homesite, 417
Homestead Book Company, 282
*Horn Book Magazine*, 315
How-to books, 23-24, 46, 52-53, 54, 55, 58,
   67, 69, 71, 73-74, 85, 109, 110, 111,
   113, 116, 119, 122, 123, 125, 131,
   139-141, 173, 179, 214, 289, 306,
   308, 352, 353, 354
   publishing, 23-24
   table of contents, 55
   title, 52-53
*How to Play Winning Poker*, 52
*Hungry Mind Review*, 308

**IBM compatibles, 37-38, 39, 107, 410, 411**
ID (Independent Distributor), 283
Illustrator, Adobe, 412
Incentive sales, 291-292
Indent, first line, 131, 213, 217
Independent book stores, 295-296
Independent Publishers Group, 273
Independent sales reps, *see* Sales rep
Index, 201, 212, 215, 298-299
Ingram Book Company, 279, 295
Interior design, 62

*International Directory of Little Magazines and
   Small Presses*, 103
*International Literary Market Place, 421*
International Standard Book Number (ISBN),
   97, 100, 262, 298, 356
Introduction, 51, 58-59, 198, 199, 200
Invoice/Invoicing, *see* Bill/billing

**JA Majors Company, 282**
Jaz Disk, 233
Jobbers, 283-285
Justified type, 129-130

***Kirkus Reviews*, 305**
Koen Books, 281
Koen Pacific distributors, 281

***Las Vegas Guide*, 59, 61, 90**
Lauriat's/ Royal Discount, 419
Layout, 197, 202-224
   laying out a book, 222-224
   planning, 202-221
Leading, 121,127-129, 213, 216
Library distributors, *see* Distributors
Library market, 297-299
Library of Congress, 97-100
   CIP (Cataloging in Publication), 98-99
   register of copyrights, 100
Library of Congress Catalog Card Number, 97-
   98, 298, 356
*Library Journal*, 305
Library-quality books, 298-299
List price, 77, 89-93, 347-350
   setting, 89-93
List/print ratio, 343-346
   8/1 list/print ratio, 346
Literary Guild, 293, 309
*Literary Market Place (LMP)*, 65, 103, 240,
   272, 276, 338, 421
Login Publishers Consortium, 273
*Los Angeles Times Book Review*, 307
L-S Distributors, 281
LTC Group, 281

**MacBarcoda, 102, 413**
Macintosh, 37-38, 39, 102, 107, 384, 385
Mail order, 289-291
Malloy Lithographing, 242
Manual paste-up, 150-151
Manuscript, 106-115
   check, 227
   edit, 109-114
   submission, 107-108

Maple-Vail Book Manufacturing, 242
Marboro Books, 295
Margins, 133-135, 202-203, 213, 216, 249, 259-260
Market, 28,68, 70, 82, 300
    academic, 300
    positioning, 82
    potential, 70-71
Market research, 49
Marketing, 80-95, 301-318, 343
    decisions, 81-82
    initial, 80-95
Mass market paperback, 83, 86
Mass-market size, 83-84, 86
Match Print, 163, 187
Mechanicals, 191-192
Microsoft Excel, 413
Microsoft Word, 39, 114, 410
Motorbooks International, 282
Musicland, 419

**Nacscorp, 283**
NAIPR (National Association of Independent Publishers Representatives), 276
National Book Network, 273
National exclusive distributors, 265-274, 344
    list of, 272-274
Negatives, storing, 259
Net Price, 77, 349
Net 30 days, 321-322
New Age books, 25-26, 66, 282, 283, 296
New Baskerville (Baskerville), 124
New Century Schoolbook (Century Schoolbook), 124, 126
New editions, 356-358
New Leaf Distributing, 283
News release, 313-314
*New York Newsday*, 307
*New York Review of Books*, 308
*New York Times Daily Book Review*, 307
*New York Times Sunday Book Review*, 307
Niche publishing, 22-23
Non-fiction books, 23-25, 53, 55, 58, 69, 71, 73-74, 85, 87, 110, 112, 123, 139, 174, 179, 306, 308, 354
    table of contents, 55

**Office**
    set-up, 39
    supplies, 40
Once-over (final proof), 229-230
On Cue, 296
*1001 Ways to Market Your Books*, 423
Open Road Publishing, 90, 351
Order form, 354-355

Orders
    increasing, 325
    invoicing, 322-324
    phone, 320
    taking, 320-326
Organizational page, 224-225
Outline, 68
Overhead, 348
Overnight delivery, 335-336
Overs, 257
Overview edit, 109-111

**Packing**
    books, 333
    boxes, 40, 327-330
    materials, 327
Packing slip, 329-330
Page check, 228-229
Page count, 51, 62, 94-95, 197-198, 201-202, 206-223
Page design, 130-137
Pagemaker, 39, 206, 234, 384
Page margins, 133-135
Page numbers, 132-133
Page proof, 303-304
Pantone Matching System (PMS), 176-177, 191-192
Paperback, 82, 83-86
    mass market, 83-86
    quality, 85
    trade, 84-85
Paperbound, *see* Paperback
Paragraph design, 130-131, 139-141, 213-214, 217
Partners Book Distributing, 281
Partnership, 32
Past due notice, 325
Paste-up, *see* Manual paste-up
Payment, 348-350
    net sales, 349-350
Percentages, 154-155
Perfect binding, 83-86, 246
Periodical, 22
*Philadelphia Inquirer*, 307
Photoshop, Adobe, 415
Pica rule, 151
Picas, 121-122
Pick-up, 261
Piggybacking, 334
PIIGS, 277, 414
Pitch letter, *see* Cover letter
Places to list your authors, 104
Places to list your books, 102-103
Places to list your company, 103
Plus Sales, 278

PMS, *see* Pantone Matching System
PO#, *see* Purchase order number
Poetry books, 25, 51, 54, 67, 71, 81, 103,
    116, 173, 213, 260, 298, 299
Point size, 213, 216, 409
    standard text, 124-125
Points, 121-122
Preface, 199-201
Premier, Adobe, 413
Premium sales, 291-292
Pre-Press,
    costs, 341
    problems, 259-261
Pre-publication date, 303
Press, going to, 231
Press release, *see* News release
Price, 59, 77, 89-93
    list, 77, 89-93, 347-350
    net, 77
Price points, 92
Pricing a book, 59, 81, 89-93
Prima Publisher, 273
Print quality, 231-233
Print quote, 240-241, 244-251
    accepting, 252-253
Print Run, 253-262
    books with sales history, 254-255
    new books, 255-256
    ordering, 253-257
    price, 258-259
    problems, 259-262
    strategy, 256-257
Printer
    choosing, 242-244
    list of, 241-242
Printing bill, 257-258
Printing, 43-45, 237-263, 341
    costs, 43-45, 341
    maintaining good price, 258-259
    output shop, 232
    presses, 238-239
    problems, 259-262
    process, 240
Printing, list of printers, 241-242
Process Colors, 175
Production, 27, 43-45,197-236, 341
    costs, 43-45, 341, 347
Profits, 41-42, 346-348
    ways to increase, 346-348
Promotion, 45
Proofing, 226-230
    cover, 194
Proofreading marks, 112
Proportional wheel (reduction wheel), 151-154

Proposal, 48, 65, 70-73
    judging, 70-73
Publication date (pub date), 303
Publicity, 302-315
    package, 310
Publish
    decision to, 26, 80-95
Publisher, 21-22
*Publishers Directory*, 103
Publishers Distribution Services, 273
*Publishers, Distributors, Wholesaler of the U.S.*,
    103
Publishers Group West, 273
Publishers Marketing Association, 104, 422
Publishers Overstock Unlimited, 295
Publishers Press, 242
*Publishers Weekly*, 276, 305, 422
Publishing costs, 40-46, 340-343
    additional, 343
    author, 342
    employee, 341-342
    marketing, 343
    postage & shipping, 343
    pre-press, 341
    printing, 341
    production, 341, 347
    publishing, 340-343
    rent, 342
    set-up, 342-343
    start-up, 40-46
    warehousing & fulfillment, 343
*Publishing Poynters*, 422
Publishing organizations, list of, 104
Publishing programs, 39, 206-208, 234, 384-
    385
    transferring, 206-208
Purchase order number (PO#), 320

**Quadtones, 163-164**
Quality Books, 98, 297-298
Quark, 39, 234, 411
Quebecor Printing/Fairfield, 242
Quote, 240-241, 244-253
    accepting, 252-253
    sample, 245
    understanding, 244-251

**Rack jobber,** *see* **Jobber**
Racks, 86
Ragged left, *see* Flush right
Ragged right, *see* Flush left
Rand McNally and Company, 242
RBW Graphic, 242
Reduction wheel, *see* Proportional wheel

Reference books, 23, 87, 88, 119, 122, 139-
    141, 282, 287, 293, 297, 298, 299, 306,
    315
Religious books, 25, 71, 72, 98, 282, 283
Remainder dealers, 294-295
Reprint, 341
Reproducing images, 159-163
    black and white, 160-161
    color copies, 189-190
    color photographic, 162-163
    color prints as black & white, 162
    color slides as black & white, 161-162
    non-photographic, 159-162
Reproduction size, 152
Resale number, 338-339
Reverse, 179
Review copy, 309-310
Reviews, 174, 302-309, 311, 315
    post-publication, 309
    pre-publication, 303-304
    sources, 305-309, 315
Richardson's Books, 282
Rose Printing Company, 242
Rough page count, 206-218, 220
Royalty, 76-79, 347
    paying, 78
    reporting, 78
R.R. Bowker, 96, 98, 102
R.R. Donnelley and Sons Company, 242
Rubilith, 148
Rules, 121
Running headers, 131-132

**S & L Sales, 295**
Saddle-stitch, 83, 89, 246
Sales, 286-291, 347
    academic, 300
    angle, 68-69
    catalog, 292
    goal, 48
    net, 349-350
    place to find, 71-72
    revenue, 347
    specialty, premium & Incentive, 291-292
Sales rep, 270-274
    choosing, 270
    finding, 276
    independent, 274-277
    individuals, 326
    territories, 275
Sample chapter, 68
Samuel French Trade, 283
Samuel Weiser, 283
*San Diego Union*, 307
*San Francisco Chronicle Book Review*, 307

*San Francisco Review of Books*, 308
*San Jose Mercury News*, 308
Sans-serif type, 122-123
Savings, planning for, 94-95
Scanner, 150
Scanning, 188-189
SCB Distributors, 273
*School Library Journal*, 306
Screens, 144-148
*Seattle Times*, 308
Self-cover, 246
Self-distribution, 265, 286-291
*Self-Publishing Manual, The*, 423
Separations, *see* Color separations
Serif type, 123-124
Setting goals, 21
Sheet-fed press, 238
Ship date, 303
Shipping, 257, 262-263, 330-336, 343
    bookrate, 331-332
    boxes, 330-335
    important documents, 335-336
    individual books, 332-333
    instructions, 263
    libraries, 335
    rush, 335-336
Shooting up & shooting down, 155
Short discount, 300
Signature, 94-95, 197-198, 201-202, 215
Silverprint, *see* Blueline
Single proprietorship, 32-34
Sizing images, 149, 152-155
*Small Press*, 306, 422
Small Press Distribution, 274
*Small Press Record of Books in Print*, 103
*Small Press Review*, 315
Smith Books/Classic Bookshops, 296, 388
Smyth-sown, 88
Software, set-up, 39
Southern Books, 282
SPAN, 422
Specialty sales, 291-292
Spell check, 114
Spine, 51-52, 54-55
    design, 173
Spine bulk, 246
Spiral binding, 83, 88, 246
Spring Arbor Distributors, 283
Standard book announcement information,
    305
Stat camera, 159-160
State abbreviations, 408
Storage, 326
Storage Media, 233
Stripping covers, 284-285

Subheadings (Subhead), 119, 215, 218
*Subject Guide to Books in Print*, 98
Submissions
    camera-ready art, 231-233
    disk, 107-108, 234-235
    electronic, 231, 234-235
    manuscript, 107
    soliciting or accepting, 67-70
Superstore, 295
SyQuest, 233

**3D Studio Max, 416**
Table of Contents, 51, 55-58, 68, 199, 200,
    208, 212, 216, 227
    positioning, 58
Taking orders, 320-326
Talman Company, The, 274
Taxes, 337-338
Terms, 251, 287-288
*Tested Advertising Methods*, 423
Testimonials, 174
Text stock, 247
Text type, 118-119
Thermal dye transfer, 186-187
Thomson-Shore, 242
Times Roman (Times), 124
Title, 52-53
Title page, 198, 199, 200, 208
Title type, 180
Toll-Free 800 Number, 290-291, 354
Total pages, 246
Trade paperback, 83, 85-86
Trade shows, 105
Trade size, 83-84
Traditional screens, 148
Trapping, 175-176, 181-182
Trim size, 246
Tritones, 163-164
Turnaround time, 243-244
Type, 116-129
    alignment, 129-130
    chaper, headline & sub-headline, 119
    design, 117-121
    sans-serif, 122-123
    selection, 122-127
    serif, 123-124
    text, 118-119
    width, 214, 217
    working with, 117-118
Type area, 247
Type attributes, 127, 142-143
Typeface, 117
    principles of using, 120-121
    running small or large, 126-127, 214, 217
Typesetting, 36

Typestyle, *see* typeface
Typo, 230
Typography, 117

**Ultimate Word Challenges, 423**
*Unabashed Self-Promotor's Guide, The*, 423
Unique Books, 99, 297-298
UPS (United Parcel Service), 235, 262, 330-
    331, 334-336
US state abbreviations, 488
*U.S.A. Today*, 308
USPS (United States Postal Service), 235, 263,
    331-332, 335-336
UV Coating, 184-185, 250

**Velo-binding, 83, 89**
Ventura Publishing, 39, 411
*Voice Literary Supplement*, 308

**Waldenbooks/Borders, 295, 419**
*Wall Street Journal*, 308
Warehousing, 338, 343
*Washington Post Book World*, 308
Web press, 238-239
W.G.P. Distributors, 295
White space, 173
Wholesale clubs, 292
Wholesalers, 278-283
    national, 279-280
    regional, 280-282
    specialized, 282-283
*Winning Casino Blackjack for the Non-
    Counter*, 50, 59-60, 351
*Winning Casino Play*, 171-172
*Winning Craps for the Serious Player*, 52
Word Perfect, 410
Word processing programs, 39, 107-108, 410
Writer
    contract, 27, 404-407
    coordinating, 109
    costs, 342
    credentials, 69
    finding, 65-67
    list of, 104
    qualifications, 69-70
*Writers Market*, 65
Writing, 73
    evaluating, 73-75
        fiction, 74-75
        how - to, 73-74
        non - fiction, 73-74
    good, bad & ugly signs, 75
    quality, 51, 59, 70

**Zip Disk, 233**

Visit the Cardoza Publishing Web Site

# www.cardozapub.com

## CARDOZA RELATED WEB SITES:

Chess City: www.chesscity.com
*Free online chess magazine*

Cardoza Entertainment: www.cardozaent.com
*Interactive gambling CD-ROM games*

Cardoza Casino: www.cardozacasino.com
*Internet on-line gambling system*

Open Road Publishing: www.openroadpub.com
*Worldwide travel guides - Be a traveler, not a tourist*

Chronicles of Xandrea: www.xandrea.com
*Online fantasy role-playing game*

Avery Cardoza is available for lectures or classes on publishing. To contact Avery, email him direct at: cardozaent@aol.com; or by phone, leave word at the New York office, (718)743-5229.